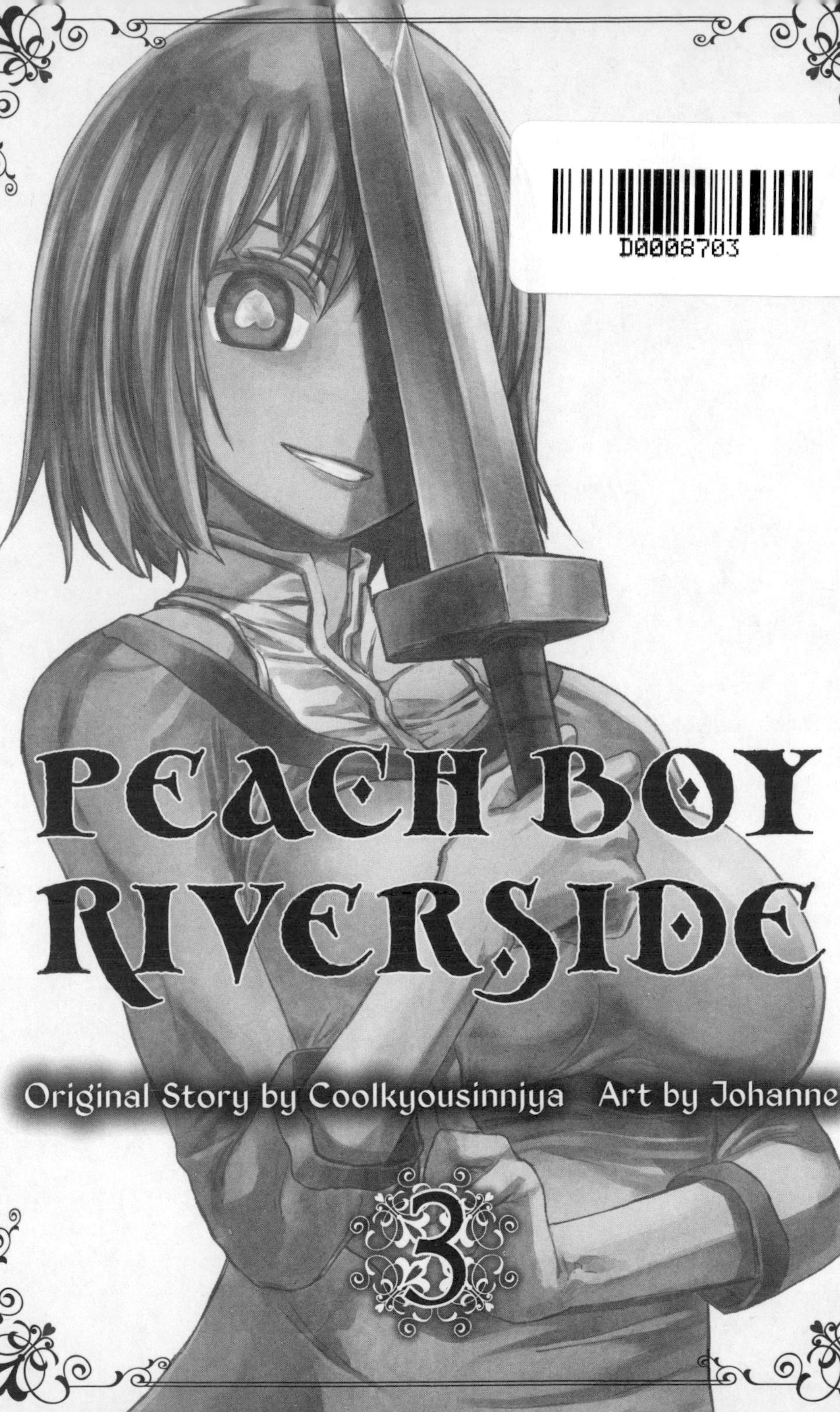

# PEACH BOY RIVERSIDE

Original Story by Coolkyousinnjya Art by Johanne

3

# CONTENTS

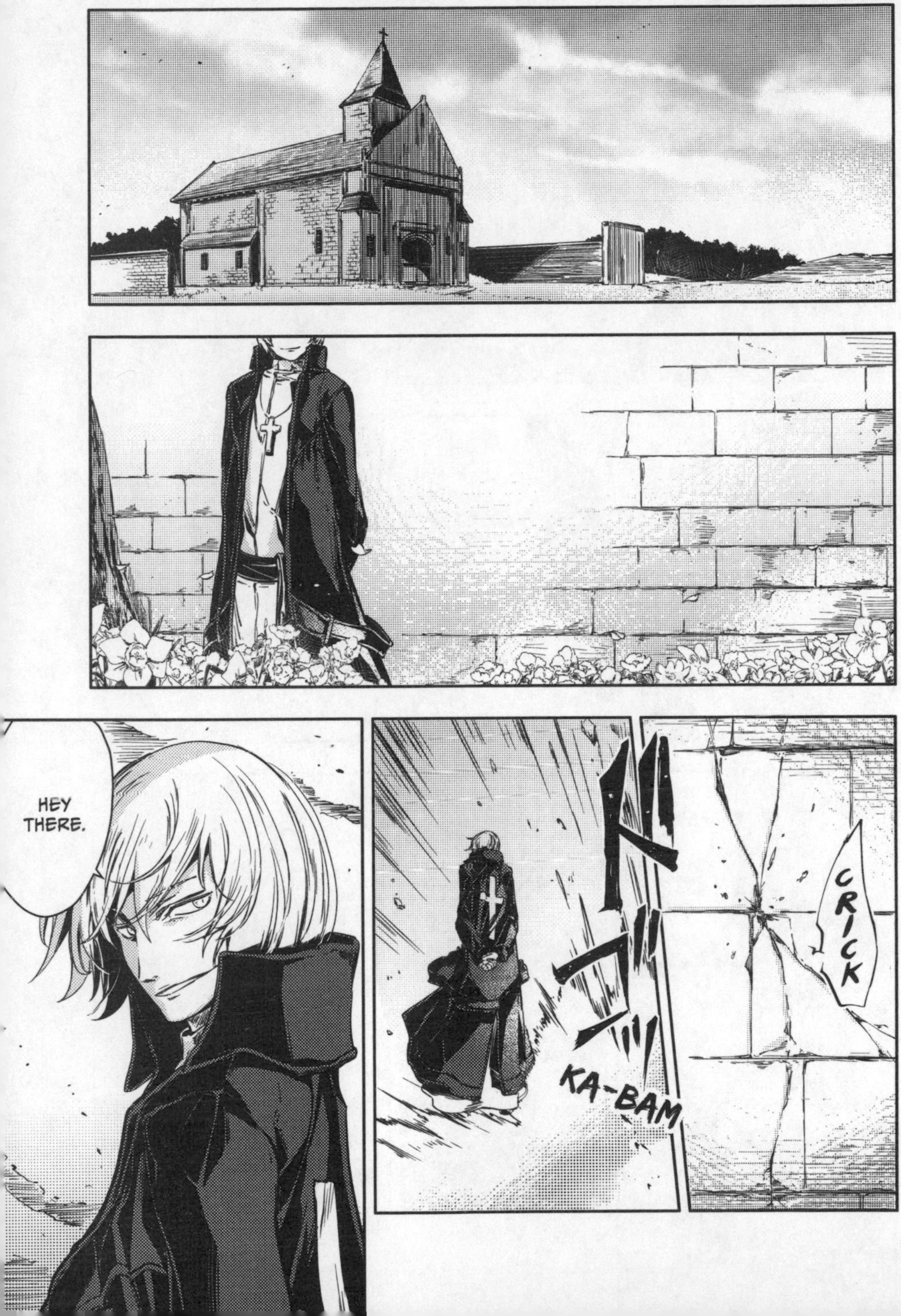
CRICK
KA-BAM
HEY THERE.

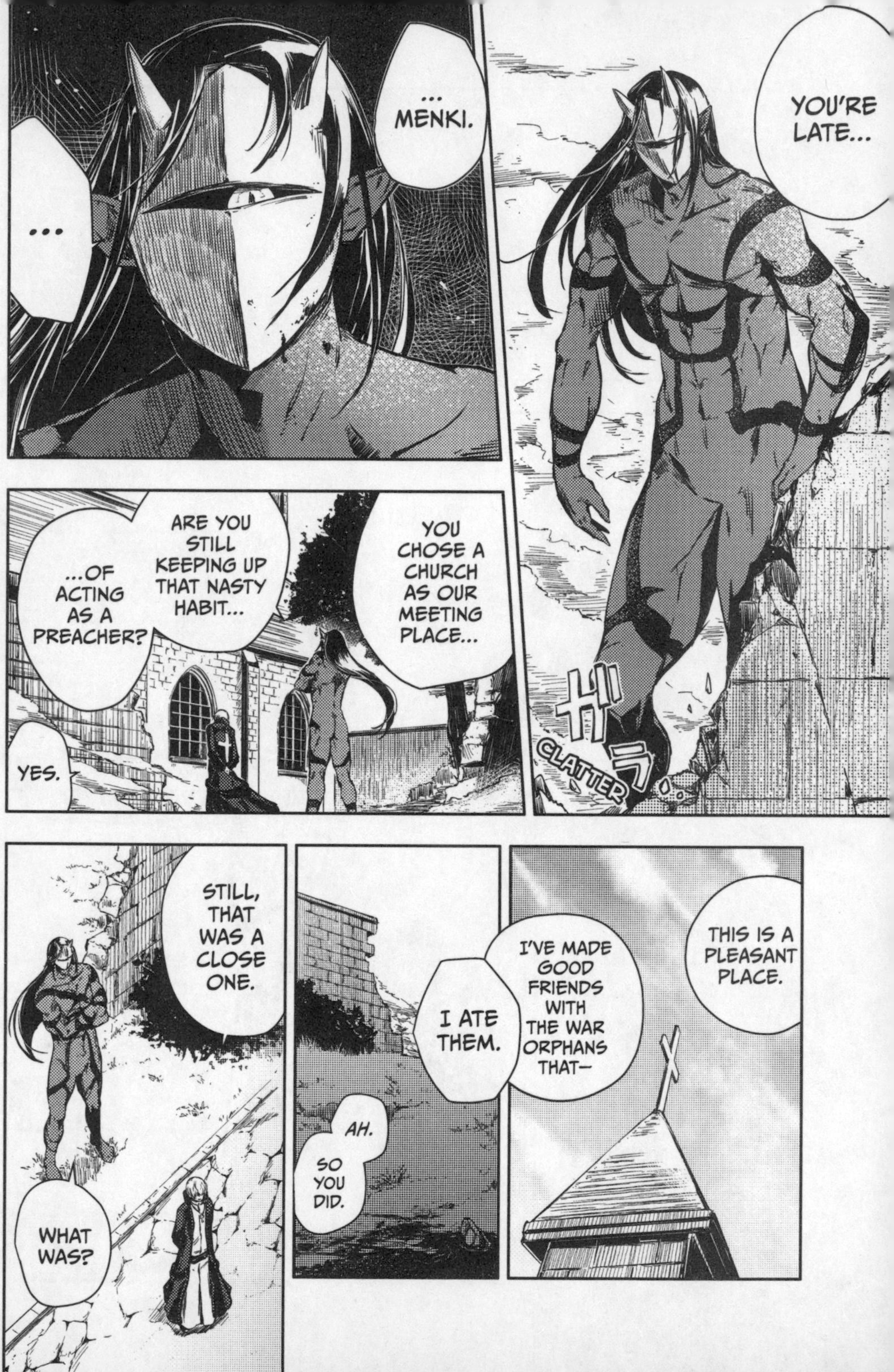
YOU'RE LATE...
ガラ
CLATTER
... MENKI.
...
YOU CHOSE A CHURCH AS OUR MEETING PLACE...
ARE YOU STILL KEEPING UP THAT NASTY HABIT...
...OF ACTING AS A PREACHER?
YES.
THIS IS A PLEASANT PLACE.
I'VE MADE GOOD FRIENDS WITH THE WAR ORPHANS THAT—
I ATE THEM.
AH.
SO YOU DID.
STILL, THAT WAS A CLOSE ONE.
WHAT WAS?

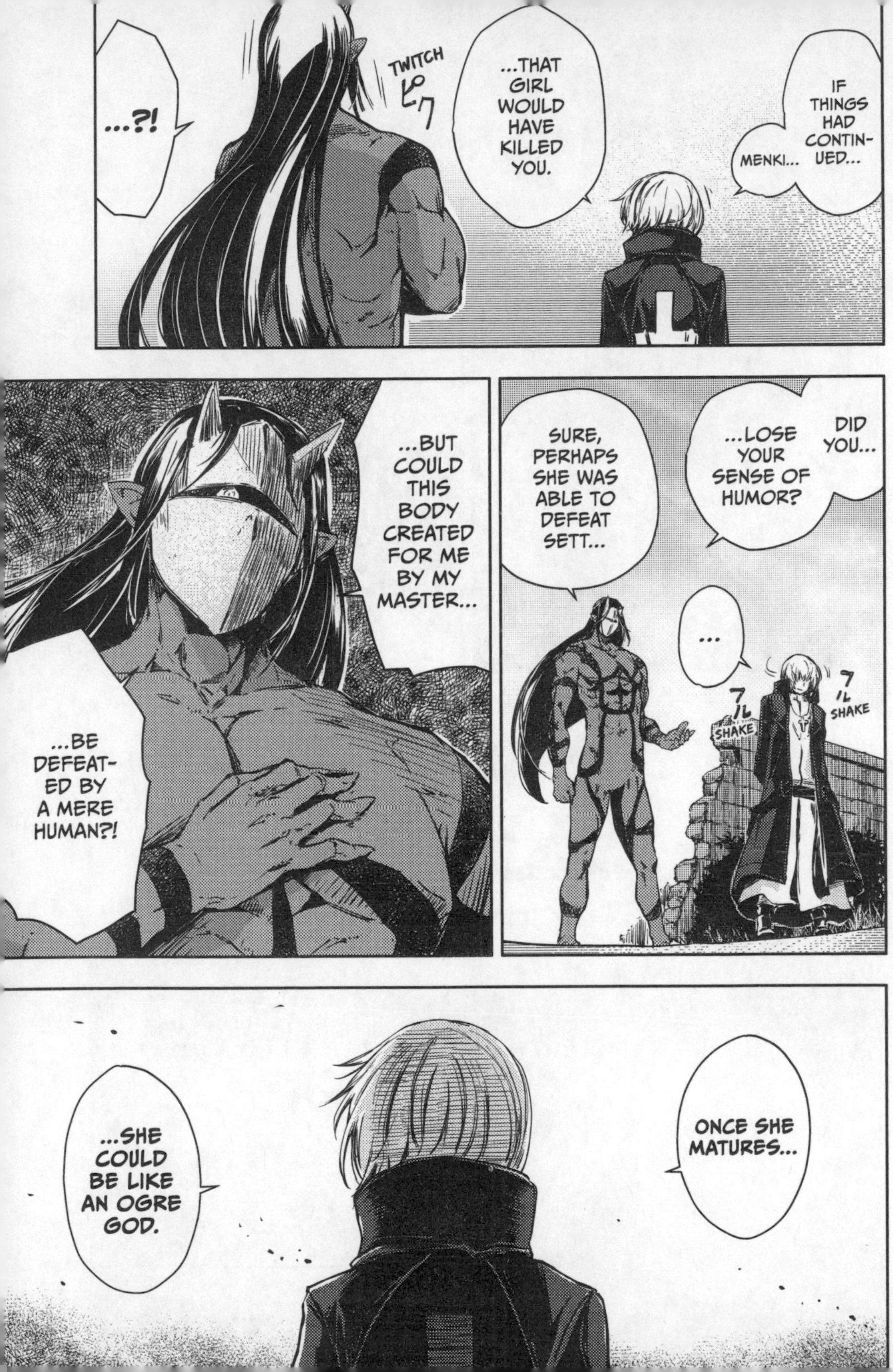
IF THINGS HAD CONTIN-UED...
MENKI...
...THAT GIRL WOULD HAVE KILLED YOU.
TWITCH
ピク
...?!
DID YOU...
...LOSE YOUR SENSE OF HUMOR?
SURE, PERHAPS SHE WAS ABLE TO DEFEAT SETT...
...
フル
SHAKE
フル
SHAKE
...BUT COULD THIS BODY CREATED FOR ME BY MY MASTER...
...BE DEFEAT-ED BY A MERE HUMAN?!
ONCE SHE MATURES...
...SHE COULD BE LIKE AN OGRE GOD.

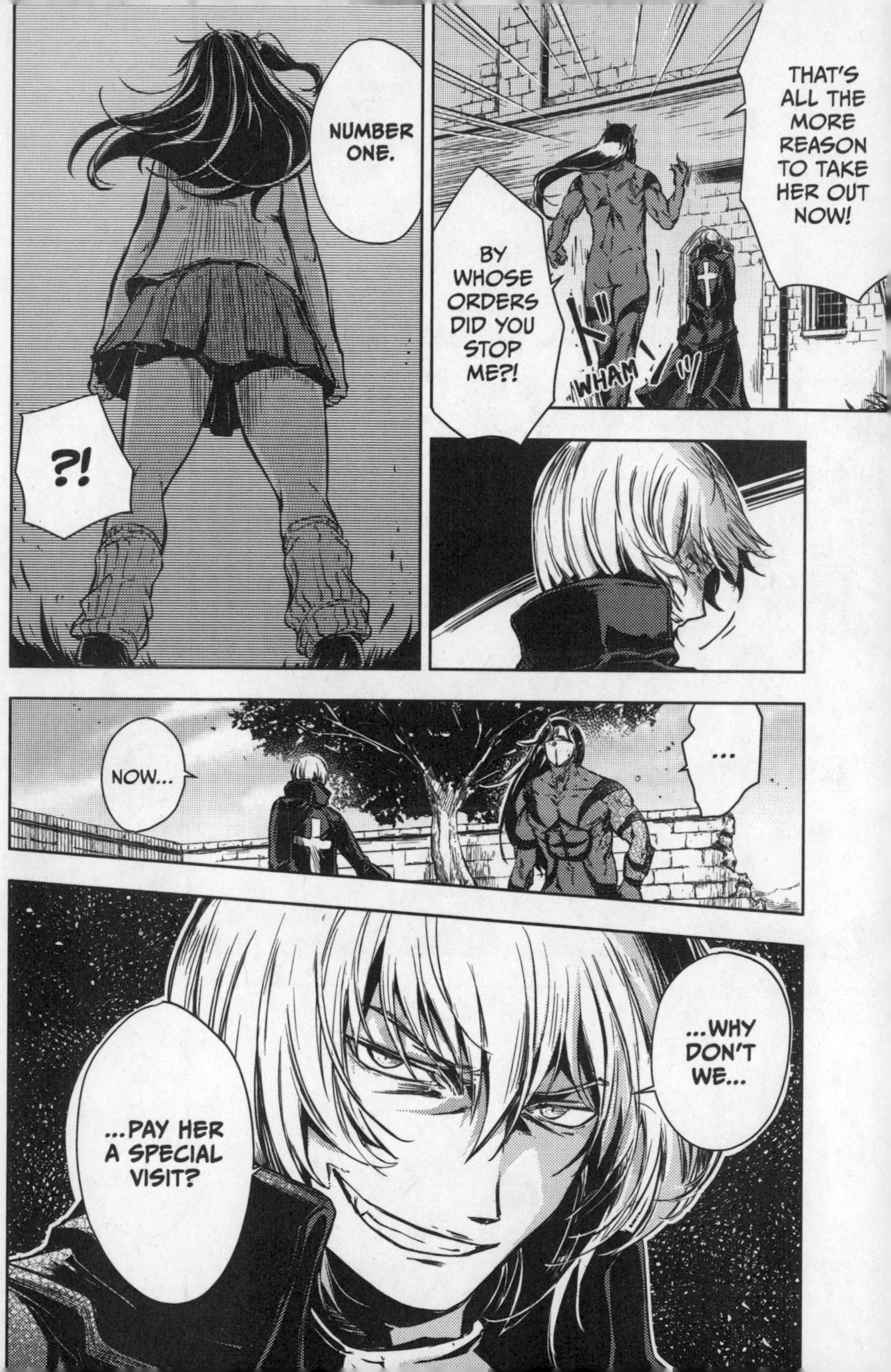
THAT'S ALL THE MORE REASON TO TAKE HER OUT NOW!
BY WHOSE ORDERS DID YOU STOP ME?!
WHAM
NUMBER ONE.
?!
...
NOW...
...WHY DON'T WE...
...PAY HER A SPECIAL VISIT?

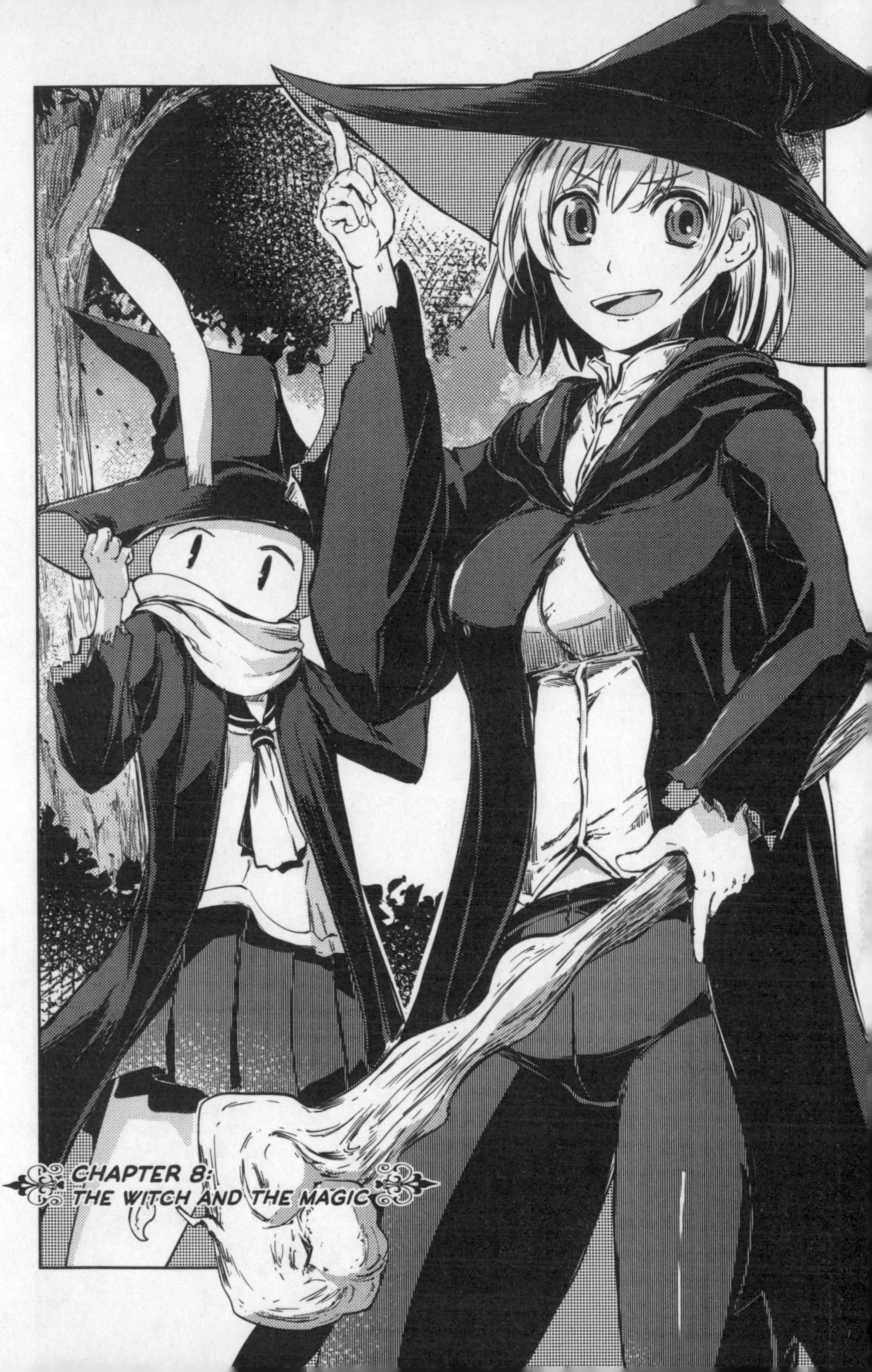
CHAPTER 8:
THE WITCH AND THE MAGIC

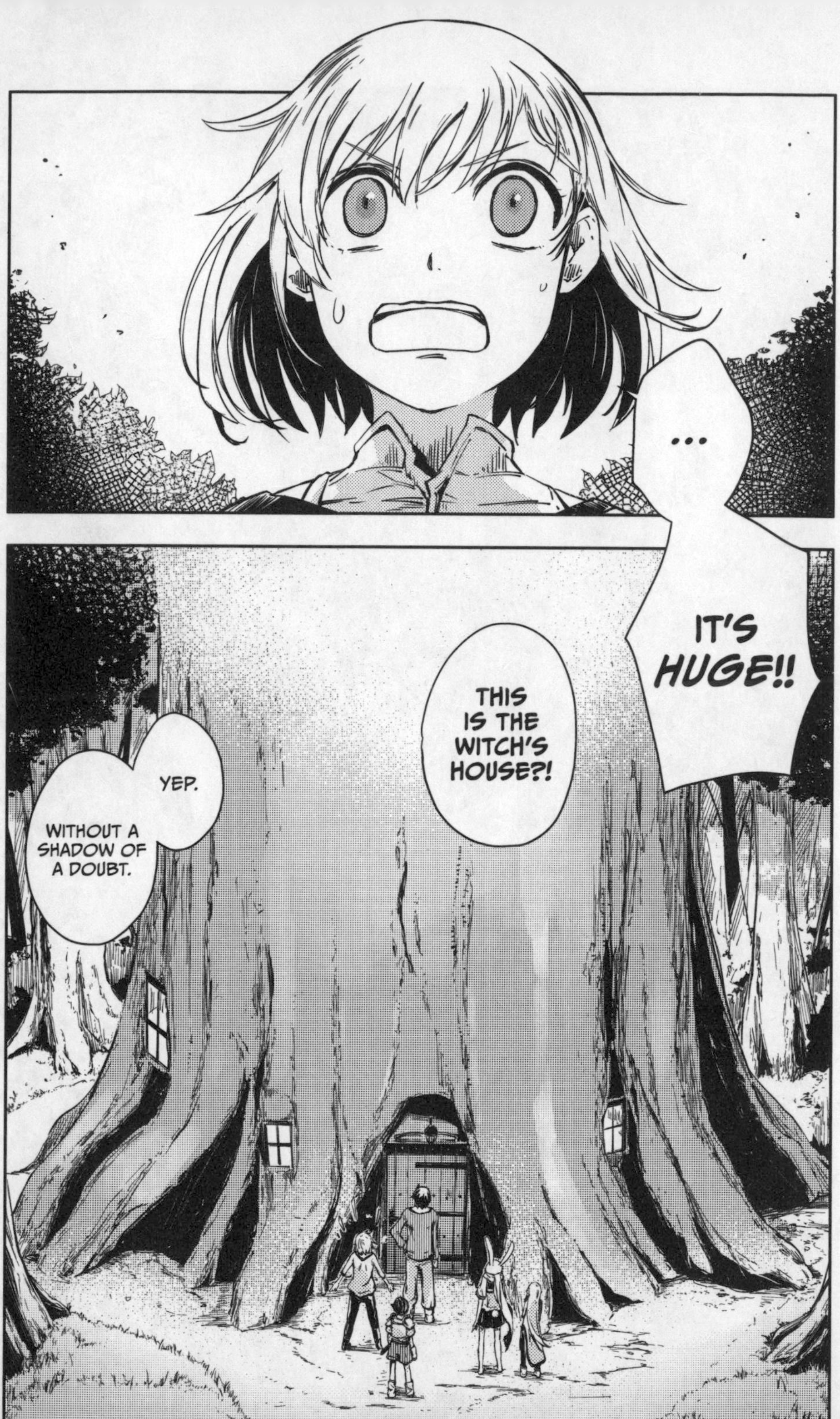
...
IT'S HUGE!!
THIS IS THE WITCH'S HOUSE?!
YEP.
WITHOUT A SHADOW OF A DOUBT.

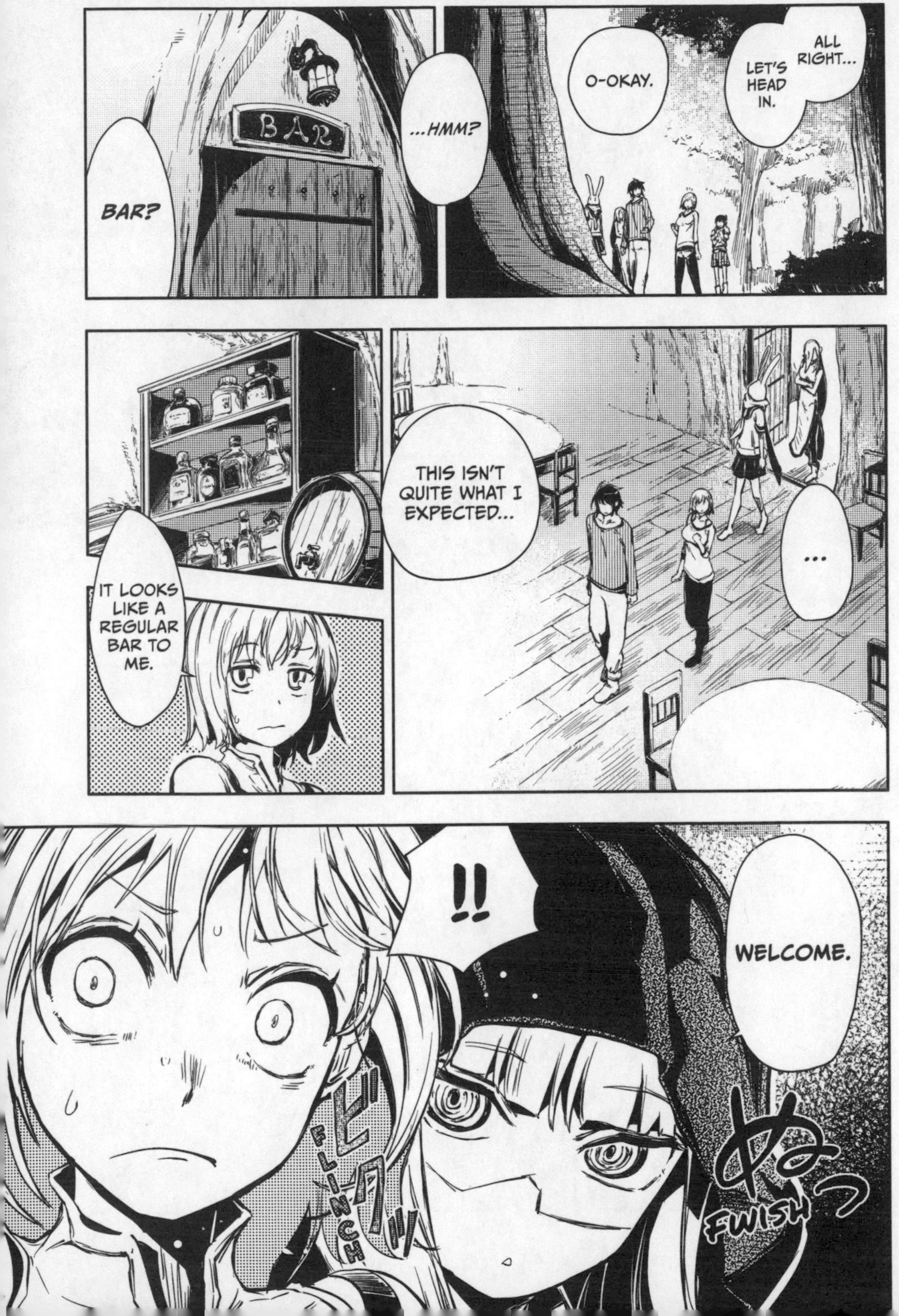
ALL RIGHT... LET'S HEAD IN.
O-OKAY.
...HMM?
BAR
BAR?
THIS ISN'T QUITE WHAT I EXPECTED...
...
IT LOOKS LIKE A REGULAR BAR TO ME.
WELCOME.
FWISH
!!
FLINCH

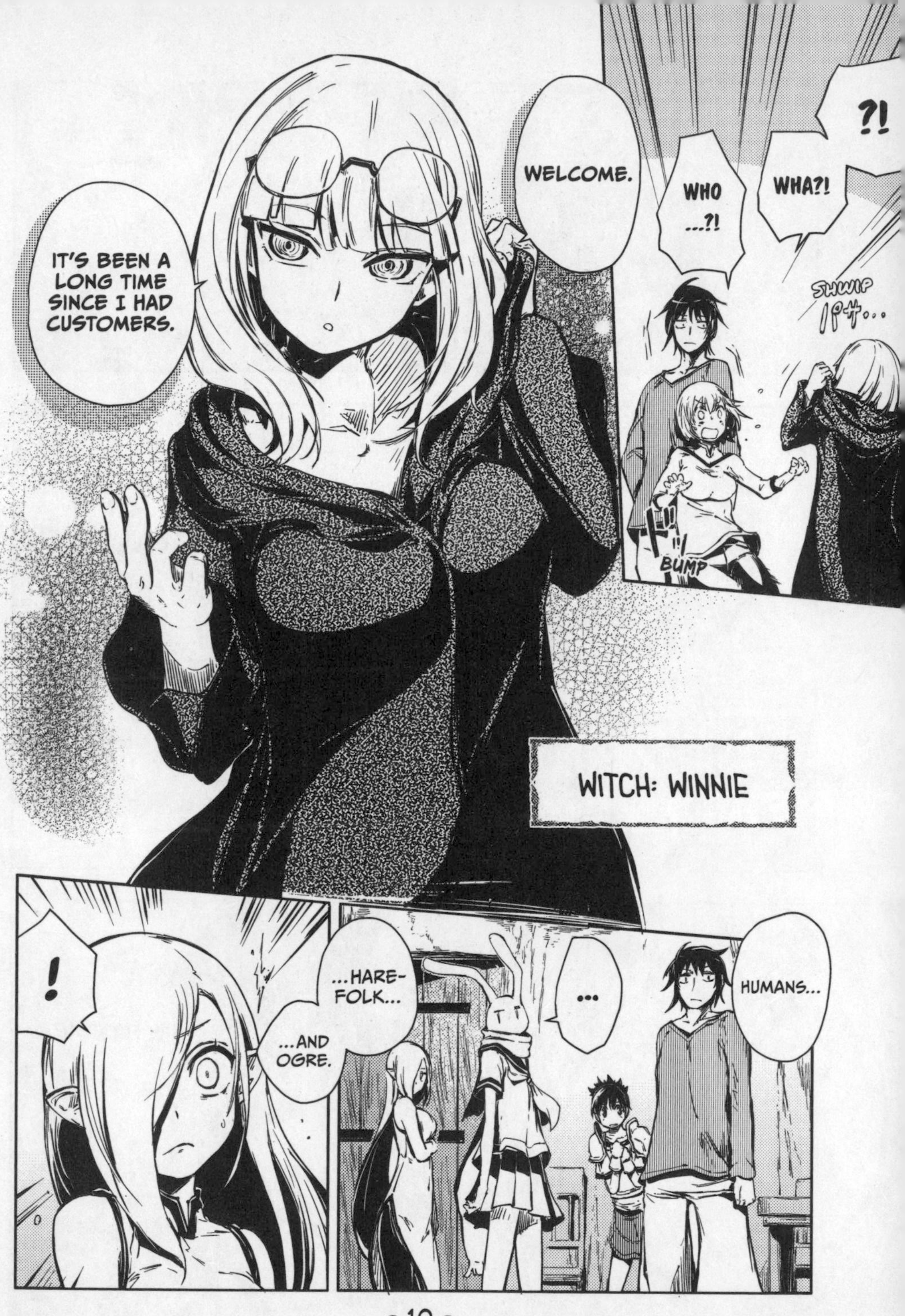
?!
WHA?!
WHO ...?!
SHWIP
BUMP
WELCOME.
IT'S BEEN A LONG TIME SINCE I HAD CUSTOMERS.
WITCH: WINNIE
HUMANS...
...
...HARE-FOLK...
...AND OGRE.
!

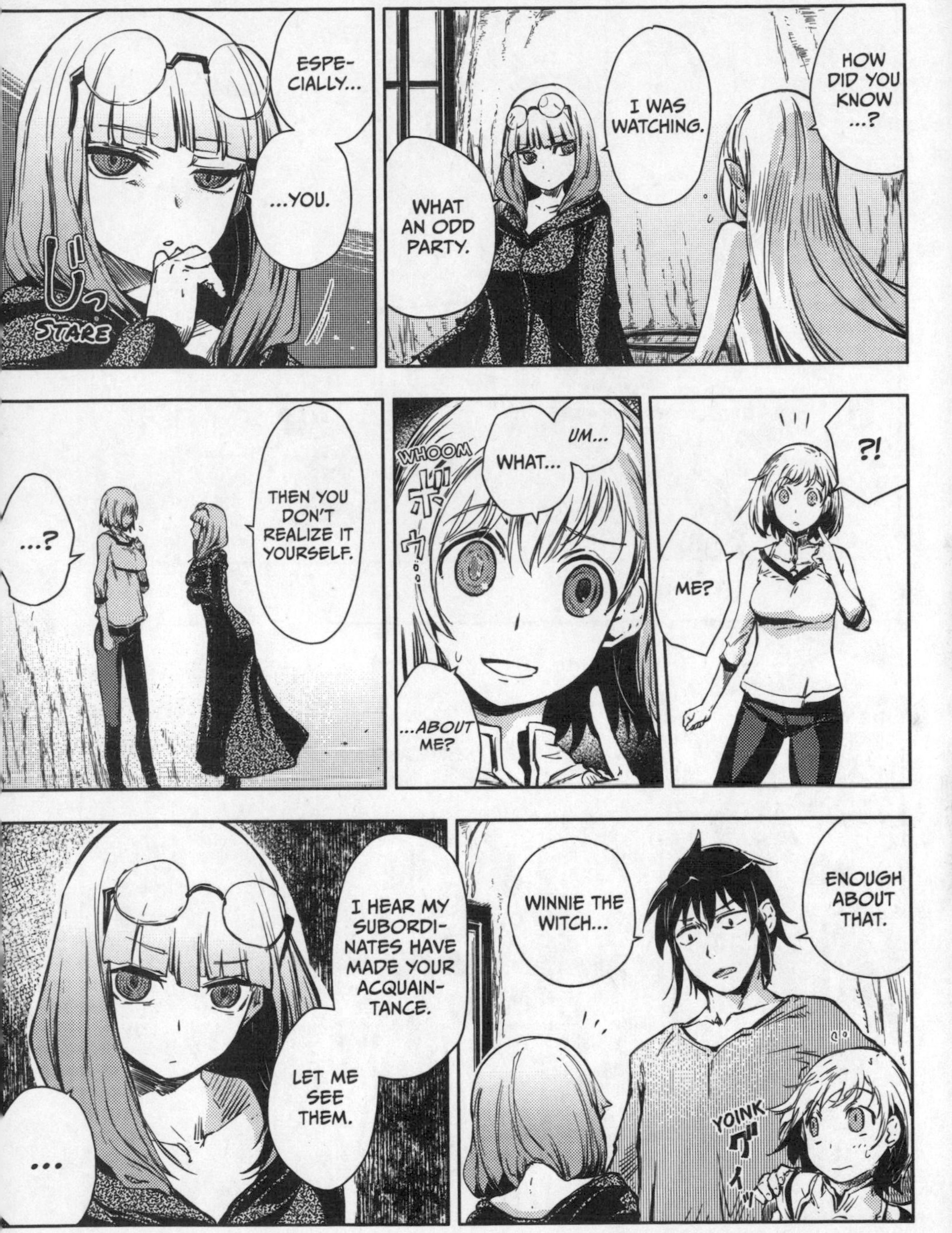
HOW DID YOU KNOW ...?
I WAS WATCHING.
WHAT AN ODD PARTY.
ESPE-CIALLY...
...YOU.
STARE
?!
ME?
UM...
WHAT...
WHOOM
...ABOUT ME?
THEN YOU DON'T REALIZE IT YOURSELF.
...?
ENOUGH ABOUT THAT.
WINNIE THE WITCH...
YOINK
I HEAR MY SUBORDI-NATES HAVE MADE YOUR ACQUAIN-TANCE.
LET ME SEE THEM.
...

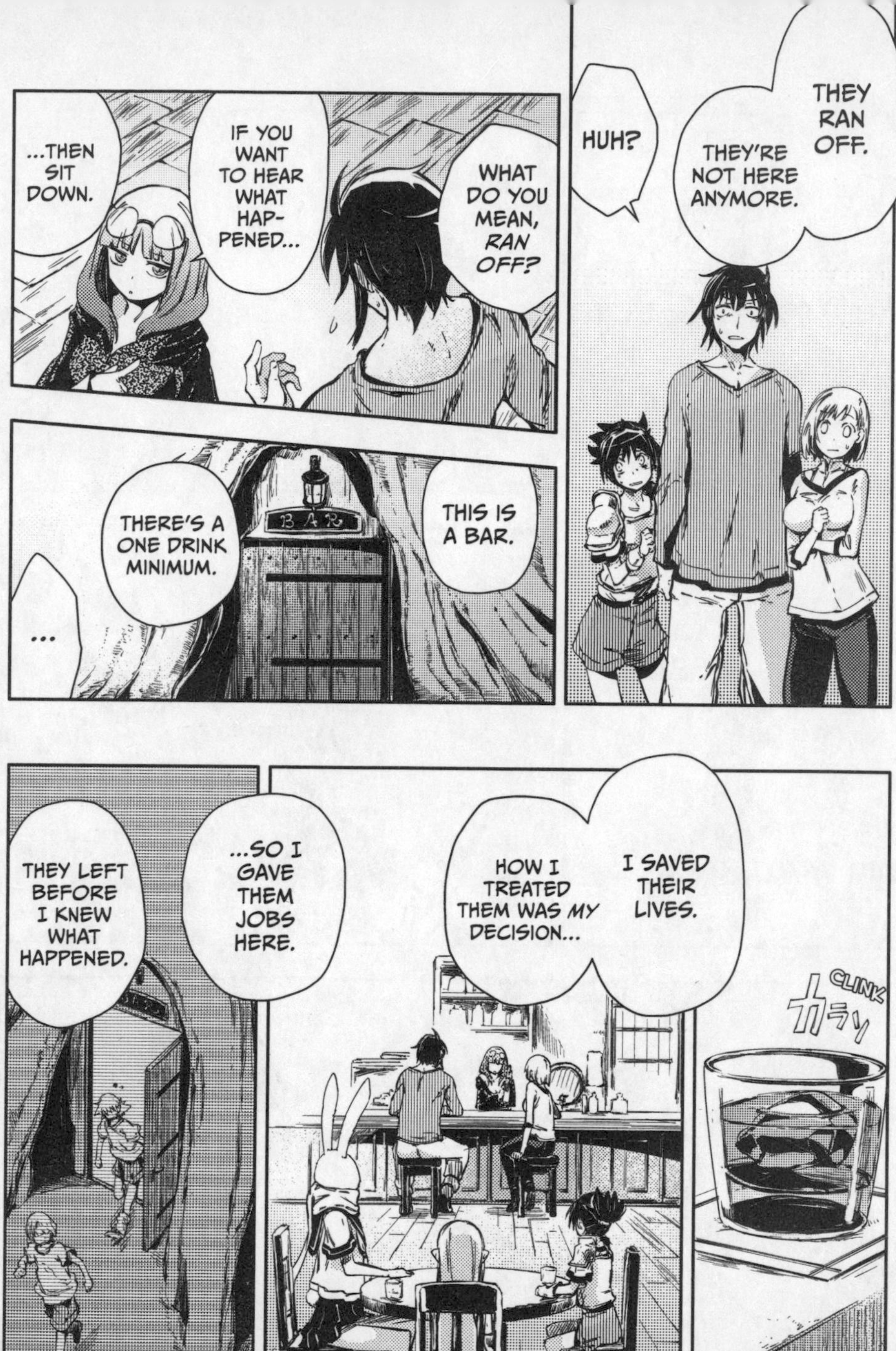
THEY RAN OFF.
THEY'RE NOT HERE ANYMORE.
HUH?
WHAT DO YOU MEAN, *RAN OFF?*
IF YOU WANT TO HEAR WHAT HAP-PENED...
...THEN SIT DOWN.
THIS IS A BAR.
THERE'S A ONE DRINK MINIMUM.
...
B A R
CLINK
カラッ
I SAVED THEIR LIVES.
HOW I TREATED THEM WAS *MY* DECISION...
...SO I GAVE THEM JOBS HERE.
THEY LEFT BEFORE I KNEW WHAT HAPPENED.

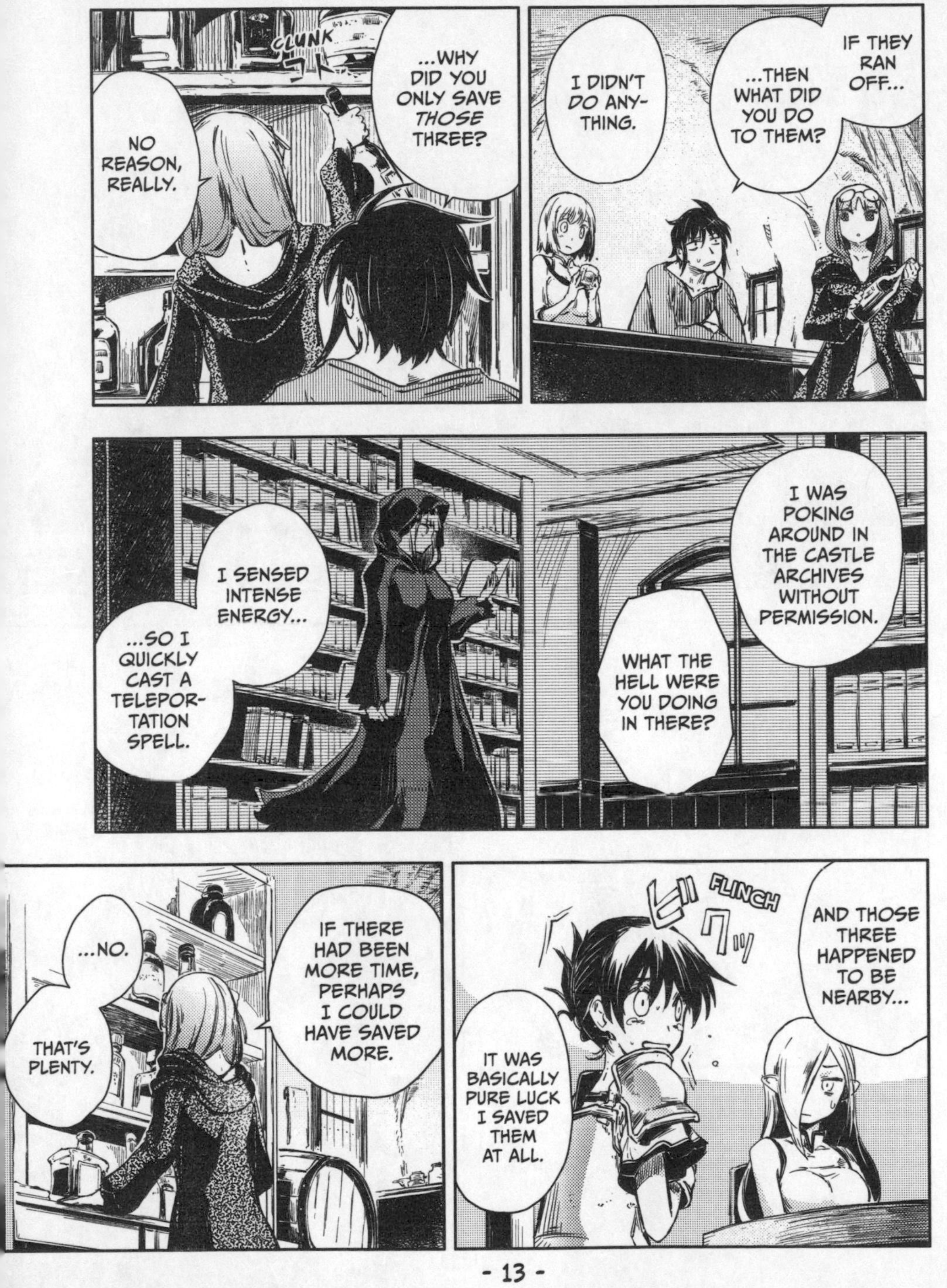
IF THEY RAN OFF...
...THEN WHAT DID YOU DO TO THEM?
I DIDN'T DO ANY-THING.
...WHY DID YOU ONLY SAVE *THOSE* THREE?
CLUNK
NO REASON, REALLY.
I WAS POKING AROUND IN THE CASTLE ARCHIVES WITHOUT PERMISSION.
WHAT THE HELL WERE YOU DOING IN THERE?
I SENSED INTENSE ENERGY...
...SO I QUICKLY CAST A TELEPOR-TATION SPELL.
FLINCH
AND THOSE THREE HAPPENED TO BE NEARBY...
IT WAS BASICALLY PURE LUCK I SAVED THEM AT ALL.
IF THERE HAD BEEN MORE TIME, PERHAPS I COULD HAVE SAVED MORE.
...NO.
THAT'S PLENTY.

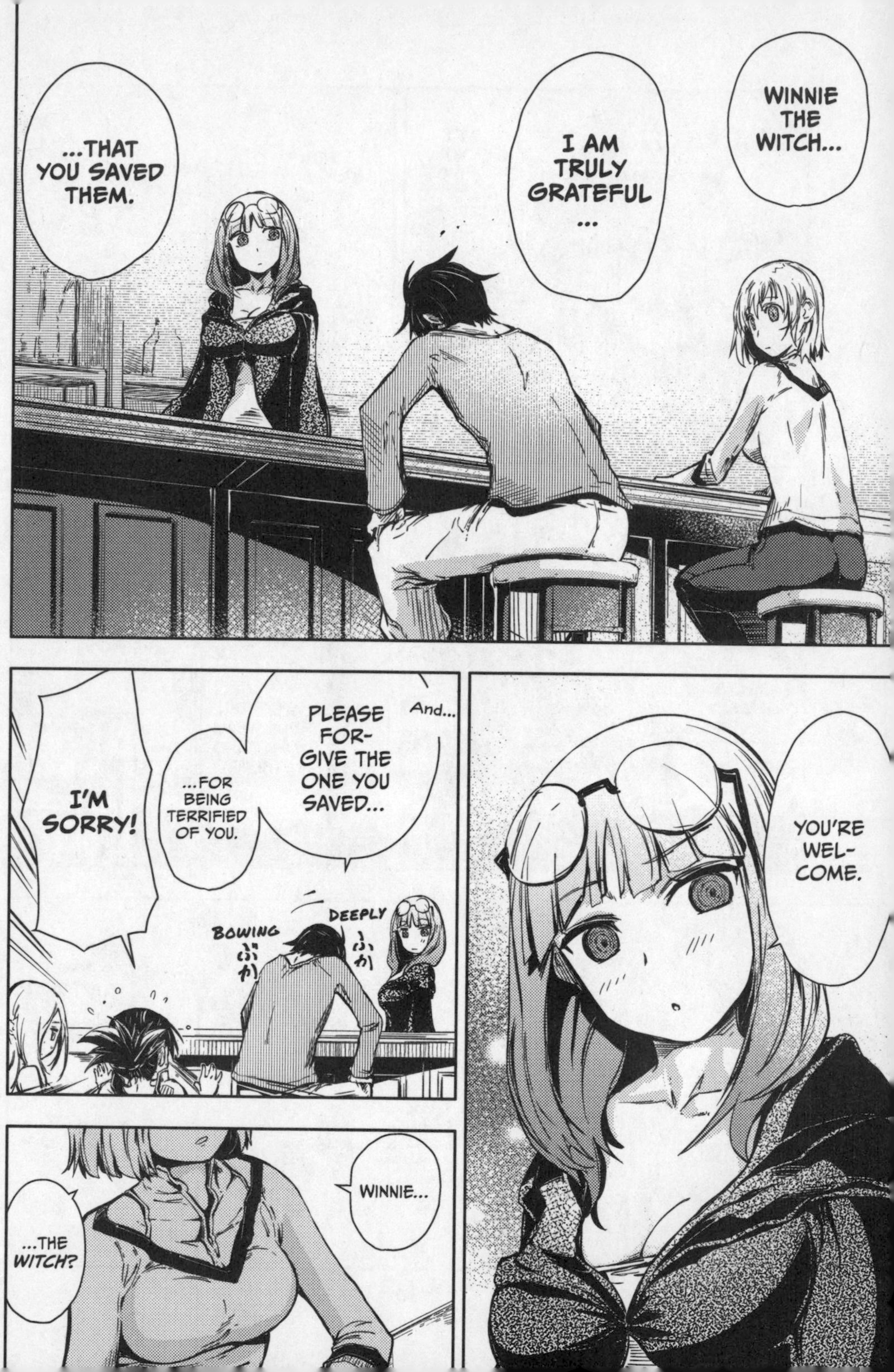
WINNIE THE WITCH...
I AM TRULY GRATEFUL ...
...THAT YOU SAVED THEM.
YOU'RE WEL-COME.
And...
PLEASE FOR-GIVE THE ONE YOU SAVED...
...FOR BEING TERRIFIED OF YOU.
I'M SORRY!
DEEPLY
ふか
BOWING
ぶか
WINNIE...
...THE WITCH?

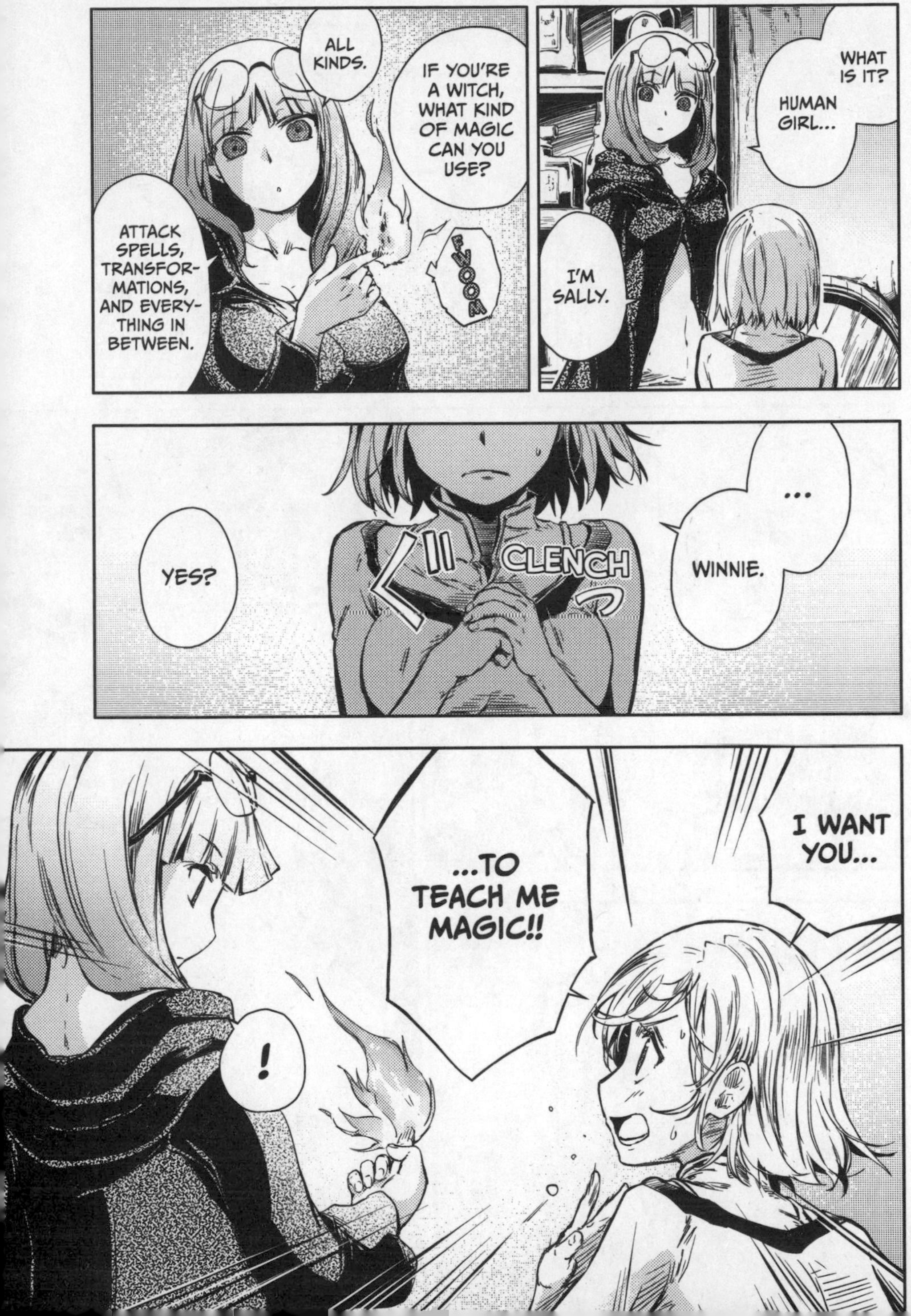
WHAT IS IT? HUMAN GIRL...
I'M SALLY.
IF YOU'RE A WITCH, WHAT KIND OF MAGIC CAN YOU USE?
ALL KINDS.
FVOOM
ATTACK SPELLS, TRANSFORMATIONS, AND EVERYTHING IN BETWEEN.
...
WINNIE.
CLENCH
YES?
I WANT YOU...
...TO TEACH ME MAGIC!!
!

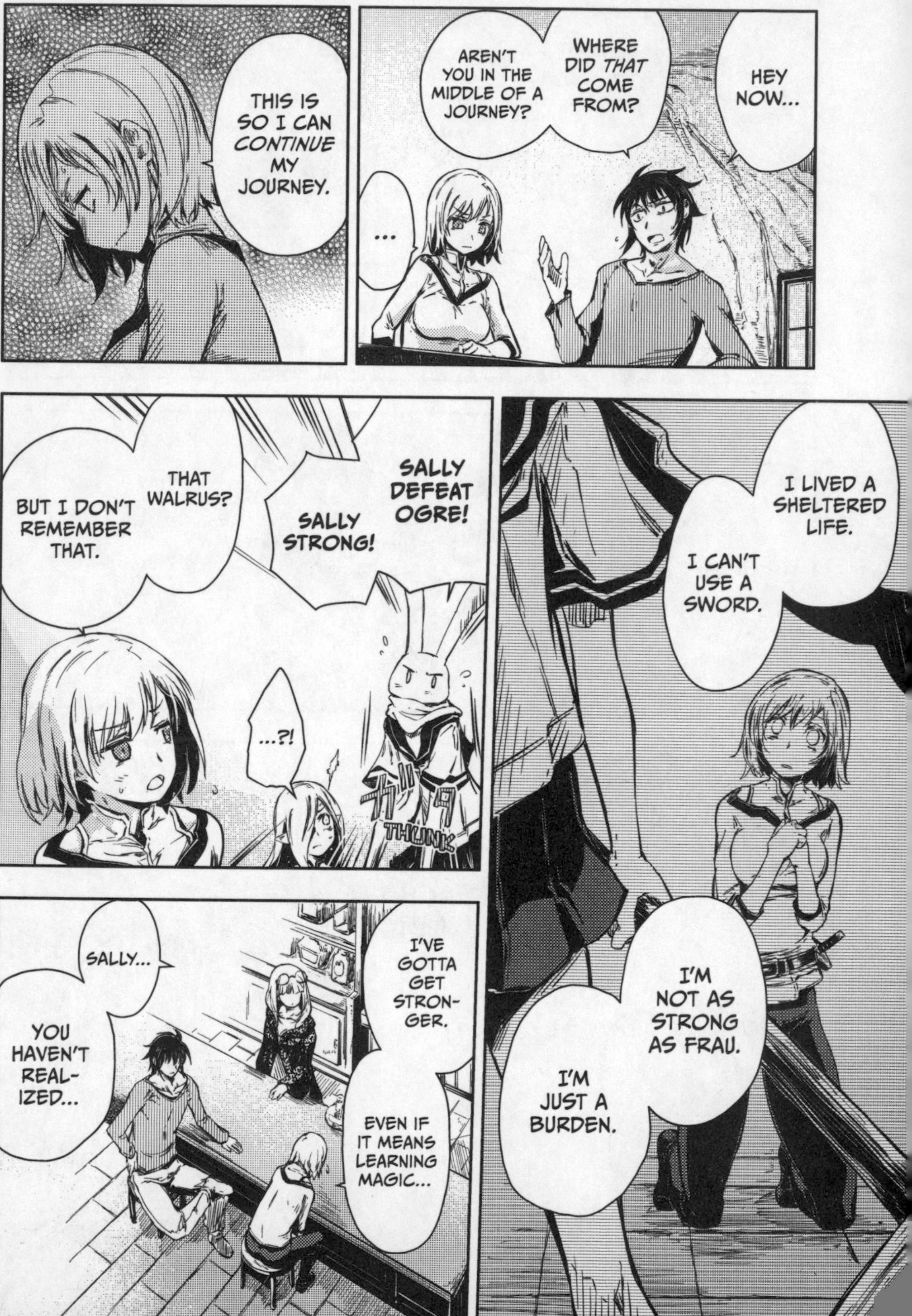
HEY NOW...
WHERE DID *THAT* COME FROM?
AREN'T YOU IN THE MIDDLE OF A JOURNEY?
...
THIS IS SO I CAN *CONTINUE* MY JOURNEY.
I LIVED A SHELTERED LIFE.
I CAN'T USE A SWORD.
I'M NOT AS STRONG AS FRAU.
I'M JUST A BURDEN.
SALLY DEFEAT OGRE!
SALLY STRONG!
THAT WALRUS?
BUT I DON'T REMEMBER THAT.
...?!
THUNK
I'VE GOTTA GET STRON-GER.
EVEN IF IT MEANS LEARNING MAGIC...
SALLY...
YOU HAVEN'T REAL-IZED...

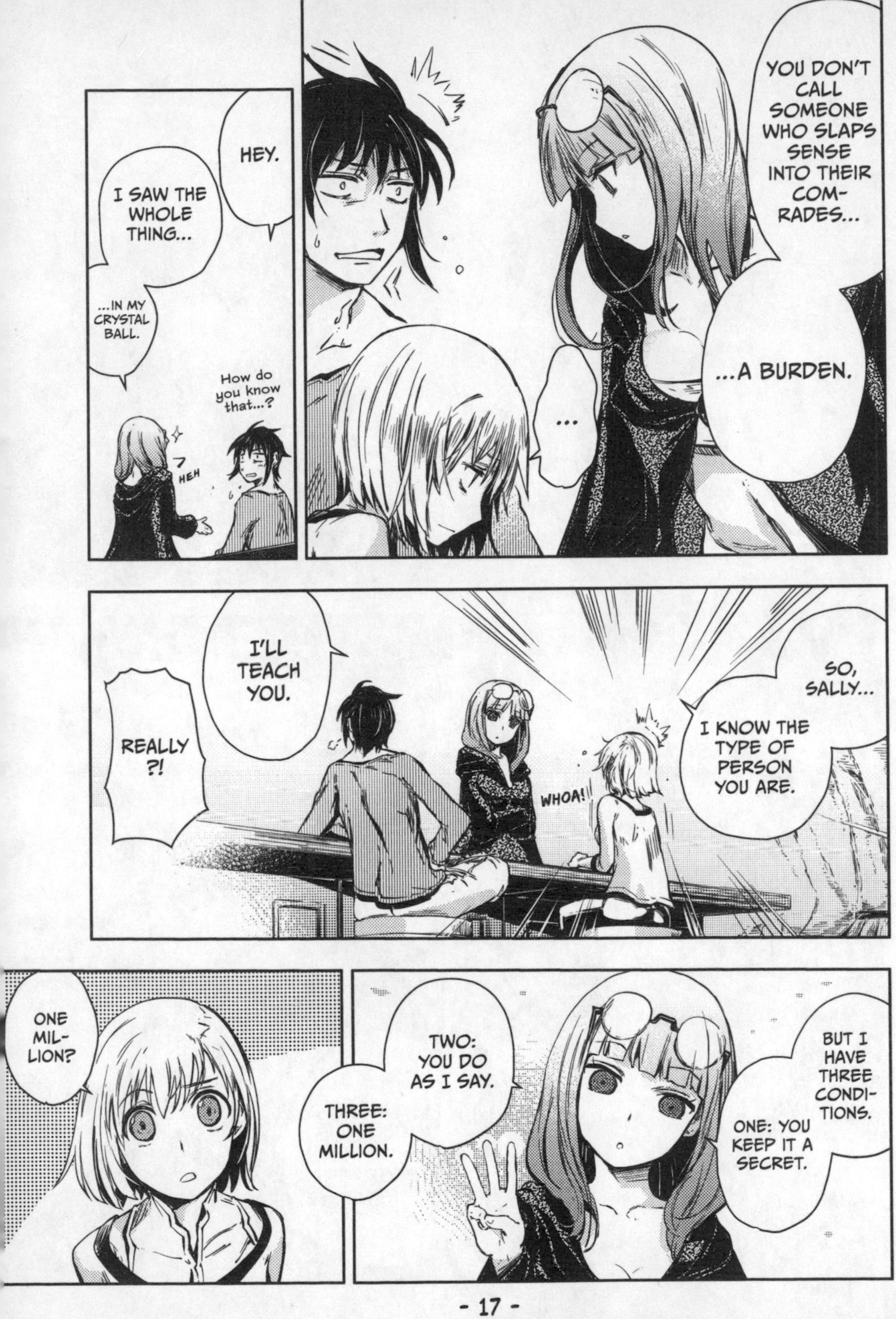
YOU DON'T CALL SOMEONE WHO SLAPS SENSE INTO THEIR COM-RADES...
...A BURDEN.
...
HEY.
I SAW THE WHOLE THING...
...IN MY CRYSTAL BALL.
How do you know that...?
HEH
SO, SALLY...
I KNOW THE TYPE OF PERSON YOU ARE.
WHOA!
I'LL TEACH YOU.
REALLY?!
BUT I HAVE THREE CONDI-TIONS.
ONE: YOU KEEP IT A SECRET.
TWO: YOU DO AS I SAY.
THREE: ONE MILLION.
ONE MIL-LION?

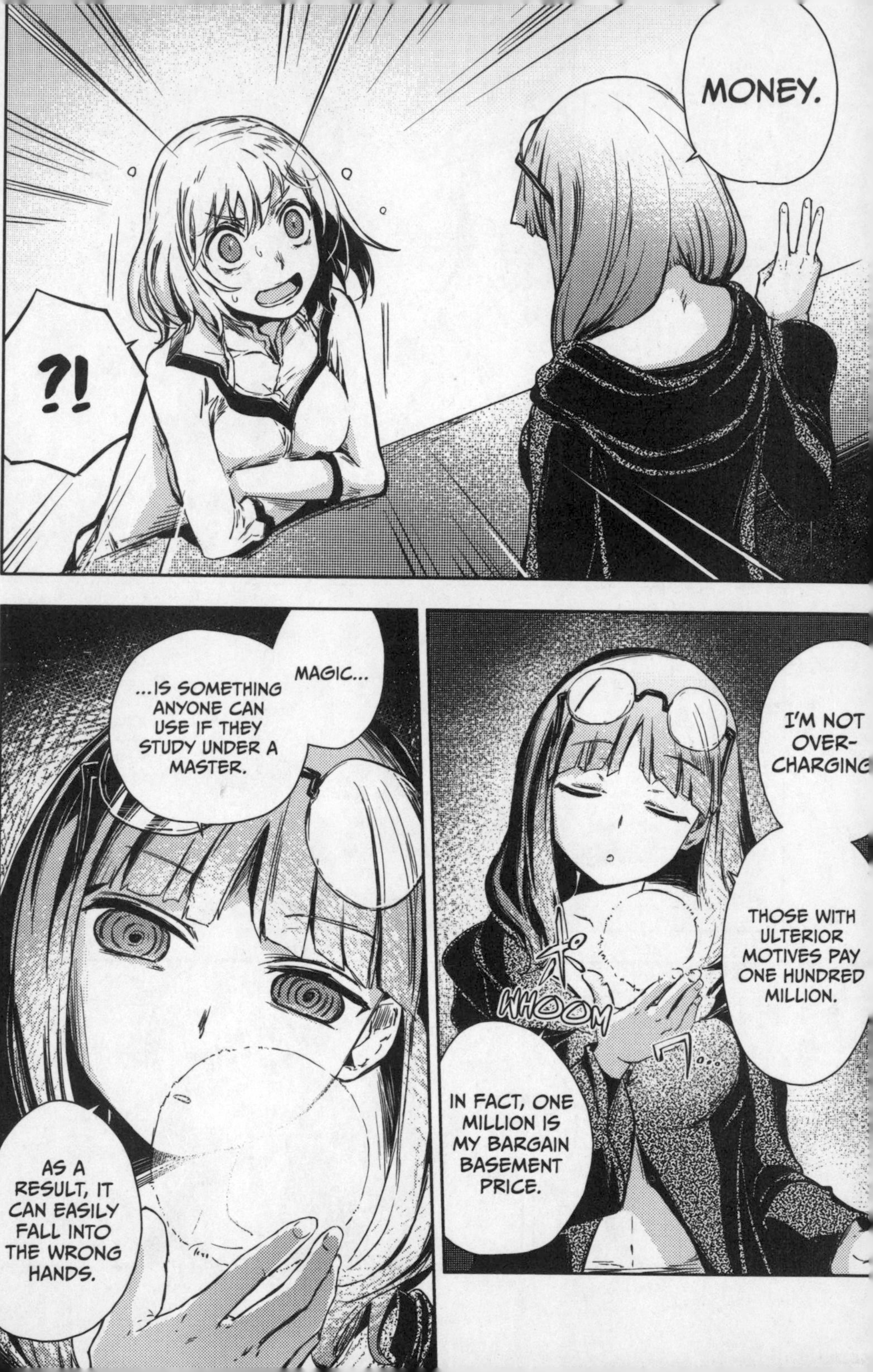
MONEY.
?!
I'M NOT OVER-CHARGING
THOSE WITH ULTERIOR MOTIVES PAY ONE HUNDRED MILLION.
WHOOM
IN FACT, ONE MILLION IS MY BARGAIN BASEMENT PRICE.
MAGIC...
...IS SOMETHING ANYONE CAN USE IF THEY STUDY UNDER A MASTER.
AS A RESULT, IT CAN EASILY FALL INTO THE WRONG HANDS.

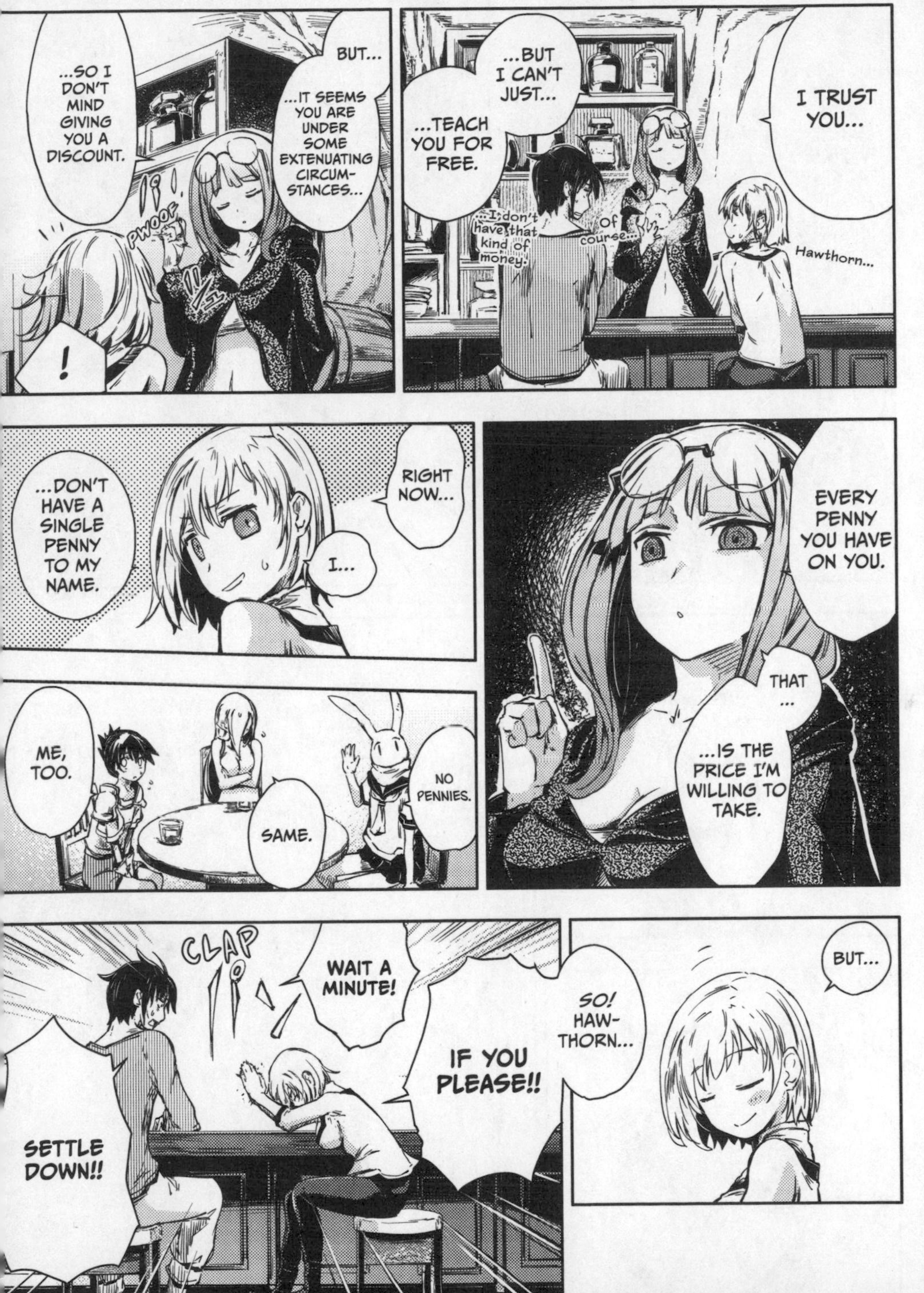
I TRUST YOU...
Hawthorn...
...BUT I CAN'T JUST...
...TEACH YOU FOR FREE.
Of course...
...I don't have that kind of money.
BUT...
...IT SEEMS YOU ARE UNDER SOME EXTENUATING CIRCUM-STANCES...
...SO I DON'T MIND GIVING YOU A DISCOUNT.
PWOOF
!
EVERY PENNY YOU HAVE ON YOU.
THAT ...
...IS THE PRICE I'M WILLING TO TAKE.
RIGHT NOW...
I...
...DON'T HAVE A SINGLE PENNY TO MY NAME.
NO PENNIES.
SAME.
ME, TOO.
BUT...
SO! HAW-THORN...
WAIT A MINUTE!
IF YOU PLEASE!!
CLAP
SETTLE DOWN!!

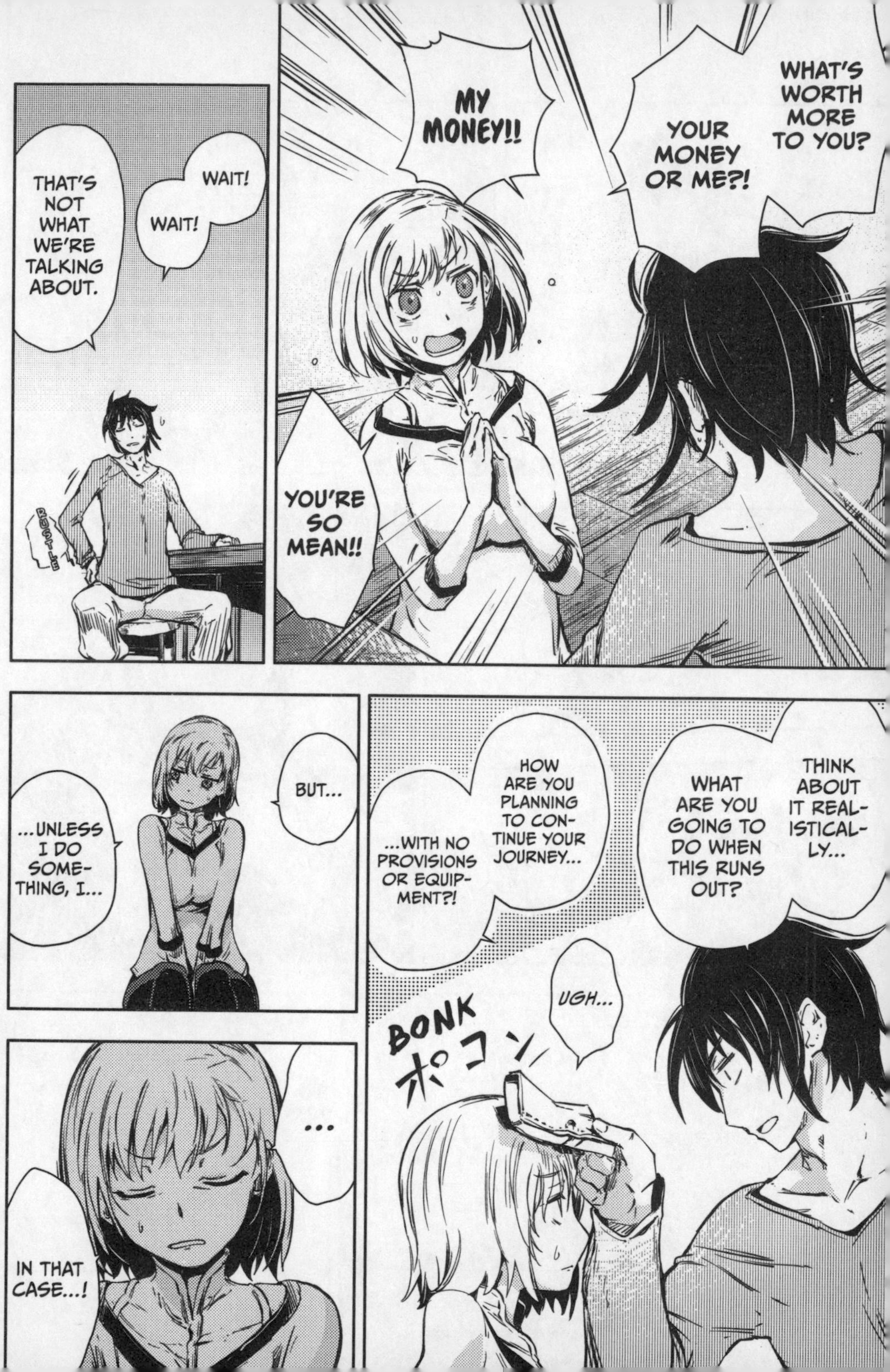
WHAT'S WORTH MORE TO YOU?
YOUR MONEY OR ME?!
MY MONEY!!
YOU'RE SO MEAN!!
WAIT!
WAIT!
THAT'S NOT WHAT WE'RE TALKING ABOUT.
RUSTLE
THINK ABOUT IT REALISTICALLY...
WHAT ARE YOU GOING TO DO WHEN THIS RUNS OUT?
HOW ARE YOU PLANNING TO CONTINUE YOUR JOURNEY...
...WITH NO PROVISIONS OR EQUIPMENT?!
BONK ポコン
UGH...
BUT...
...UNLESS I DO SOMETHING, I...
...
IN THAT CASE...!

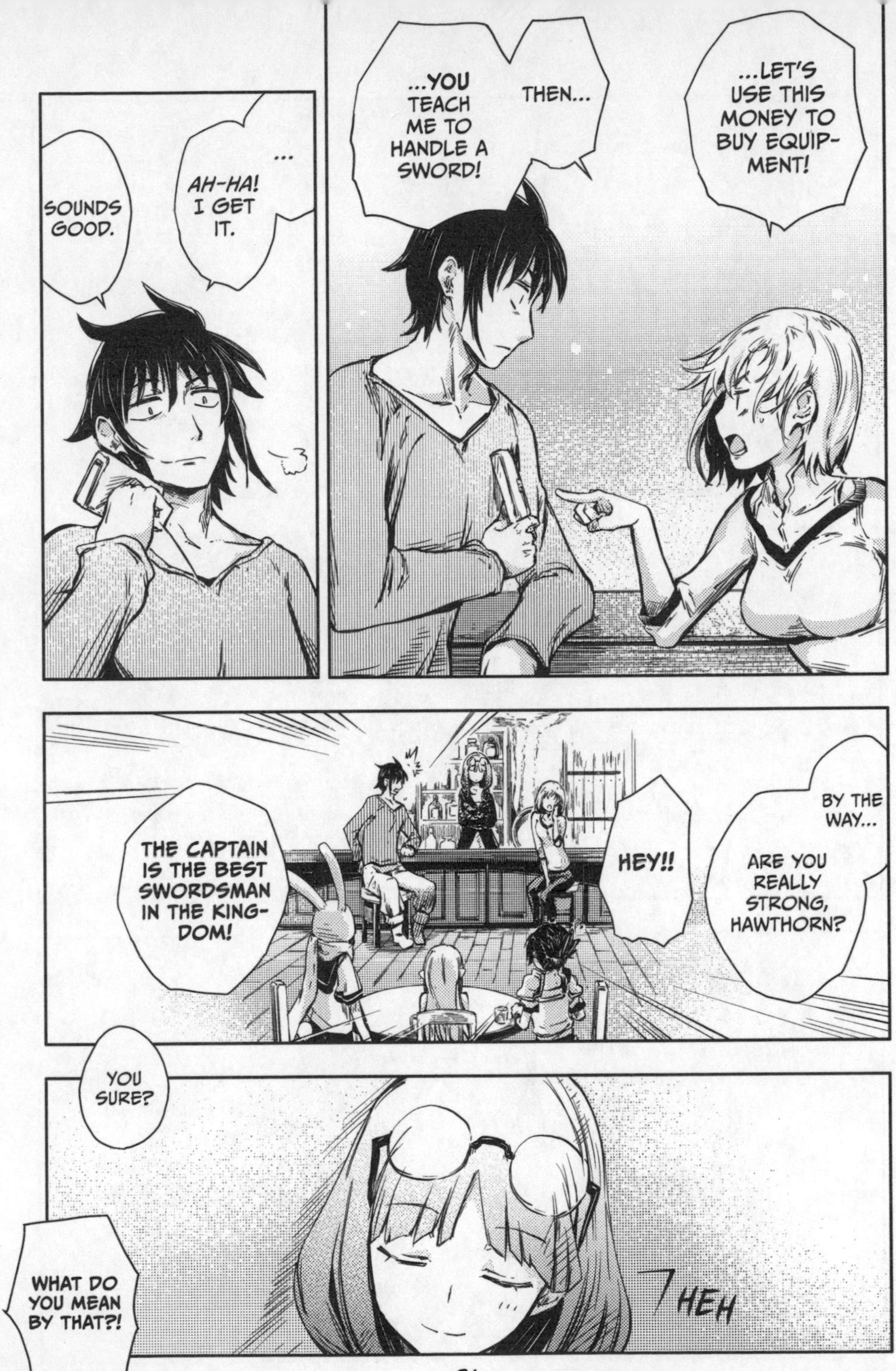
...LET'S USE THIS MONEY TO BUY EQUIPMENT!
THEN...
...YOU TEACH ME TO HANDLE A SWORD!
...
AH-HA! I GET IT.
SOUNDS GOOD.
BY THE WAY...
ARE YOU REALLY STRONG, HAWTHORN?
HEY!!
THE CAPTAIN IS THE BEST SWORDSMAN IN THE KINGDOM!
HEH
YOU SURE?
WHAT DO YOU MEAN BY THAT?!

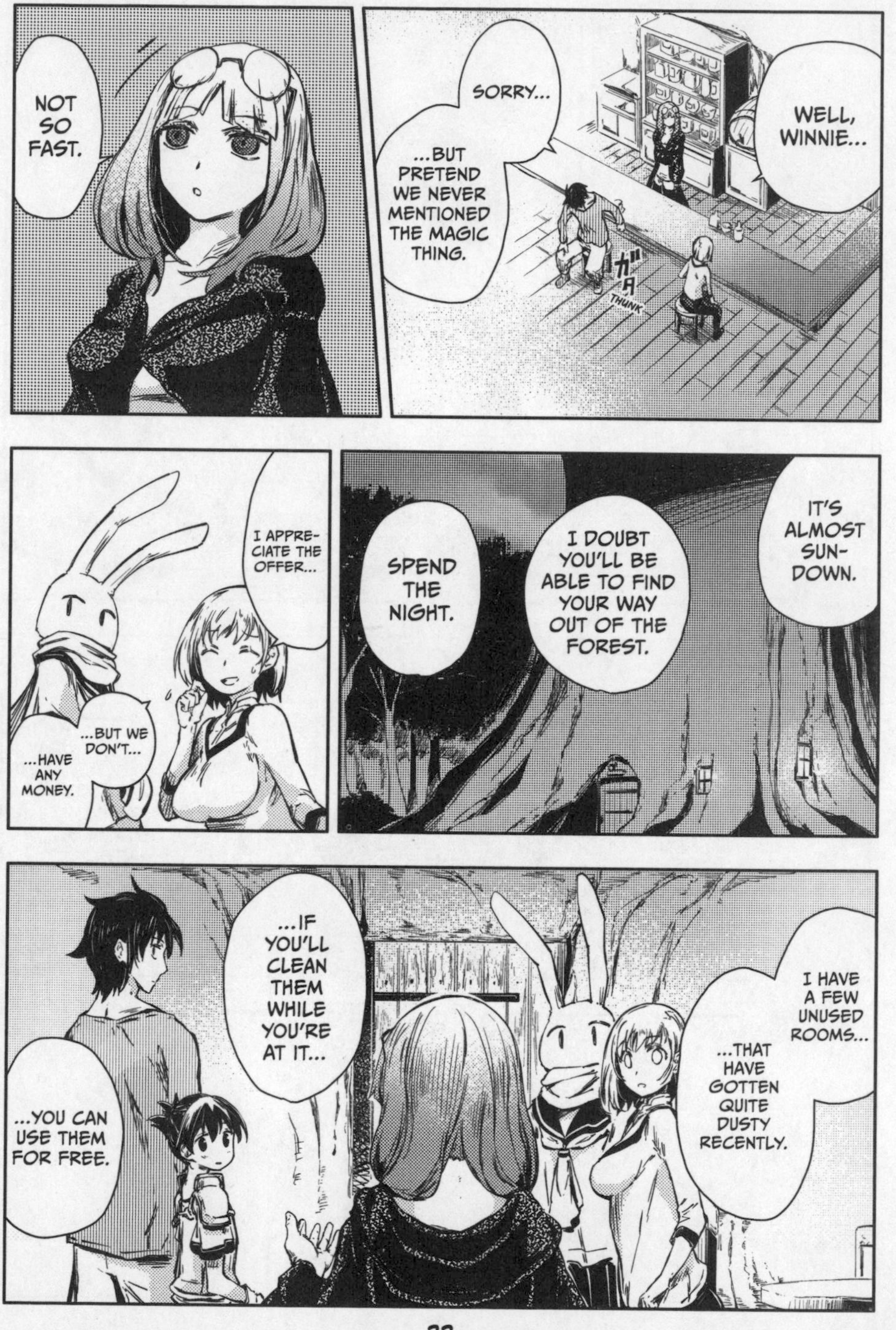
WELL, WINNIE...
SORRY...
...BUT PRETEND WE NEVER MENTIONED THE MAGIC THING.
THUNK
NOT SO FAST.
IT'S ALMOST SUN-DOWN.
I DOUBT YOU'LL BE ABLE TO FIND YOUR WAY OUT OF THE FOREST.
SPEND THE NIGHT.
I APPRE-CIATE THE OFFER...
...BUT WE DON'T...
...HAVE ANY MONEY.
I HAVE A FEW UNUSED ROOMS...
...THAT HAVE GOTTEN QUITE DUSTY RECENTLY.
...IF YOU'LL CLEAN THEM WHILE YOU'RE AT IT...
...YOU CAN USE THEM FOR FREE.

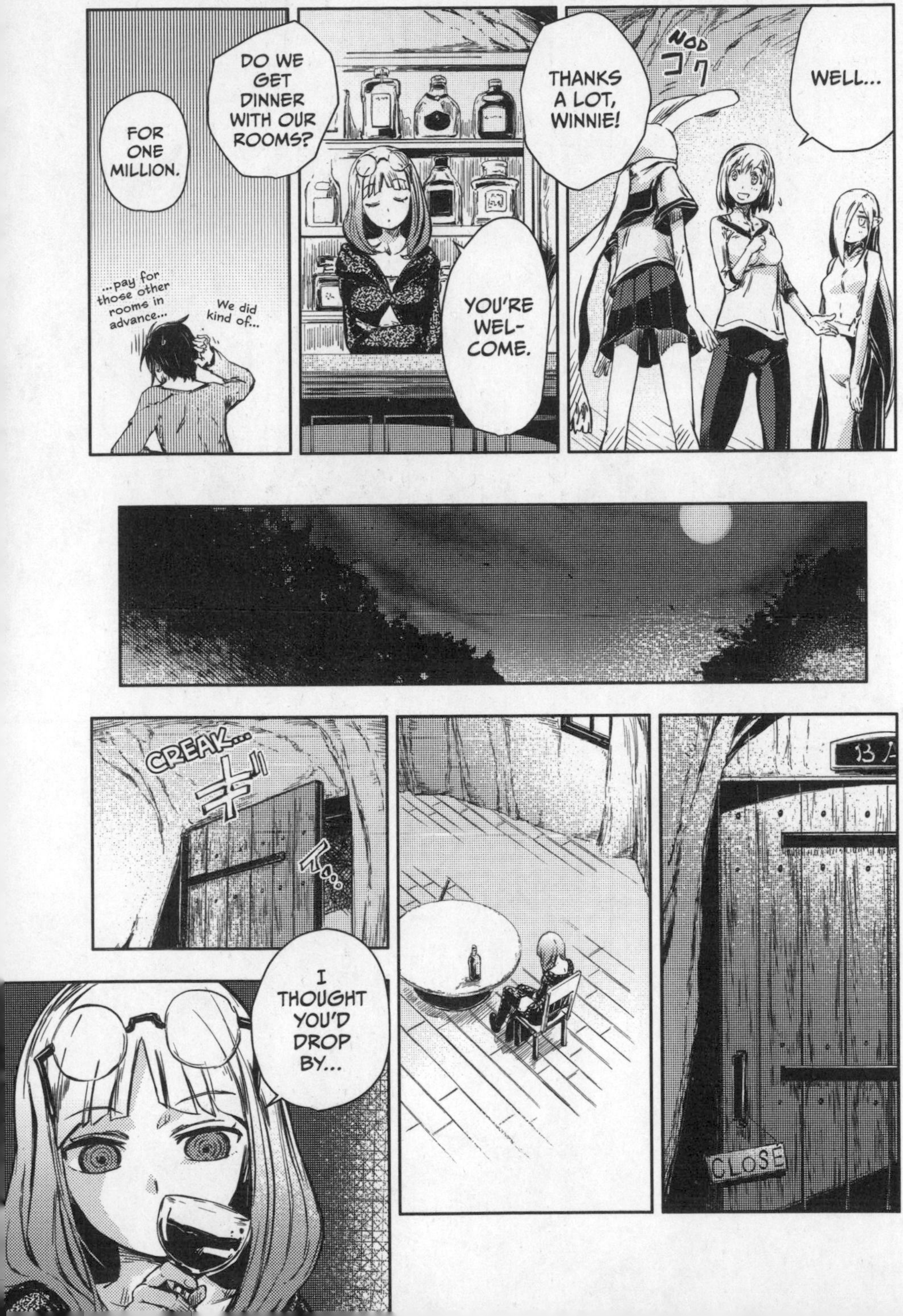
WELL...
NOD
コク
THANKS A LOT, WINNIE!
YOU'RE WEL-COME.
DO WE GET DINNER WITH OUR ROOMS?
FOR ONE MILLION.
We did kind of...
...pay for those other rooms in advance...
BA
CLOSE
CREAK...
キィ...
I THOUGHT YOU'D DROP BY...

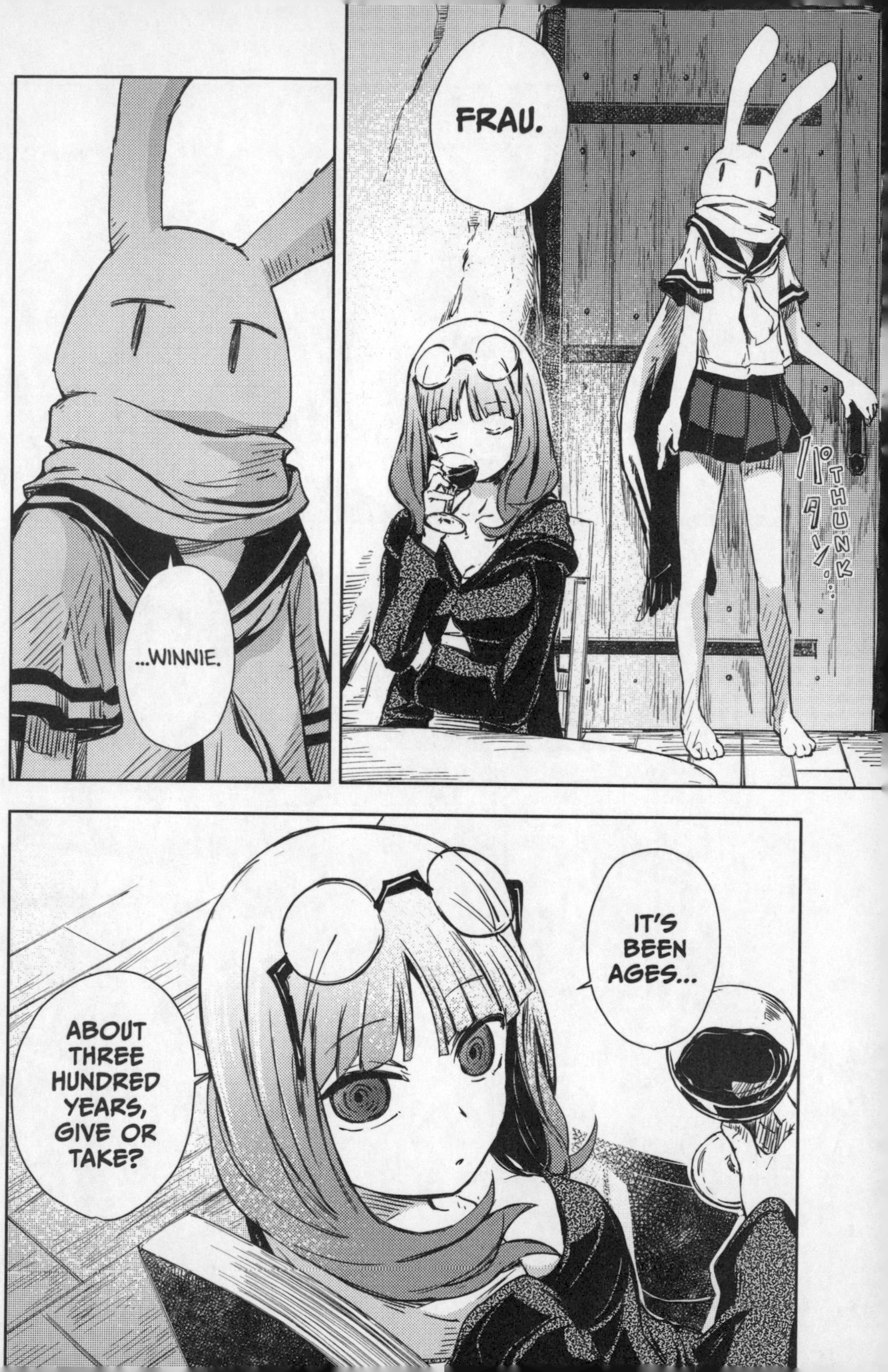
FRAU.
THUNK
...WINNIE.
IT'S BEEN AGES...
ABOUT THREE HUNDRED YEARS, GIVE OR TAKE?

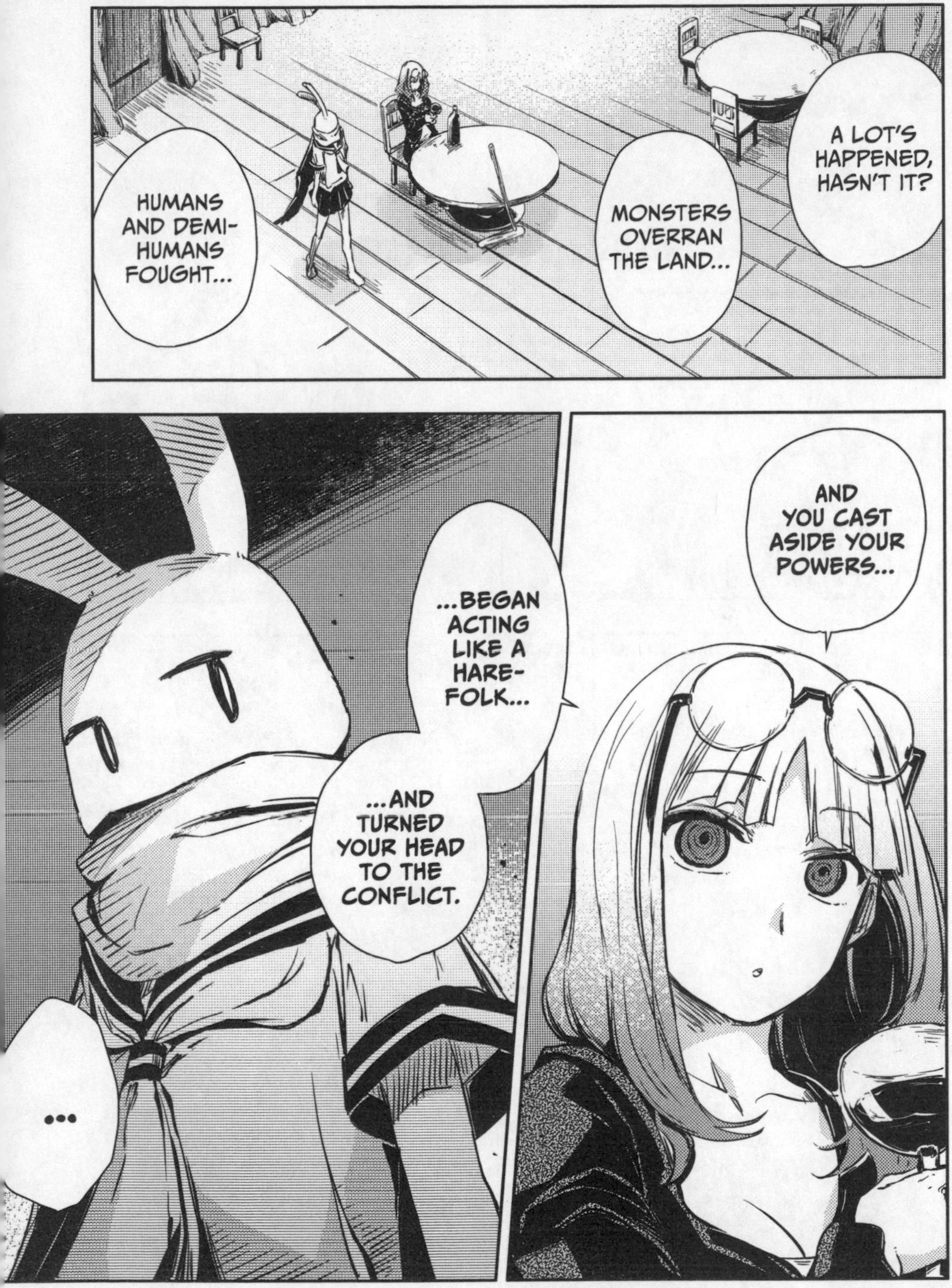
A LOT'S HAPPENED, HASN'T IT?
MONSTERS OVERRAN THE LAND...
HUMANS AND DEMI-HUMANS FOUGHT...
AND YOU CAST ASIDE YOUR POWERS...
...BEGAN ACTING LIKE A HARE-FOLK...
...AND TURNED YOUR HEAD TO THE CONFLICT.
...

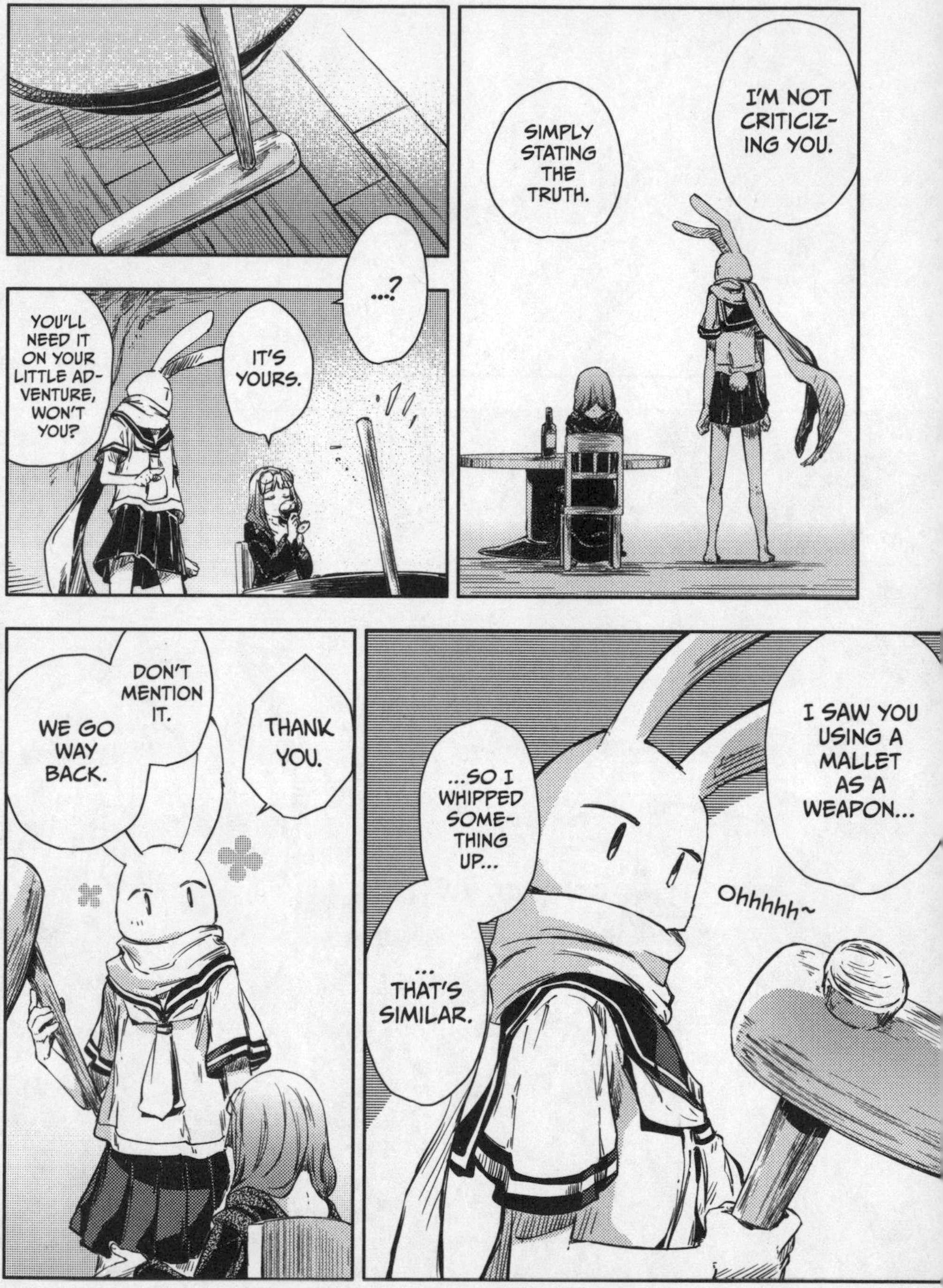
I'M NOT CRITICIZING YOU.
SIMPLY STATING THE TRUTH.
...?
IT'S YOURS.
YOU'LL NEED IT ON YOUR LITTLE ADVENTURE, WON'T YOU?
I SAW YOU USING A MALLET AS A WEAPON...
...SO I WHIPPED SOMETHING UP...
Ohhhhh~
... THAT'S SIMILAR.
THANK YOU.
DON'T MENTION IT.
WE GO WAY BACK.

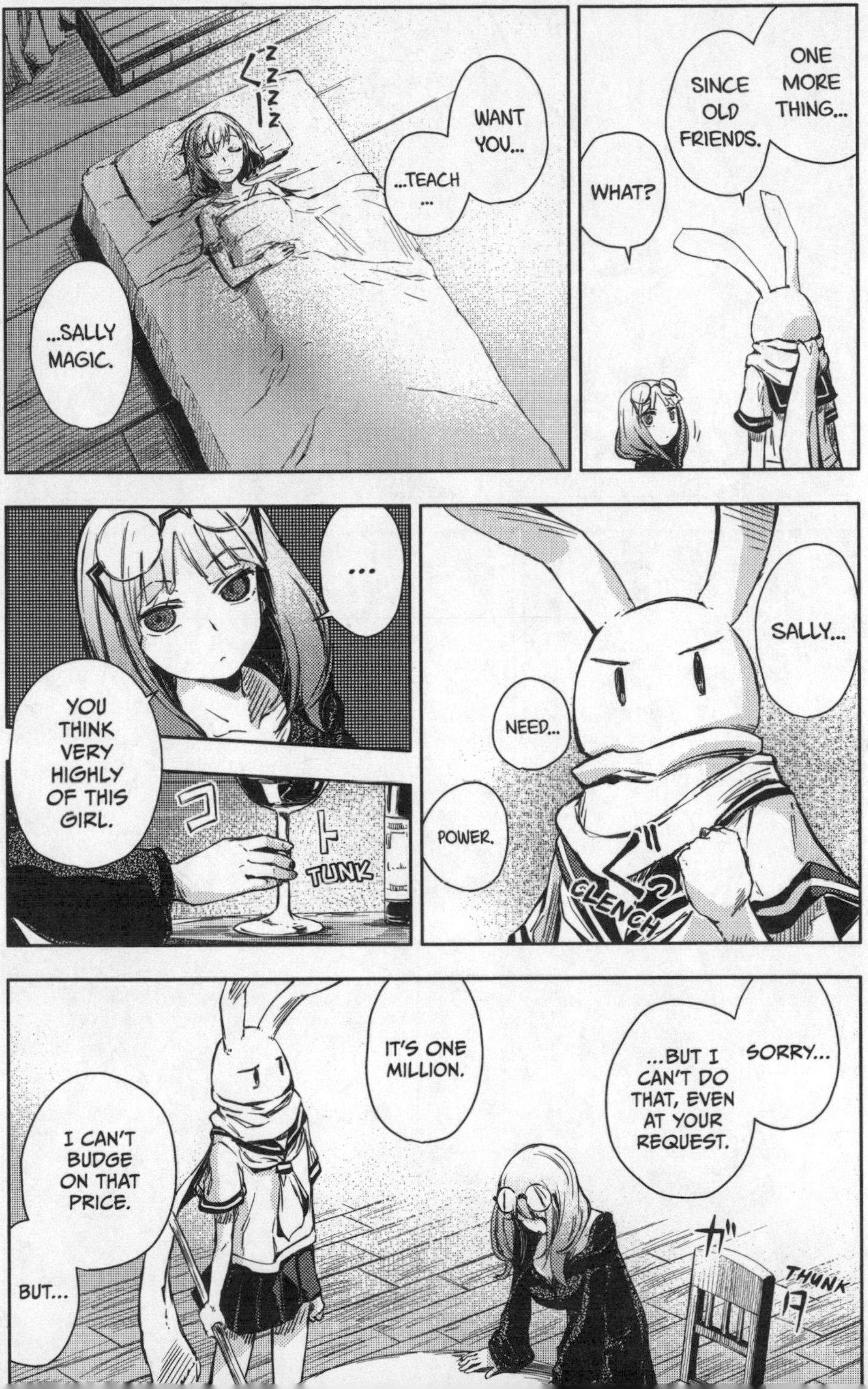
ONE MORE THING...
SINCE OLD FRIENDS.
WHAT?
Z Z Z Z
WANT YOU...
...TEACH ...
...SALLY MAGIC.
SALLY...
NEED...
POWER.
CLENCH
...
YOU THINK VERY HIGHLY OF THIS GIRL.
TUNK
SORRY...
...BUT I CAN'T DO THAT, EVEN AT YOUR REQUEST.
IT'S ONE MILLION.
I CAN'T BUDGE ON THAT PRICE.
BUT...
THUNK

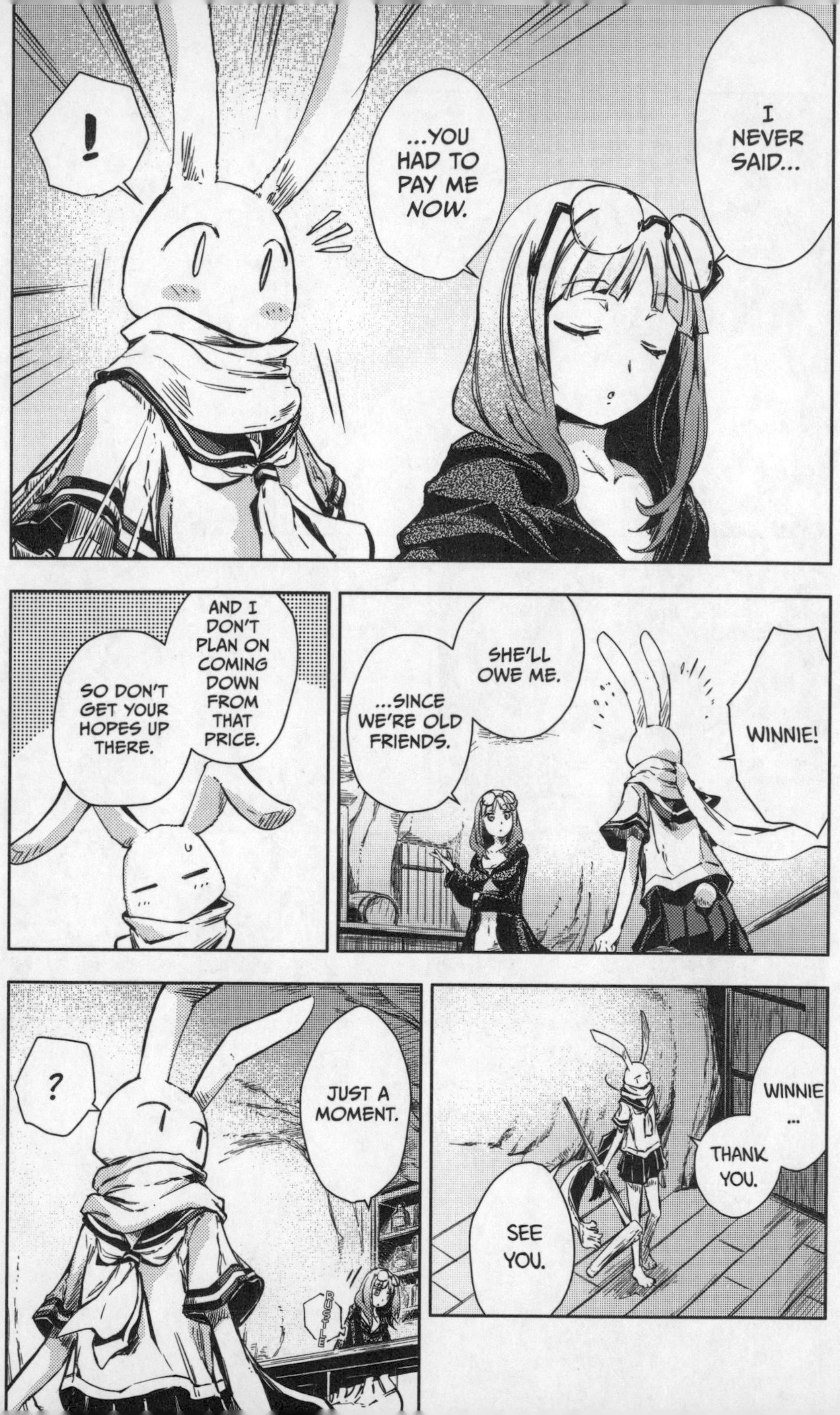
I NEVER SAID...
...YOU HAD TO PAY ME *NOW.*
!
WINNIE!
SHE'LL OWE ME.
...SINCE WE'RE OLD FRIENDS.
AND I DON'T PLAN ON COMING DOWN FROM THAT PRICE.
SO DON'T GET YOUR HOPES UP THERE.
WINNIE ...
THANK YOU.
SEE YOU.
JUST A MOMENT.
?
RUSTLE

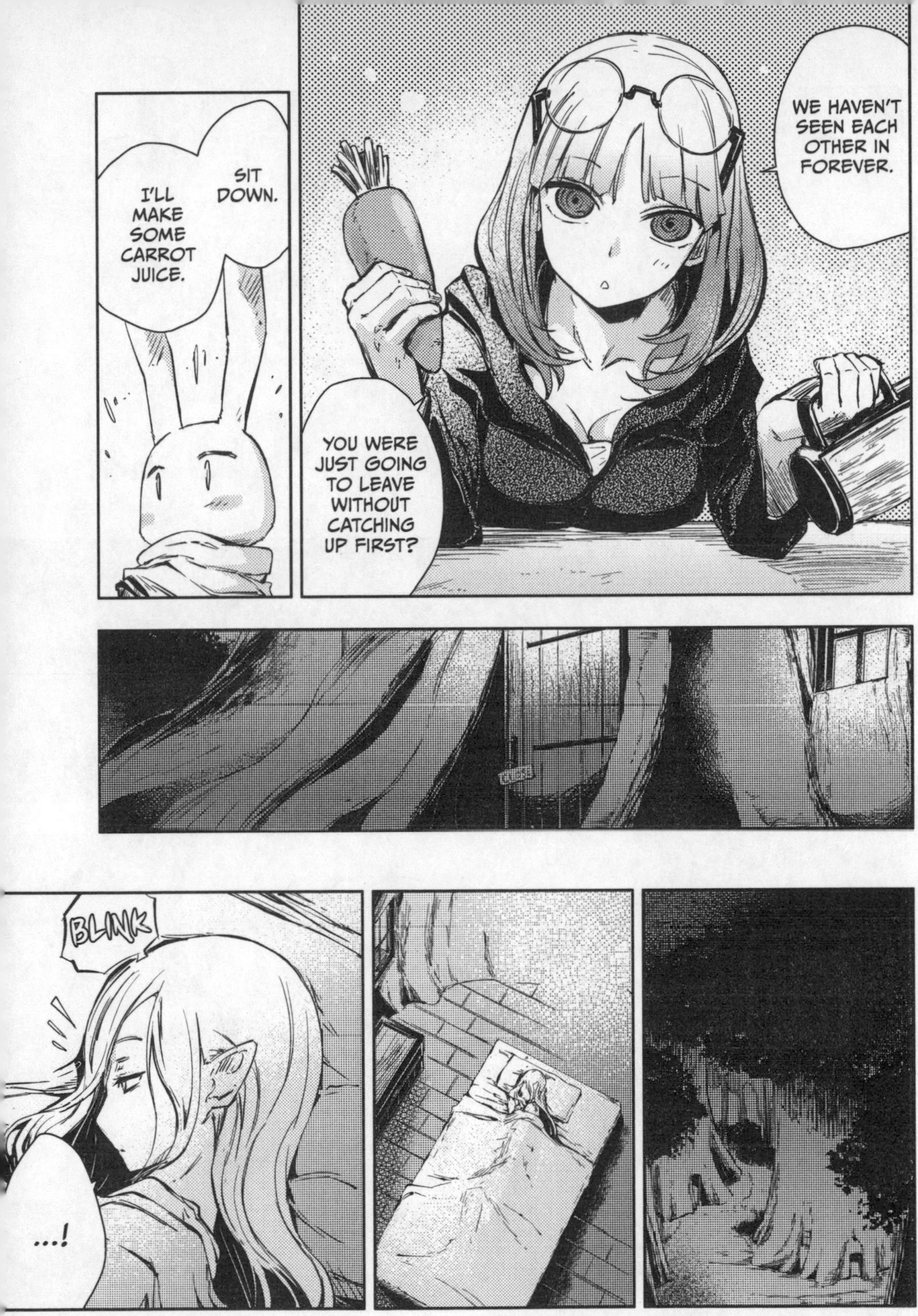
WE HAVEN'T SEEN EACH OTHER IN FOREVER.
YOU WERE JUST GOING TO LEAVE WITHOUT CATCHING UP FIRST?
SIT DOWN.
I'LL MAKE SOME CARROT JUICE.
BLINK
...!

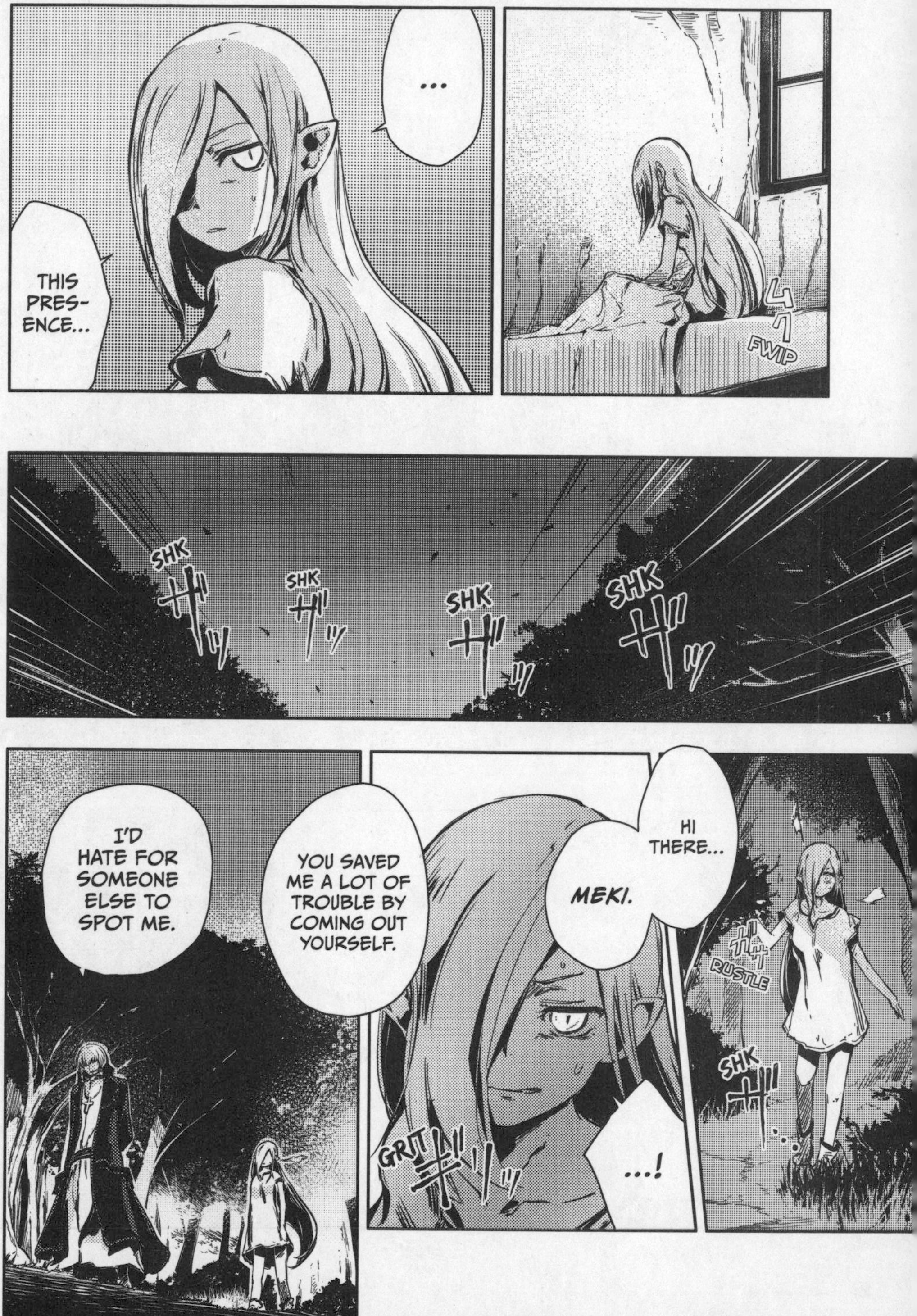
FWIP
...
THIS PRESENCE...
SHK
SHK
SHK
SHK
HI THERE...
MEKI.
RUSTLE
SHK
...!
GRIT
YOU SAVED ME A LOT OF TROUBLE BY COMING OUT YOURSELF.
I'D HATE FOR SOMEONE ELSE TO SPOT ME.

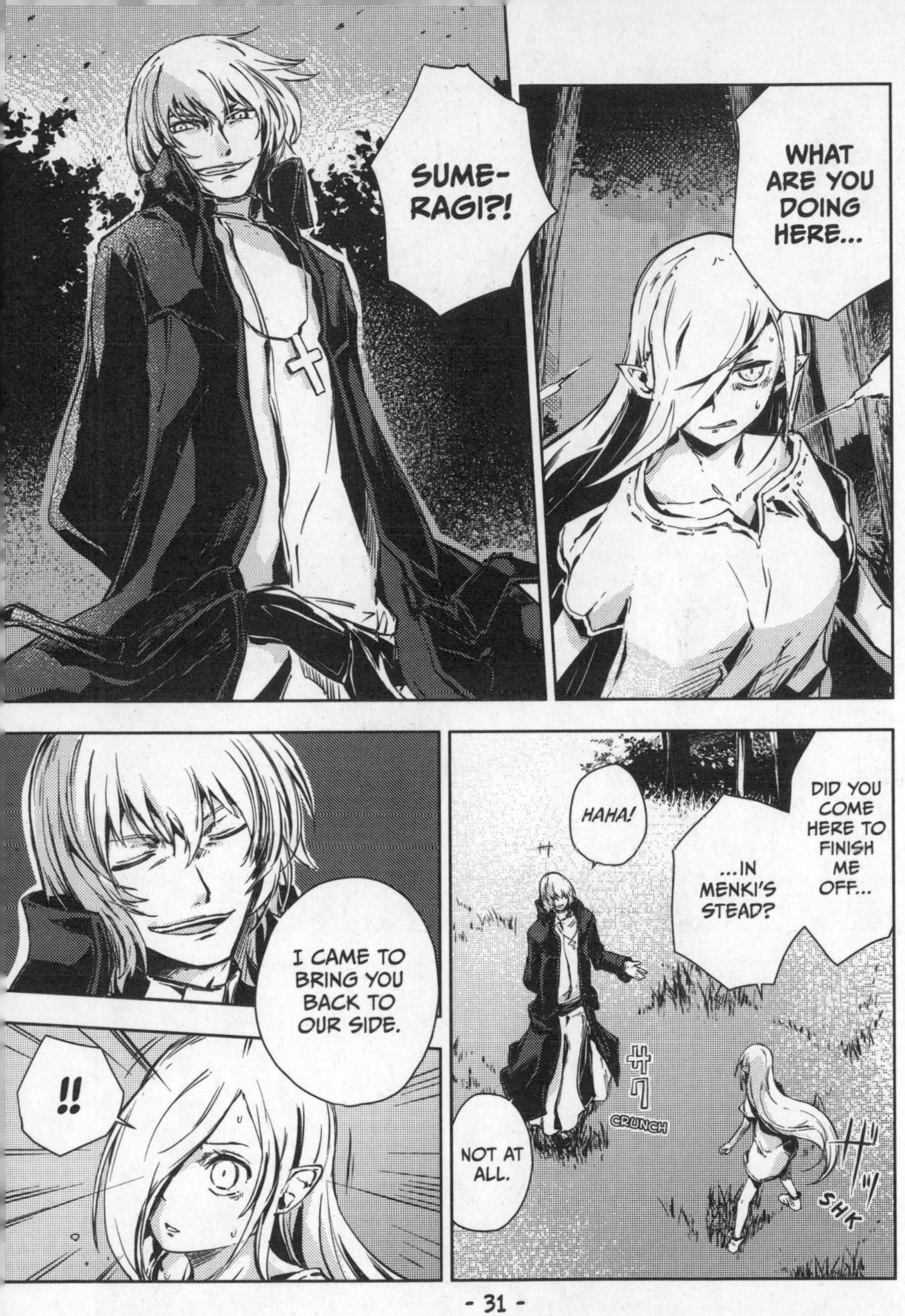
WHAT ARE YOU DOING HERE...
SUME-RAGI?!
DID YOU COME HERE TO FINISH ME OFF...
...IN MENKI'S STEAD?
HAHA!
SHK
CRUNCH
NOT AT ALL.
I CAME TO BRING YOU BACK TO OUR SIDE.
!!

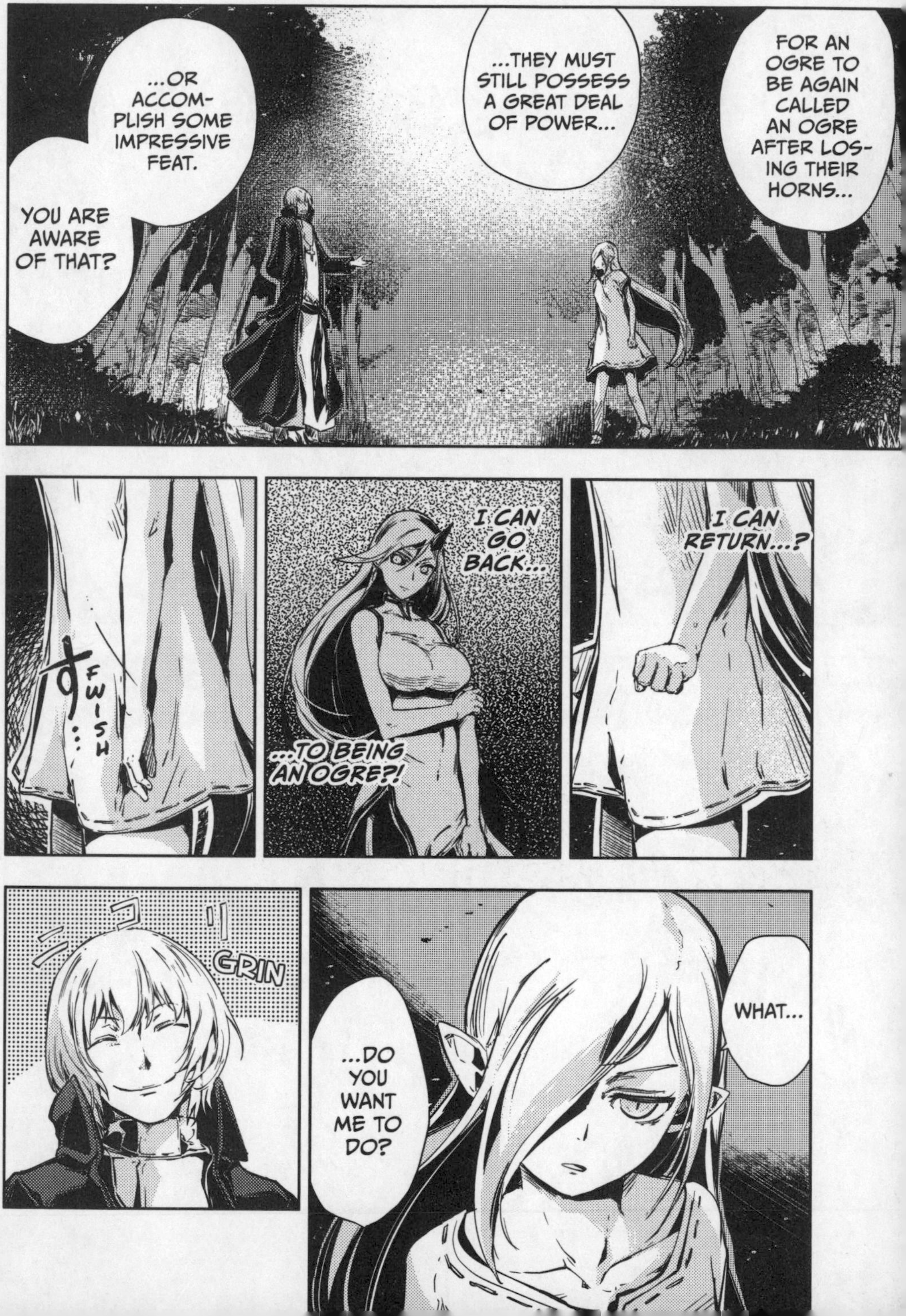
FOR AN OGRE TO BE AGAIN CALLED AN OGRE AFTER LOS-ING THEIR HORNS...
...THEY MUST STILL POSSESS A GREAT DEAL OF POWER...
...OR ACCOM-PLISH SOME IMPRESSIVE FEAT.
YOU ARE AWARE OF THAT?
I CAN RETURN...?
I CAN GO BACK...
...TO BEING AN OGRE?!
FWISH
WHAT...
...DO YOU WANT ME TO DO?
GRIN

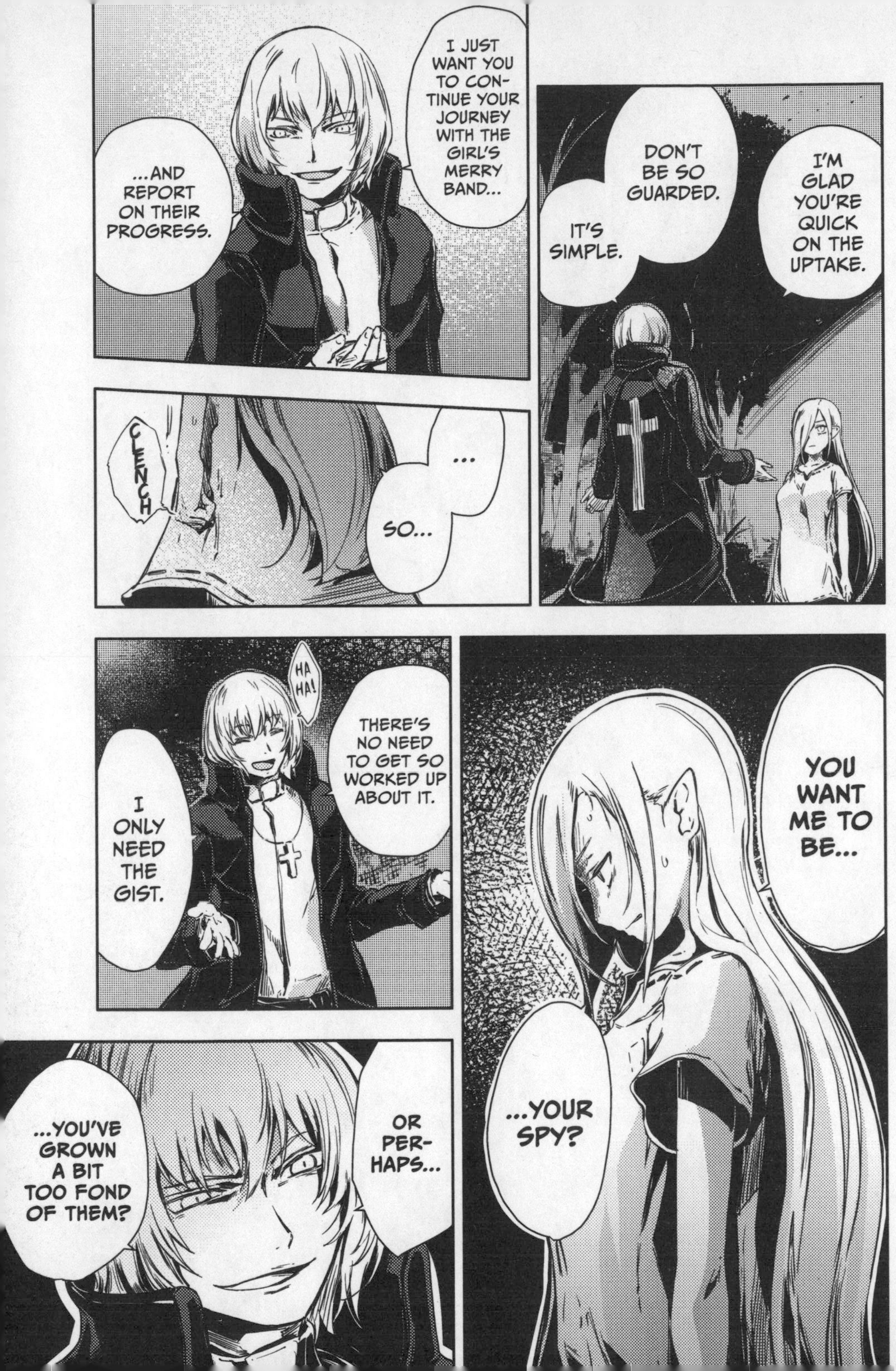
I'M GLAD YOU'RE QUICK ON THE UPTAKE.
DON'T BE SO GUARDED.
IT'S SIMPLE.
I JUST WANT YOU TO CON-TINUE YOUR JOURNEY WITH THE GIRL'S MERRY BAND...
...AND REPORT ON THEIR PROGRESS.
...
SO...
CLENCH
YOU WANT ME TO BE...
...YOUR SPY?
HA HA!
THERE'S NO NEED TO GET SO WORKED UP ABOUT IT.
I ONLY NEED THE GIST.
OR PER-HAPS...
...YOU'VE GROWN A BIT TOO FOND OF THEM?

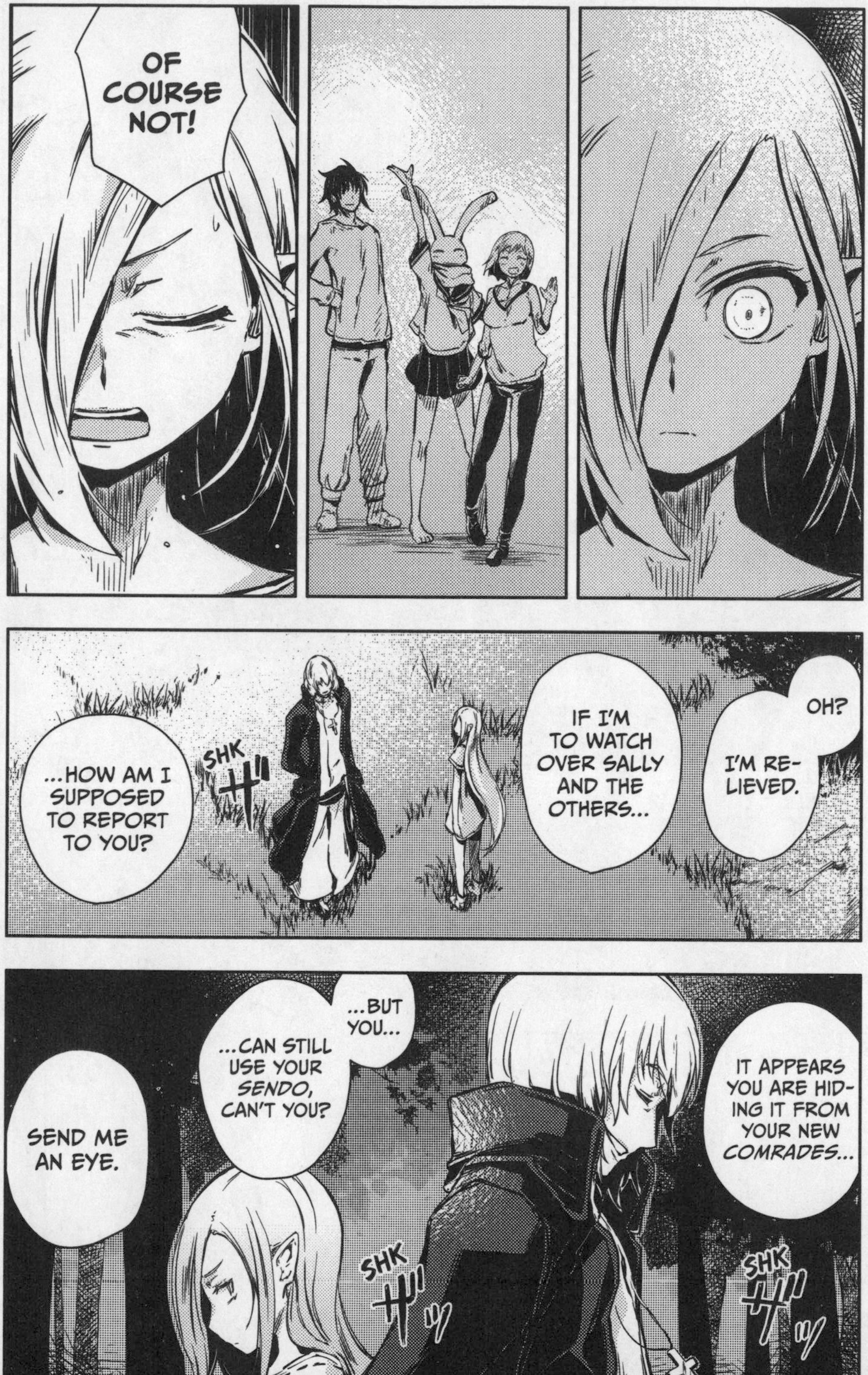
OF COURSE NOT!
OH?
I'M RE-LIEVED.
IF I'M TO WATCH OVER SALLY AND THE OTHERS...
SHK
...HOW AM I SUPPOSED TO REPORT TO YOU?
IT APPEARS YOU ARE HID-ING IT FROM YOUR NEW COMRADES...
SHK
...BUT YOU...
...CAN STILL USE YOUR SENDO, CAN'T YOU?
SHK
SEND ME AN EYE.

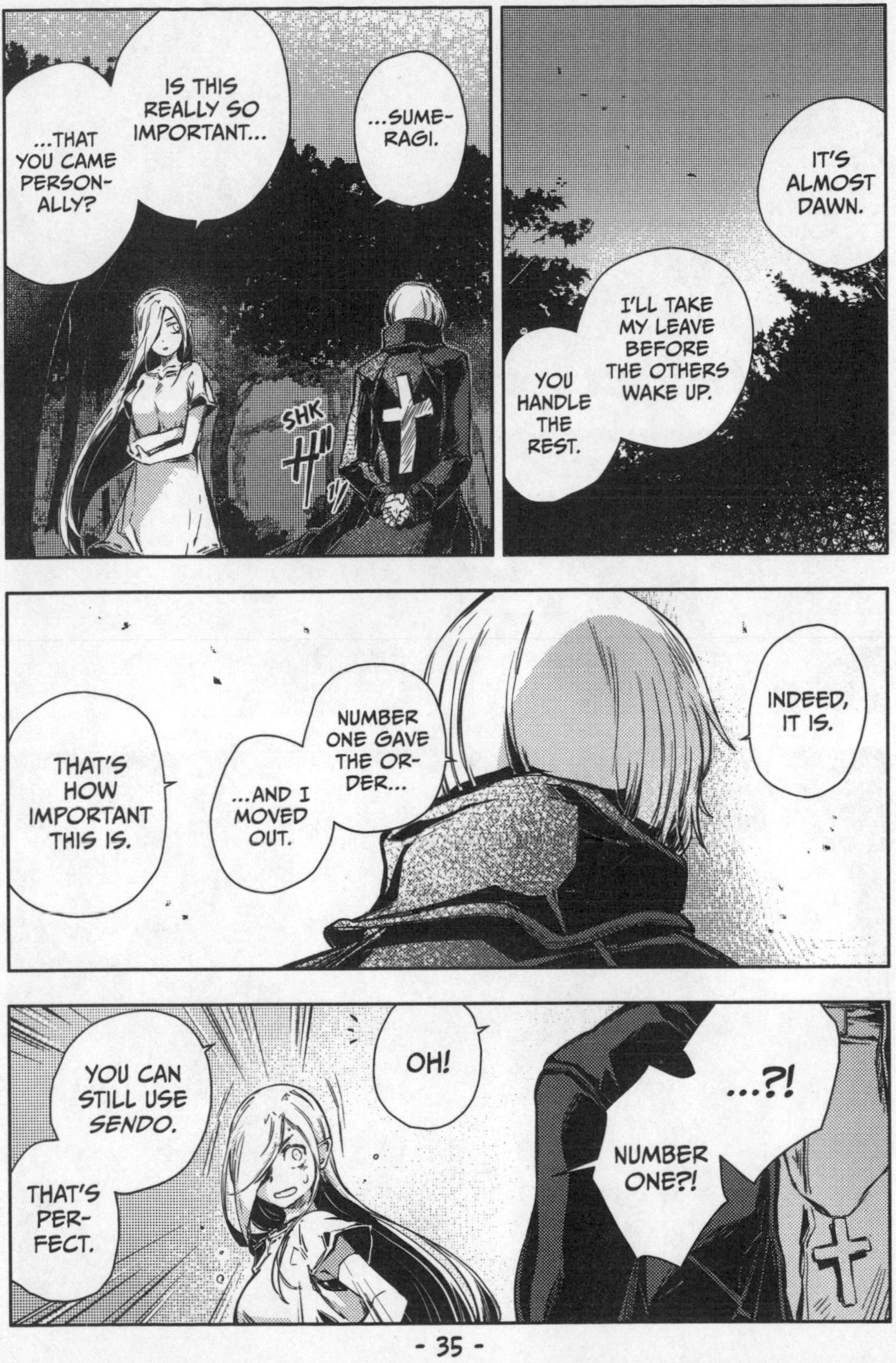
IT'S ALMOST DAWN.
I'LL TAKE MY LEAVE BEFORE THE OTHERS WAKE UP.
YOU HANDLE THE REST.
...SUME-RAGI.
IS THIS REALLY SO IMPORTANT...
...THAT YOU CAME PERSON-ALLY?
SHK
INDEED, IT IS.
NUMBER ONE GAVE THE OR-DER...
...AND I MOVED OUT.
THAT'S HOW IMPORTANT THIS IS.
...?!
NUMBER ONE?!
OH!
YOU CAN STILL USE SENDO.
THAT'S PER-FECT.

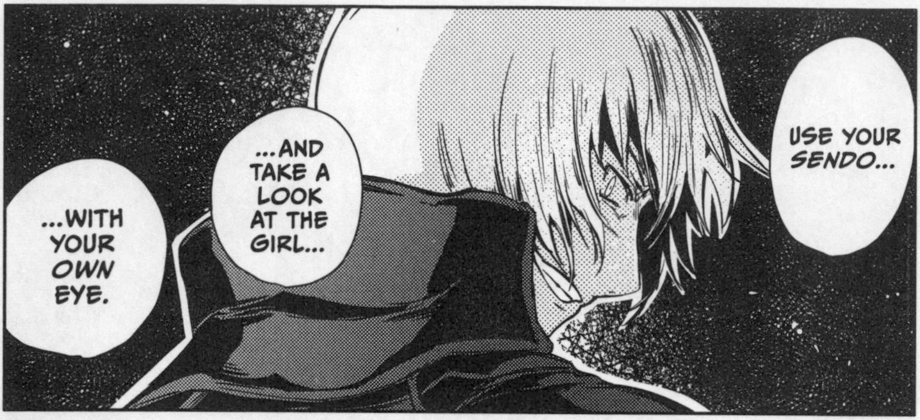
USE YOUR SENDO...
...AND TAKE A LOOK AT THE GIRL...
...WITH YOUR OWN EYE.

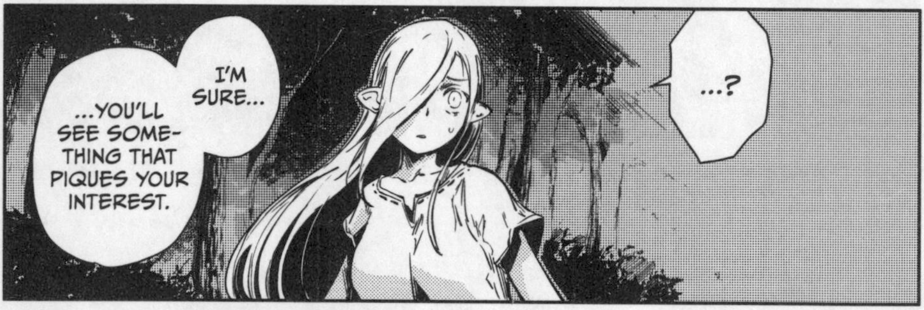
...?
I'M SURE...
...YOU'LL SEE SOMETHING THAT PIQUES YOUR INTEREST.

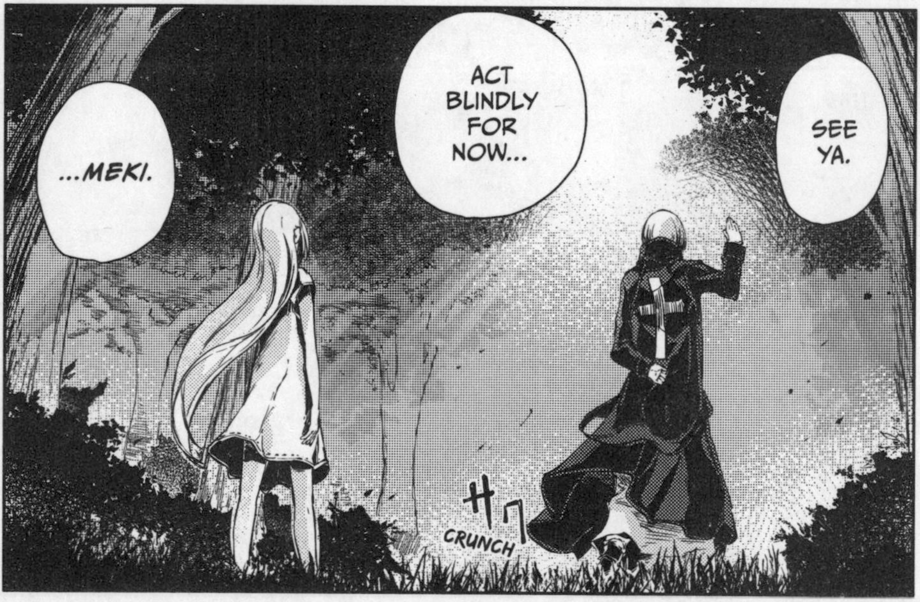
SEE YA.
ACT BLINDLY FOR NOW...
...MEKI.
CRUNCH

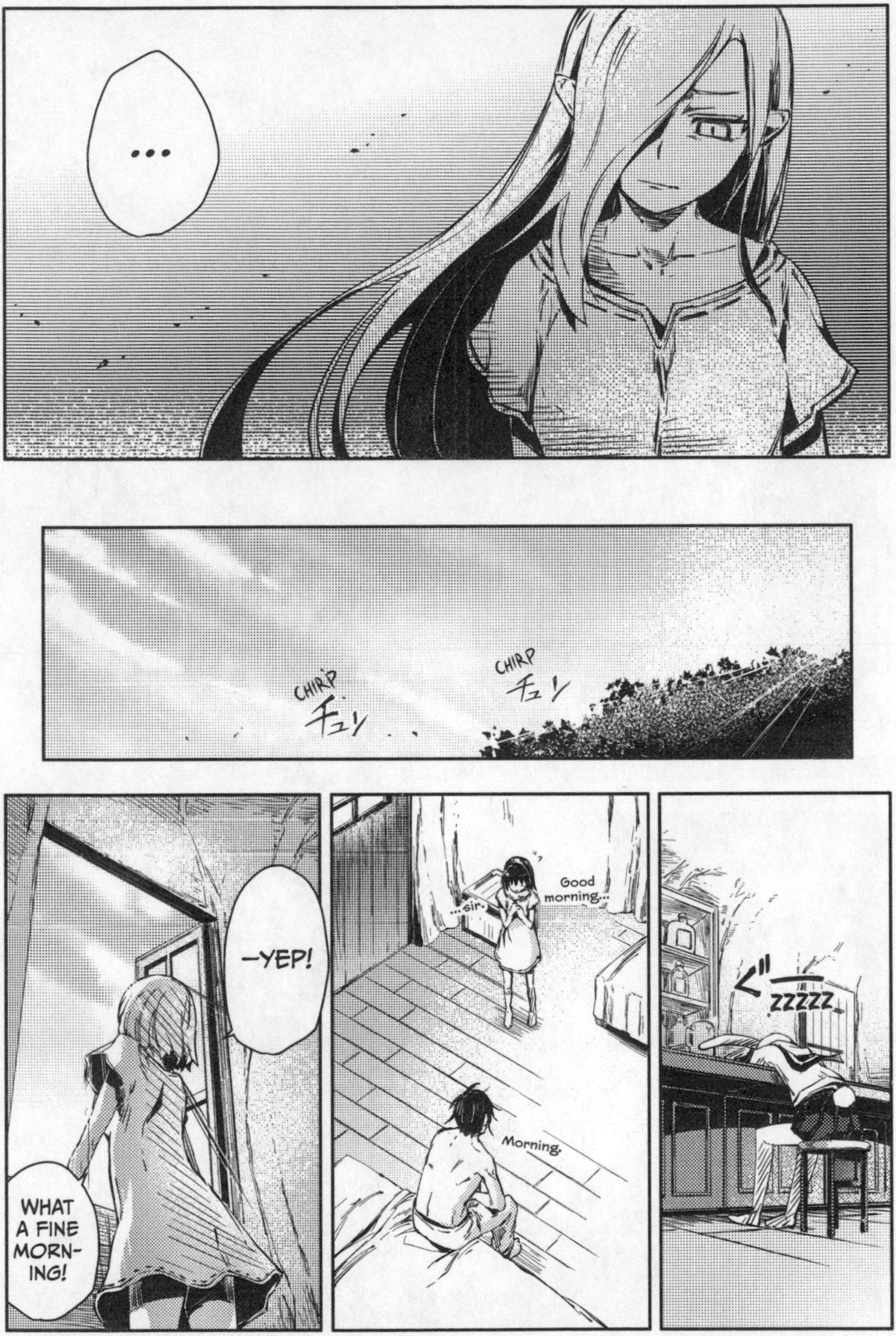
...
CHIRP
チュン
CHIRP
チュン
ぐー
ZZZZZ
Good morning...
...sir.
Morning.
—YEP!
WHAT A FINE MORNING!

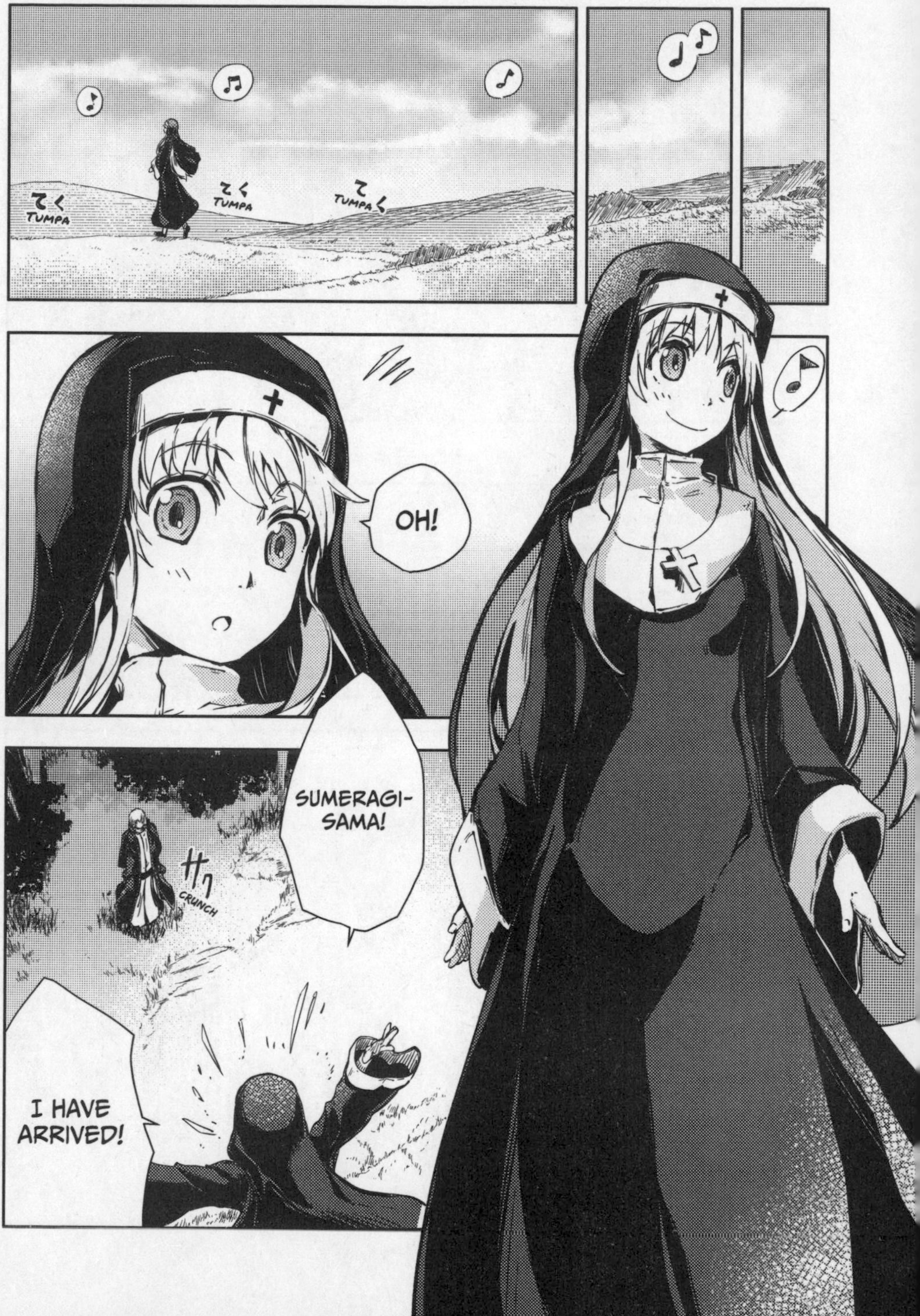

てく
TUMPA
てく
TUMPA
てく
TUMPA
OH!
SUMERAGI-SAMA!
サク
CRUNCH
I HAVE ARRIVED!

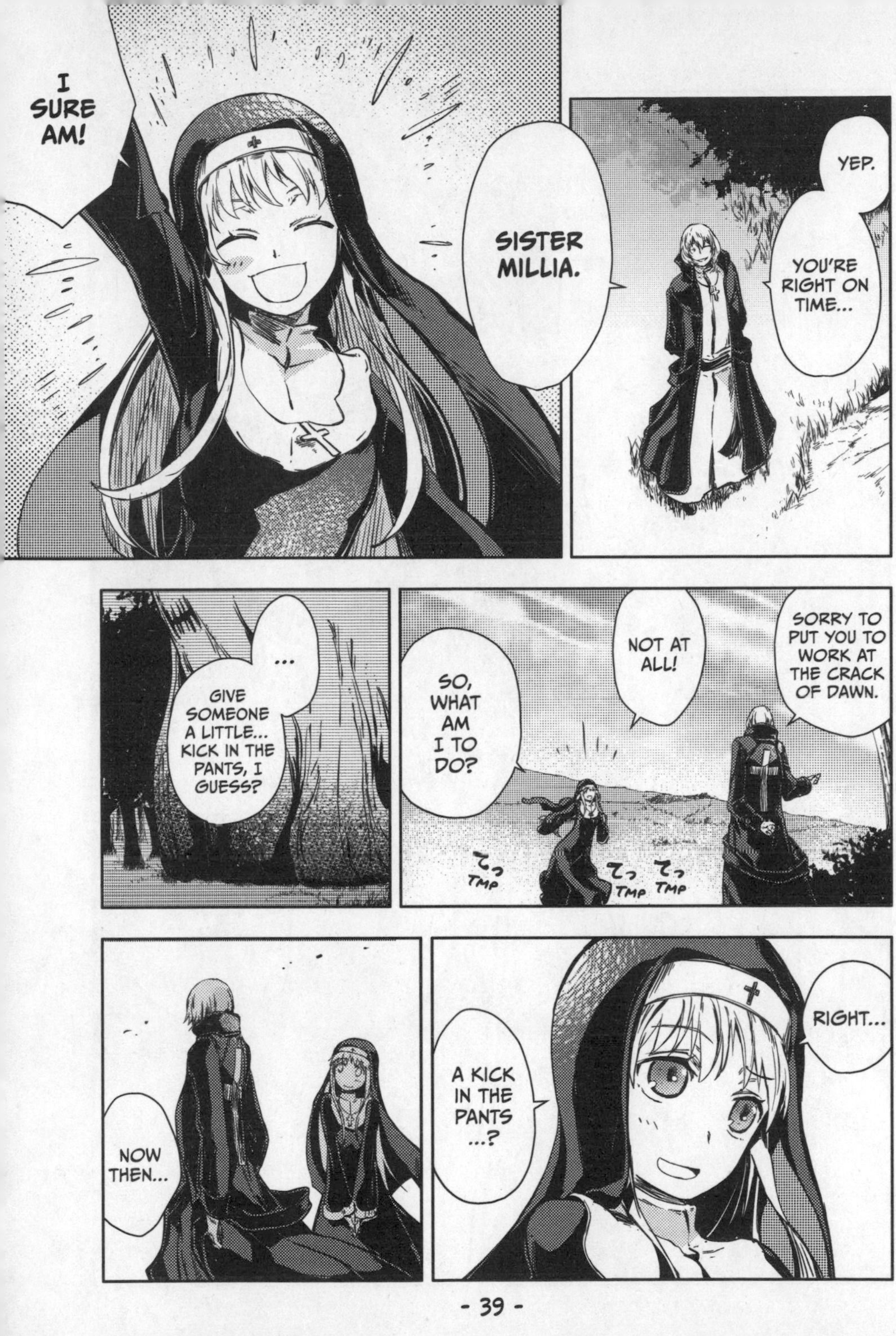
YEP.
YOU'RE RIGHT ON TIME...
SISTER MILLIA.
I SURE AM!
SORRY TO PUT YOU TO WORK AT THE CRACK OF DAWN.
NOT AT ALL!
SO, WHAT AM I TO DO?
てっ TMP
てっ TMP
てっ TMP
...
GIVE SOMEONE A LITTLE... KICK IN THE PANTS, I GUESS?
RIGHT...
A KICK IN THE PANTS ...?
NOW THEN...

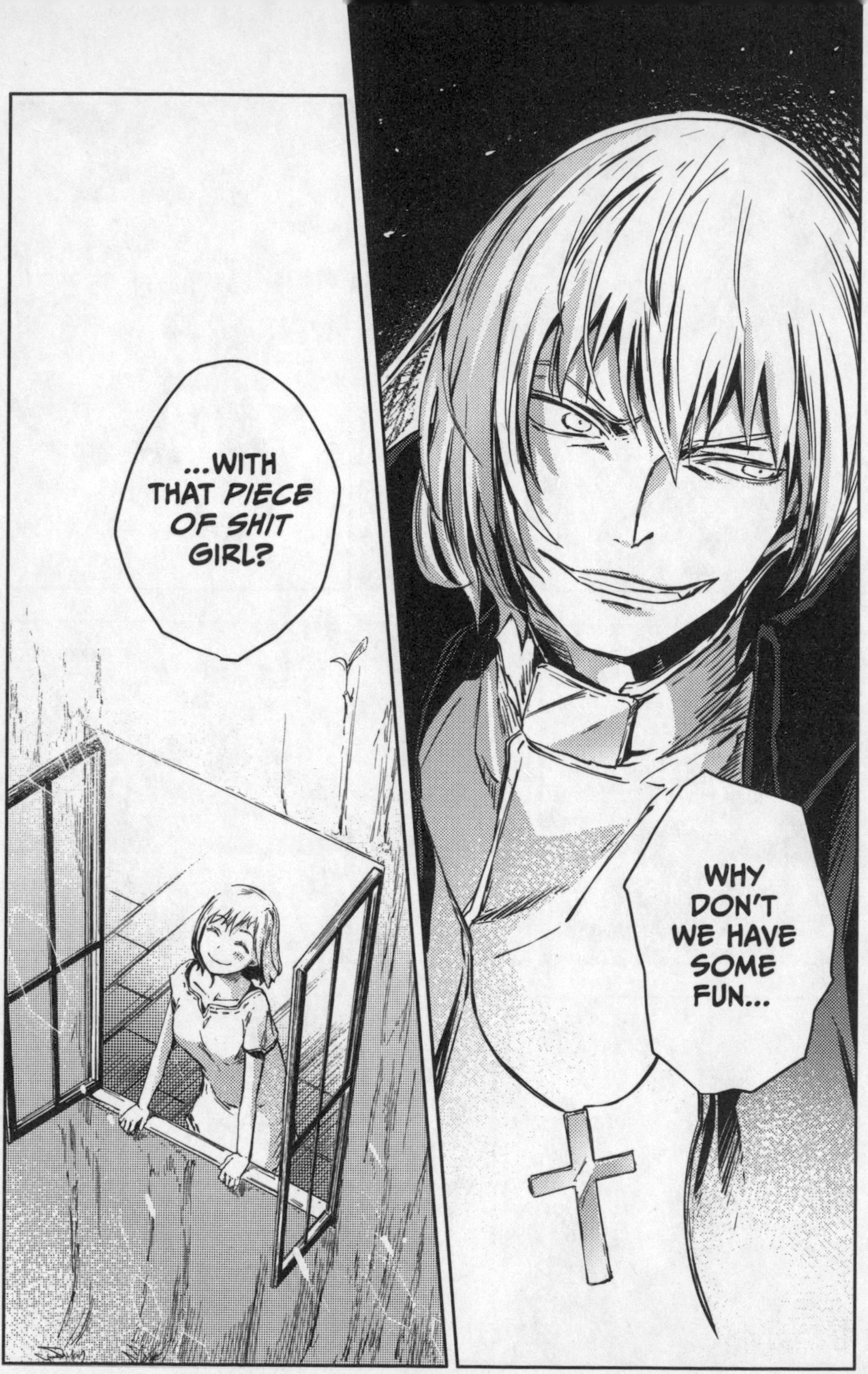
WHY DON'T WE HAVE SOME FUN...
...WITH THAT *PIECE* OF SHIT GIRL?

Was it just my imagination or did I hear Sumeragi-sama use foul language?
AHEM!
It was your imagination.

# PEACH BOY RIVERSIDE

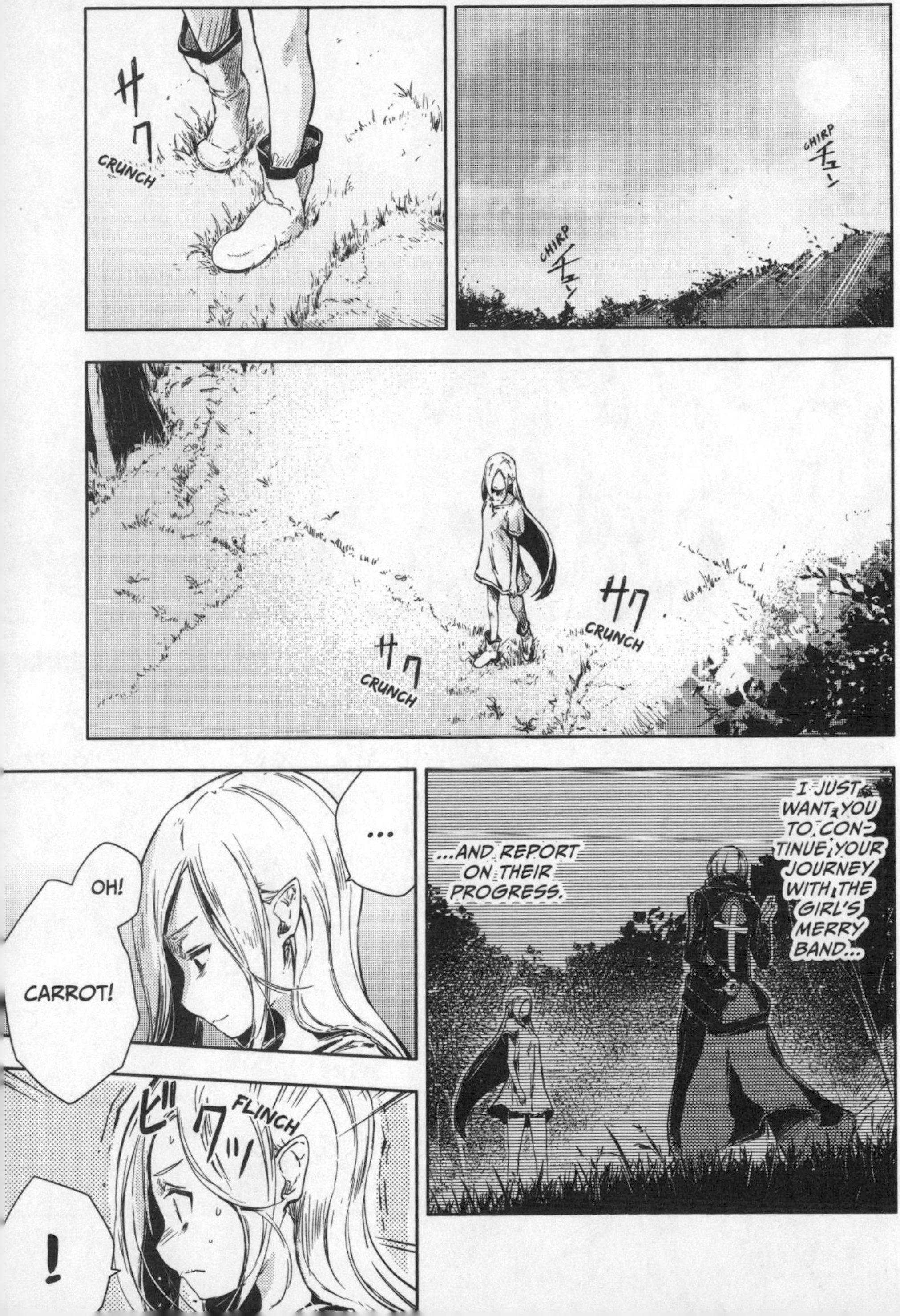
CHIRP
CHIRP
サク
CRUNCH
サク
CRUNCH
サク
CRUNCH
I JUST WANT YOU TO CONTINUE YOUR JOURNEY WITH THE GIRL'S MERRY BAND...
...AND REPORT ON THEIR PROGRESS.
...
OH!
CARROT!
FLINCH
!

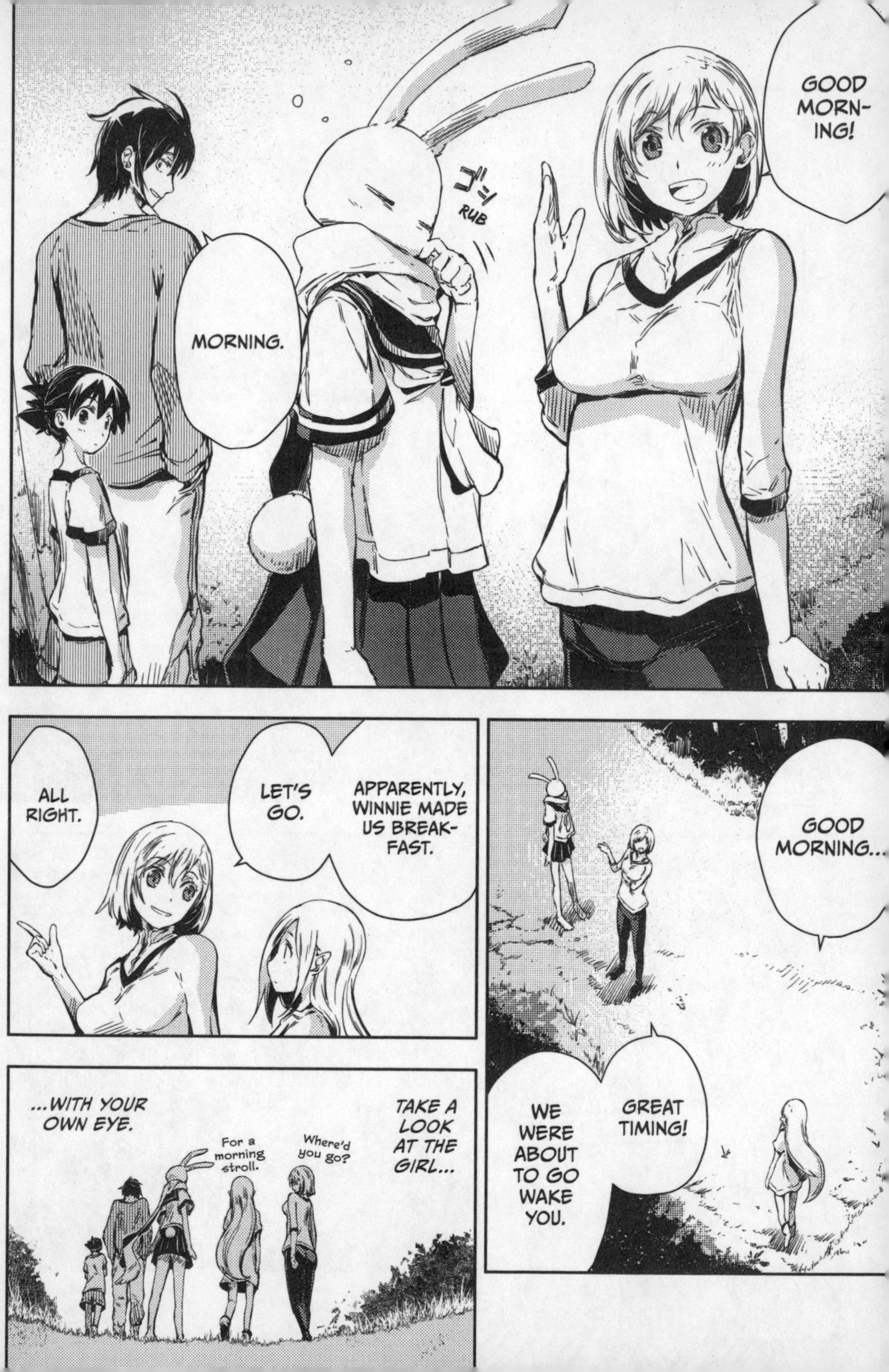
GOOD MORNING!
ゴシ
RUB
MORNING.
GOOD MORNING...
GREAT TIMING!
WE WERE ABOUT TO GO WAKE YOU.
APPARENTLY, WINNIE MADE US BREAKFAST.
LET'S GO.
ALL RIGHT.
TAKE A LOOK AT THE GIRL...
Where'd you go?
For a morning stroll.
...WITH YOUR OWN EYE.

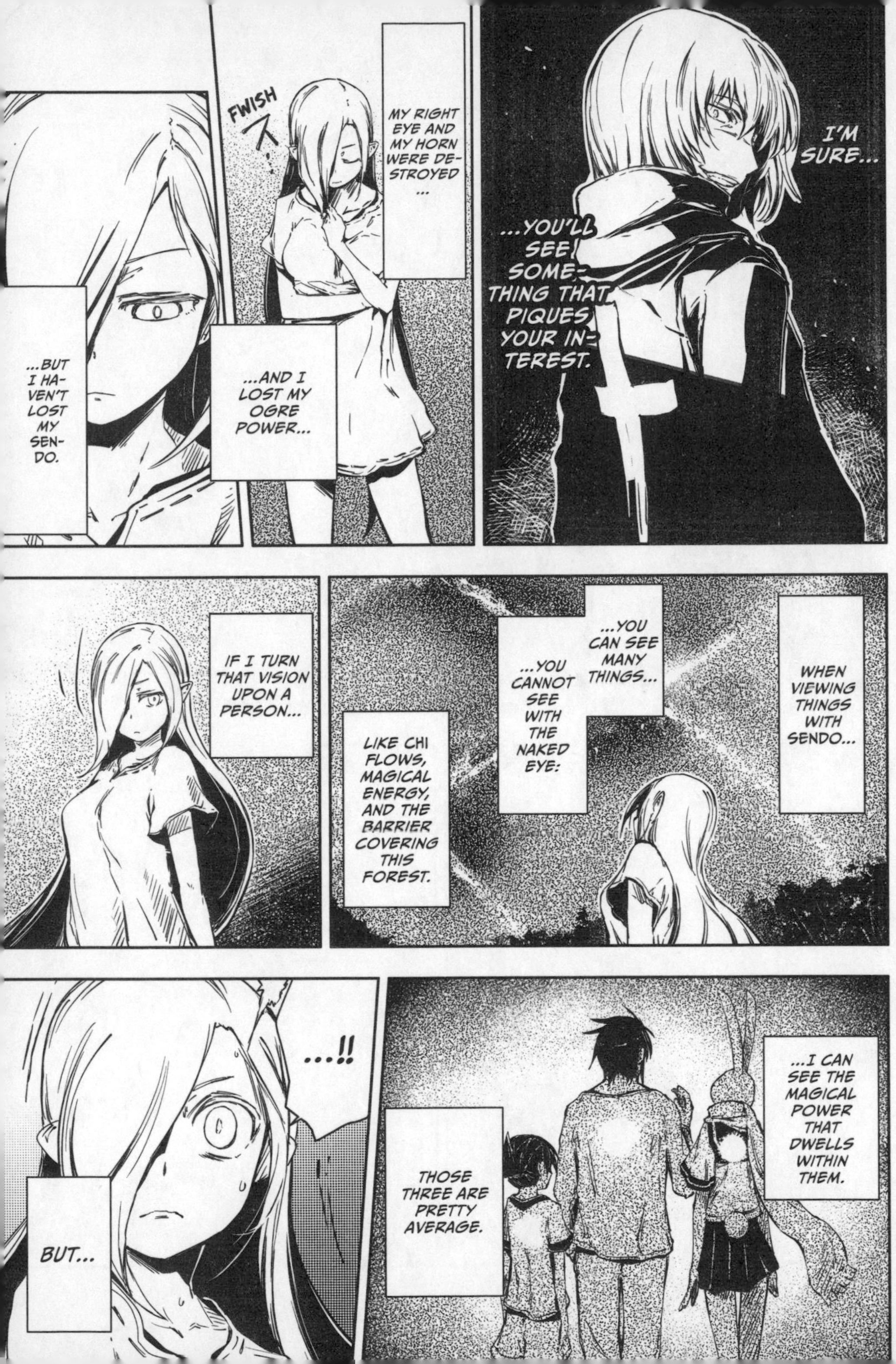
I'M SURE...
...YOU'LL SEE SOMETHING THAT PIQUES YOUR INTEREST.
FWISH
MY RIGHT EYE AND MY HORN WERE DESTROYED...
...AND I LOST MY OGRE POWER...
...BUT I HAVEN'T LOST MY SENDO.
WHEN VIEWING THINGS WITH SENDO...
...YOU CAN SEE MANY THINGS...
...YOU CANNOT SEE WITH THE NAKED EYE:
LIKE CHI FLOWS, MAGICAL ENERGY, AND THE BARRIER COVERING THIS FOREST.
IF I TURN THAT VISION UPON A PERSON...
...I CAN SEE THE MAGICAL POWER THAT DWELLS WITHIN THEM.
THOSE THREE ARE PRETTY AVERAGE.
...!!
BUT...

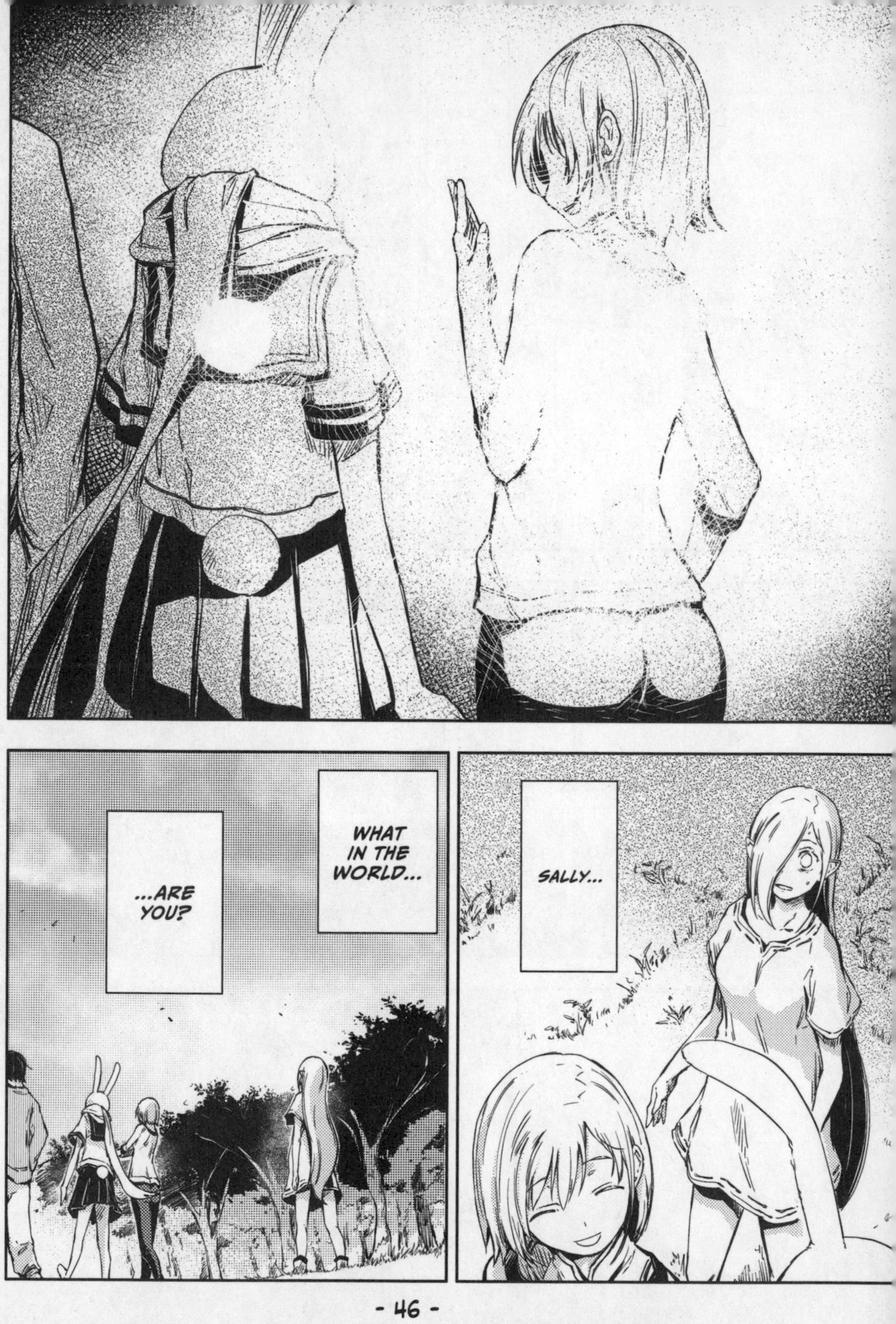
SALLY...
WHAT IN THE WORLD...
...ARE YOU?

# CHAPTER 9: HAWTHORN AND THE TRUTH

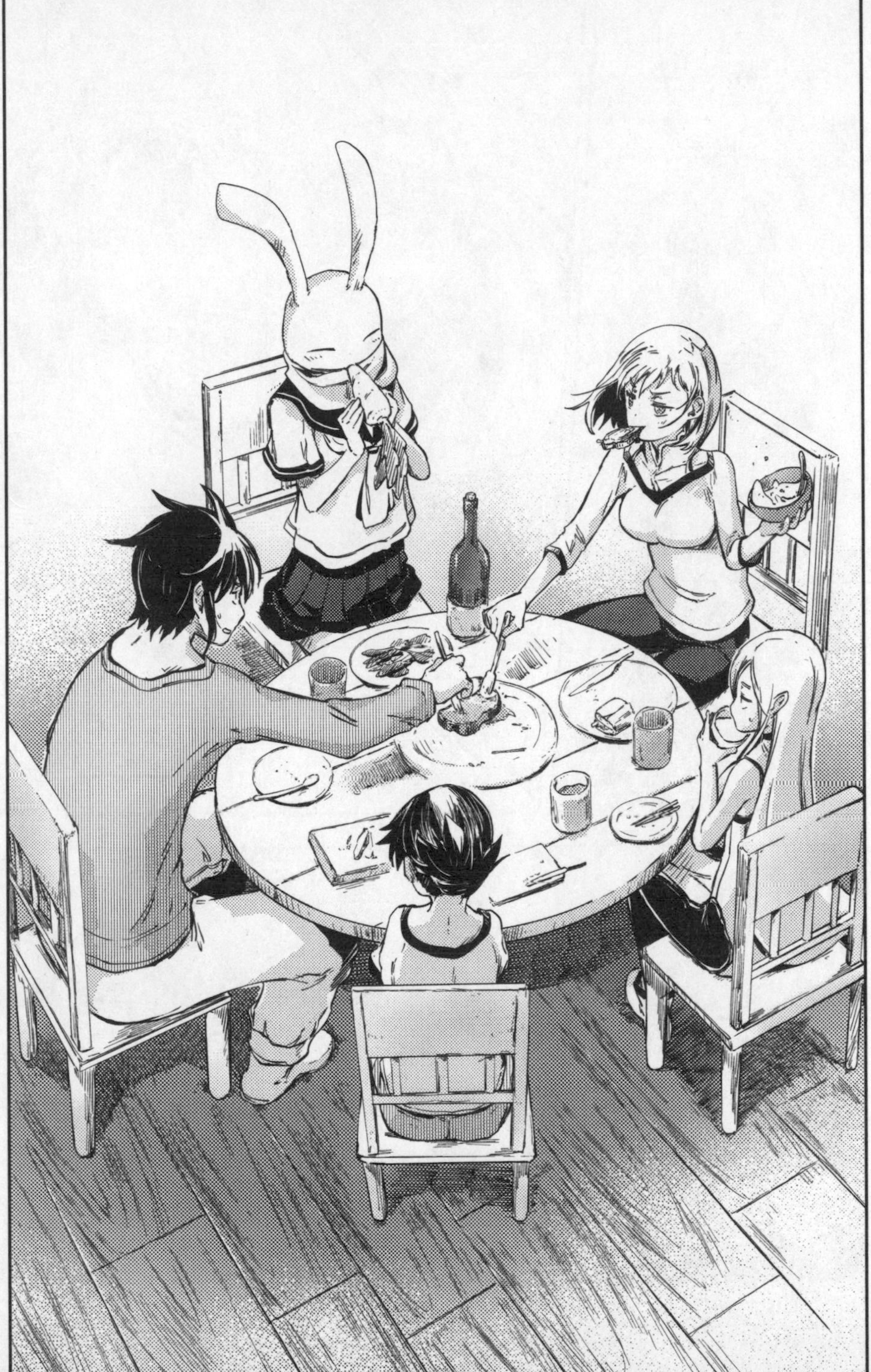

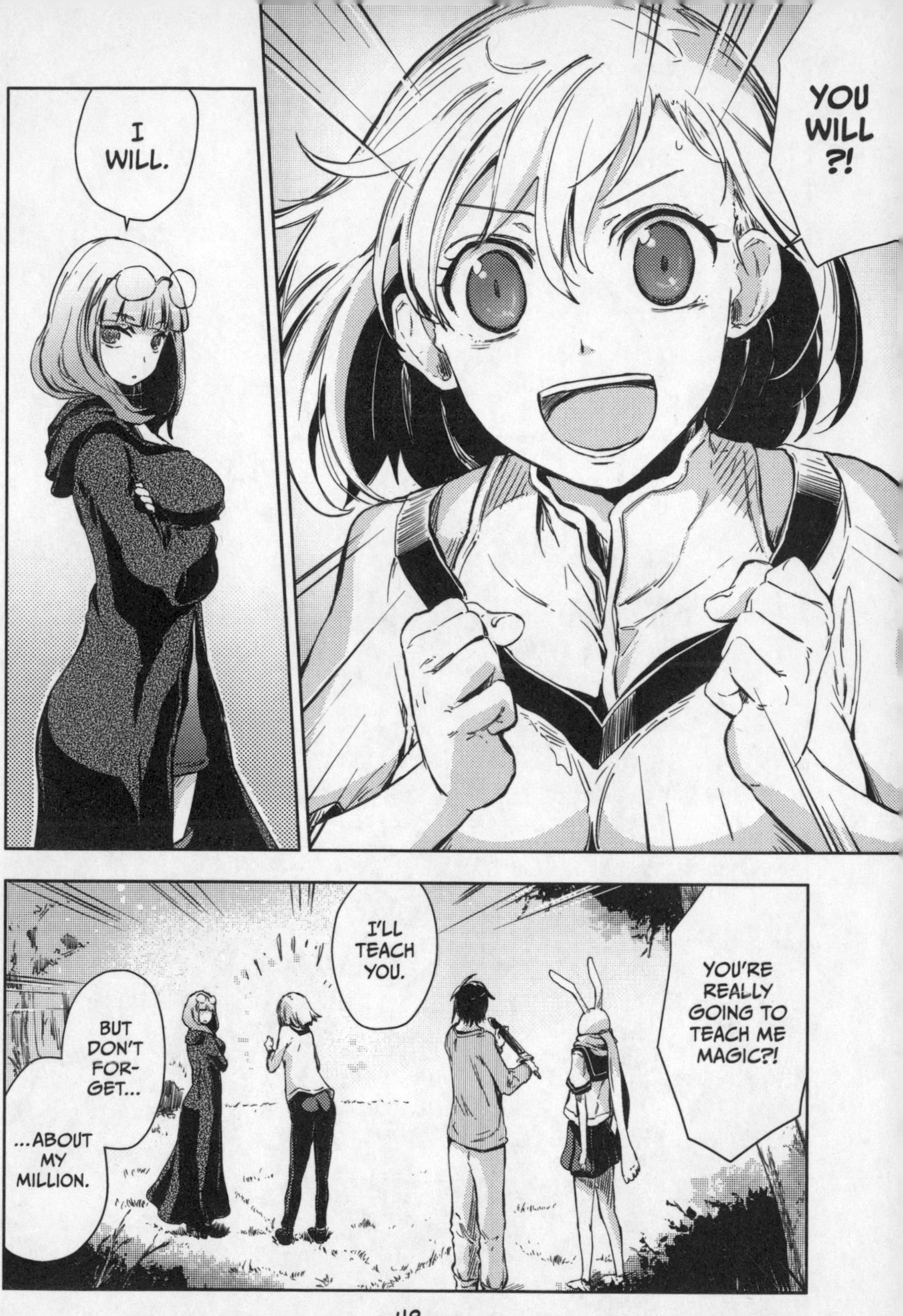
YOU WILL ?!
I WILL.
YOU'RE REALLY GOING TO TEACH ME MAGIC?!
I'LL TEACH YOU.
BUT DON'T FOR-GET...
...ABOUT MY MILLION.

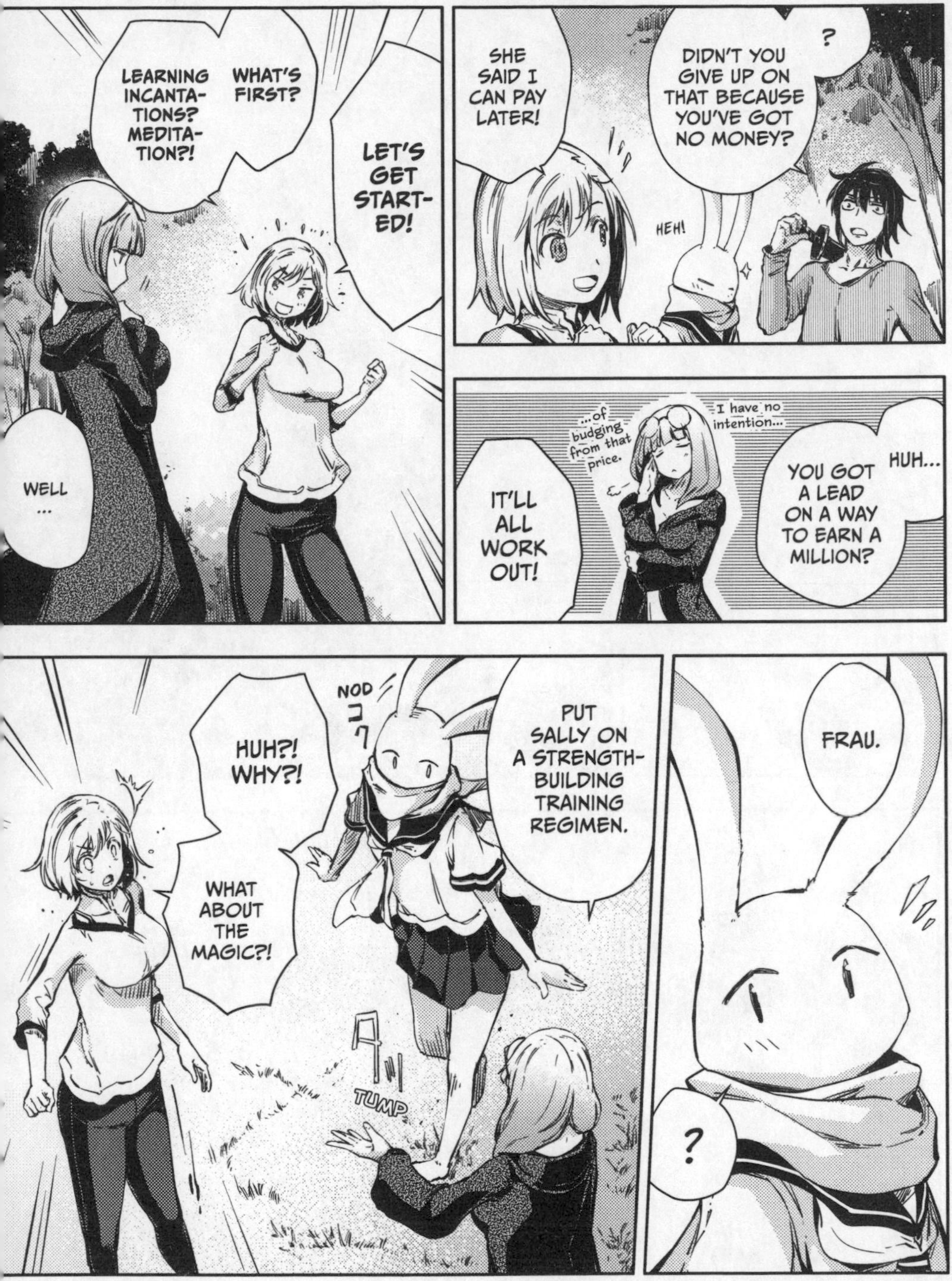
?
DIDN'T YOU GIVE UP ON THAT BECAUSE YOU'VE GOT NO MONEY?
SHE SAID I CAN PAY LATER!
HEH!
HUH...
YOU GOT A LEAD ON A WAY TO EARN A MILLION?
I have no intention...
...of budging from that price.
IT'LL ALL WORK OUT!
LET'S GET START-ED!
WHAT'S FIRST?
LEARNING INCANTA-TIONS? MEDITA-TION?!
WELL ...
FRAU.
?
PUT SALLY ON A STRENGTH-BUILDING TRAINING REGIMEN.
NOD
HUH?! WHY?!
WHAT ABOUT THE MAGIC?!
TUMP

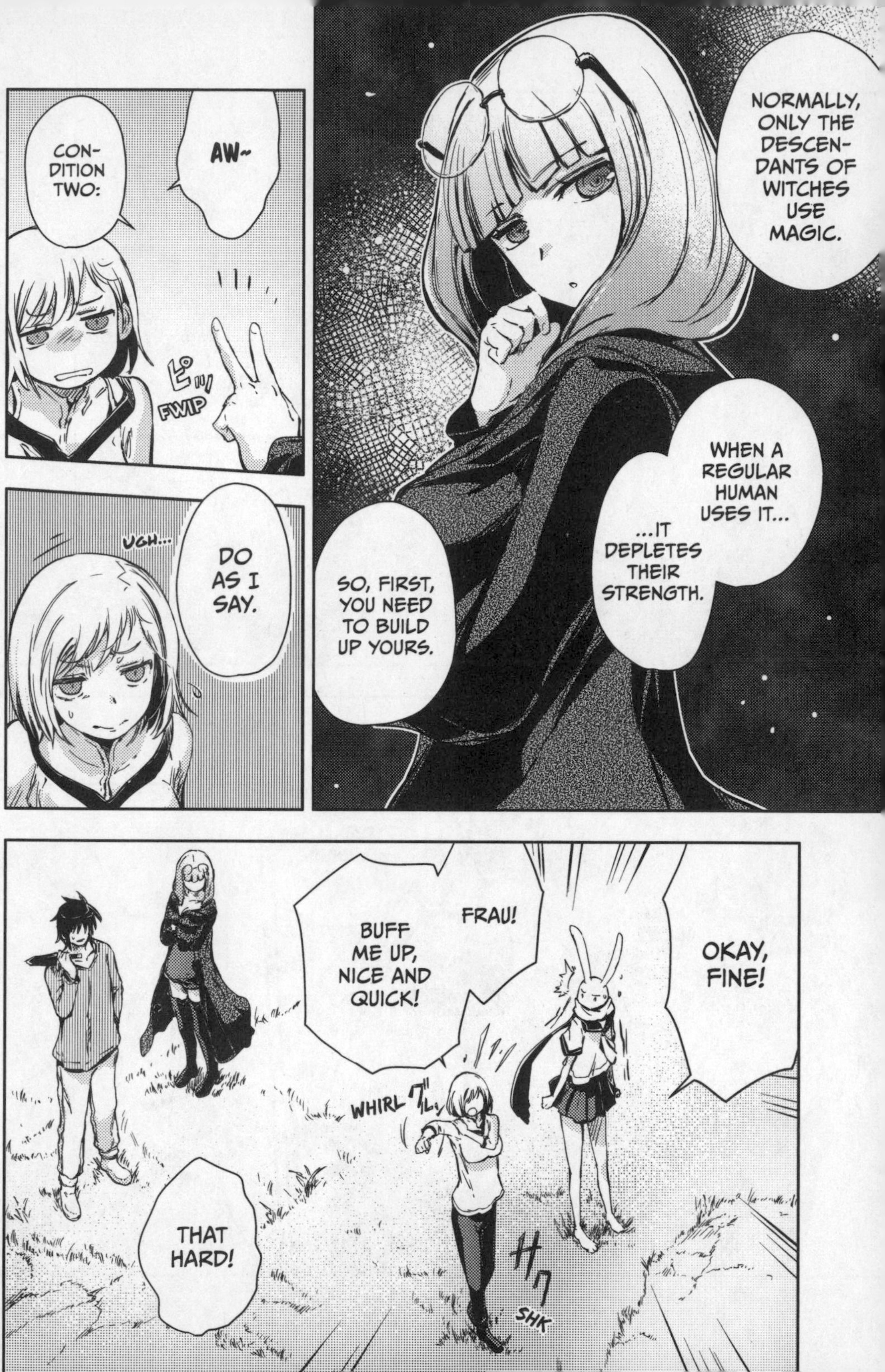
NORMALLY, ONLY THE DESCEN-DANTS OF WITCHES USE MAGIC.
WHEN A REGULAR HUMAN USES IT...
...IT DEPLETES THEIR STRENGTH.
SO, FIRST, YOU NEED TO BUILD UP YOURS.
AW~
CON-DITION TWO:
FWIP
DO AS I SAY.
UGH...
OKAY, FINE!
FRAU!
BUFF ME UP, NICE AND QUICK!
WHIRL
SHK
THAT HARD!

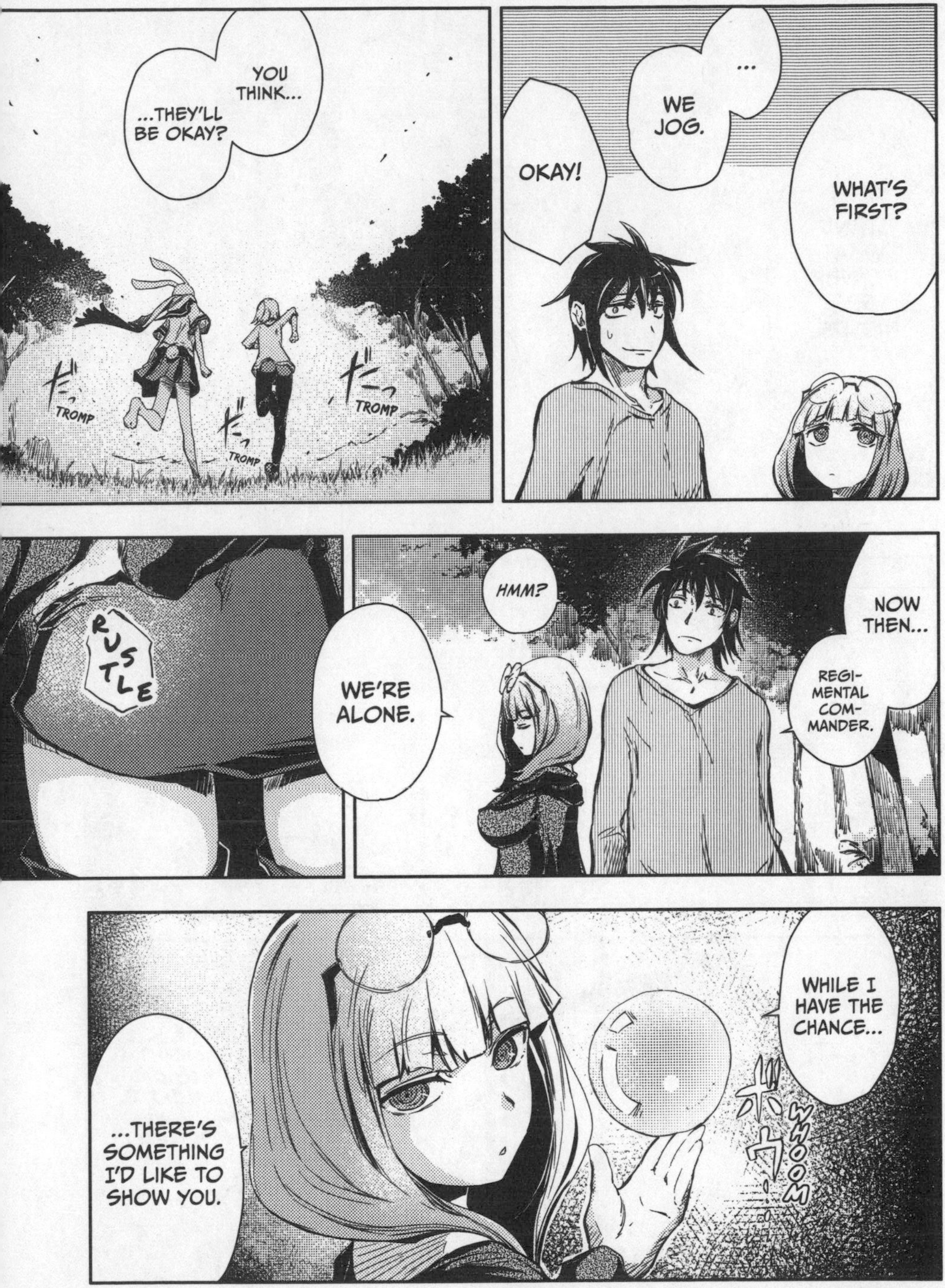
WHAT'S FIRST?
...
WE JOG.
OKAY!
YOU THINK... ...THEY'LL BE OKAY?
TROMP
TROMP
TROMP
NOW THEN... REGI-MENTAL COM-MANDER.
HMM?
WE'RE ALONE.
RUSTLE
WHILE I HAVE THE CHANCE...
WHOOM
...THERE'S SOMETHING I'D LIKE TO SHOW YOU.

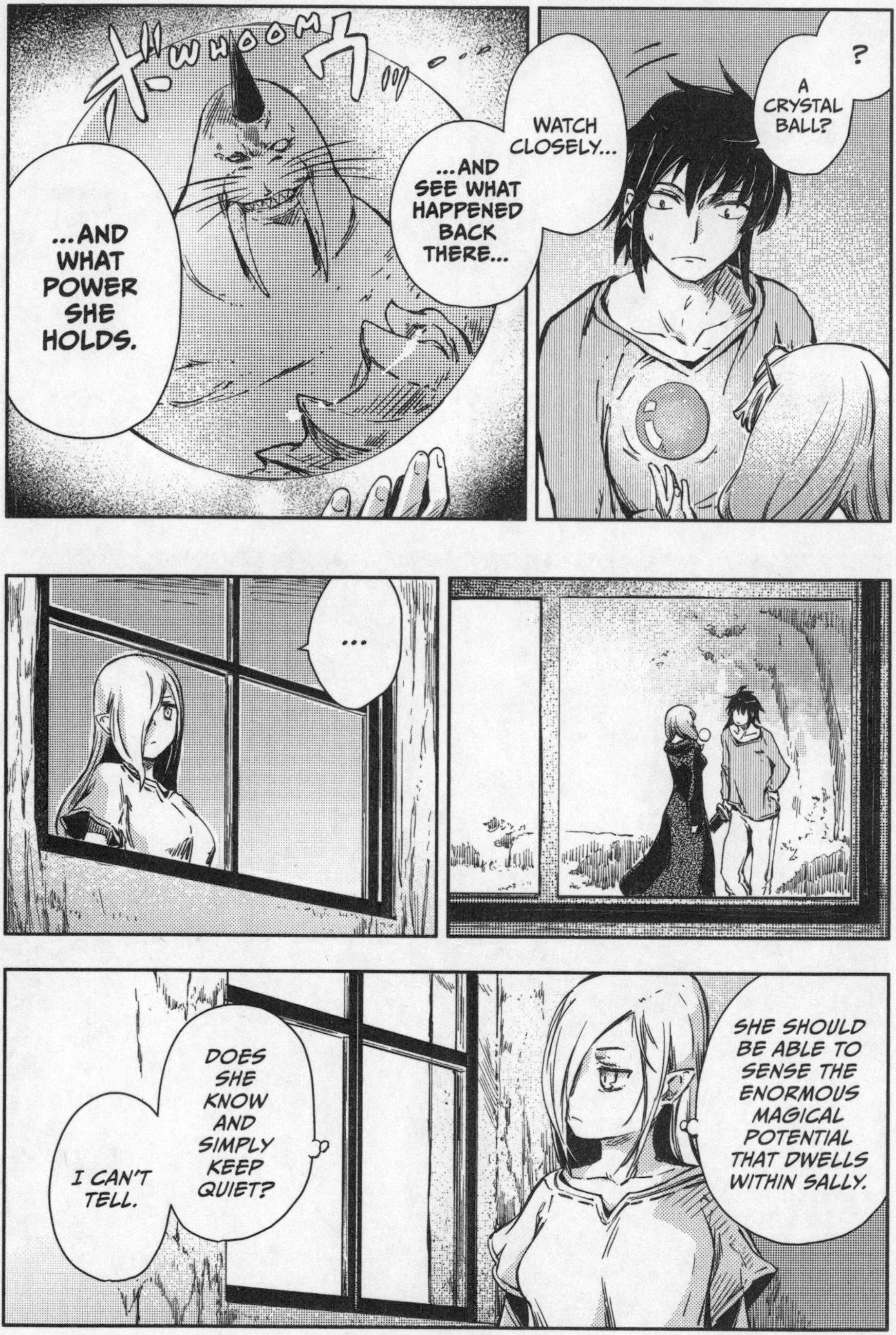
?
A CRYSTAL BALL?
WATCH CLOSELY...
...AND SEE WHAT HAPPENED BACK THERE...
WHOOOM
...AND WHAT POWER SHE HOLDS.
...
SHE SHOULD BE ABLE TO SENSE THE ENORMOUS MAGICAL POTENTIAL THAT DWELLS WITHIN SALLY.
DOES SHE KNOW AND SIMPLY KEEP QUIET?
I CAN'T TELL.

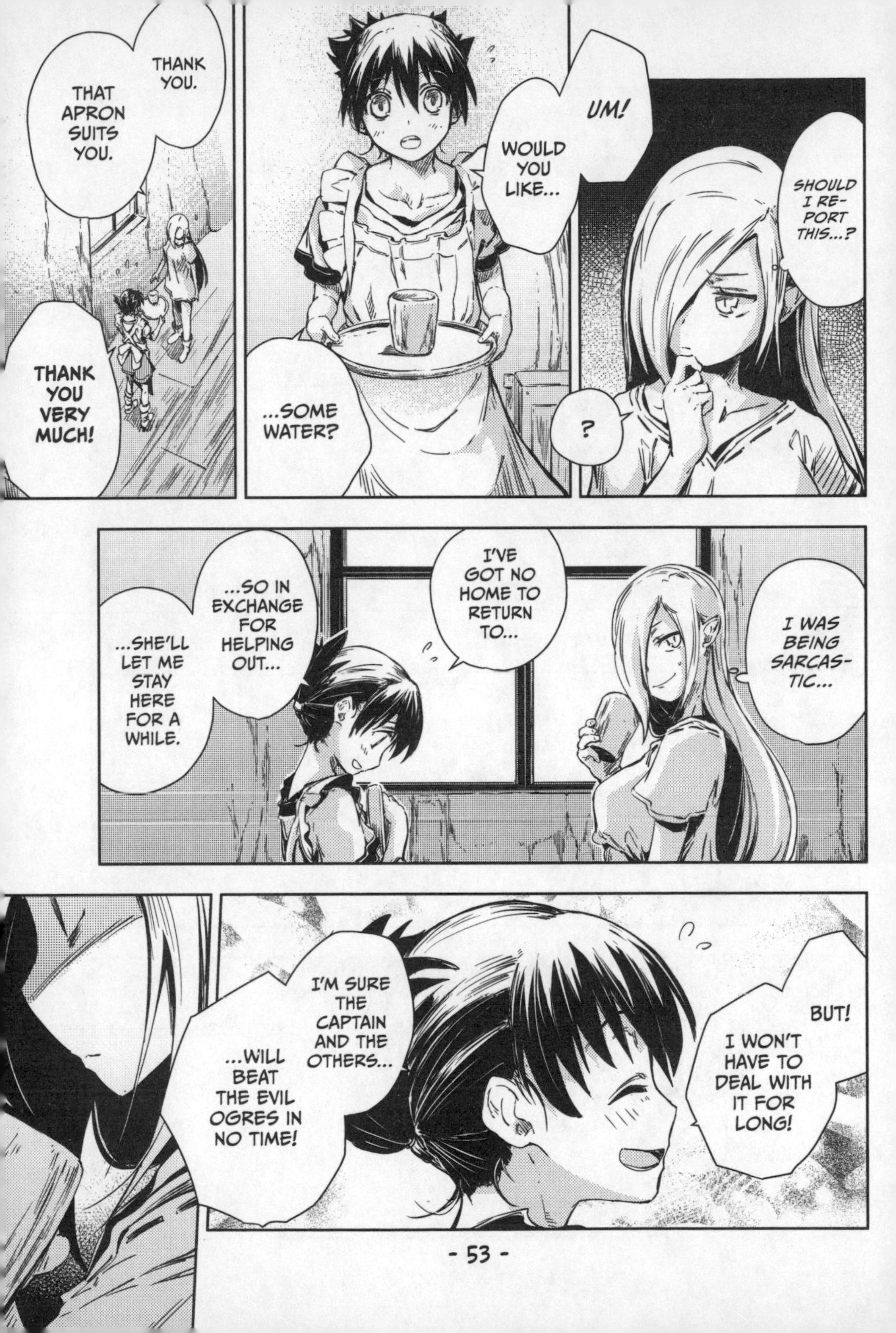
SHOULD I RE-PORT THIS...?
?
UM!
WOULD YOU LIKE...
...SOME WATER?
THANK YOU.
THAT APRON SUITS YOU.
THANK YOU VERY MUCH!
I WAS BEING SARCAS-TIC...
I'VE GOT NO HOME TO RETURN TO...
...SO IN EXCHANGE FOR HELPING OUT...
...SHE'LL LET ME STAY HERE FOR A WHILE.
BUT!
I WON'T HAVE TO DEAL WITH IT FOR LONG!
I'M SURE THE CAPTAIN AND THE OTHERS...
...WILL BEAT THE EVIL OGRES IN NO TIME!

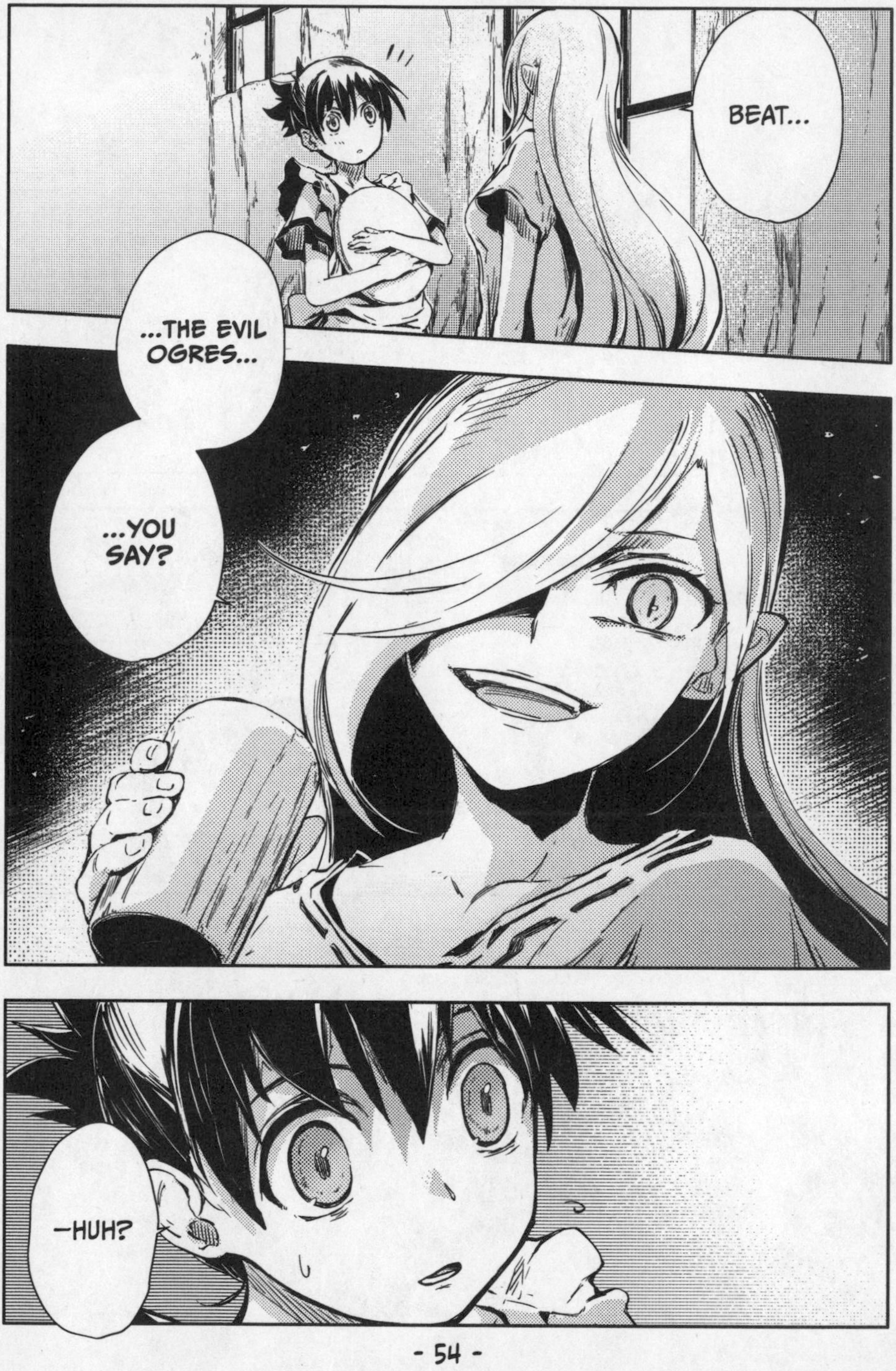
BEAT...
...THE EVIL OGRES...
...YOU SAY?
—HUH?

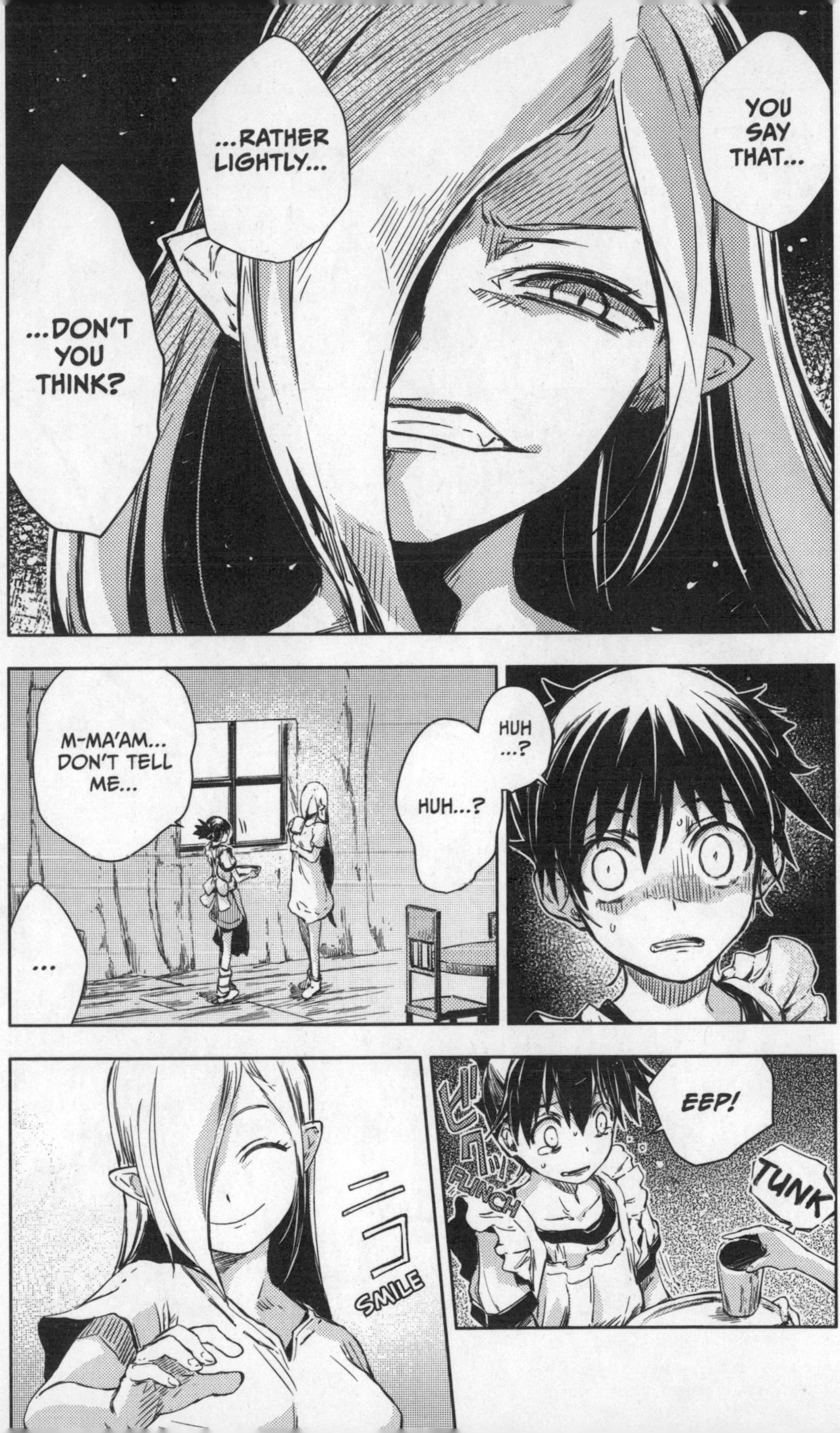
YOU SAY THAT...
...RATHER LIGHTLY...
...DON'T YOU THINK?
HUH ...?
HUH...?
M-MA'AM... DON'T TELL ME...
...
EEP!
TUNK
FLINCH
SMILE

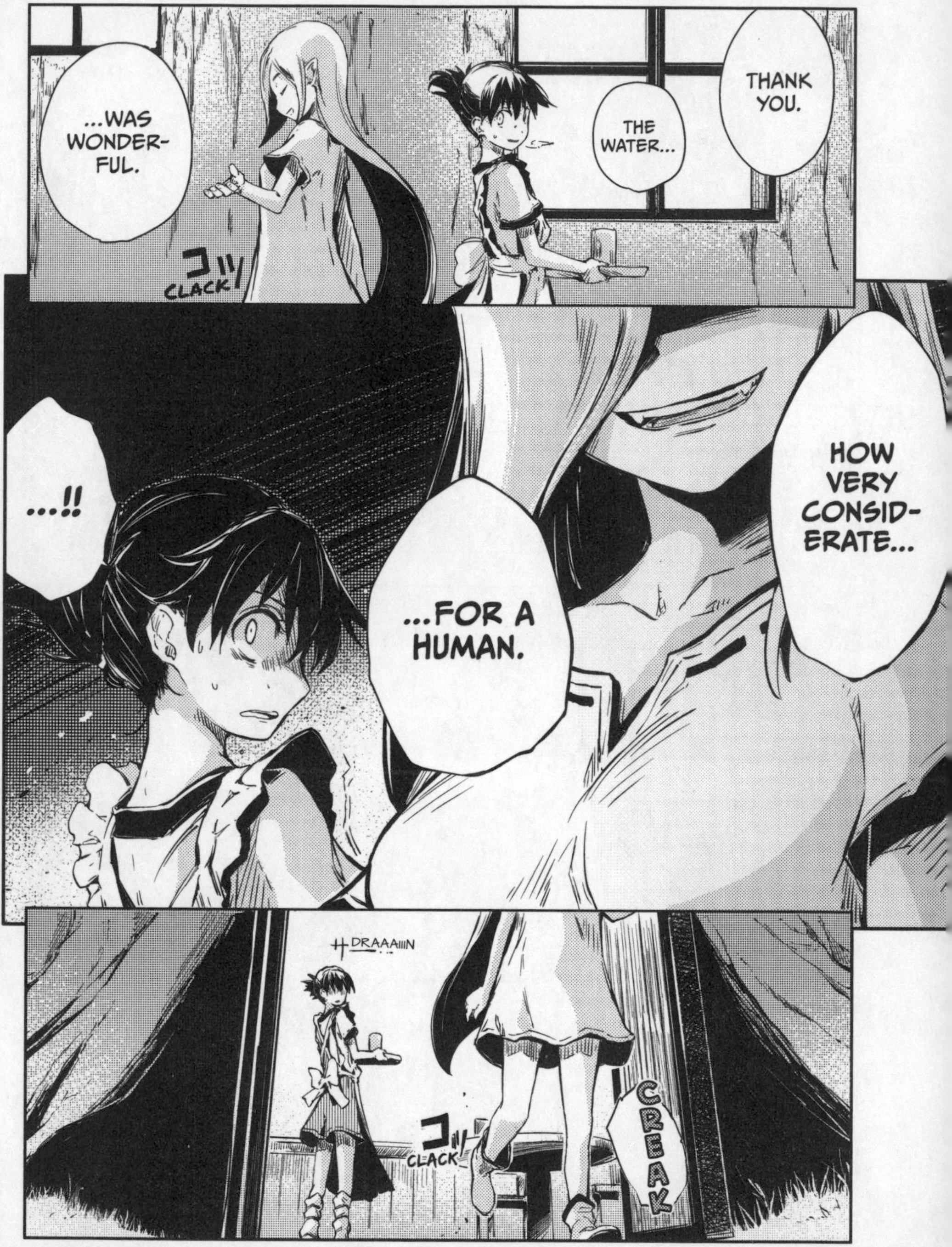
THANK YOU.
THE WATER...
...WAS WONDERFUL.
CLACK
HOW VERY CONSIDERATE...
...FOR A HUMAN.
...!!
DRAAAIIIN
CREAK
CLACK

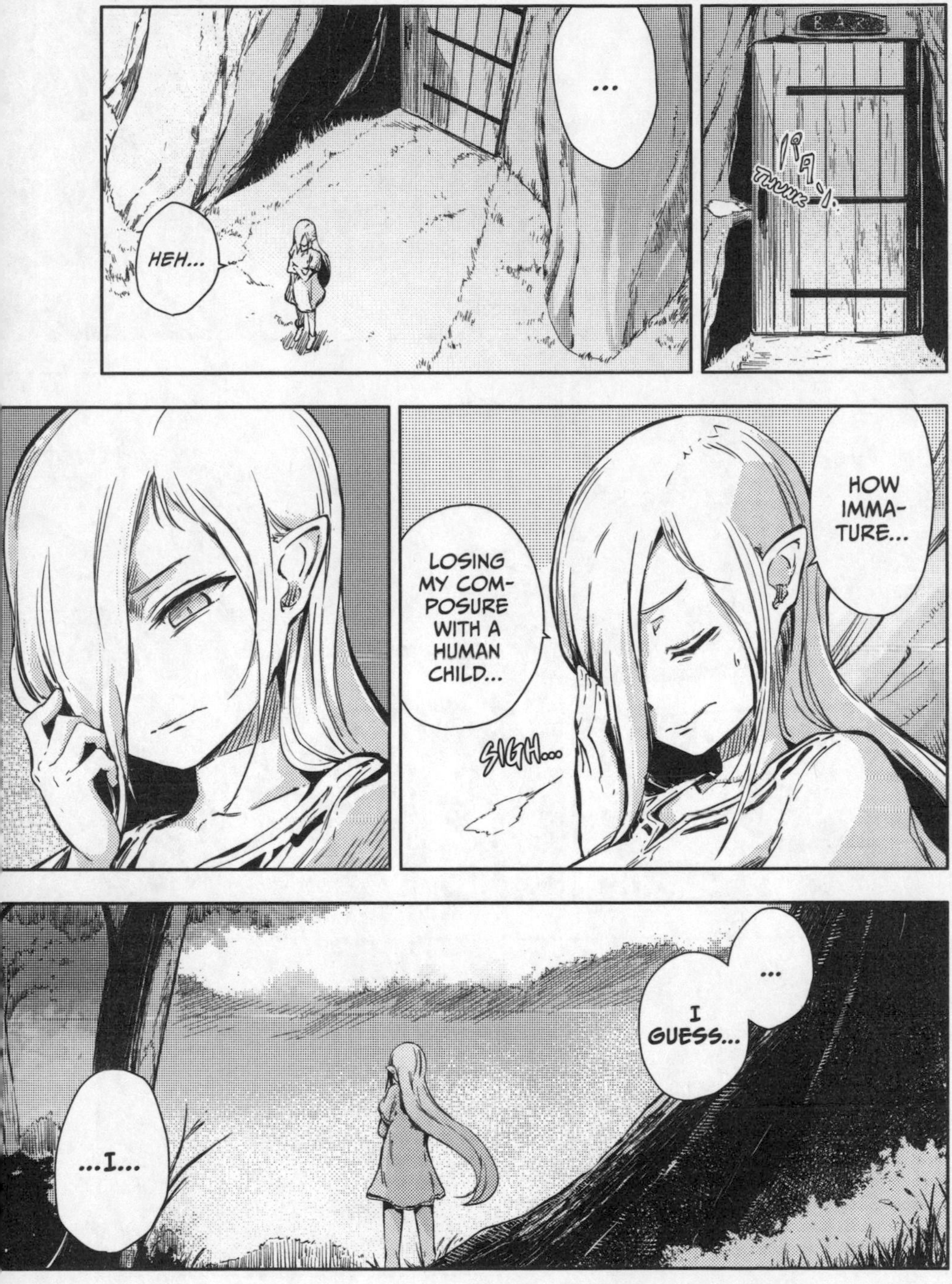
BAR
THUNK
...
HEH...
HOW IMMA-TURE...
LOSING MY COM-POSURE WITH A HUMAN CHILD...
SIGH...
... I GUESS...
...I...

HUFF

HUFF

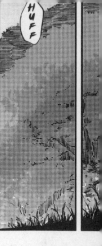

HUFF

たーっ TUMP

たーっ TUMP

たーっ TUMP

...WHY DON'T WE GET STARTED?

NOW...

NICE JOB.

YOU TOO, FRAU.

GOOD JOB!

WE'RE BACK...

SIGH...

STAGGER よろ...

WHEEZE

—HUH?

HUUUUUH?!

HUFF

IT'S TIME FOR YOUR SWORD TRAINING.

HERE, TAKE YOURS.

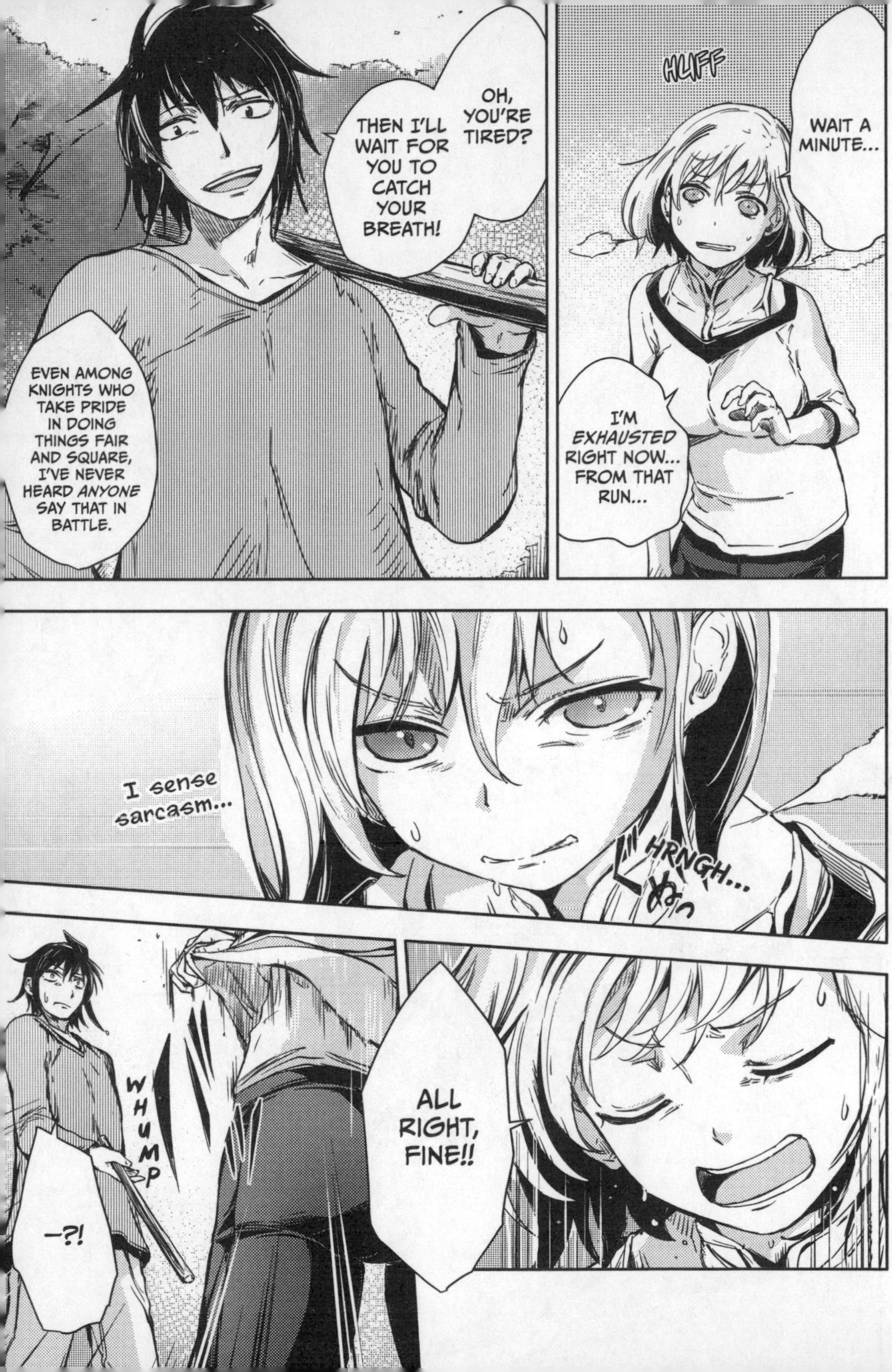
HUFF
WAIT A MINUTE...
I'M *EXHAUSTED* RIGHT NOW... FROM THAT RUN...
OH, YOU'RE TIRED?
THEN I'LL WAIT FOR YOU TO CATCH YOUR BREATH!
EVEN AMONG KNIGHTS WHO TAKE PRIDE IN DOING THINGS FAIR AND SQUARE, I'VE NEVER HEARD *ANYONE* SAY THAT IN BATTLE.
I sense sarcasm...
HRNGH...
ぬっ
ALL RIGHT, FINE!!
WHUMP
—?!

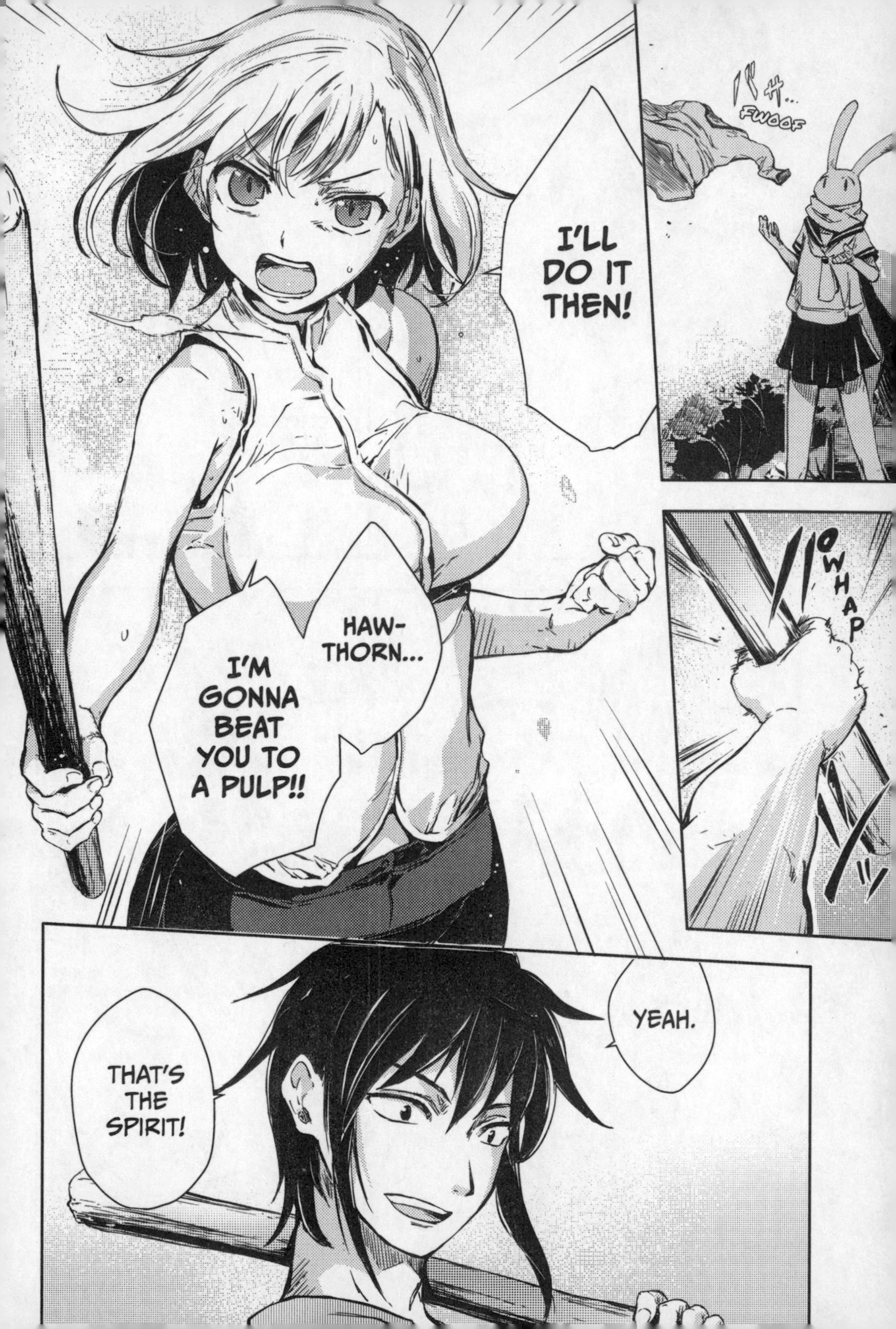
FWOOF
WHAP
I'LL DO IT THEN!
HAW-THORN...
I'M GONNA BEAT YOU TO A PULP!!
YEAH.
THAT'S THE SPIRIT!

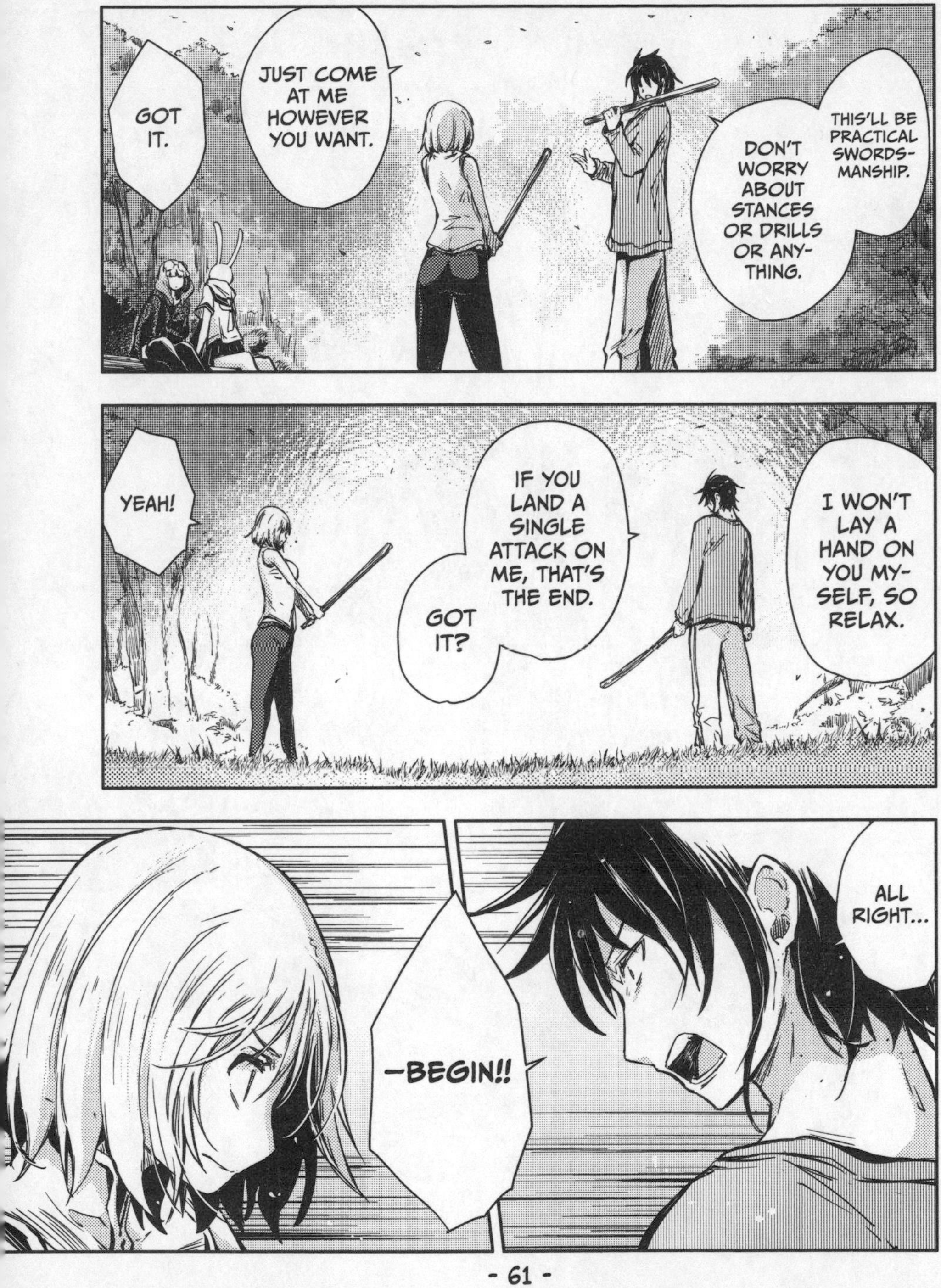
THIS'LL BE PRACTICAL SWORDS-MANSHIP.
DON'T WORRY ABOUT STANCES OR DRILLS OR ANY-THING.
JUST COME AT ME HOWEVER YOU WANT.
GOT IT.
I WON'T LAY A HAND ON YOU MY-SELF, SO RELAX.
IF YOU LAND A SINGLE ATTACK ON ME, THAT'S THE END.
GOT IT?
YEAH!
ALL RIGHT...
—BEGIN!!

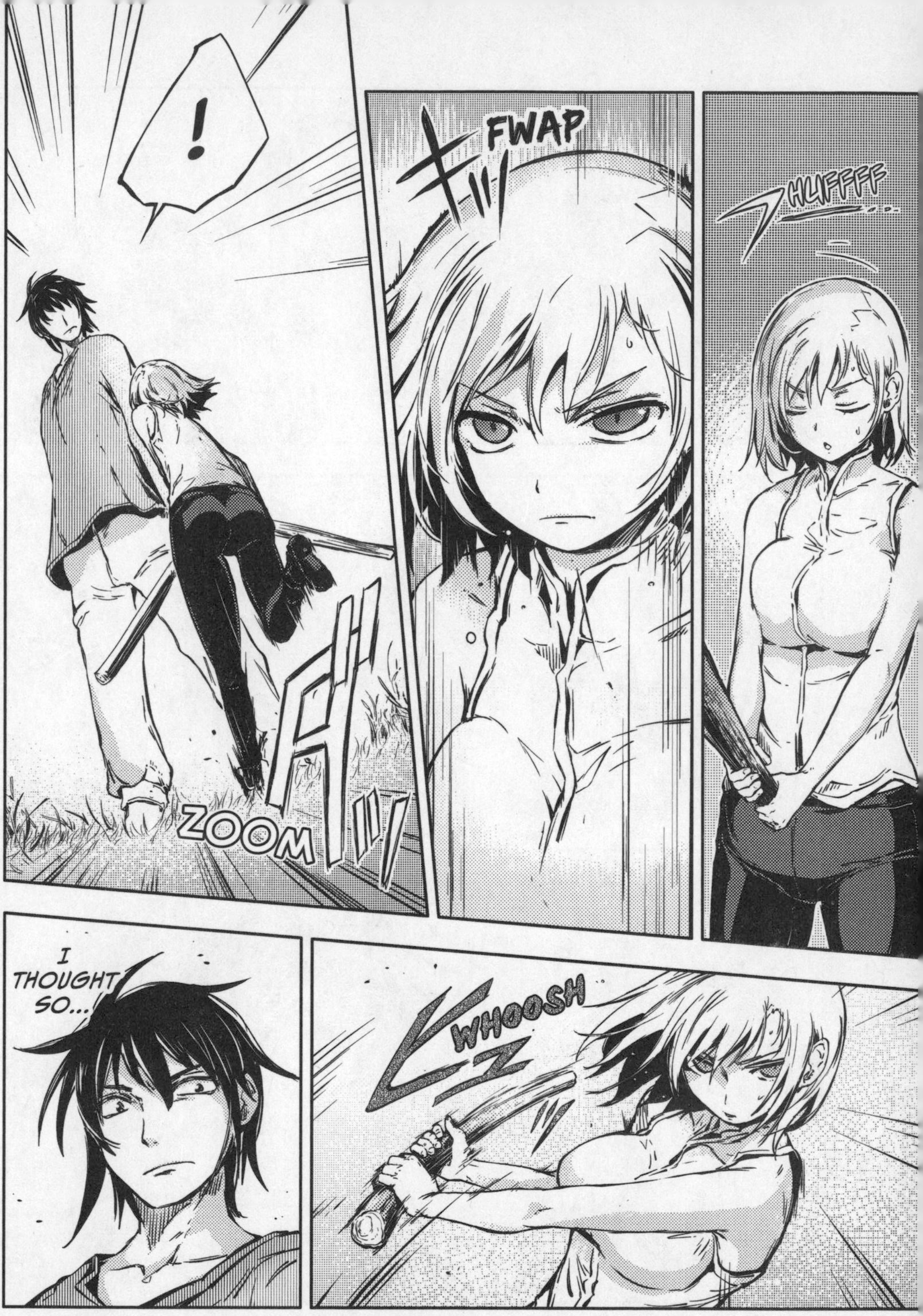
HUFFFFF
FWAP
!
ZOOM
WHOOSH
I THOUGHT SO...

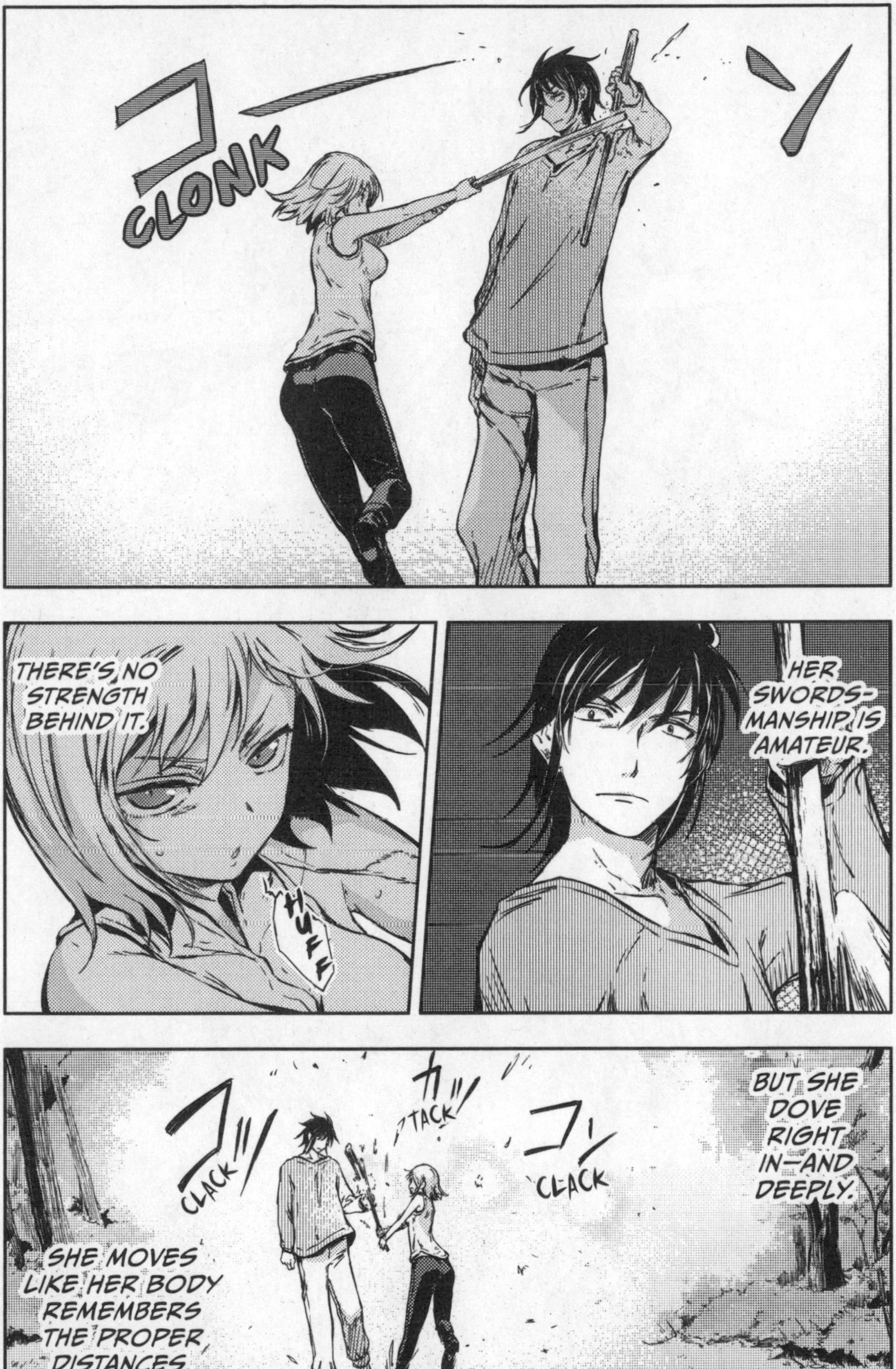
CLONK
HER SWORDS-MANSHIP IS AMATEUR.
THERE'S NO STRENGTH BEHIND IT.
HUFF
BUT SHE DOVE RIGHT IN—AND DEEPLY.
CLACK
TACK
CLACK
SHE MOVES LIKE HER BODY REMEMBERS THE PROPER DISTANCES.

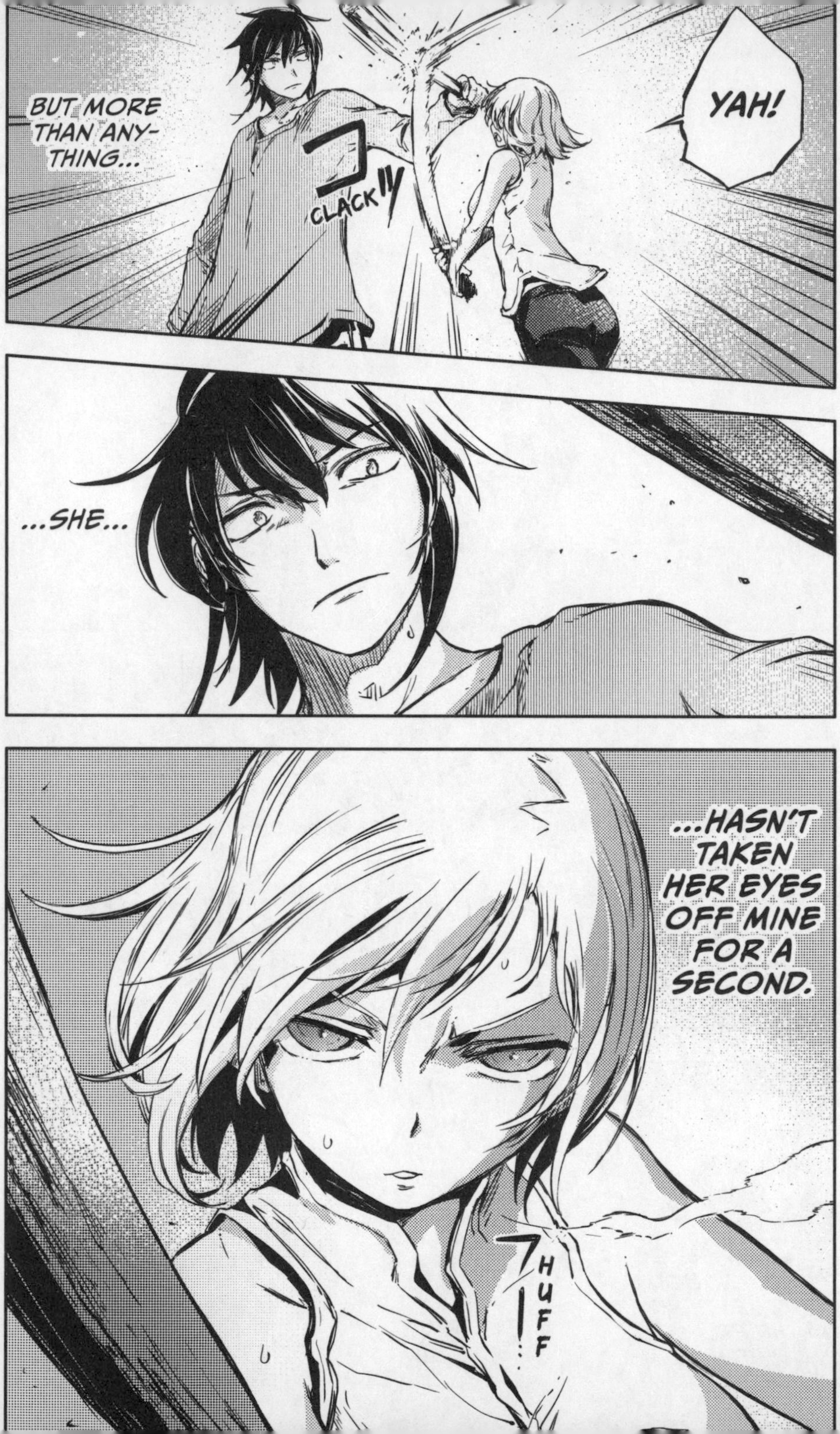
YAH!
BUT MORE THAN ANY-THING...
CLACK
...SHE...
...HASN'T TAKEN HER EYES OFF MINE FOR A SECOND.
HUFF

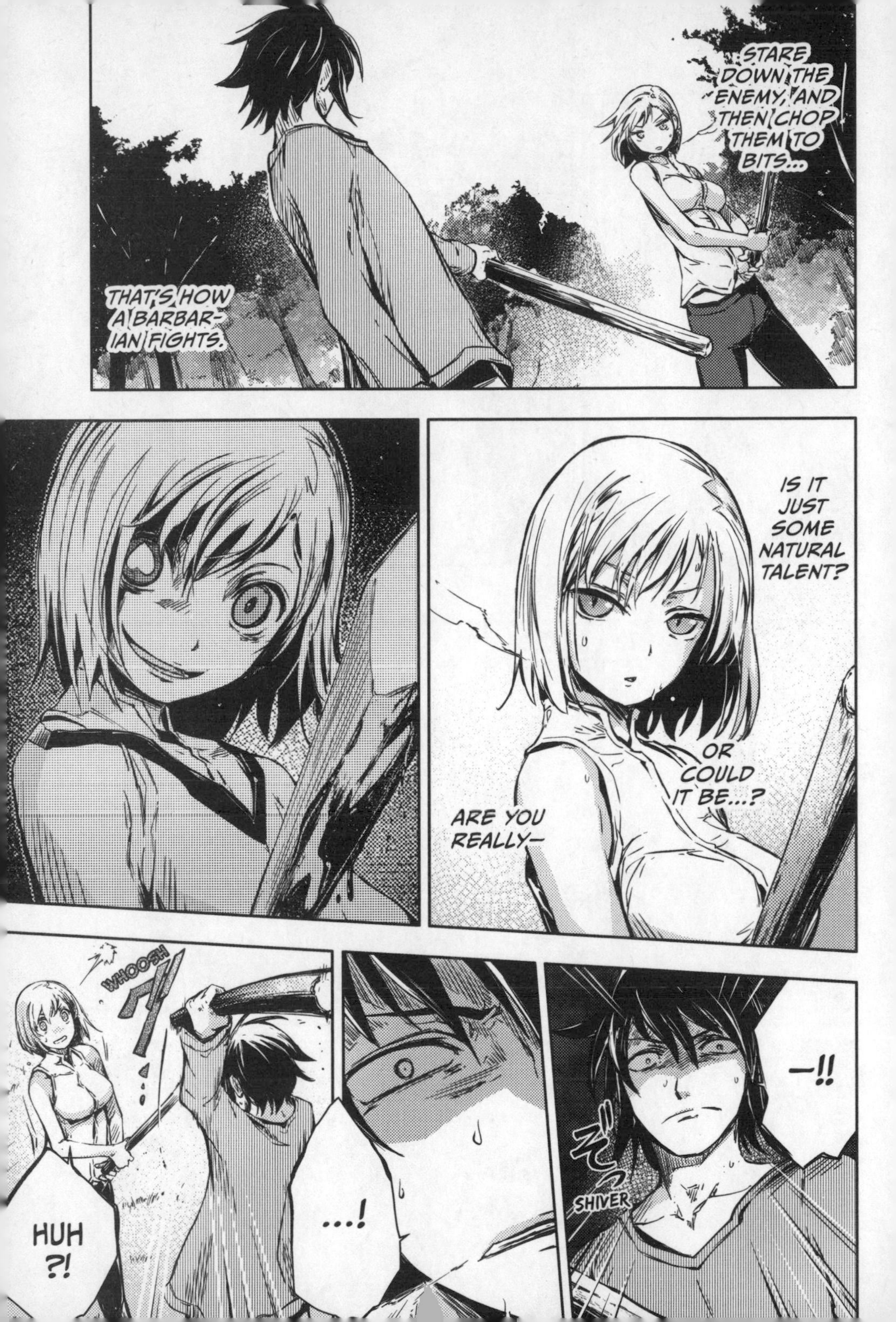
STARE DOWN THE ENEMY, AND THEN CHOP THEM TO BITS...
THAT'S HOW A BARBAR-IAN FIGHTS.
IS IT JUST SOME NATURAL TALENT?
OR COULD IT BE...?
ARE YOU REALLY—
—!!
SHIVER
...!
WHOOSH
HUH ?!

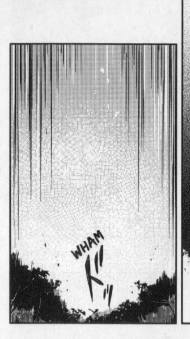

WHAM

SKREEK

HUFF

HAW-THORN?!

WHOA
...

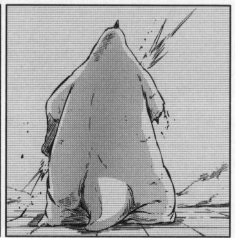

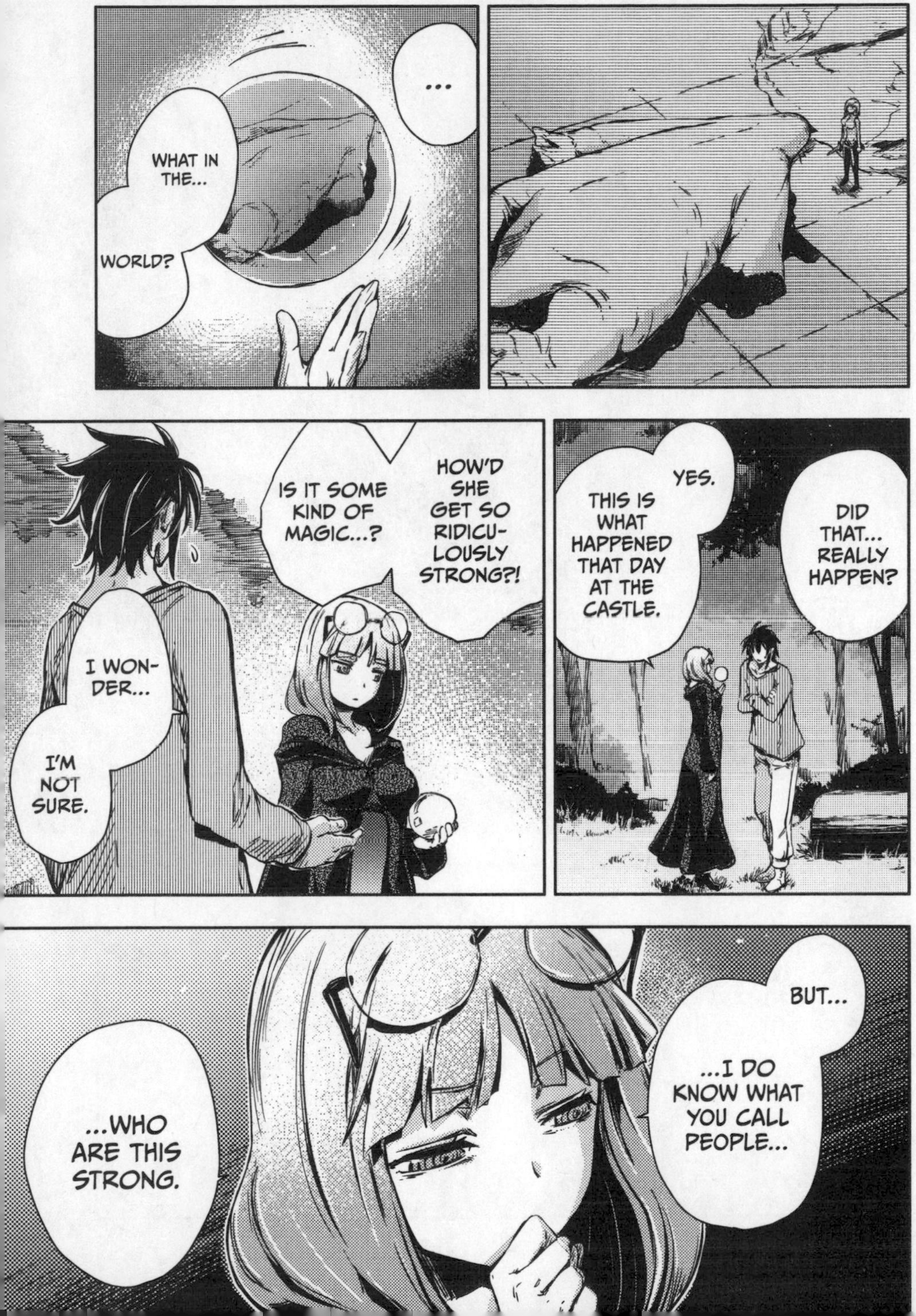
...
WHAT IN THE...
WORLD?
DID THAT... REALLY HAPPEN?
YES.
THIS IS WHAT HAPPENED THAT DAY AT THE CASTLE.
HOW'D SHE GET SO RIDICULOUSLY STRONG?!
IS IT SOME KIND OF MAGIC...?
I WONDER...
I'M NOT SURE.
BUT...
...I DO KNOW WHAT YOU CALL PEOPLE...
...WHO ARE THIS STRONG.

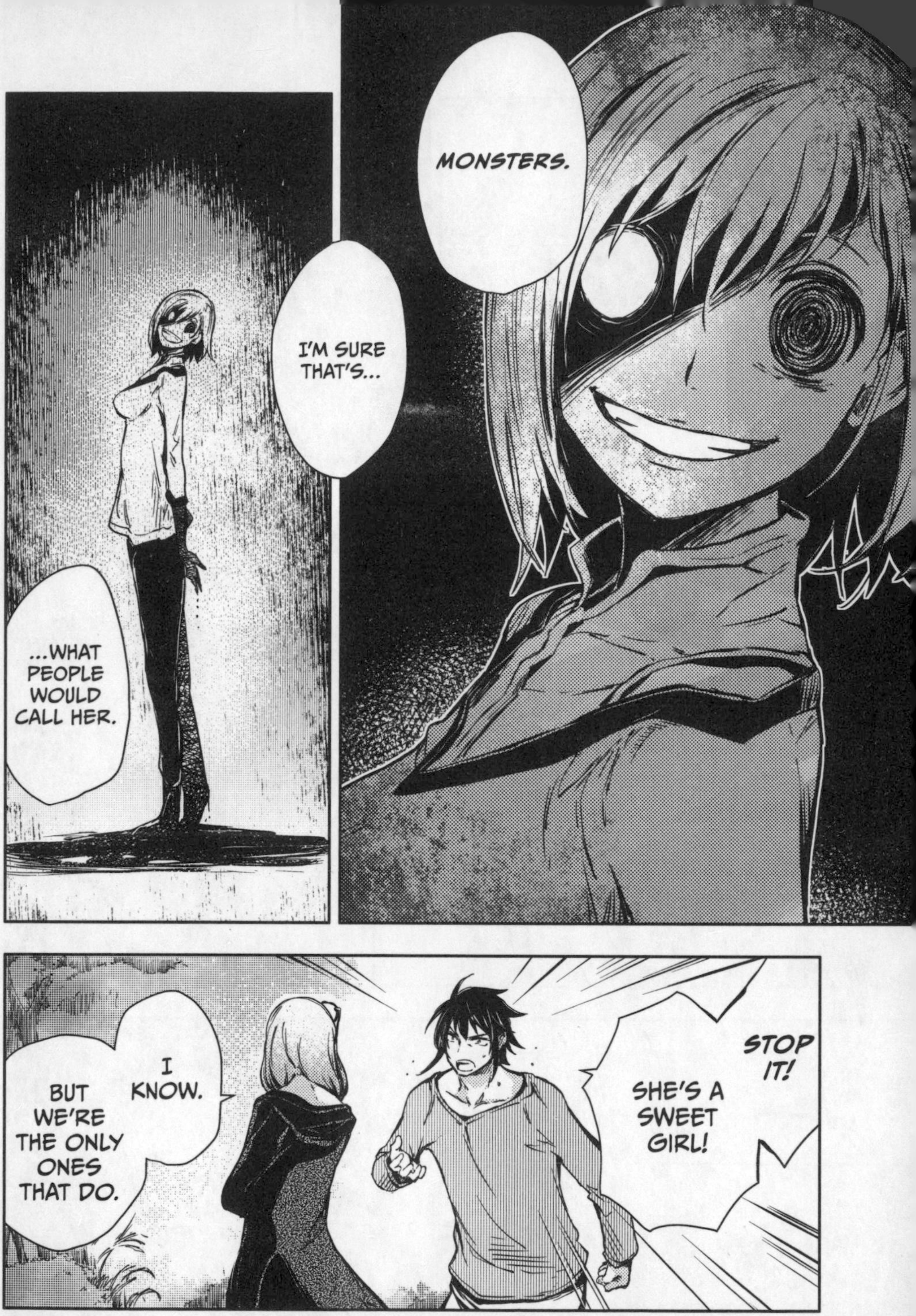
MONSTERS.
I'M SURE THAT'S...
...WHAT PEOPLE WOULD CALL HER.
STOP IT!
SHE'S A SWEET GIRL!
I KNOW.
BUT WE'RE THE ONLY ONES THAT DO.

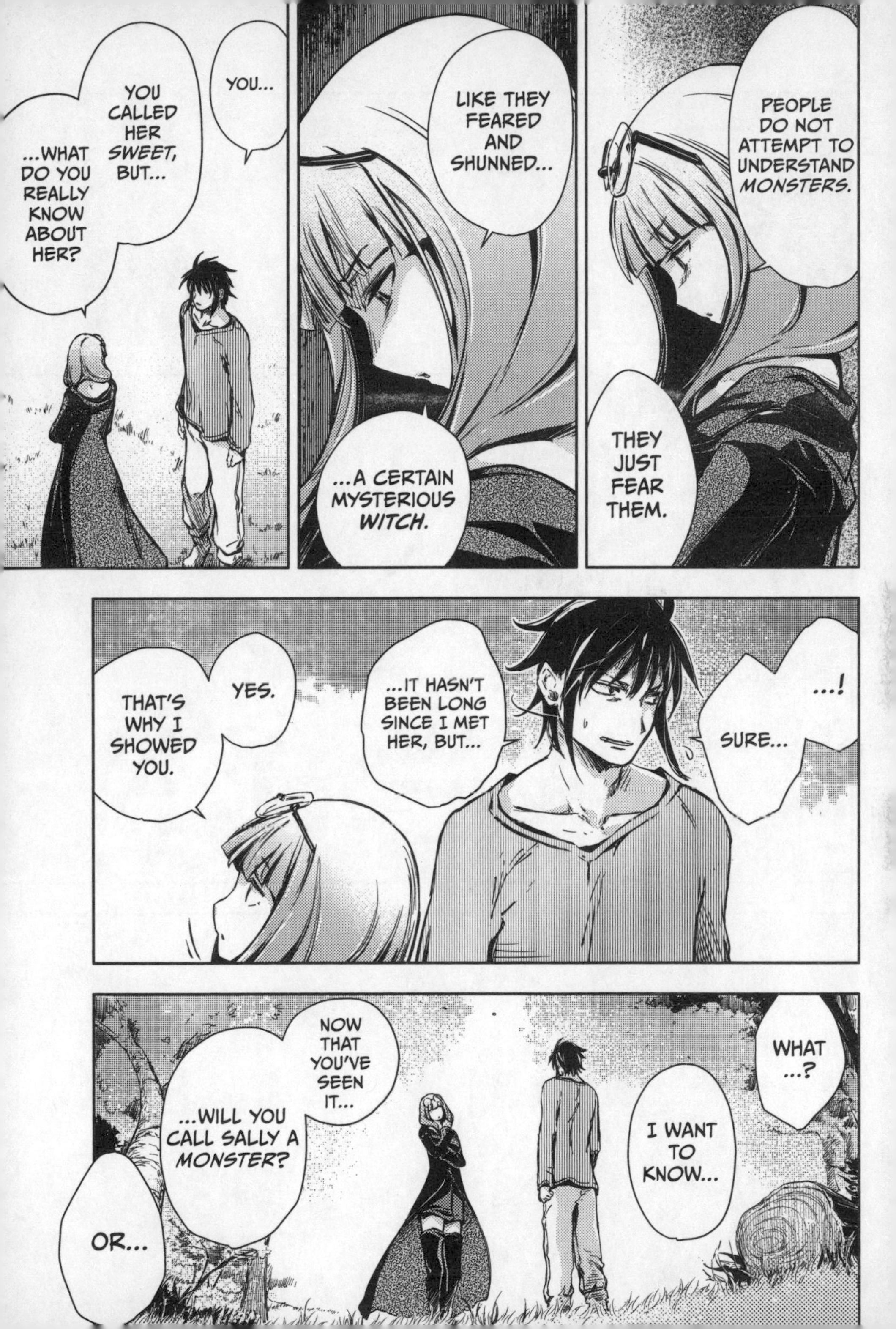
PEOPLE DO NOT ATTEMPT TO UNDERSTAND MONSTERS.
THEY JUST FEAR THEM.
LIKE THEY FEARED AND SHUNNED...
...A CERTAIN MYSTERIOUS WITCH.
YOU...
YOU CALLED HER SWEET, BUT...
...WHAT DO YOU REALLY KNOW ABOUT HER?
...!
SURE...
...IT HASN'T BEEN LONG SINCE I MET HER, BUT...
YES.
THAT'S WHY I SHOWED YOU.
WHAT ...?
I WANT TO KNOW...
NOW THAT YOU'VE SEEN IT...
...WILL YOU CALL SALLY A MONSTER?
OR...

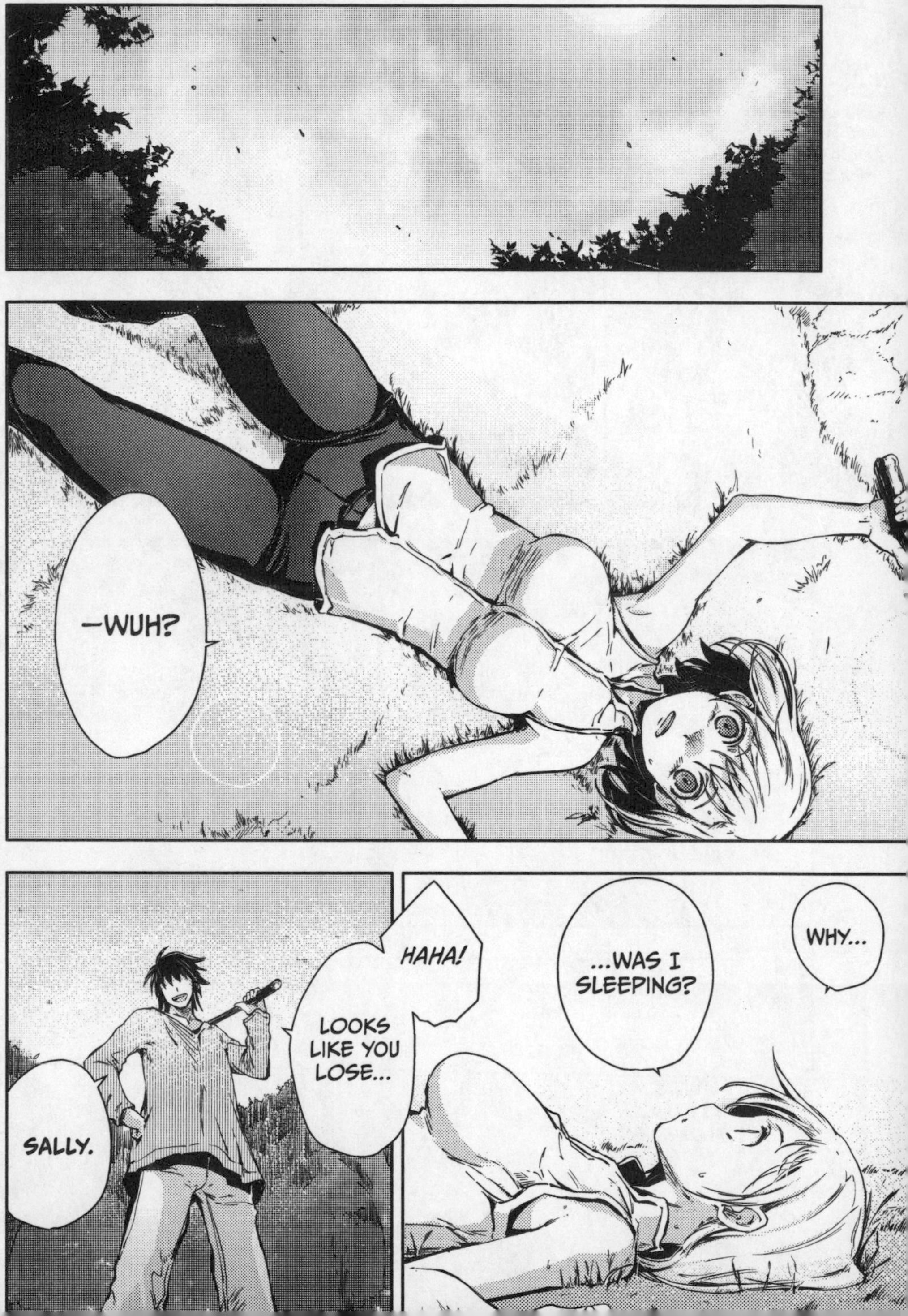
—WUH?
WHY...
...WAS I SLEEPING?
HAHA!
LOOKS LIKE YOU LOSE...
SALLY.

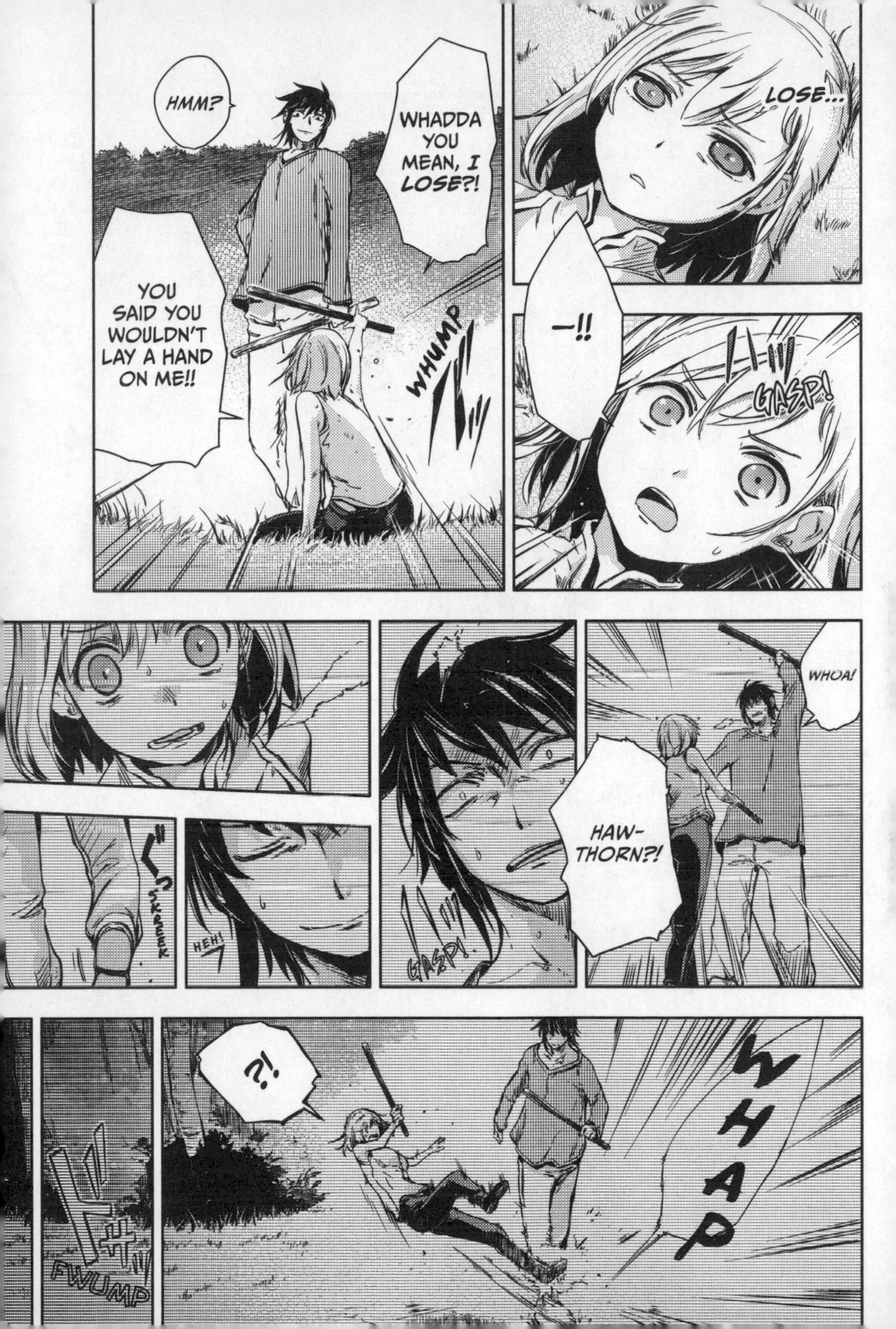
LOSE...
—!!
GASP!
HMM?
WHADDA YOU MEAN, I LOSE?!
YOU SAID YOU WOULDN'T LAY A HAND ON ME!!
WHUMP
WHOA!
HAW-THORN?!
GASP!
HEH!
SKREEK
?!
WHAP
FWUMP

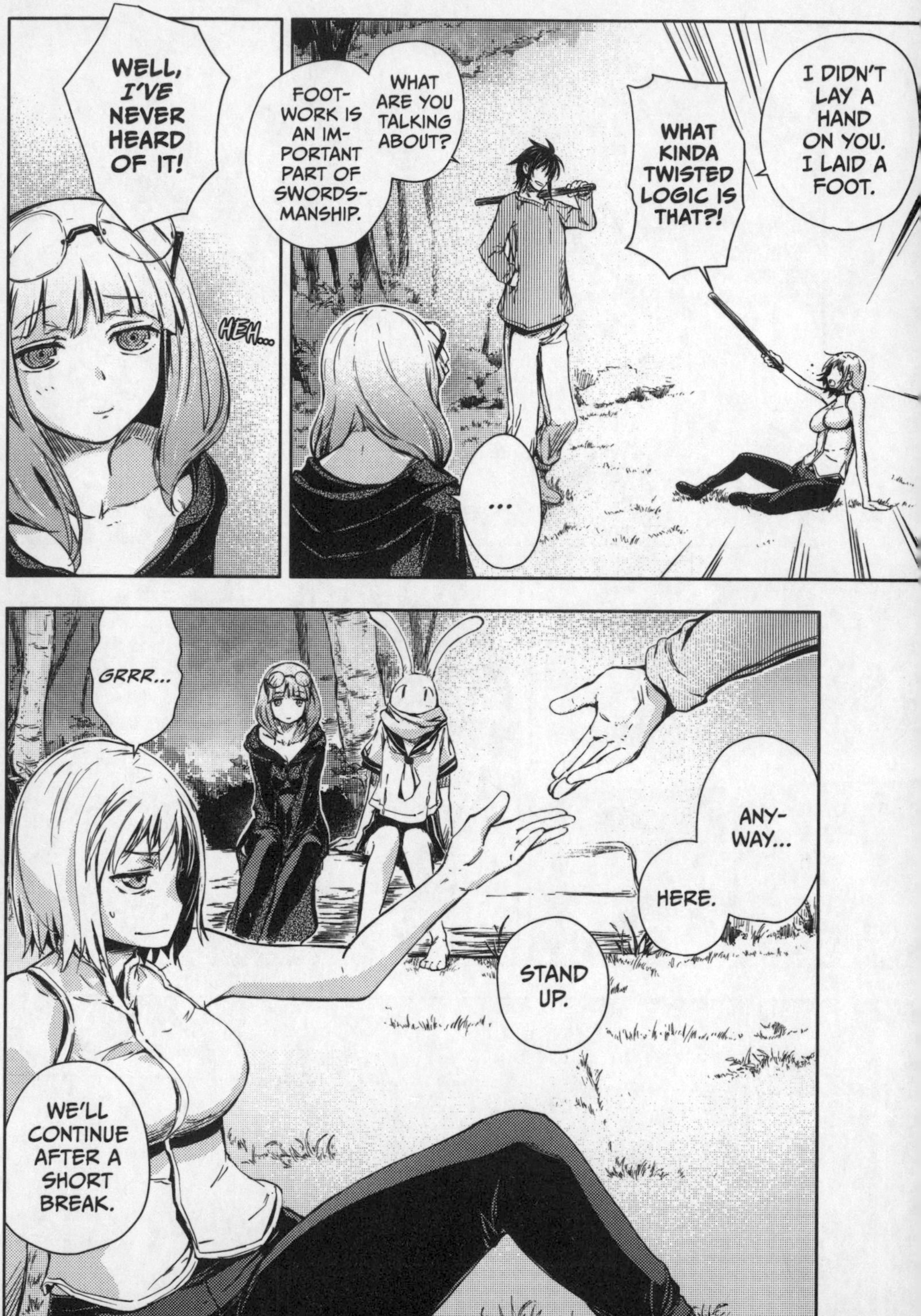
I DIDN'T LAY A HAND ON YOU. I LAID A FOOT.
WHAT KINDA TWISTED LOGIC IS THAT?!
WHAT ARE YOU TALKING ABOUT?
FOOT-WORK IS AN IM-PORTANT PART OF SWORDS-MANSHIP.
...
WELL, I'VE NEVER HEARD OF IT!
HEH...
ANY-WAY...
HERE.
STAND UP.
GRRR...
WE'LL CONTINUE AFTER A SHORT BREAK.

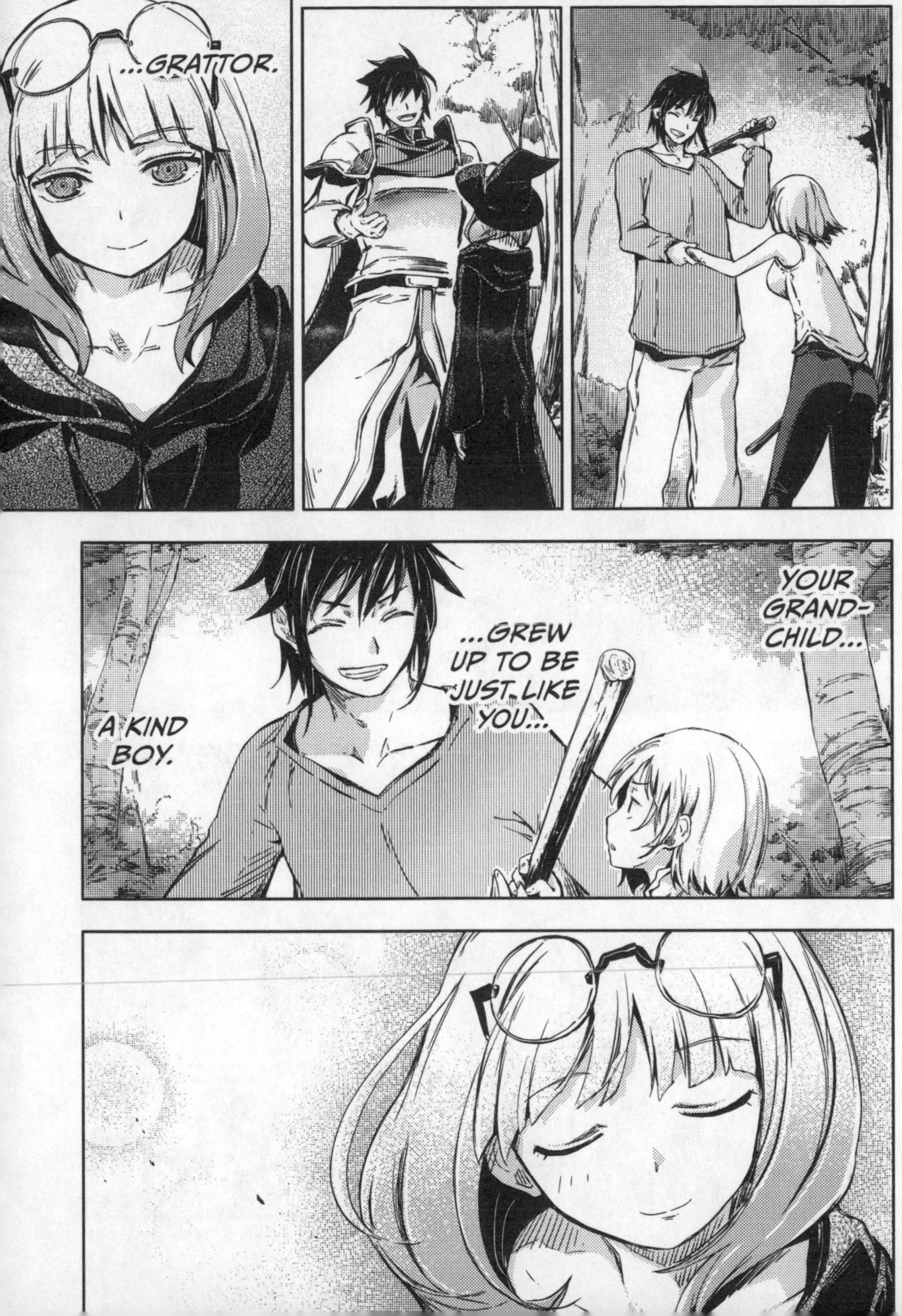
...GRATTOR.
YOUR GRAND-CHILD...
...GREW UP TO BE JUST LIKE YOU...
A KIND BOY.

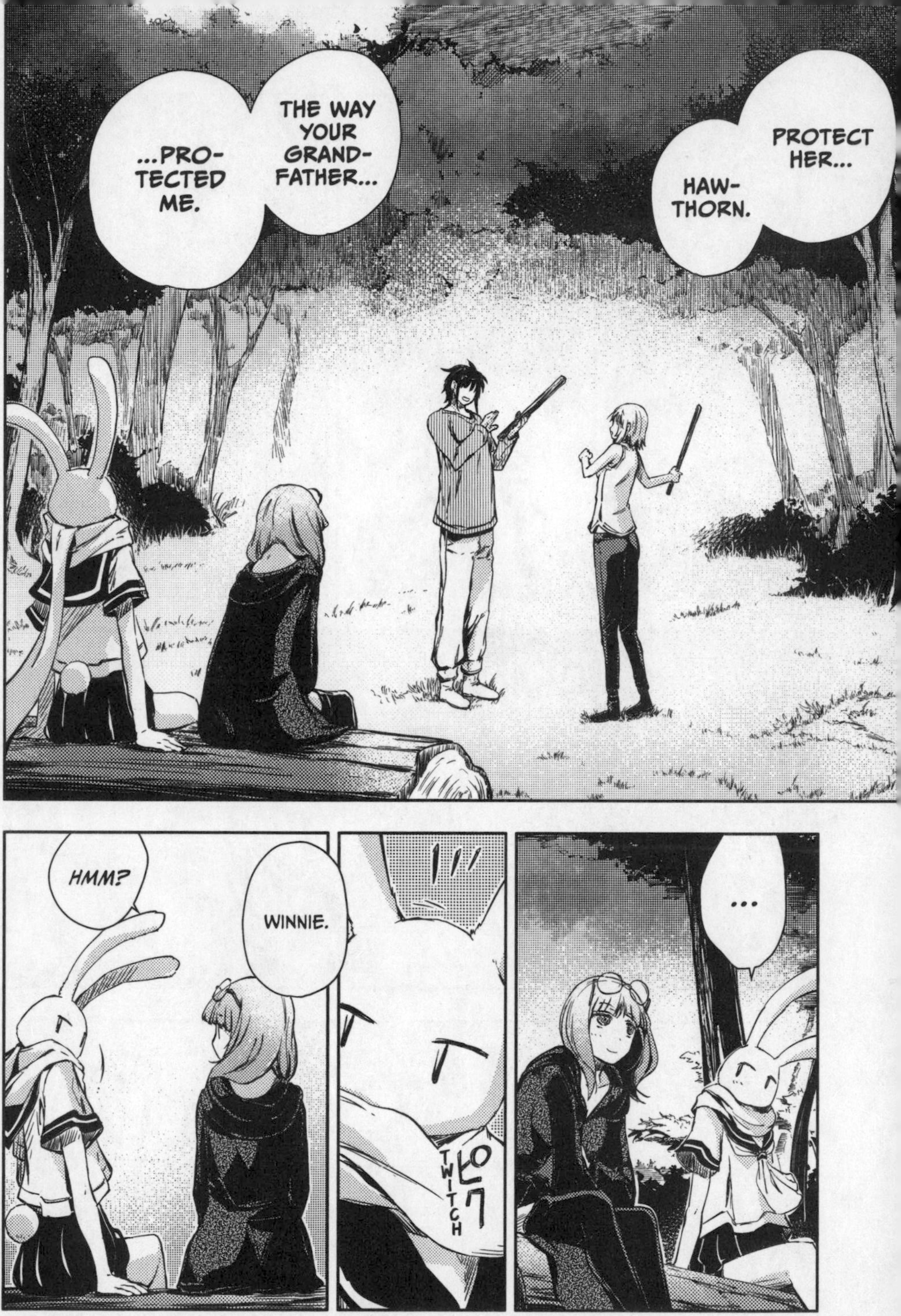
PROTECT HER...
HAW-THORN.
THE WAY YOUR GRAND-FATHER...
...PRO-TECTED ME.
...
TWITCH
WINNIE.
HMM?

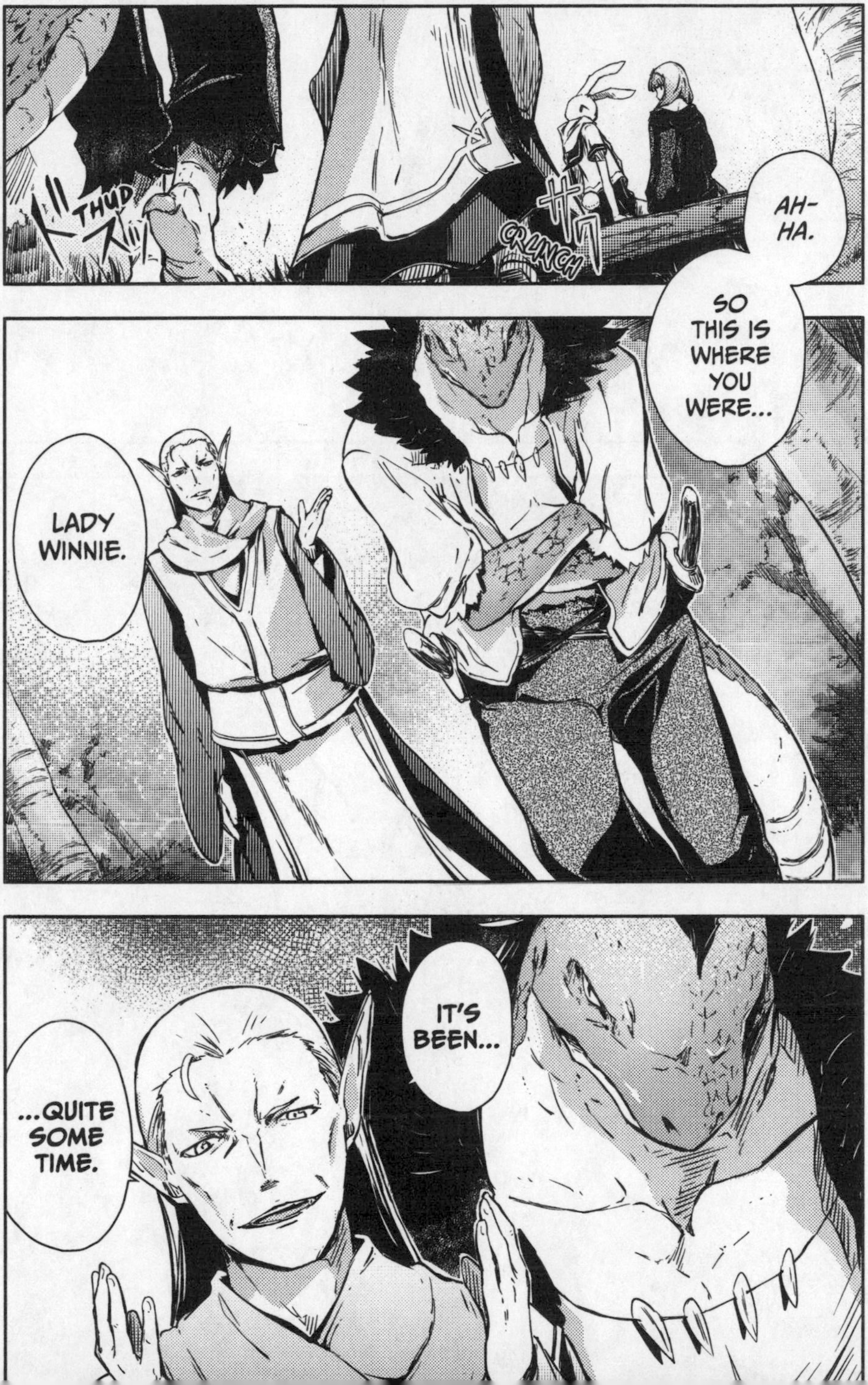
AH-HA.
CRUNCH
THUD
SO THIS IS WHERE YOU WERE...
LADY WINNIE.
IT'S BEEN...
...QUITE SOME TIME.

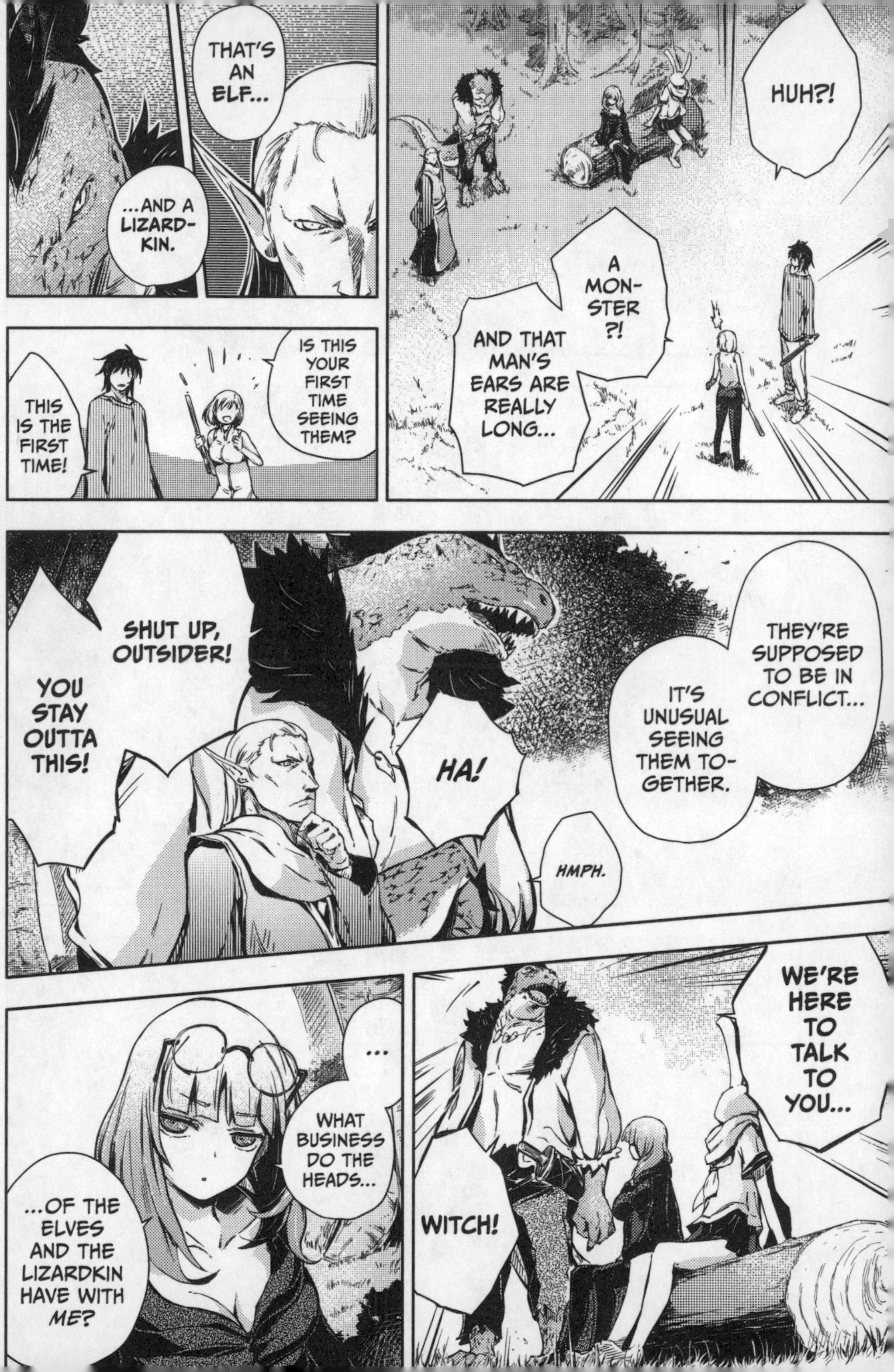
HUH?!
A MONSTER?!
AND THAT MAN'S EARS ARE REALLY LONG...
THAT'S AN ELF...
...AND A LIZARDKIN.
IS THIS YOUR FIRST TIME SEEING THEM?
THIS IS THE FIRST TIME!
THEY'RE SUPPOSED TO BE IN CONFLICT...
IT'S UNUSUAL SEEING THEM TOGETHER.
HA!
HMPH.
SHUT UP, OUTSIDER!
YOU STAY OUTTA THIS!
WE'RE HERE TO TALK TO YOU...
WITCH!
...
WHAT BUSINESS DO THE HEADS...
...OF THE ELVES AND THE LIZARDKIN HAVE WITH *ME*?

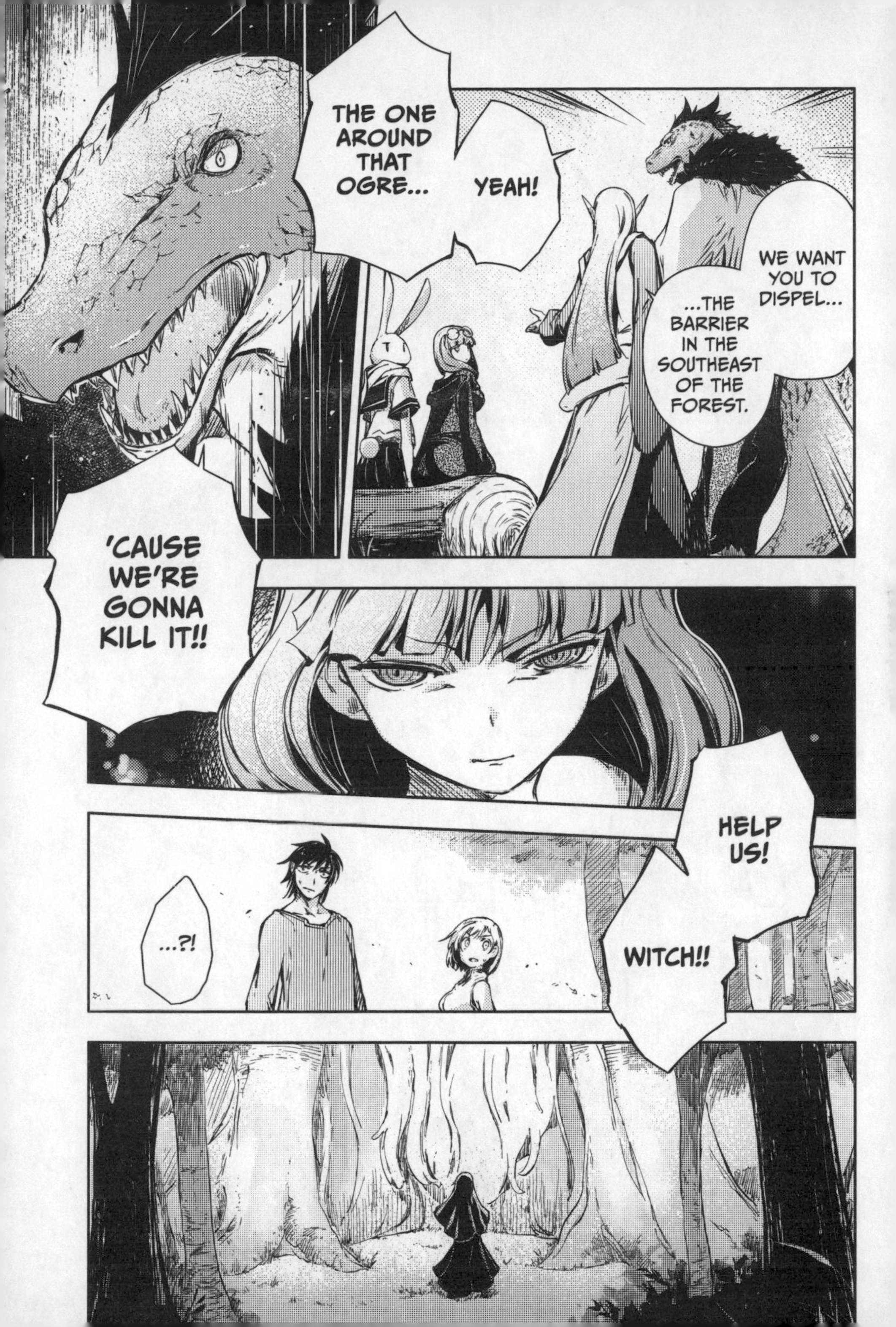
WE WANT YOU TO DISPEL...
...THE BARRIER IN THE SOUTHEAST OF THE FOREST.
THE ONE AROUND THAT OGRE...
YEAH!
'CAUSE WE'RE GONNA KILL IT!!
HELP US!
WITCH!!
...?!

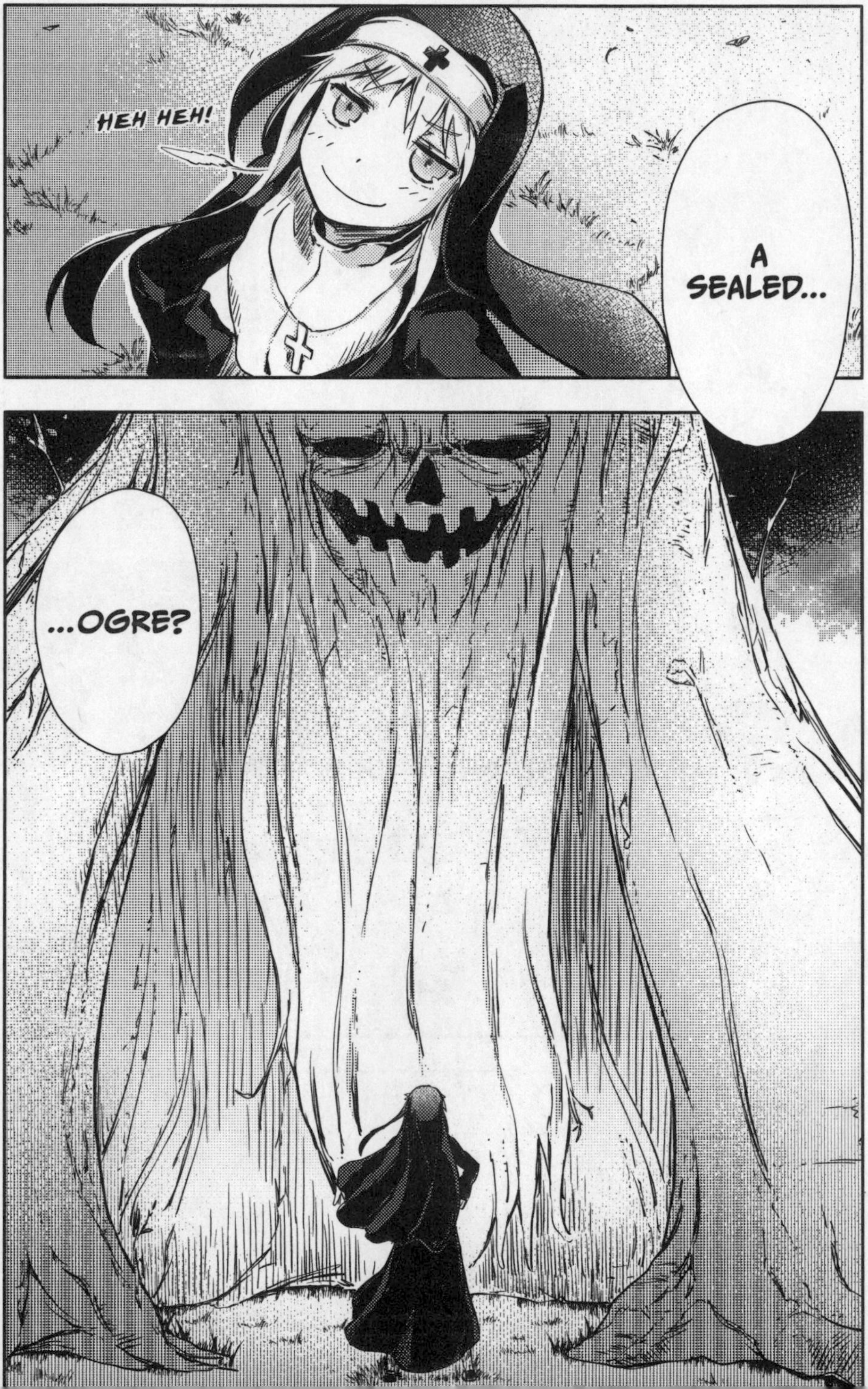
HEH HEH!
A SEALED...
...OGRE?

## CHAPTER 10: IDEALS AND REALITY

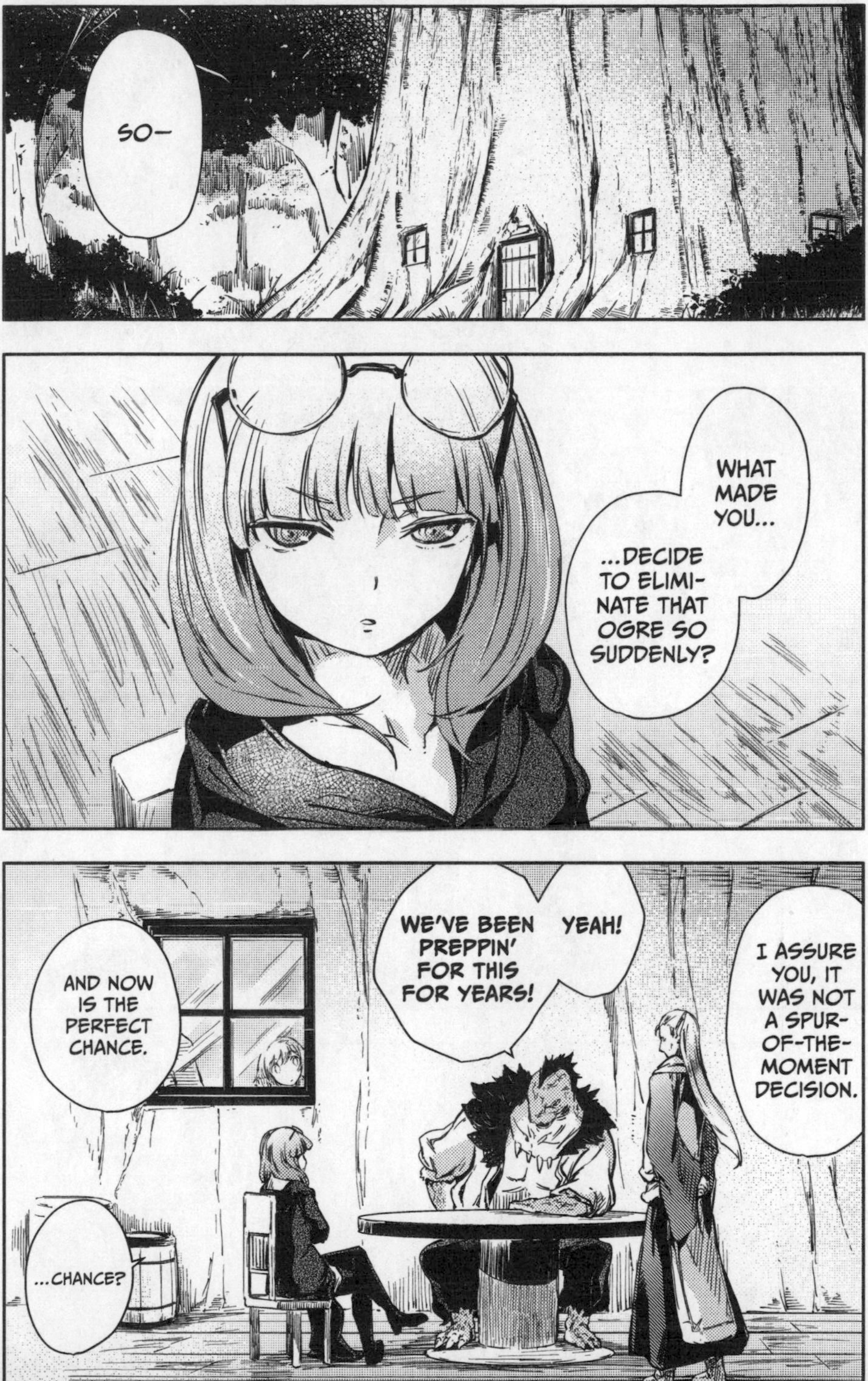
SO—
WHAT MADE YOU...
...DECIDE TO ELIMI-NATE THAT OGRE SO SUDDENLY?
I ASSURE YOU, IT WAS NOT A SPUR-OF-THE-MOMENT DECISION.
YEAH!
WE'VE BEEN PREPPIN' FOR THIS FOR YEARS!
AND NOW IS THE PERFECT CHANCE.
...CHANCE?

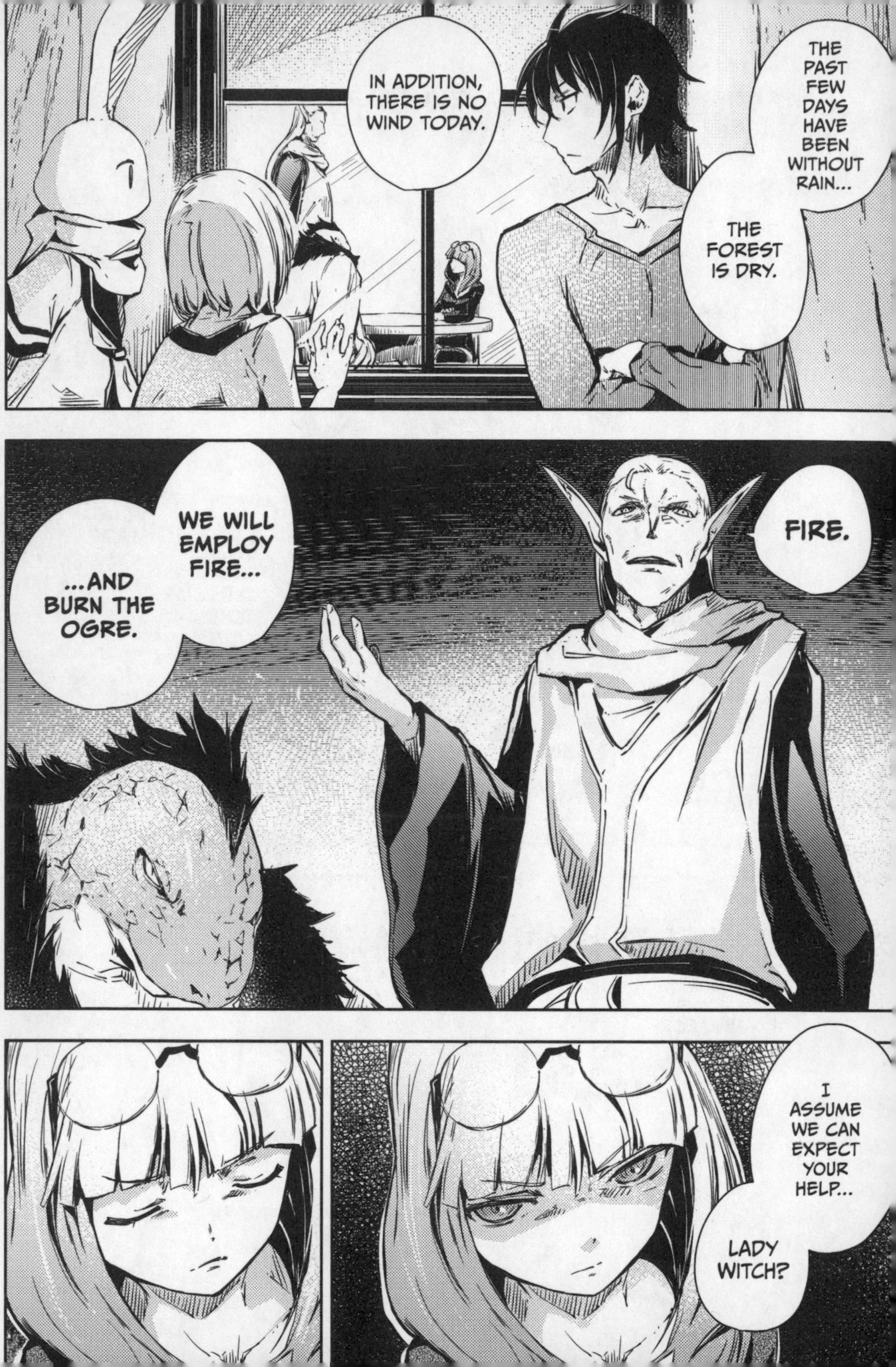
THE PAST FEW DAYS HAVE BEEN WITHOUT RAIN...
THE FOREST IS DRY.
IN ADDITION, THERE IS NO WIND TODAY.
FIRE.
WE WILL EMPLOY FIRE...
...AND BURN THE OGRE.
I ASSUME WE CAN EXPECT YOUR HELP...
LADY WITCH?

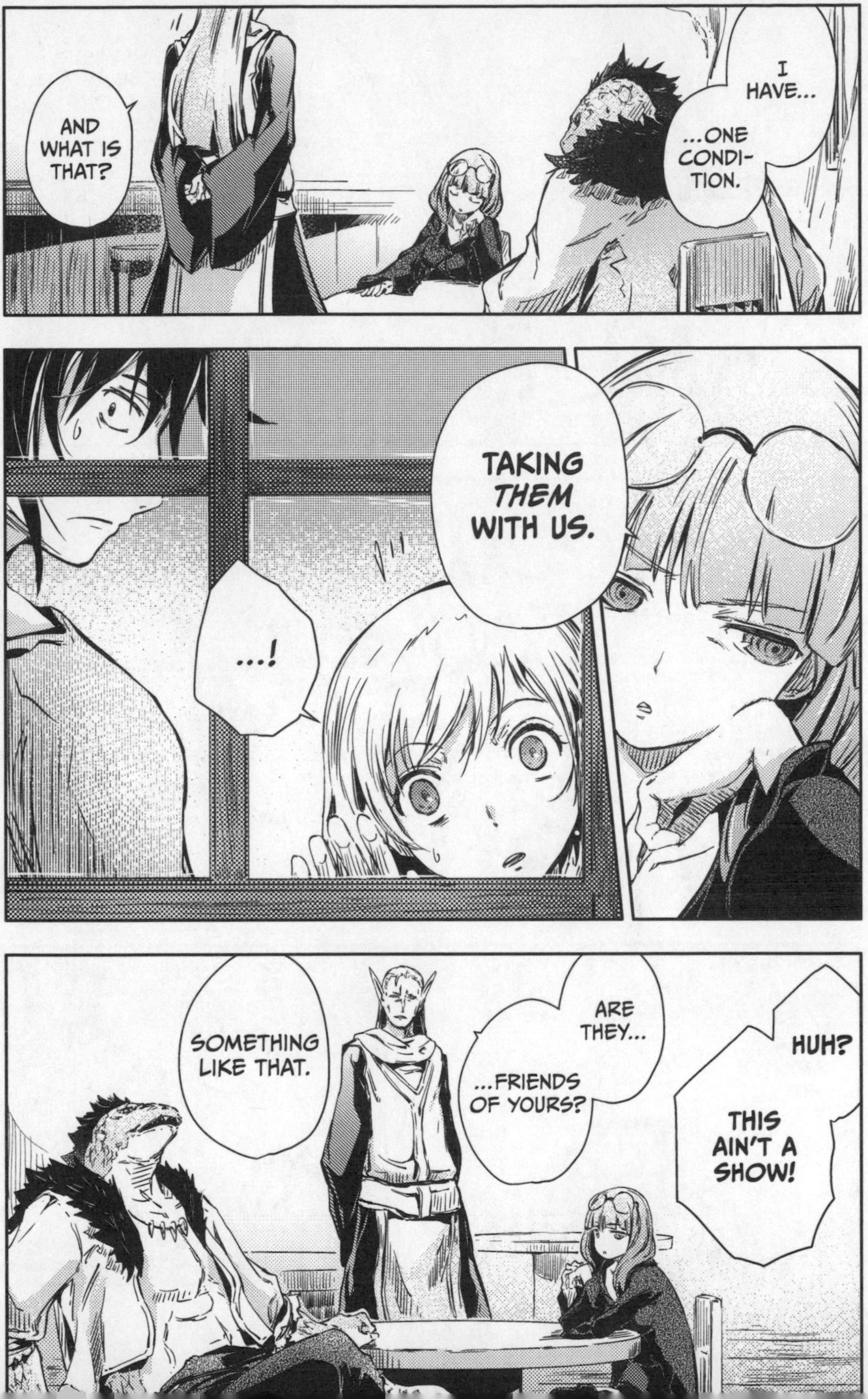
I HAVE...
...ONE CONDITION.
AND WHAT IS THAT?
TAKING THEM WITH US.
...!
HUH?
THIS AIN'T A SHOW!
ARE THEY...
...FRIENDS OF YOURS?
SOMETHING LIKE THAT.

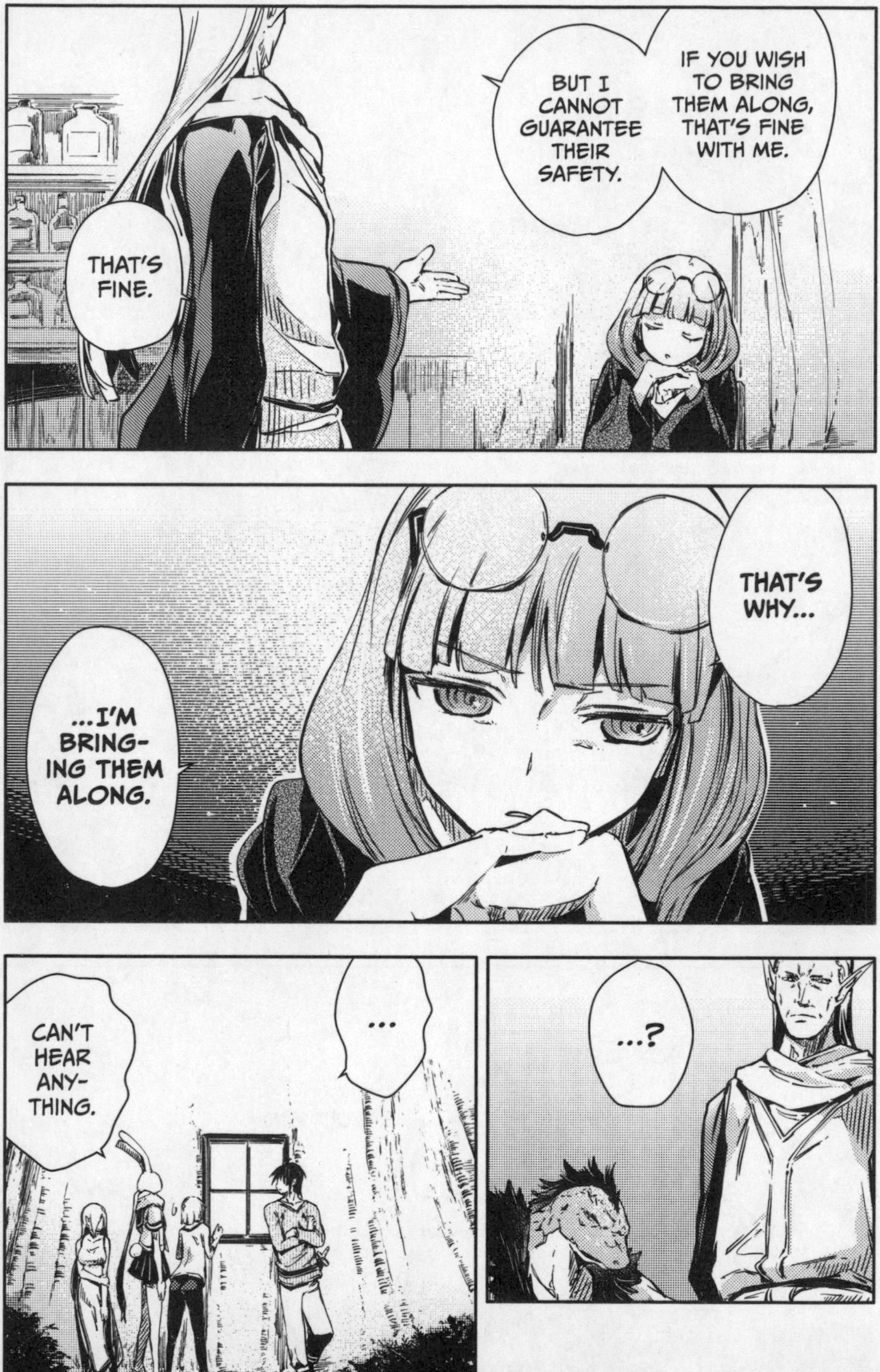
IF YOU WISH TO BRING THEM ALONG, THAT'S FINE WITH ME.
BUT I CANNOT GUARANTEE THEIR SAFETY.
THAT'S FINE.
THAT'S WHY...
...I'M BRING-ING THEM ALONG.
...?
...
CAN'T HEAR ANY-THING.

## CHAPTER 10: IDEALS AND REALITY

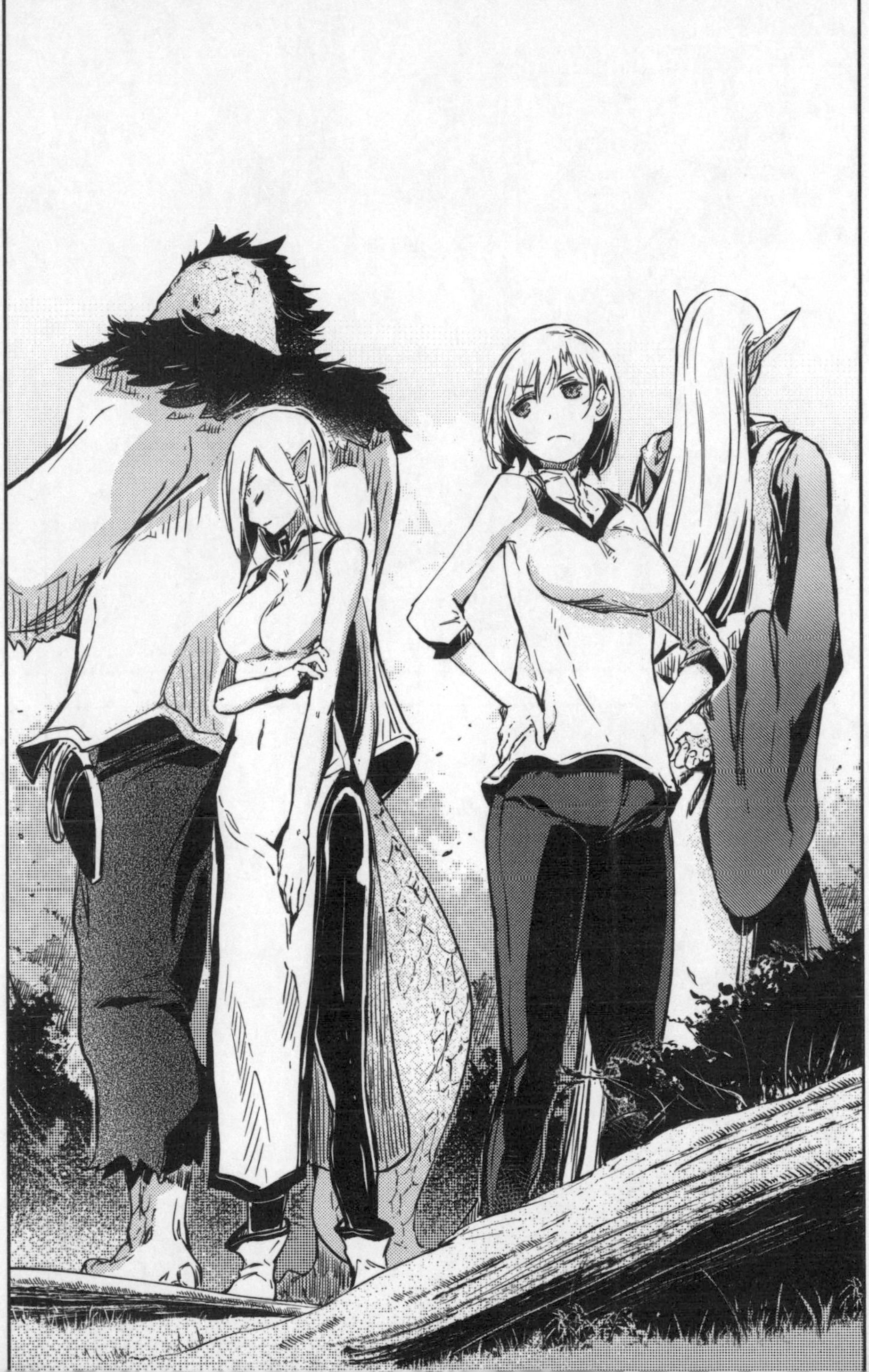

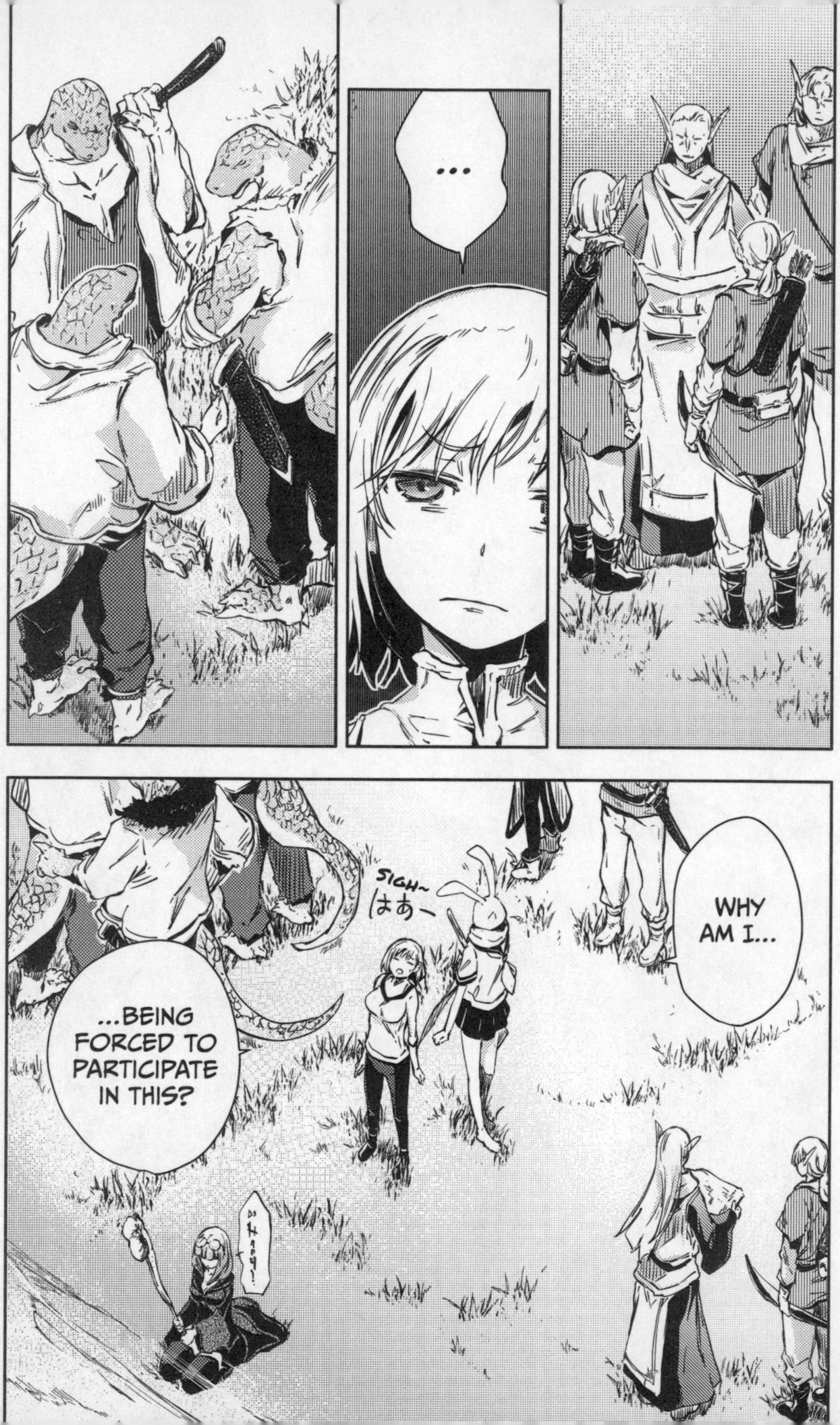
...
WHY AM I...
SIGH~
はあ~
...BEING FORCED TO PARTICIPATE IN THIS?

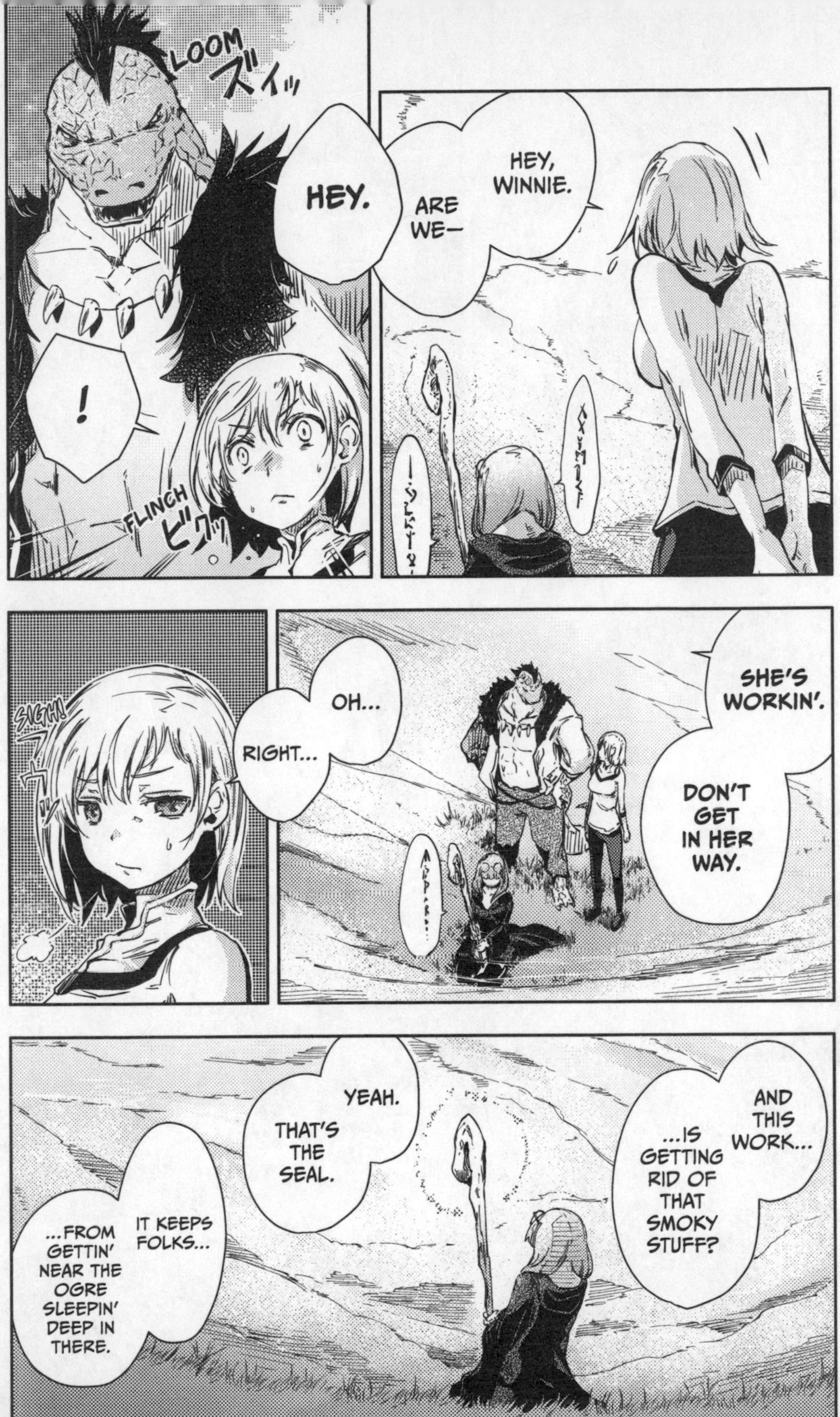
HEY, WINNIE.
ARE WE—
LOOM ズイッ
HEY.
!
FLINCH ビクッ
SHE'S WORKIN'.
DON'T GET IN HER WAY.
OH...
RIGHT...
SIGH!
AND THIS WORK...
...IS GETTING RID OF THAT SMOKY STUFF?
YEAH.
THAT'S THE SEAL.
IT KEEPS FOLKS...
...FROM GETTIN' NEAR THE OGRE SLEEPIN' DEEP IN THERE.

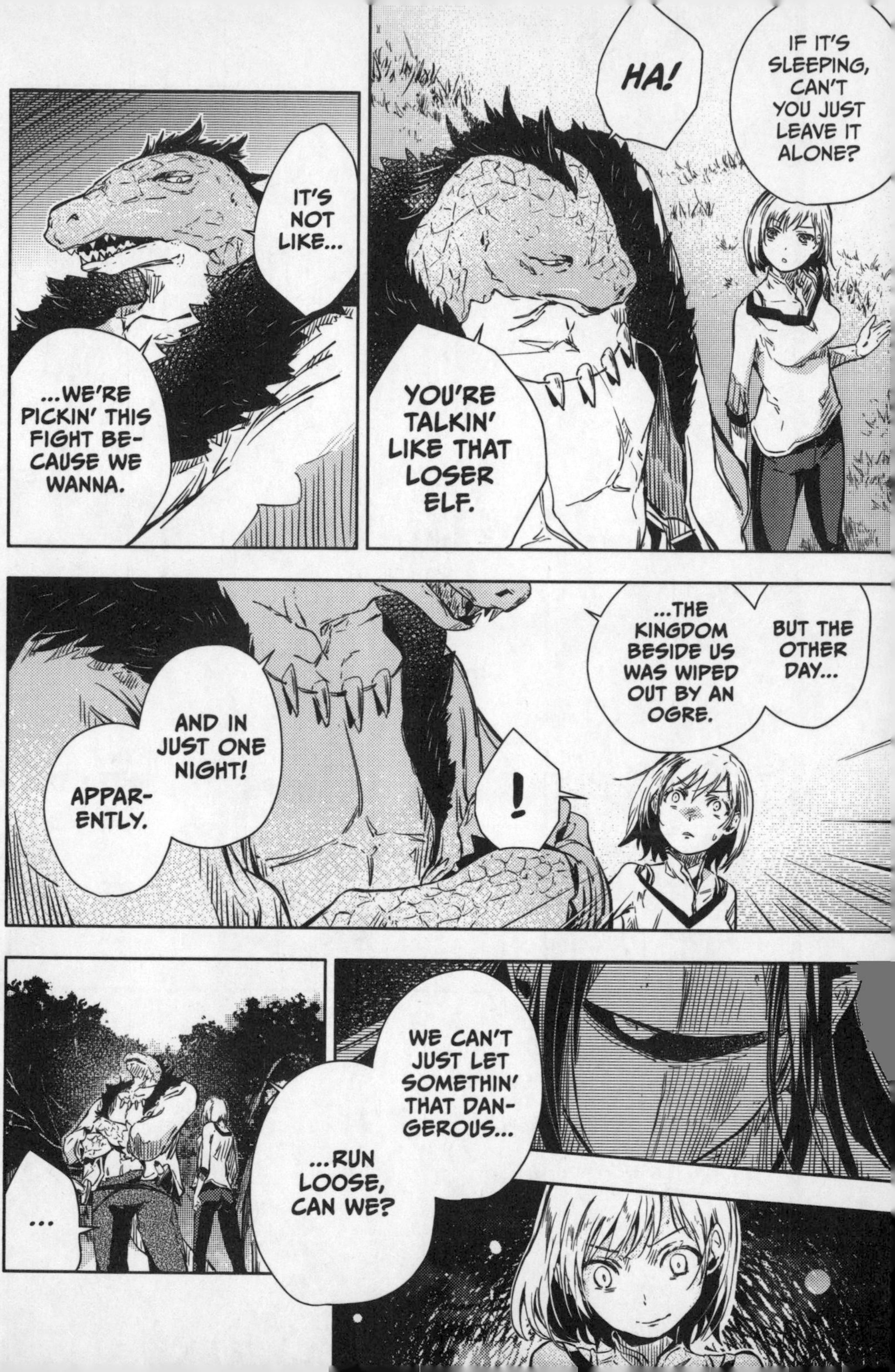
IF IT'S SLEEPING, CAN'T YOU JUST LEAVE IT ALONE?
HA!
YOU'RE TALKIN' LIKE THAT LOSER ELF.
IT'S NOT LIKE...
...WE'RE PICKIN' THIS FIGHT BE-CAUSE WE WANNA.
BUT THE OTHER DAY...
...THE KINGDOM BESIDE US WAS WIPED OUT BY AN OGRE.
!
AND IN JUST ONE NIGHT!
APPAR-ENTLY.
WE CAN'T JUST LET SOMETHIN' THAT DAN-GEROUS...
...RUN LOOSE, CAN WE?
...

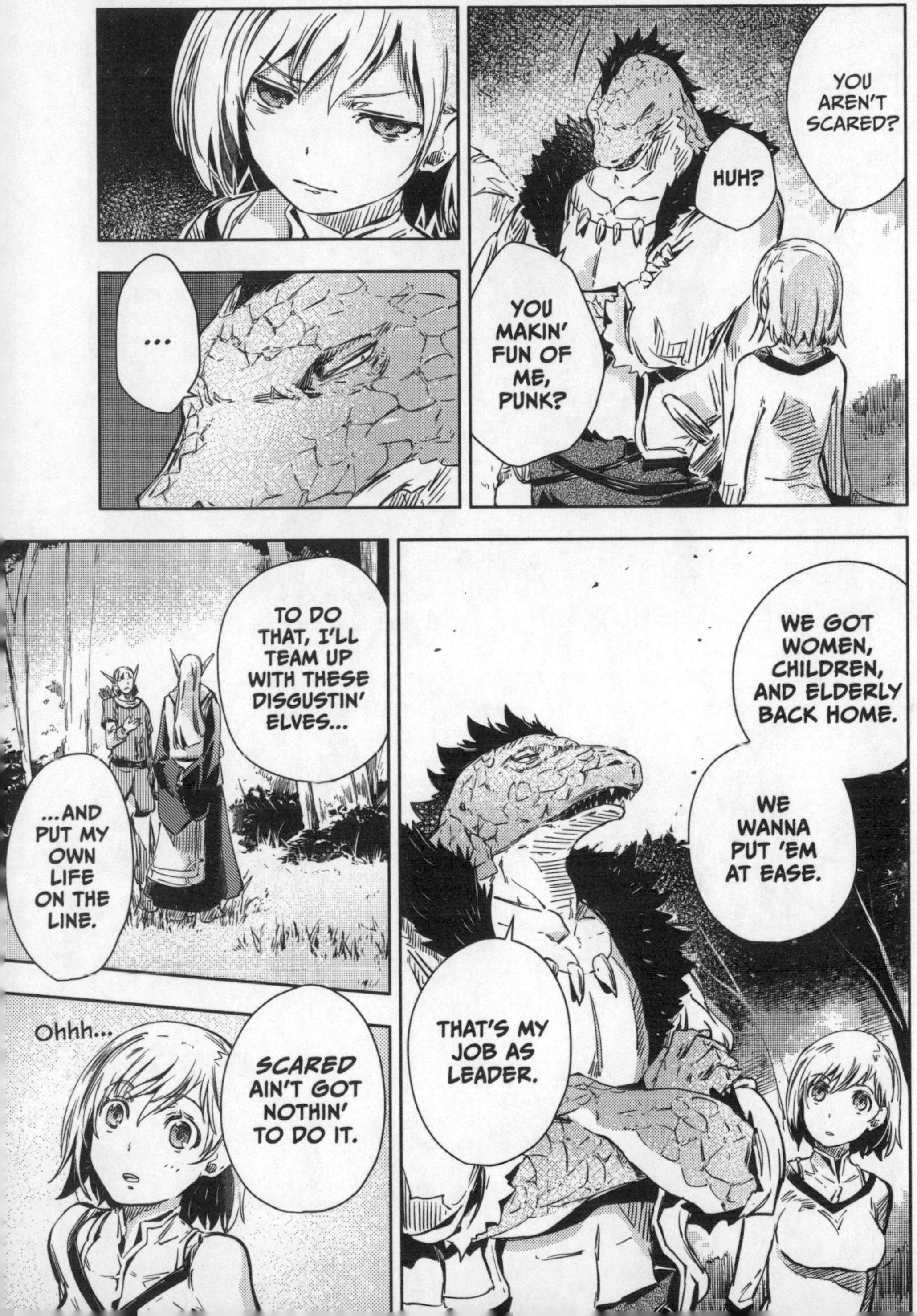
YOU AREN'T SCARED?
HUH?
YOU MAKIN' FUN OF ME, PUNK?
...
WE GOT WOMEN, CHILDREN, AND ELDERLY BACK HOME.
WE WANNA PUT 'EM AT EASE.
THAT'S MY JOB AS LEADER.
TO DO THAT, I'LL TEAM UP WITH THESE DISGUSTIN' ELVES...
...AND PUT MY OWN LIFE ON THE LINE.
SCARED AIN'T GOT NOTHIN' TO DO IT.
Ohhh...

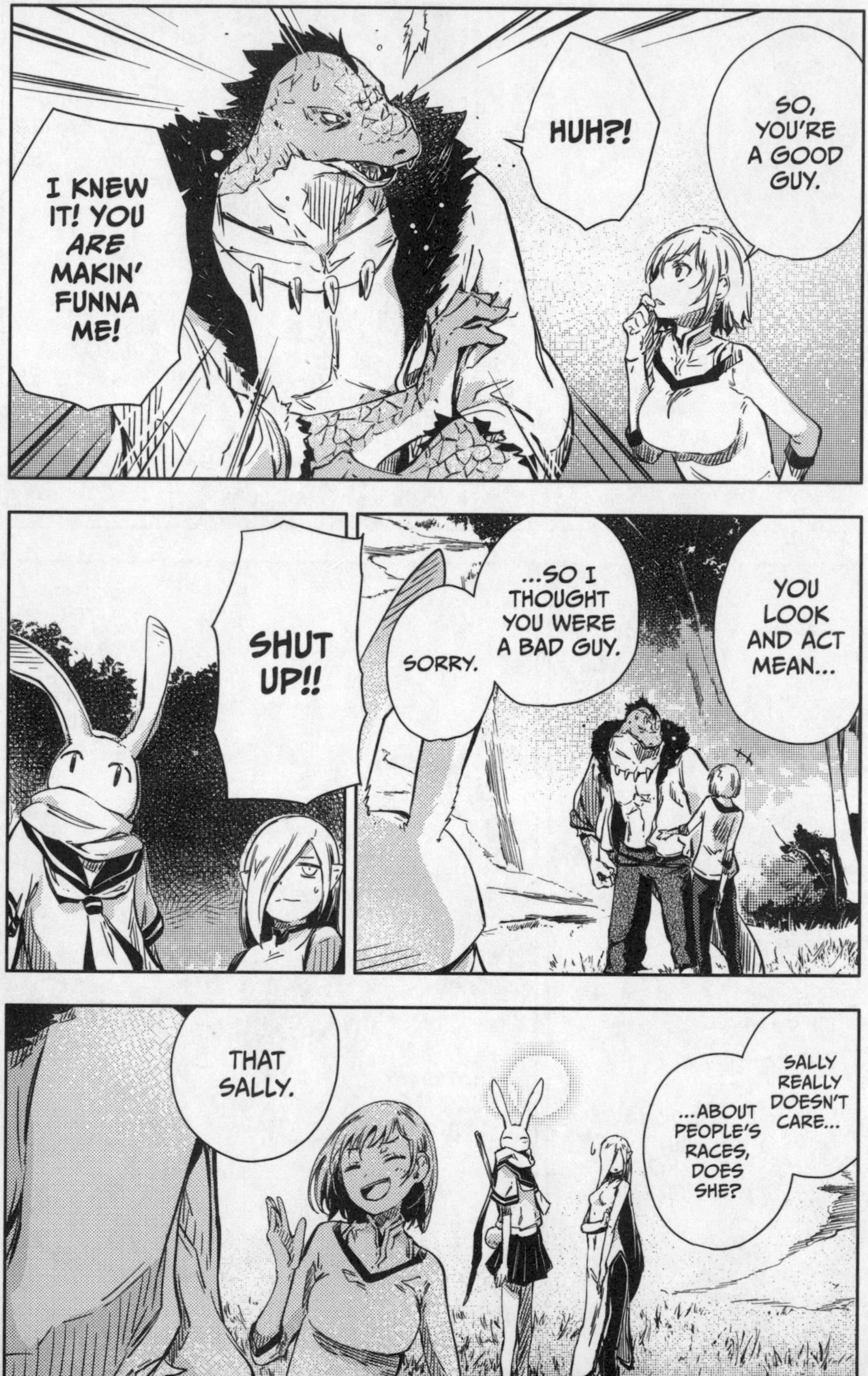
SO, YOU'RE A GOOD GUY.
HUH?!
I KNEW IT! YOU *ARE* MAKIN' FUNNA ME!
YOU LOOK AND ACT MEAN...
...SO I THOUGHT YOU WERE A BAD GUY.
SORRY.
SHUT UP!!
SALLY REALLY DOESN'T CARE...
...ABOUT PEOPLE'S RACES, DOES SHE?
THAT SALLY.

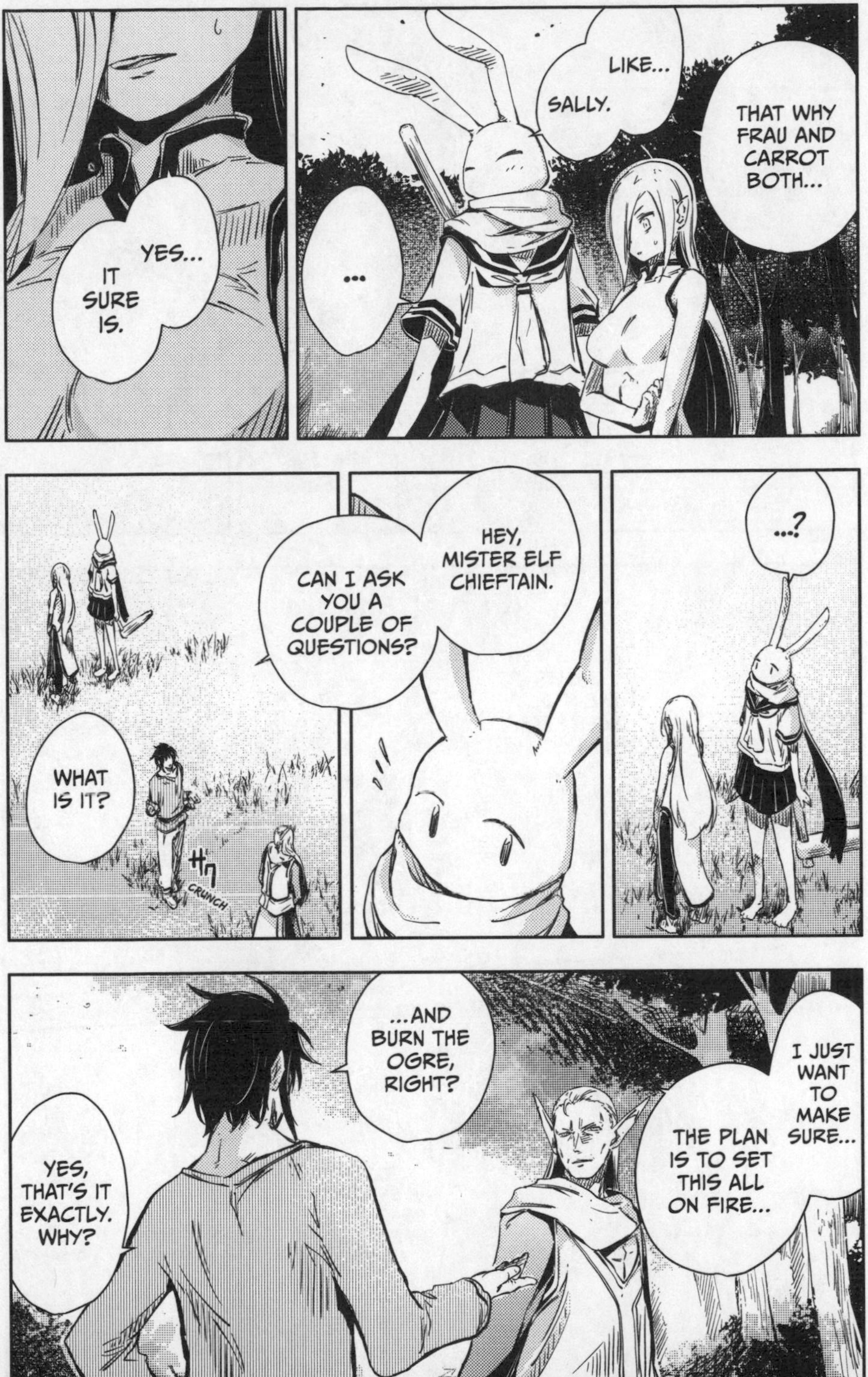
THAT WHY FRAU AND CARROT BOTH...
LIKE... SALLY.
...
YES... IT SURE IS.
...?
HEY, MISTER ELF CHIEFTAIN.
CAN I ASK YOU A COUPLE OF QUESTIONS?
WHAT IS IT?
CRUNCH
I JUST WANT TO MAKE SURE...
THE PLAN IS TO SET THIS ALL ON FIRE...
...AND BURN THE OGRE, RIGHT?
YES, THAT'S IT EXACTLY. WHY?

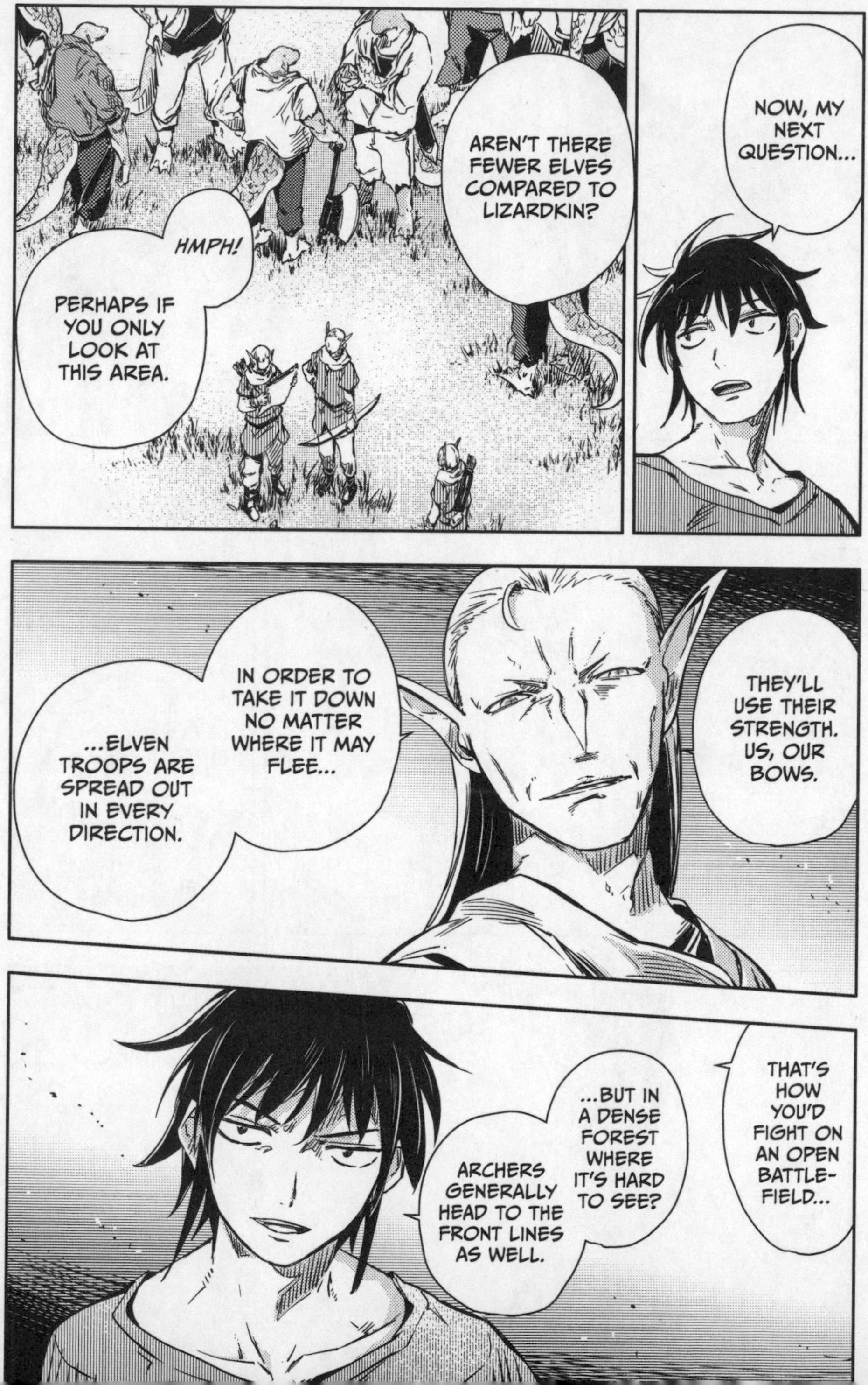
NOW, MY NEXT QUESTION...
AREN'T THERE FEWER ELVES COMPARED TO LIZARDKIN?
HMPH!
PERHAPS IF YOU ONLY LOOK AT THIS AREA.
THEY'LL USE THEIR STRENGTH. US, OUR BOWS.
IN ORDER TO TAKE IT DOWN NO MATTER WHERE IT MAY FLEE...
...ELVEN TROOPS ARE SPREAD OUT IN EVERY DIRECTION.
THAT'S HOW YOU'D FIGHT ON AN OPEN BATTLE-FIELD...
...BUT IN A DENSE FOREST WHERE IT'S HARD TO SEE?
ARCHERS GENERALLY HEAD TO THE FRONT LINES AS WELL.

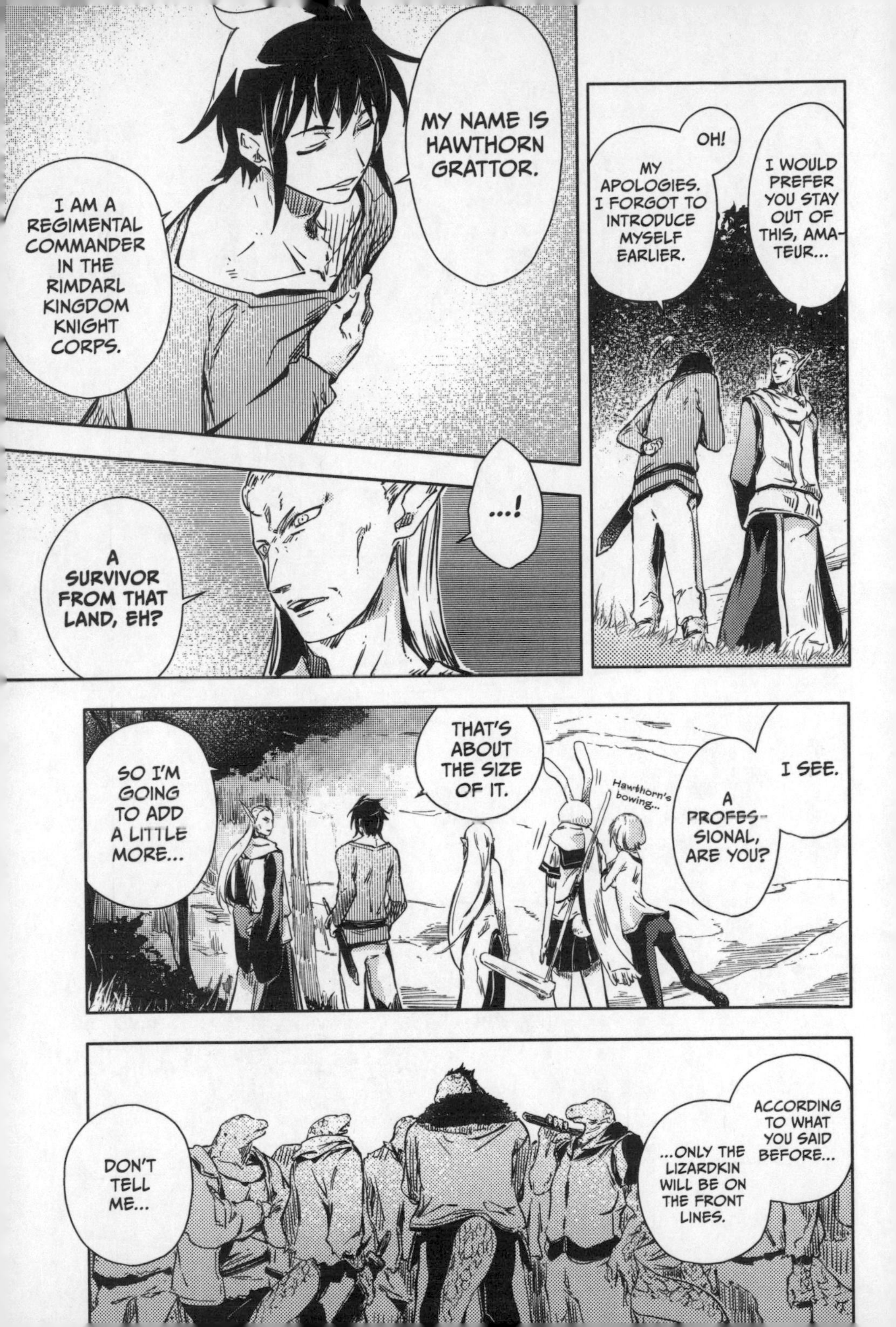
I WOULD PREFER YOU STAY OUT OF THIS, AMATEUR...
OH!
MY APOLOGIES. I FORGOT TO INTRODUCE MYSELF EARLIER.
MY NAME IS HAWTHORN GRATTOR.
I AM A REGIMENTAL COMMANDER IN THE RIMDARL KINGDOM KNIGHT CORPS.
...!
A SURVIVOR FROM THAT LAND, EH?
I SEE.
A PROFESSIONAL, ARE YOU?
Hawthorn's bowing...
THAT'S ABOUT THE SIZE OF IT.
SO I'M GOING TO ADD A LITTLE MORE...
ACCORDING TO WHAT YOU SAID BEFORE...
...ONLY THE LIZARDKIN WILL BE ON THE FRONT LINES.
DON'T TELL ME...

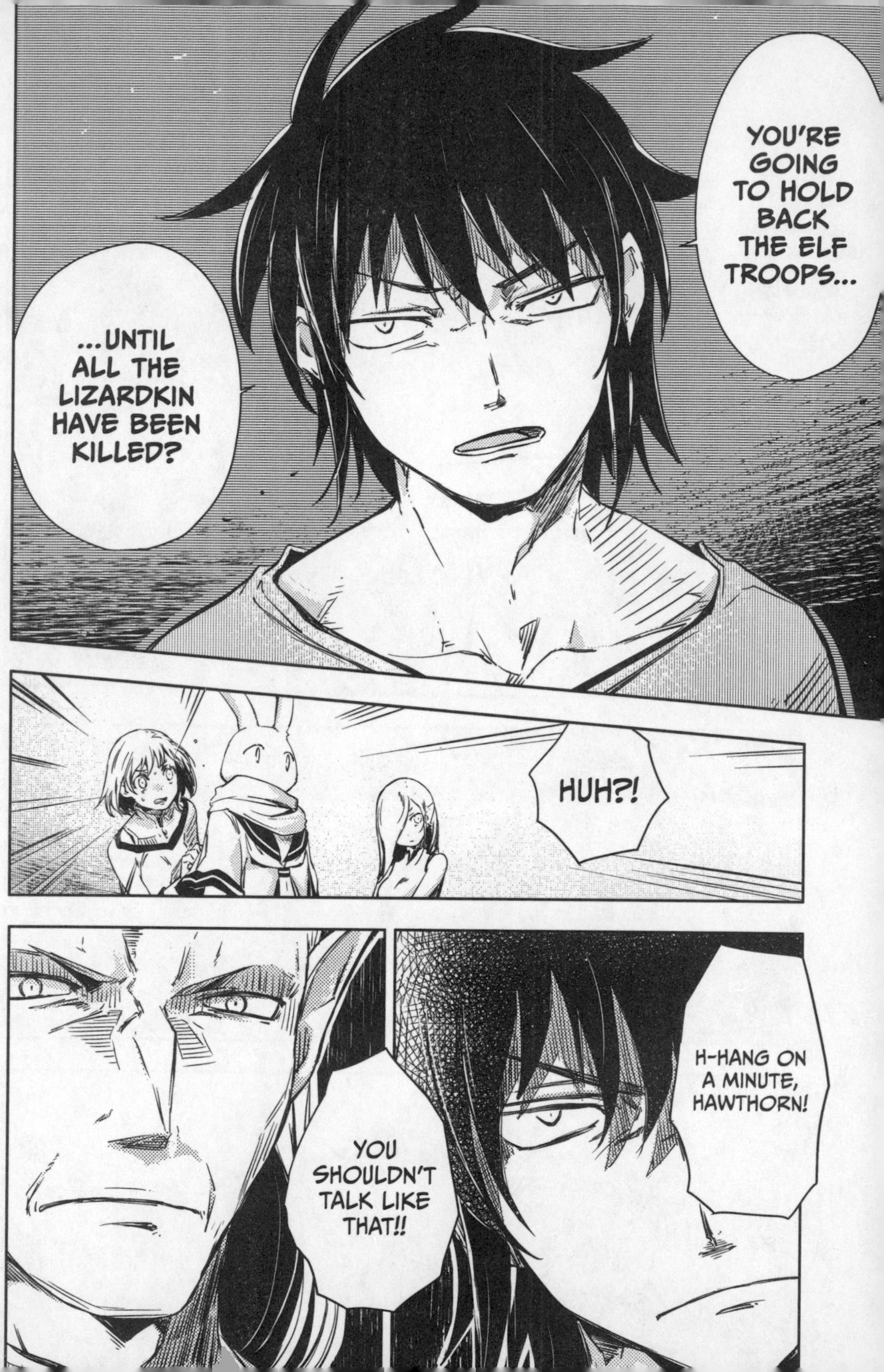
YOU'RE GOING TO HOLD BACK THE ELF TROOPS...
...UNTIL ALL THE LIZARDKIN HAVE BEEN KILLED?
HUH?!
H-HANG ON A MINUTE, HAWTHORN!
YOU SHOULDN'T TALK LIKE THAT!!

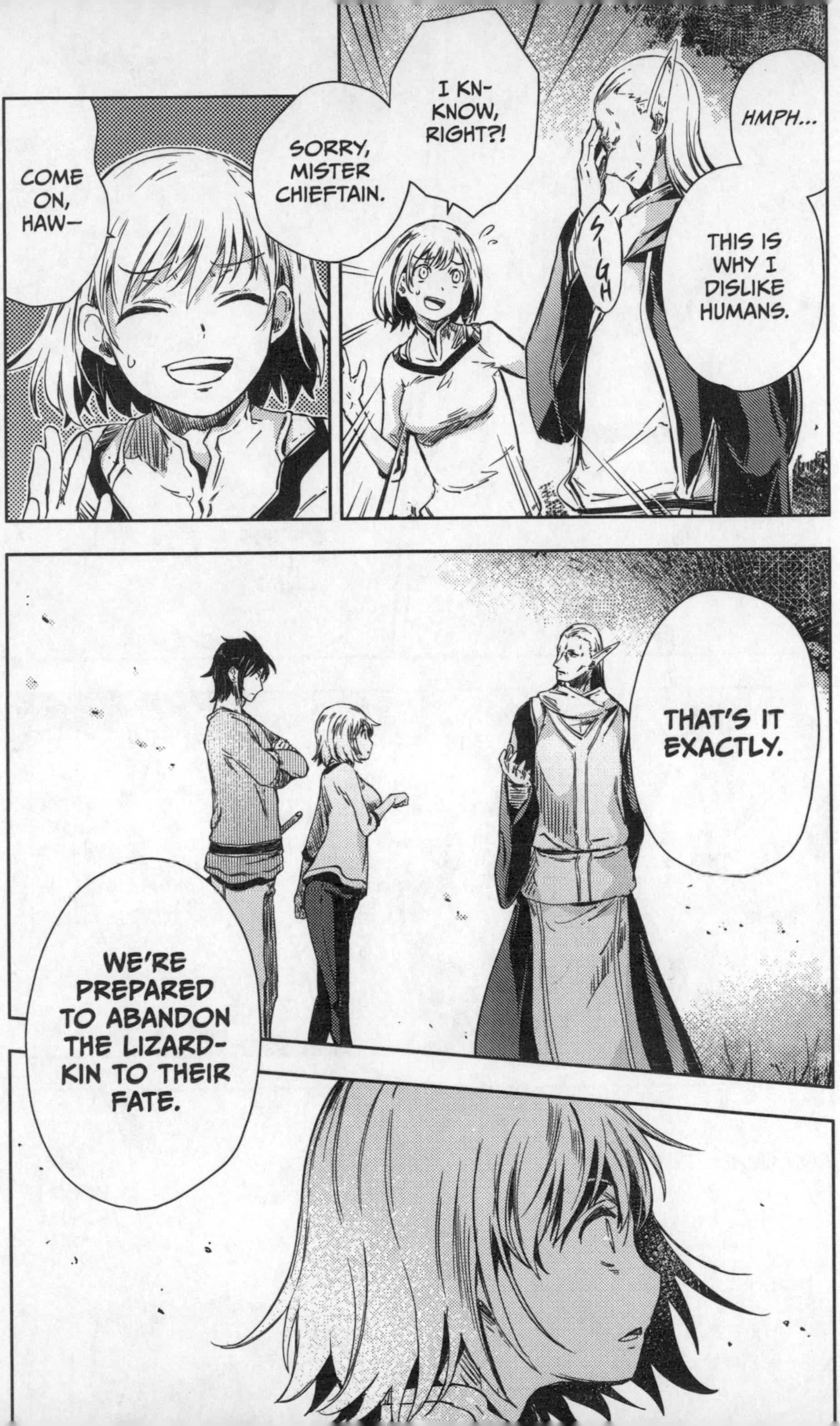
HMPH...
THIS IS WHY I DISLIKE HUMANS.
SIGH
I KN-KNOW, RIGHT?!
SORRY, MISTER CHIEFTAIN.
COME ON, HAW—
THAT'S IT EXACTLY.
WE'RE PREPARED TO ABANDON THE LIZARD-KIN TO THEIR FATE.

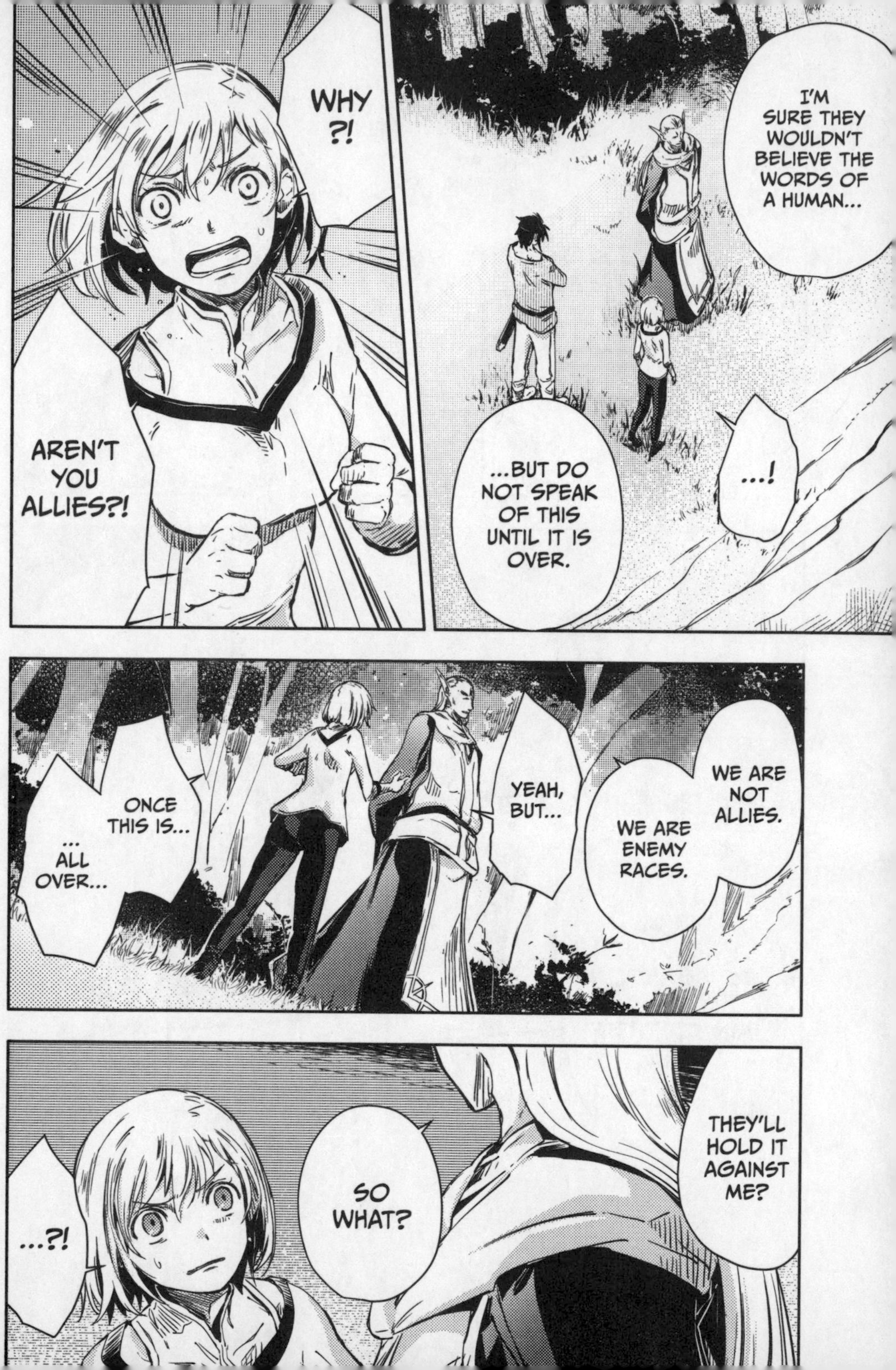
I'M SURE THEY WOULDN'T BELIEVE THE WORDS OF A HUMAN...
...BUT DO NOT SPEAK OF THIS UNTIL IT IS OVER.
...!
WHY?!
AREN'T YOU ALLIES?!
WE ARE NOT ALLIES.
WE ARE ENEMY RACES.
YEAH, BUT...
ONCE THIS IS...
...ALL OVER...
THEY'LL HOLD IT AGAINST ME?
SO WHAT?
...?!

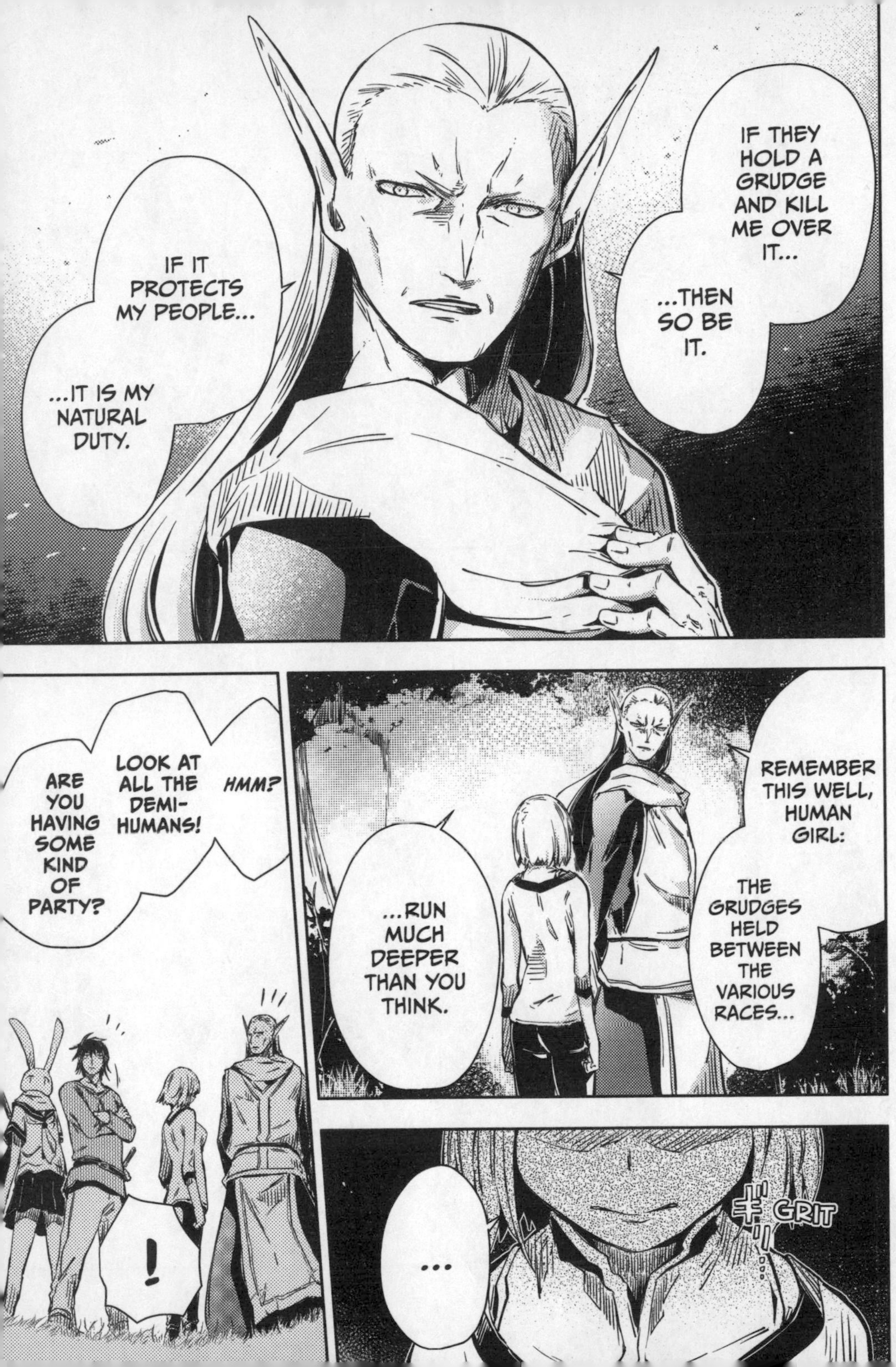
IF THEY HOLD A GRUDGE AND KILL ME OVER IT...
...THEN SO BE IT.
IF IT PROTECTS MY PEOPLE...
...IT IS MY NATURAL DUTY.
REMEMBER THIS WELL, HUMAN GIRL:
THE GRUDGES HELD BETWEEN THE VARIOUS RACES...
...RUN MUCH DEEPER THAN YOU THINK.
GRIT
...
HMM?
LOOK AT ALL THE DEMI-HUMANS!
ARE YOU HAVING SOME KIND OF PARTY?
!

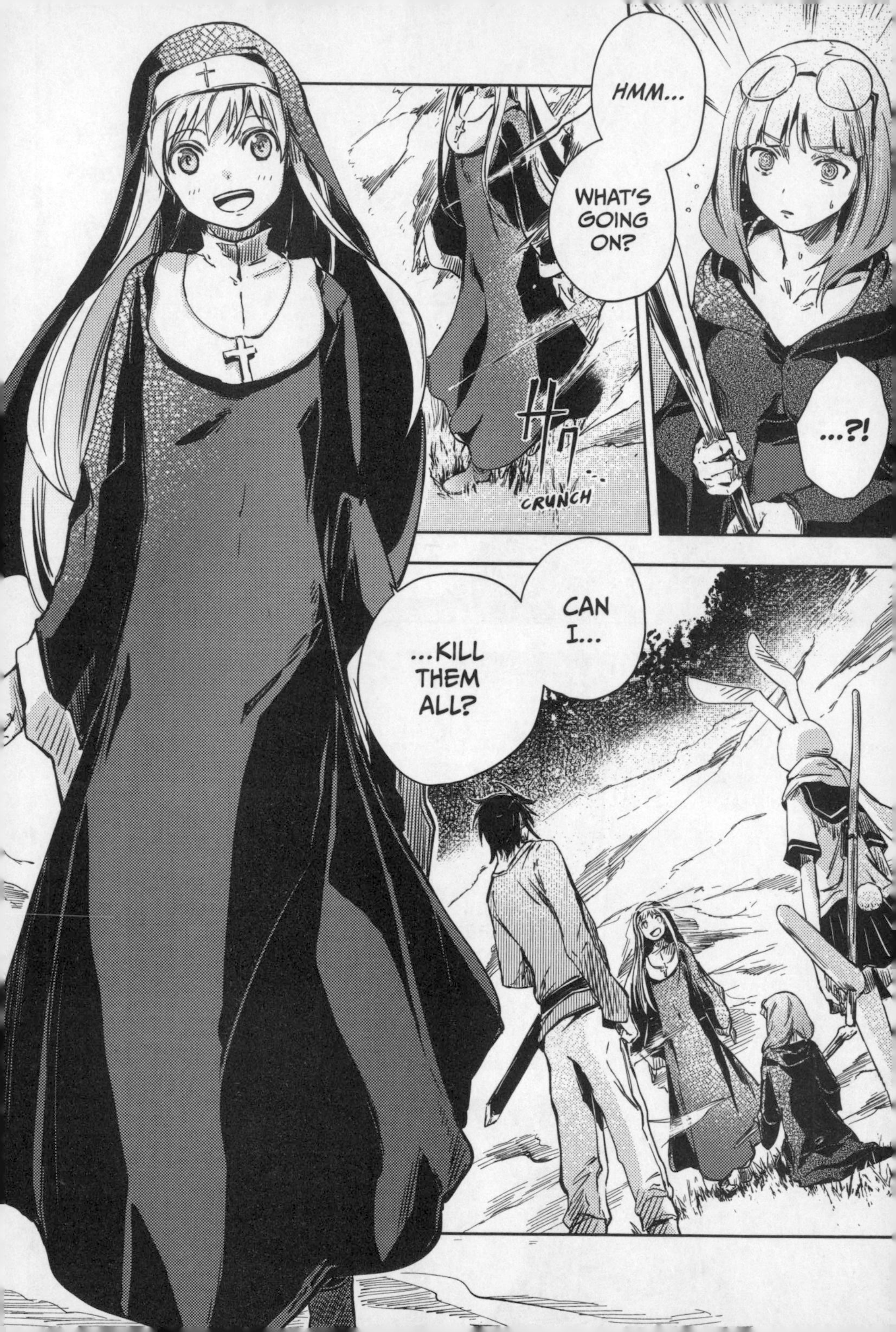
HMM...
WHAT'S GOING ON?
...?!
CRUNCH
CAN I...
...KILL THEM ALL?

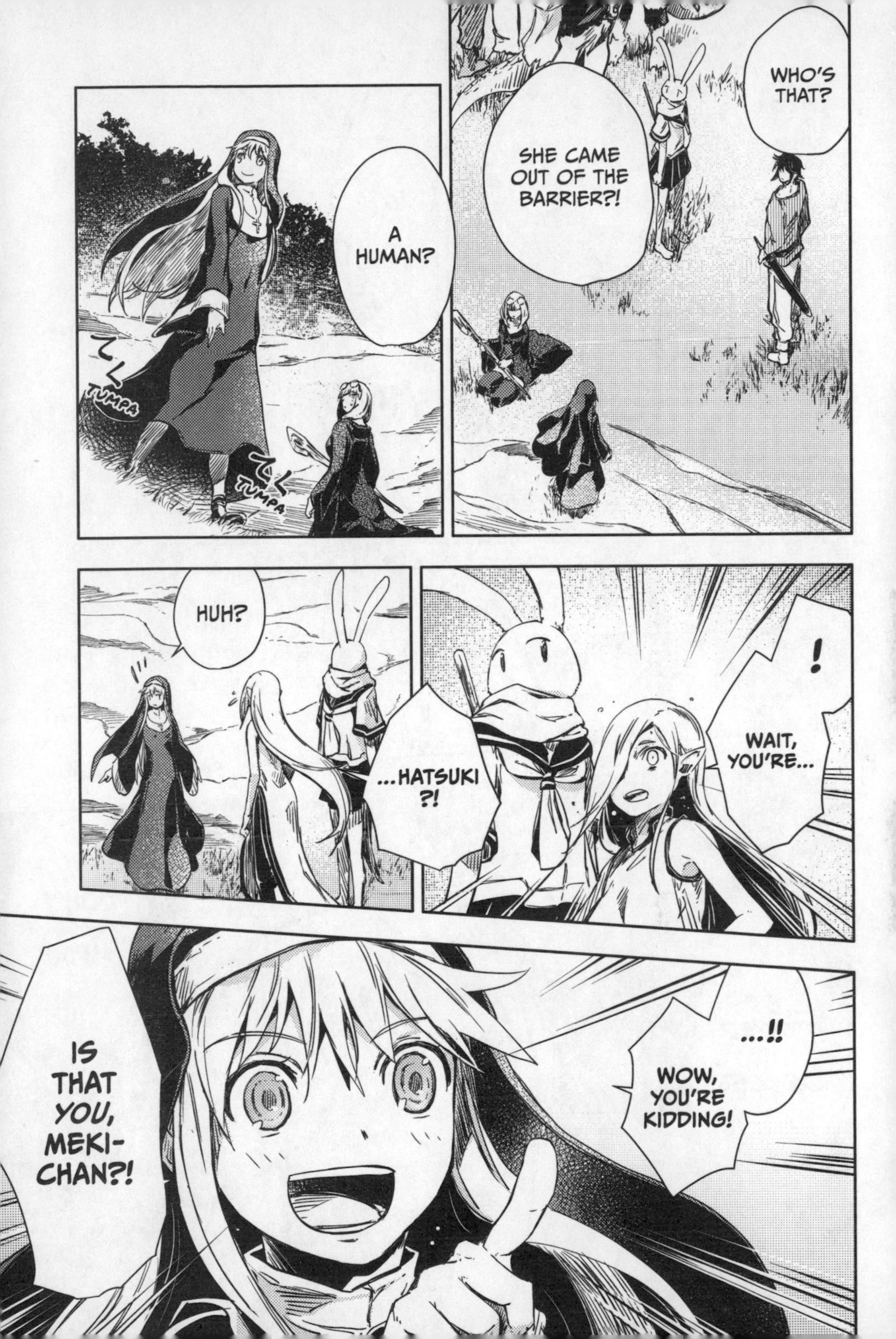
WHO'S THAT?
SHE CAME OUT OF THE BARRIER?!
A HUMAN?
てく TUMPA
てく TUMPA
!
WAIT, YOU'RE...
...HATSUKI ?!
HUH?
...!!
WOW, YOU'RE KIDDING!
IS THAT YOU, MEKI-CHAN?!

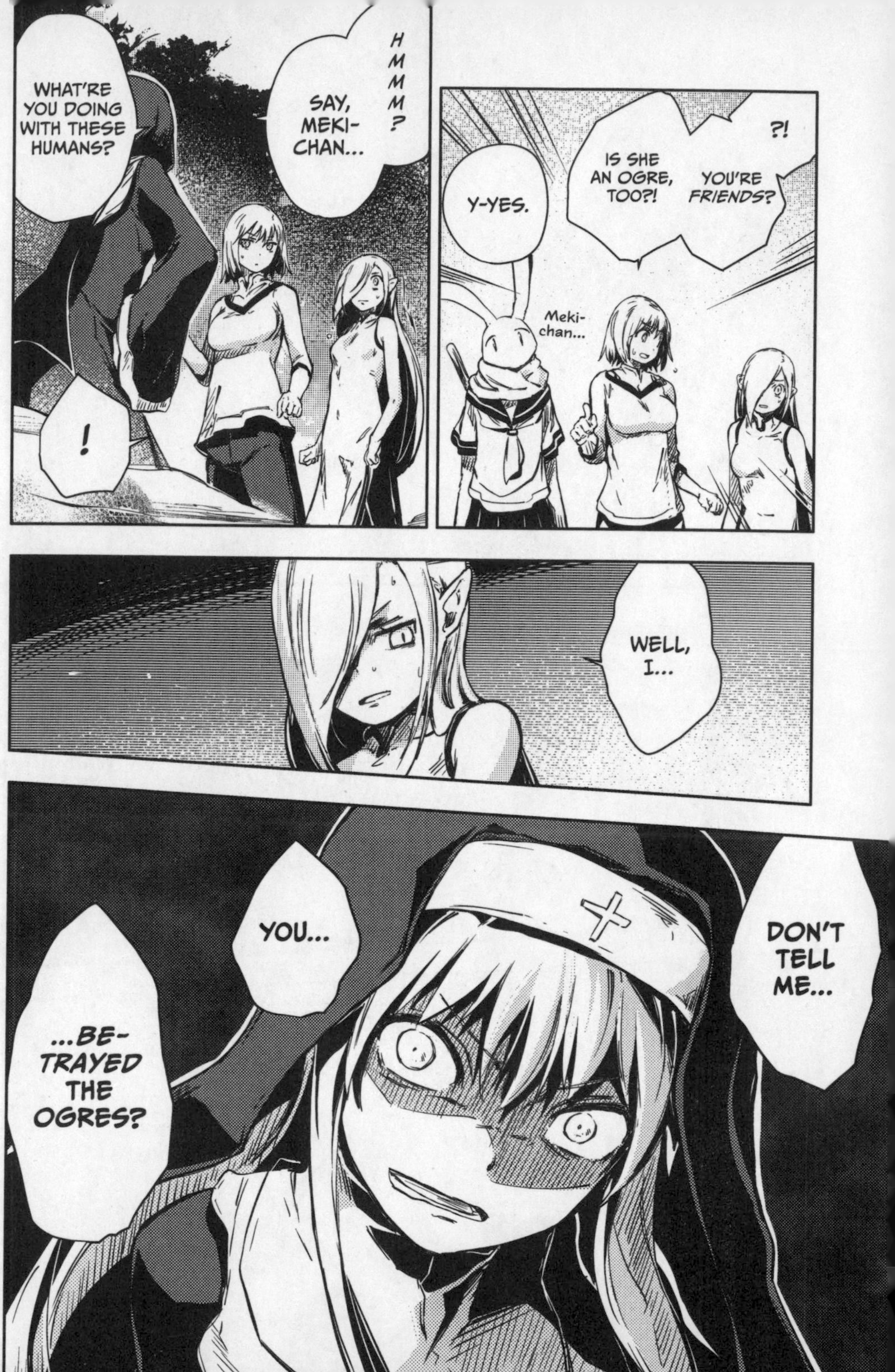
?!
YOU'RE FRIENDS?
IS SHE AN OGRE, TOO?!
Y-YES.
Meki-chan...
HMMMM?
SAY, MEKI-CHAN...
WHAT'RE YOU DOING WITH THESE HUMANS?
!
WELL, I...
DON'T TELL ME...
YOU...
...BE-TRAYED THE OGRES?

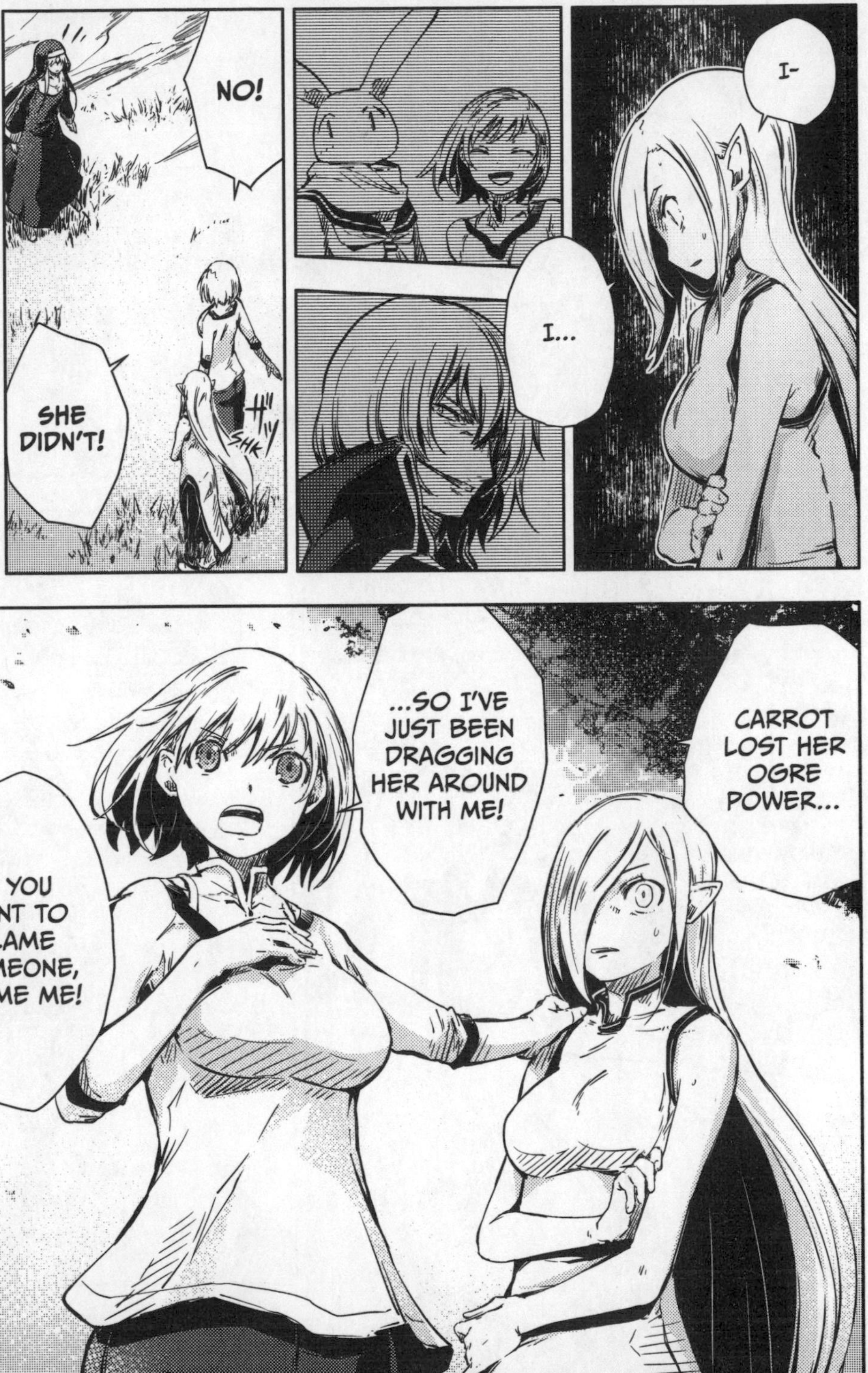
I-
I...
NO!
SHE DIDN'T!
SHK
CARROT LOST HER OGRE POWER...
...SO I'VE JUST BEEN DRAGGING HER AROUND WITH ME!
IF YOU WANT TO BLAME SOMEONE, BLAME ME!

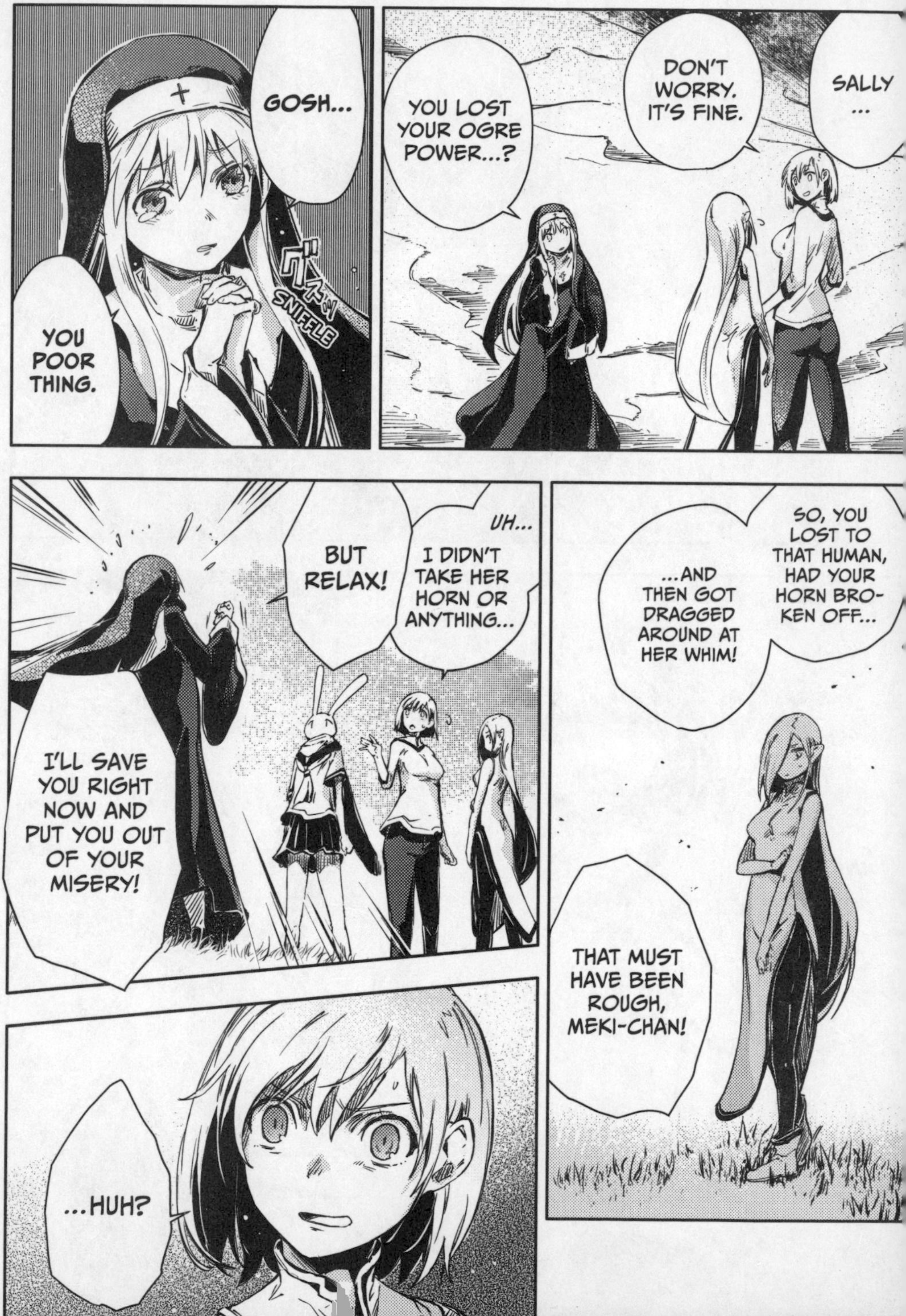
SALLY ...
DON'T WORRY. IT'S FINE.
YOU LOST YOUR OGRE POWER...?
GOSH...
SNIFFLE
YOU POOR THING.
SO, YOU LOST TO THAT HUMAN, HAD YOUR HORN BRO-KEN OFF...
...AND THEN GOT DRAGGED AROUND AT HER WHIM!
THAT MUST HAVE BEEN ROUGH, MEKI-CHAN!
UH... I DIDN'T TAKE HER HORN OR ANYTHING...
BUT RELAX!
I'LL SAVE YOU RIGHT NOW AND PUT YOU OUT OF YOUR MISERY!
...HUH?

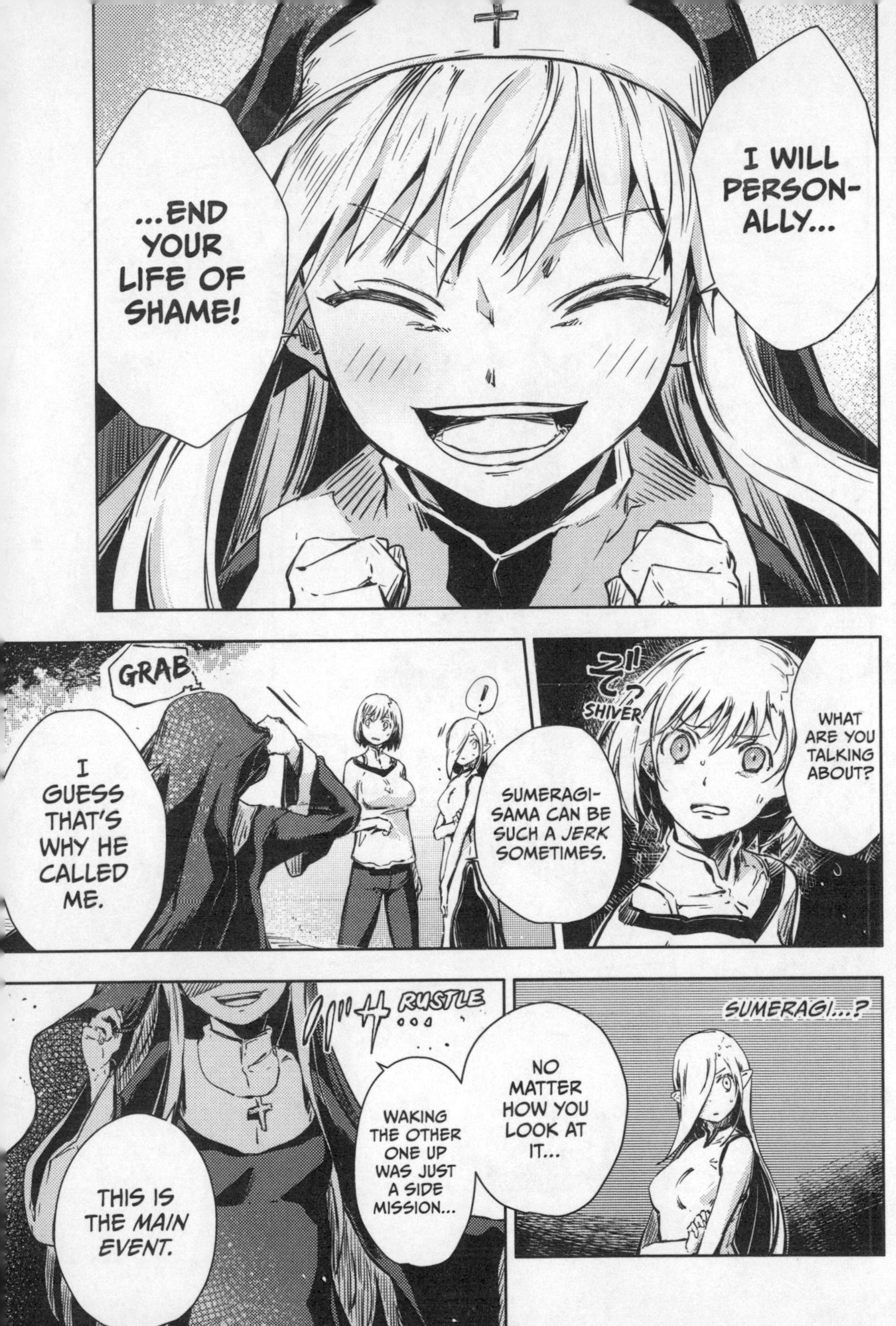
I WILL PERSON-ALLY...
...END YOUR LIFE OF SHAME!
ぞ
SHIVER
WHAT ARE YOU TALKING ABOUT?
GRAB
!
SUMERAGI-SAMA CAN BE SUCH A *JERK* SOMETIMES.
I GUESS THAT'S WHY HE CALLED ME.
*SUMERAGI...?*
*RUSTLE*
NO MATTER HOW YOU LOOK AT IT...
WAKING THE OTHER ONE UP WAS JUST A SIDE MISSION...
THIS IS THE *MAIN EVENT.*

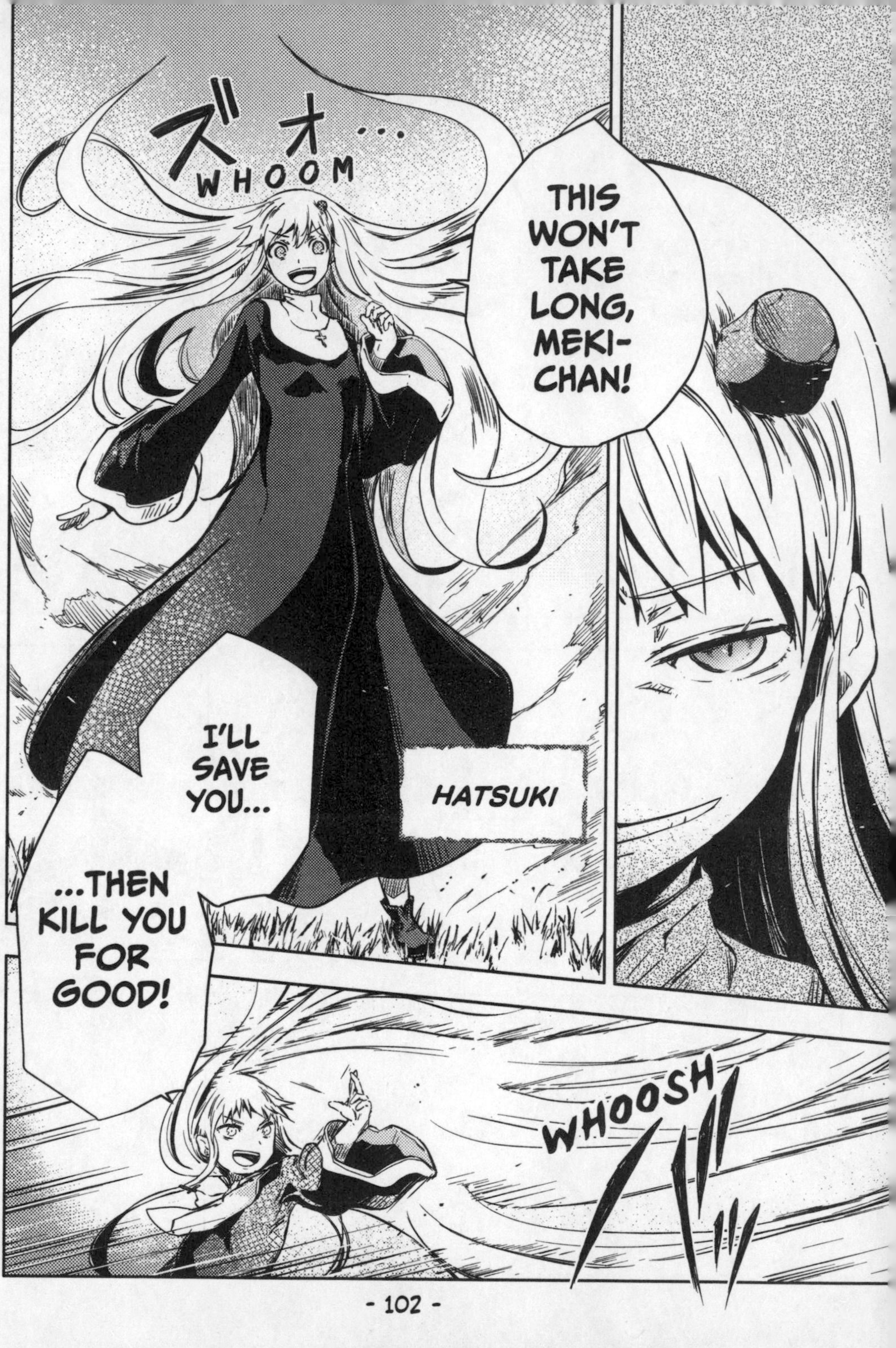
THIS WON'T TAKE LONG, MEKI-CHAN!
ズオ…
WHOOM
I'LL SAVE YOU...
HATSUKI
...THEN KILL YOU FOR GOOD!
WHOOSH

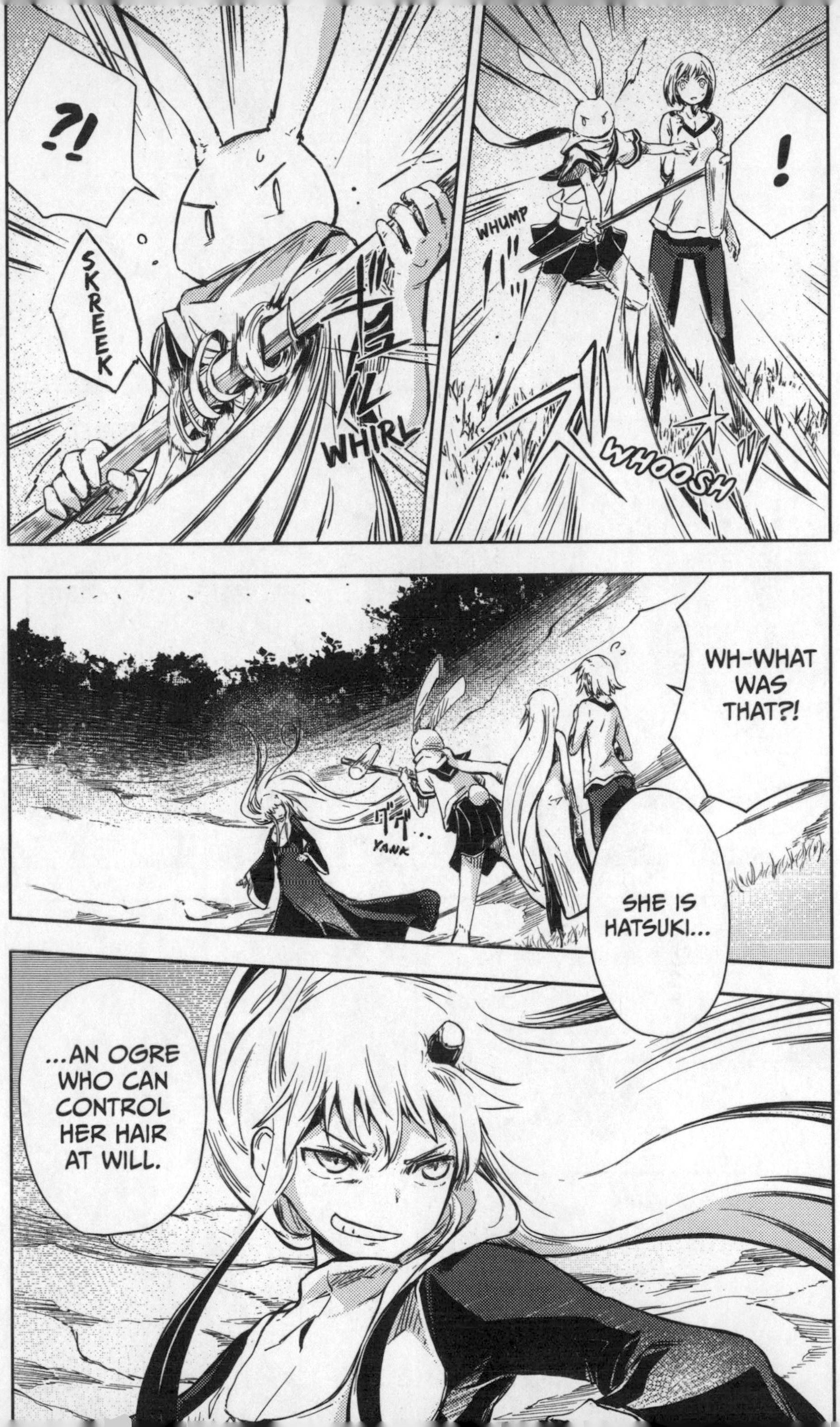
!
WHUMP
WHOOSH
?!
SKREEK
WHIRL
WH-WHAT WAS THAT?!
YANK
SHE IS HATSUKI...
...AN OGRE WHO CAN CONTROL HER HAIR AT WILL.

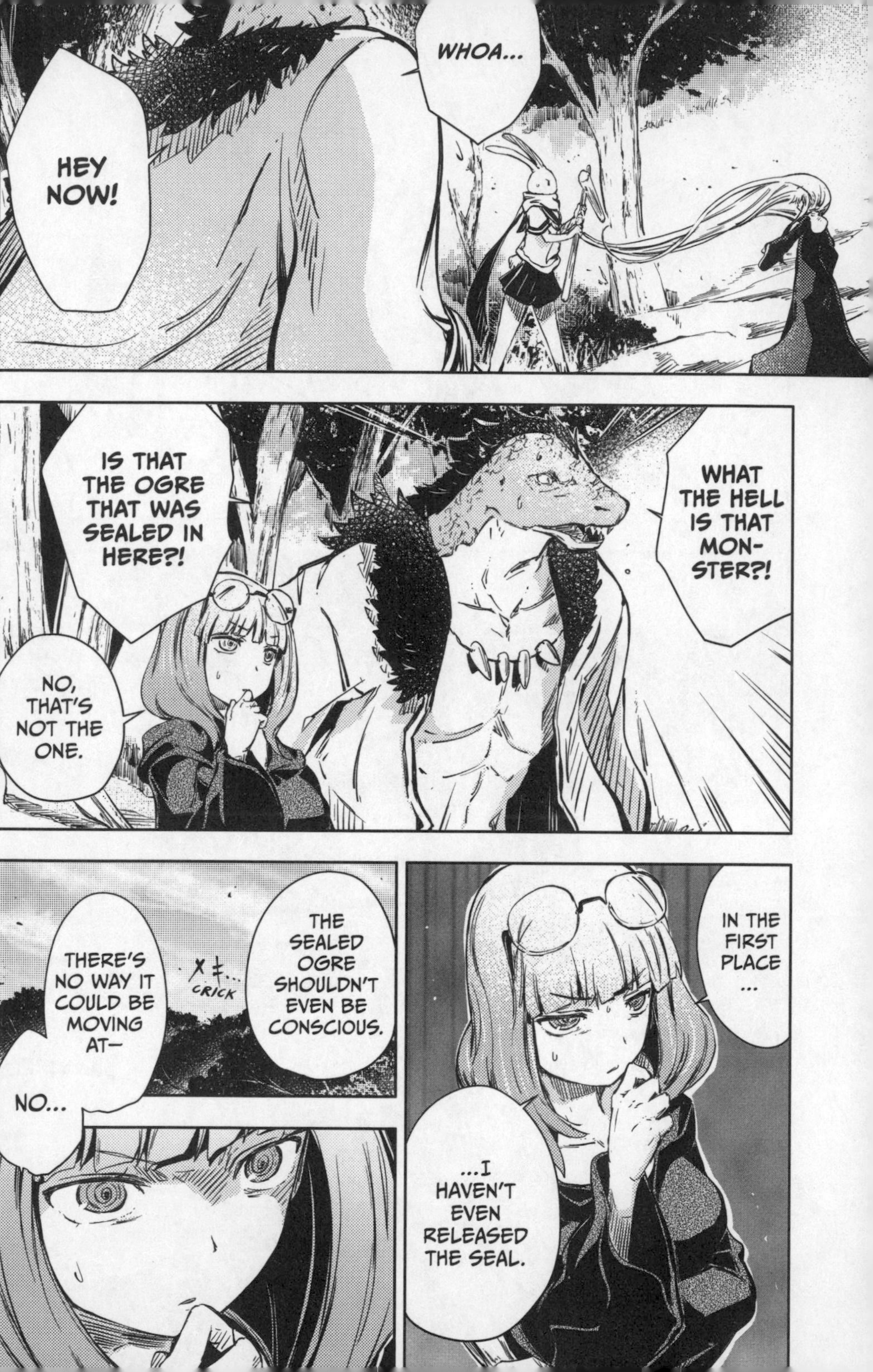
WHOA...
HEY NOW!
WHAT THE HELL IS THAT MONSTER?!
IS THAT THE OGRE THAT WAS SEALED IN HERE?!
NO, THAT'S NOT THE ONE.
IN THE FIRST PLACE ...
...I HAVEN'T EVEN RELEASED THE SEAL.
THE SEALED OGRE SHOULDN'T EVEN BE CONSCIOUS.
CRICK
THERE'S NO WAY IT COULD BE MOVING AT—
NO...

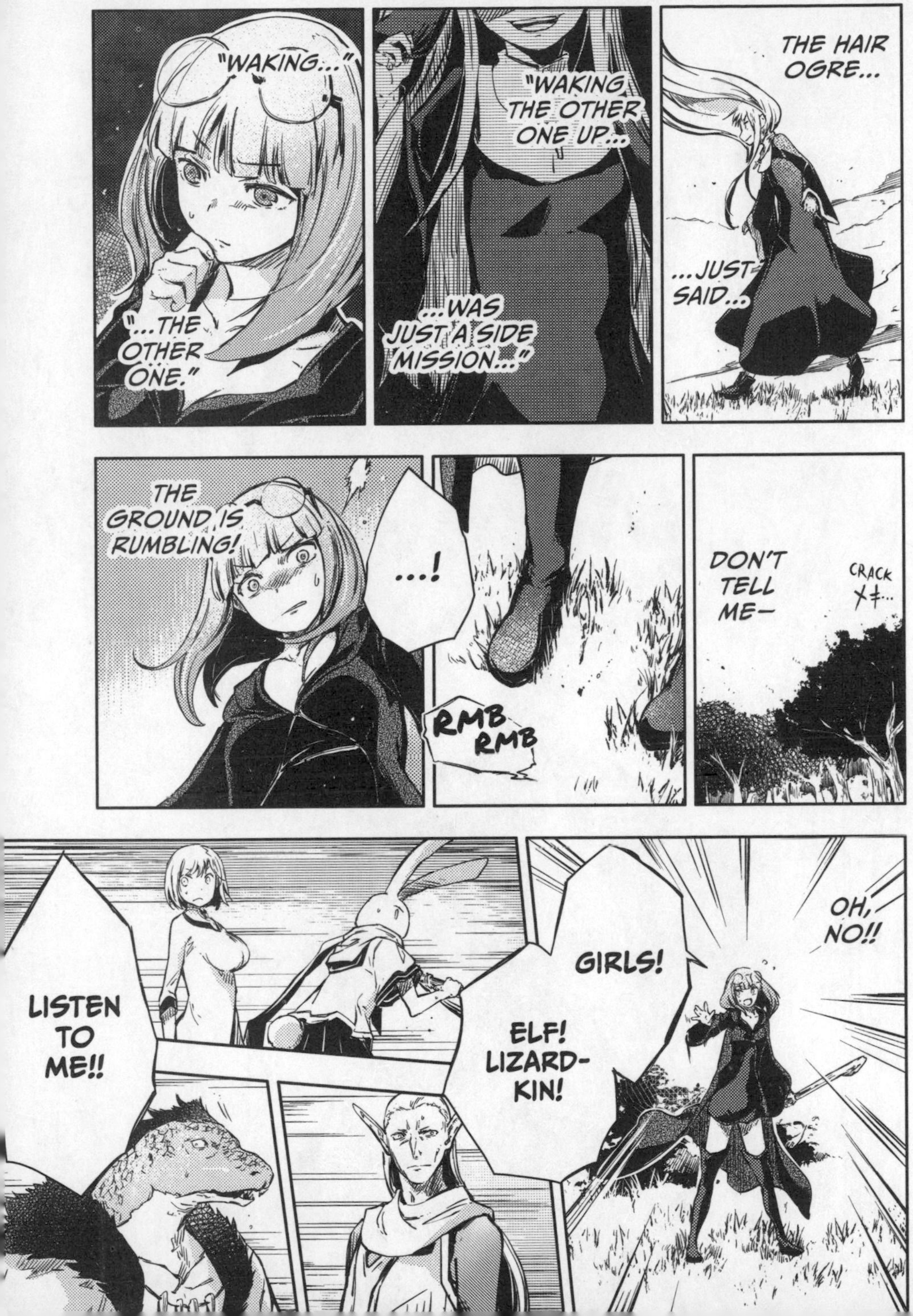
THE HAIR OGRE...
...JUST SAID...
"WAKING THE OTHER ONE UP...
...WAS JUST A SIDE MISSION..."
"WAKING..."
"...THE OTHER ONE."
DON'T TELL ME—
CRACK
メキ...
RMB RMB
...!
THE GROUND IS RUMBLING!
OH, NO!!
GIRLS!
ELF! LIZARD-KIN!
LISTEN TO ME!!

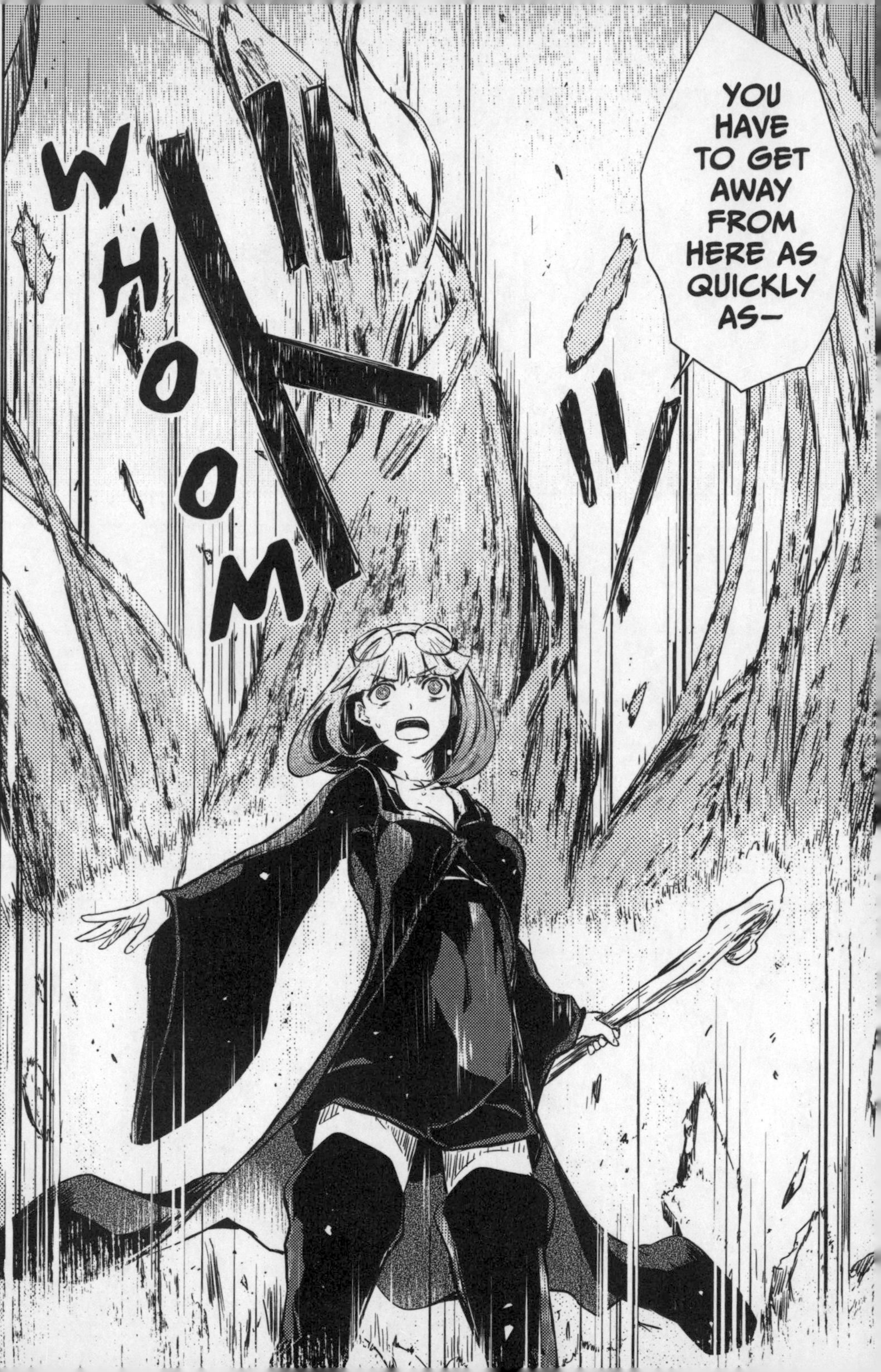
YOU HAVE TO GET AWAY FROM HERE AS QUICKLY AS—
WHOOM

—I WASN'T FAST ENOUGH!

CRICK

!

TSK!

...TREE ROOTS?!

WH-WHAT ARE ALL THESE?!

BWUMP

BWUMP

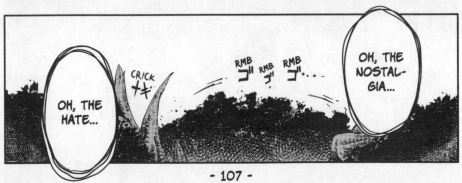

OH, THE HATE...

CRICK

RMB RMB RMB....

OH, THE NOSTAL-GIA...

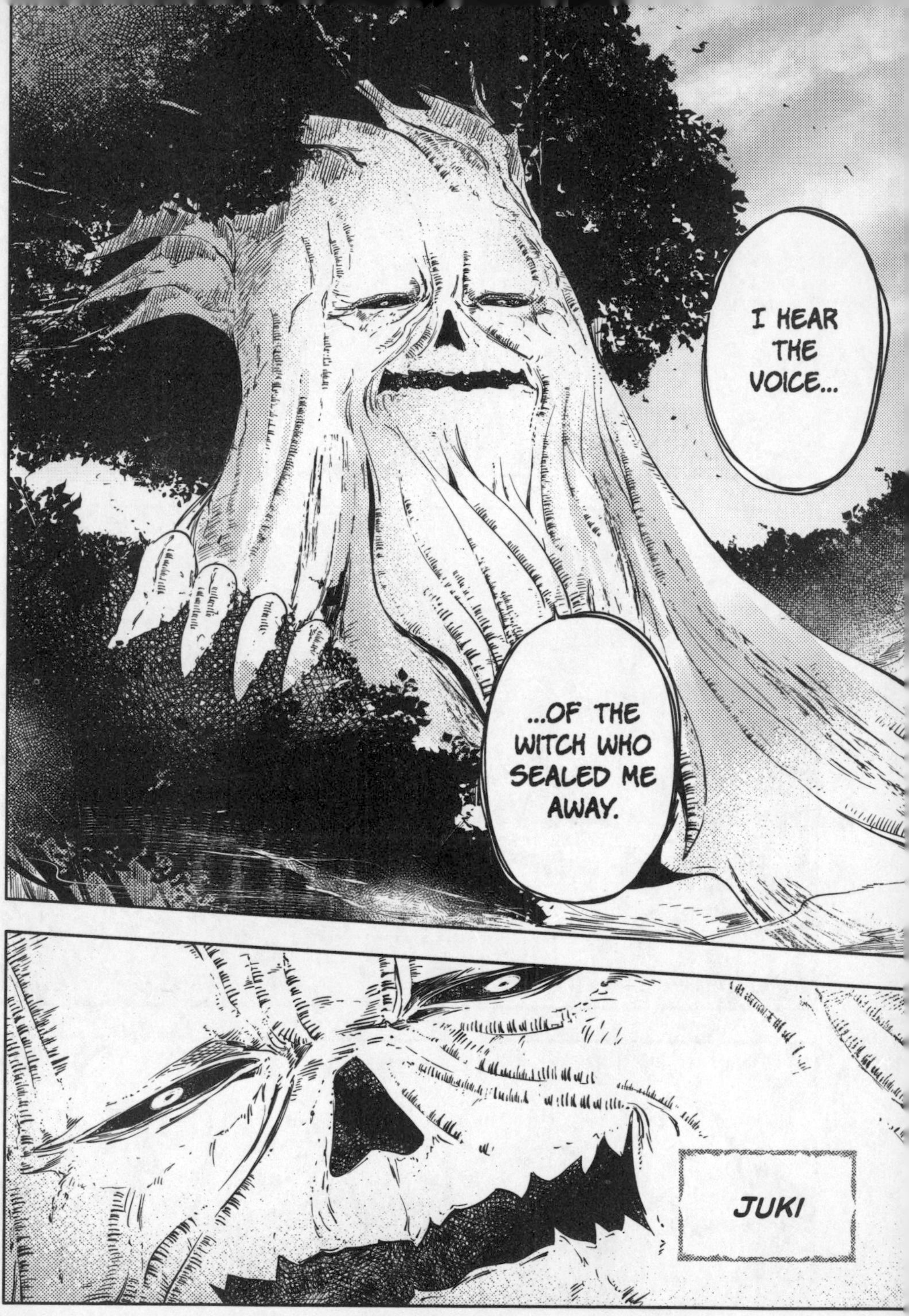
I HEAR THE VOICE...
...OF THE WITCH WHO SEALED ME AWAY.
JUKI

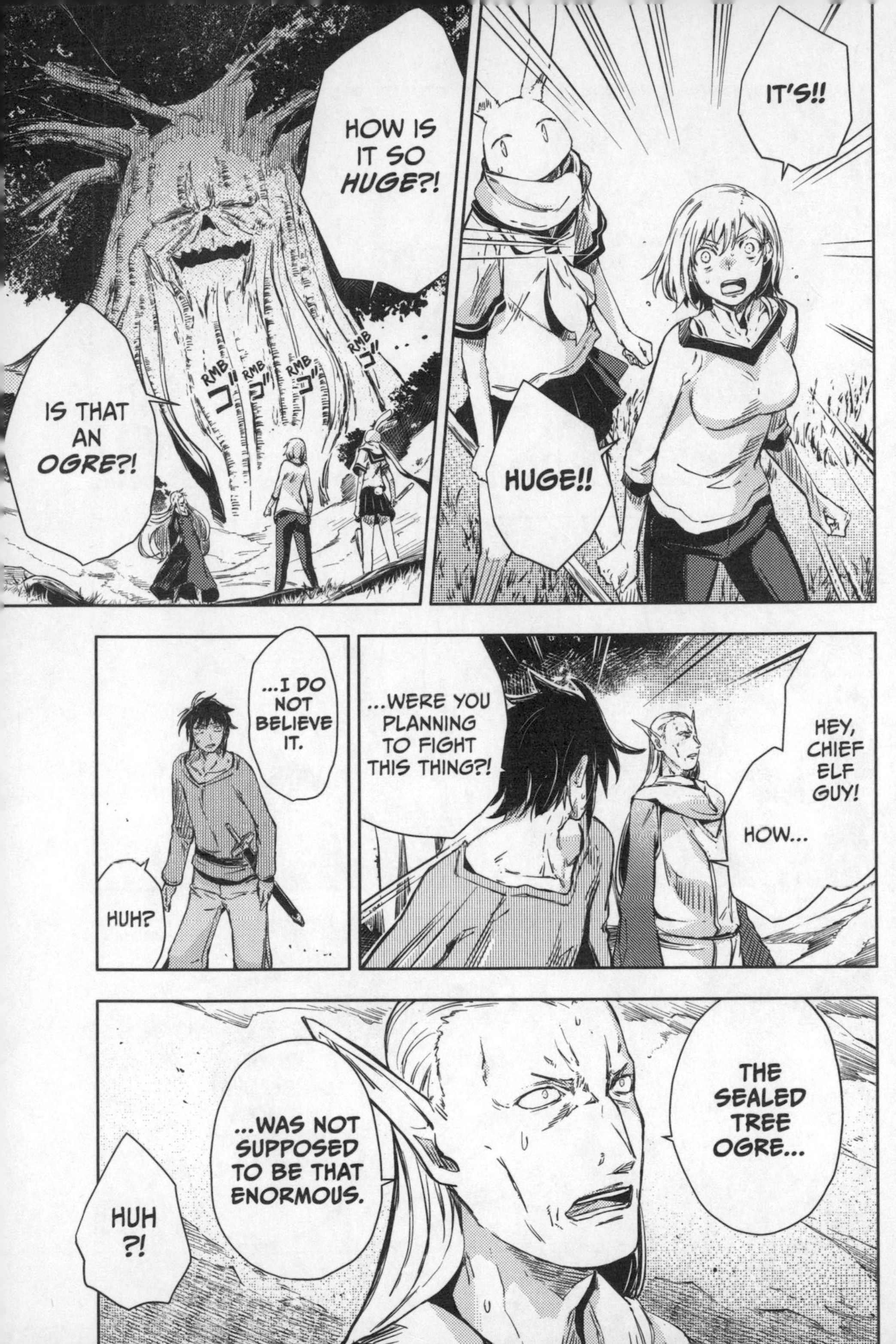
IT'S!!
HUGE!!
HOW IS IT SO HUGE?!
RMB
RMB
RMB
RMB
IS THAT AN OGRE?!
HEY, CHIEF ELF GUY!
HOW...
...WERE YOU PLANNING TO FIGHT THIS THING?!
...I DO NOT BELIEVE IT.
HUH?
THE SEALED TREE OGRE...
...WAS NOT SUPPOSED TO BE THAT ENORMOUS.
HUH?!

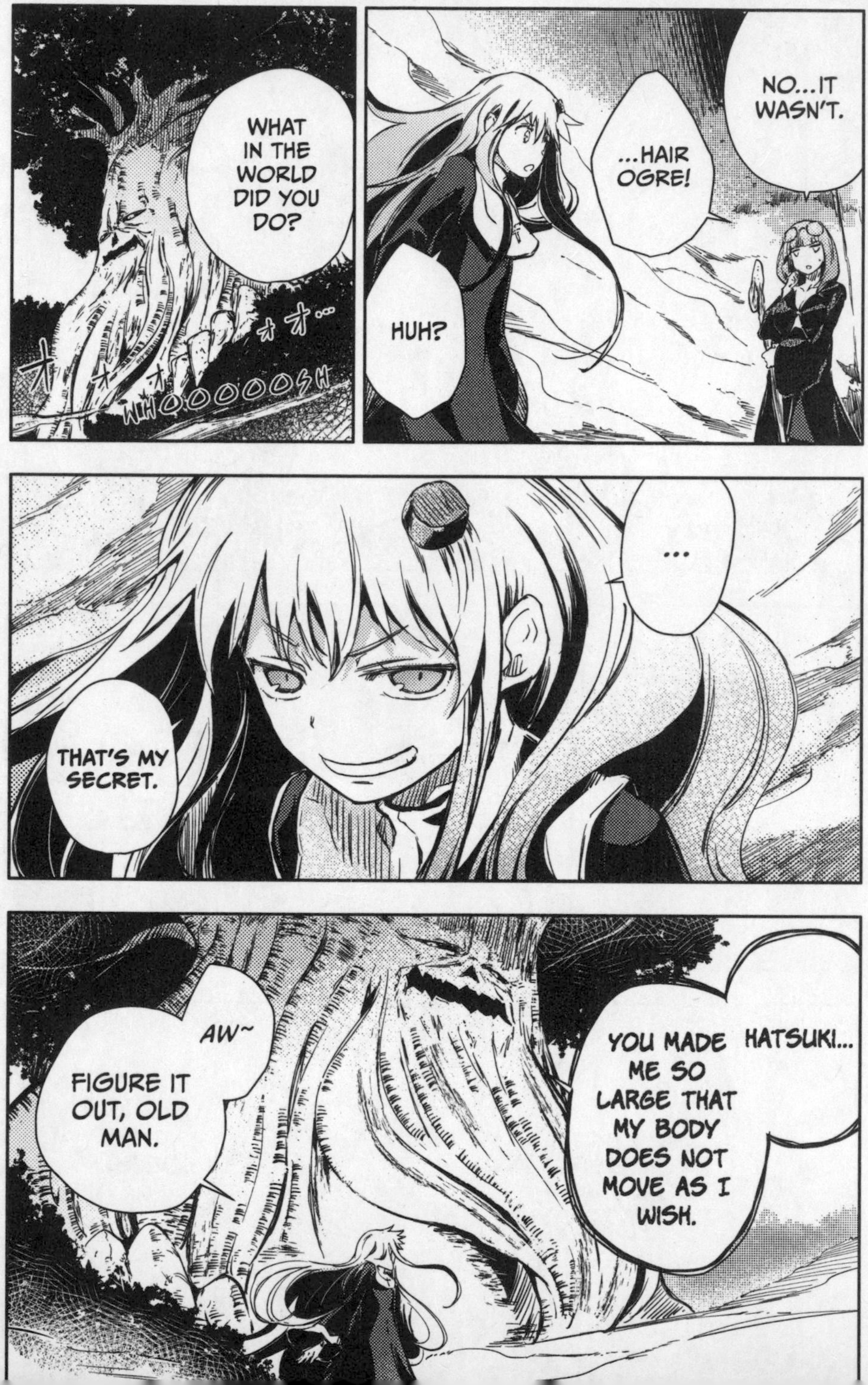
NO...IT WASN'T.
...HAIR OGRE!
HUH?
WHAT IN THE WORLD DID YOU DO?
WHOOOOOOSH
...
THAT'S MY SECRET.
HATSUKI...
YOU MADE ME SO LARGE THAT MY BODY DOES NOT MOVE AS I WISH.
AW~
FIGURE IT OUT, OLD MAN.

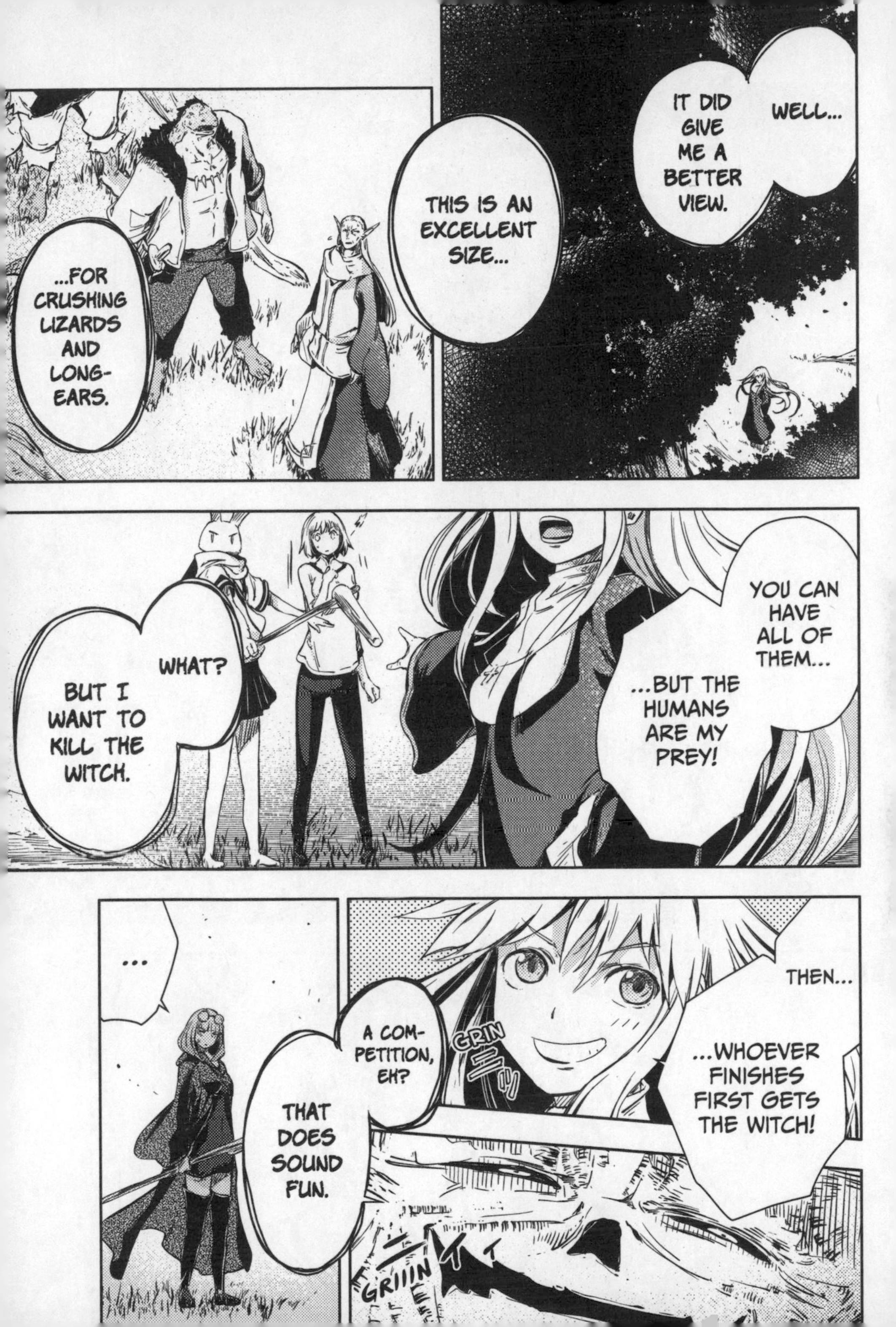
WELL...
IT DID GIVE ME A BETTER VIEW.
THIS IS AN EXCELLENT SIZE...
...FOR CRUSHING LIZARDS AND LONG-EARS.
YOU CAN HAVE ALL OF THEM...
...BUT THE HUMANS ARE MY PREY!
WHAT?
BUT I WANT TO KILL THE WITCH.
THEN...
...WHOEVER FINISHES FIRST GETS THE WITCH!
GRIN
A COMPETITION, EH?
THAT DOES SOUND FUN.
GRIIIN
...

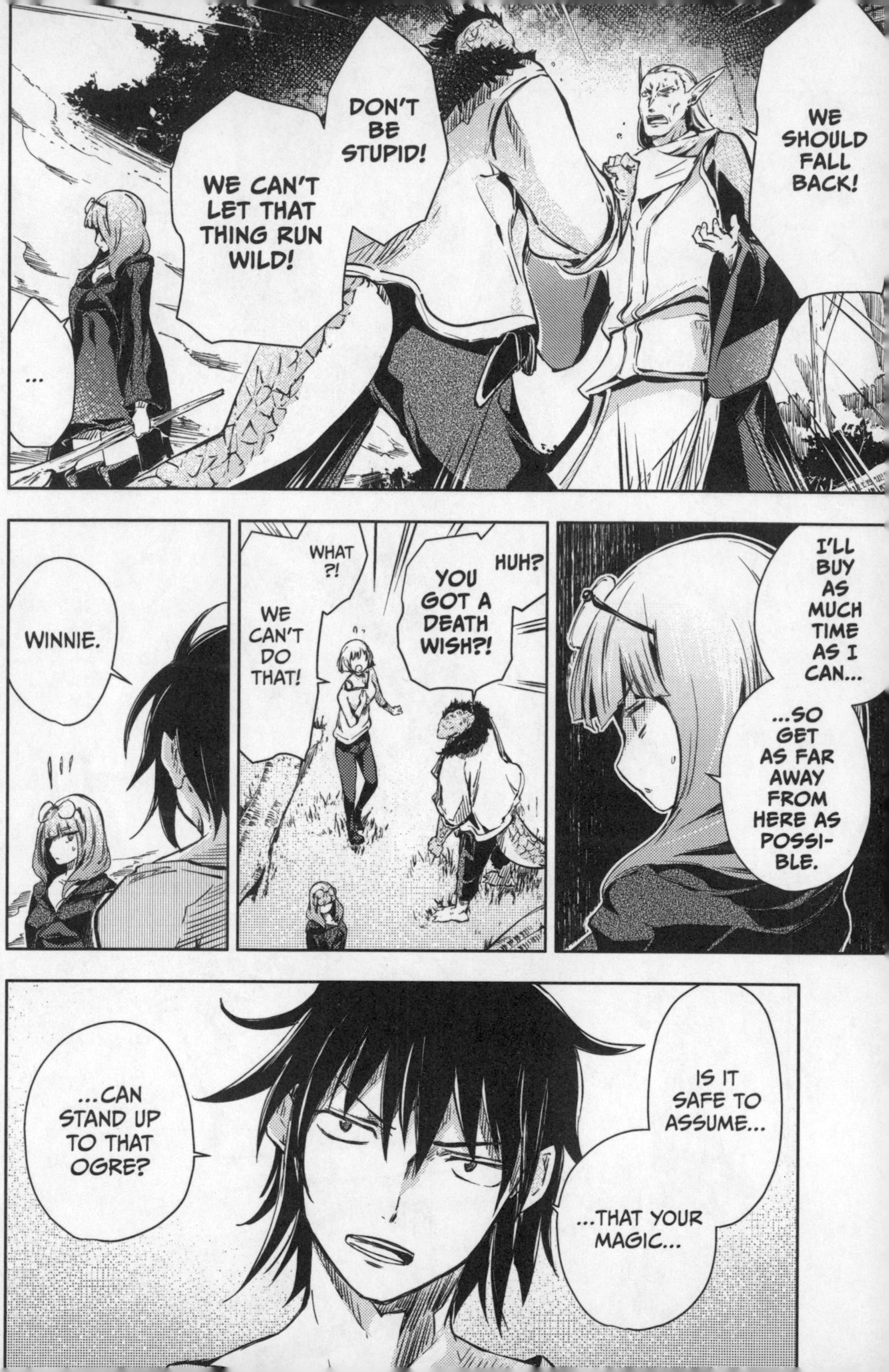
WE SHOULD FALL BACK!
DON'T BE STUPID!
WE CAN'T LET THAT THING RUN WILD!
...
I'LL BUY AS MUCH TIME AS I CAN...
...SO GET AS FAR AWAY FROM HERE AS POSSI-BLE.
HUH?
YOU GOT A DEATH WISH?!
WHAT?!
WE CAN'T DO THAT!
WINNIE.
IS IT SAFE TO ASSUME...
...THAT YOUR MAGIC...
...CAN STAND UP TO THAT OGRE?

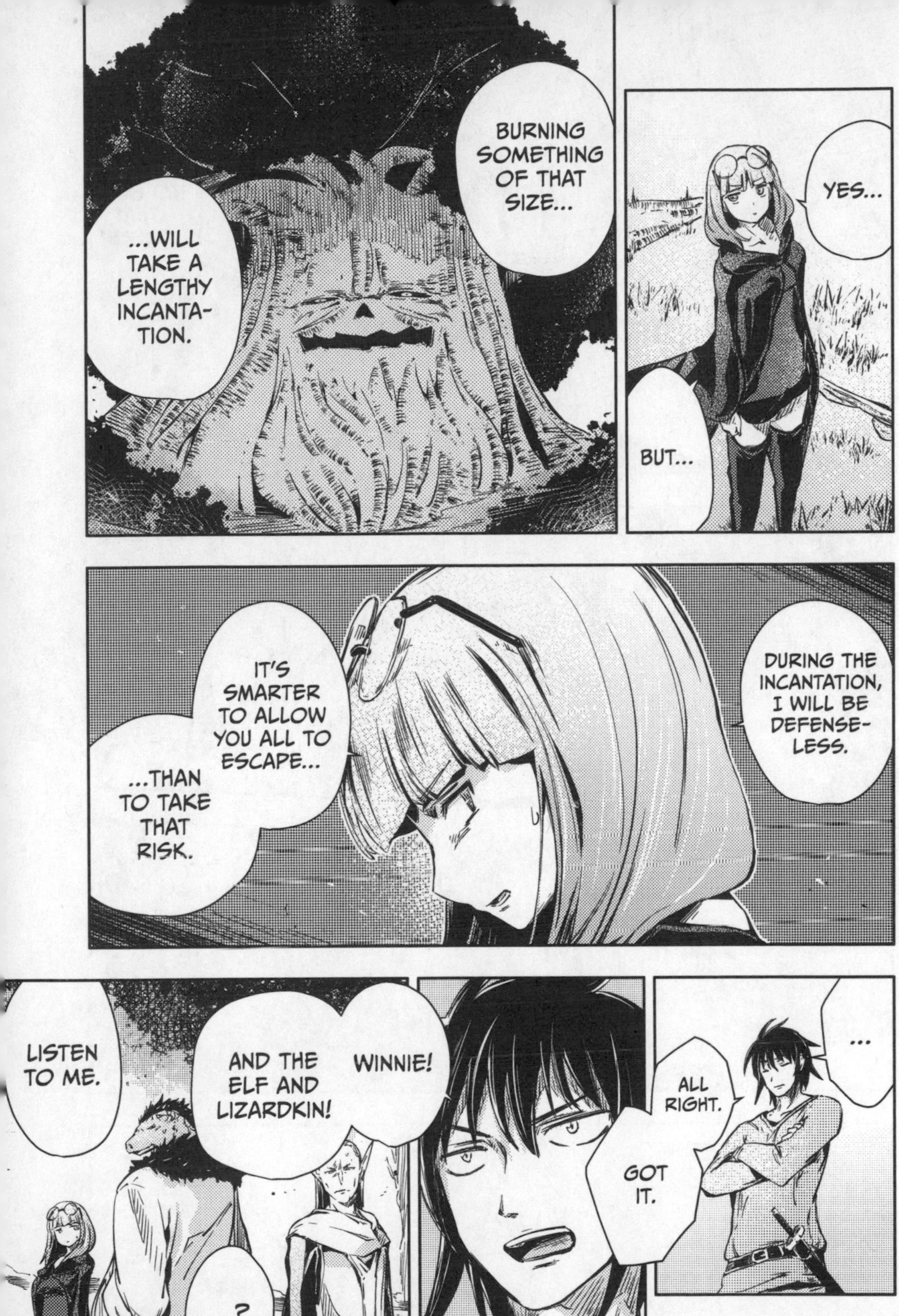
YES...
BUT...
BURNING SOMETHING OF THAT SIZE...
...WILL TAKE A LENGTHY INCANTATION.
DURING THE INCANTATION, I WILL BE DEFENSELESS.
IT'S SMARTER TO ALLOW YOU ALL TO ESCAPE...
...THAN TO TAKE THAT RISK.
...
ALL RIGHT.
GOT IT.
WINNIE!
AND THE ELF AND LIZARDKIN!
LISTEN TO ME.
...?

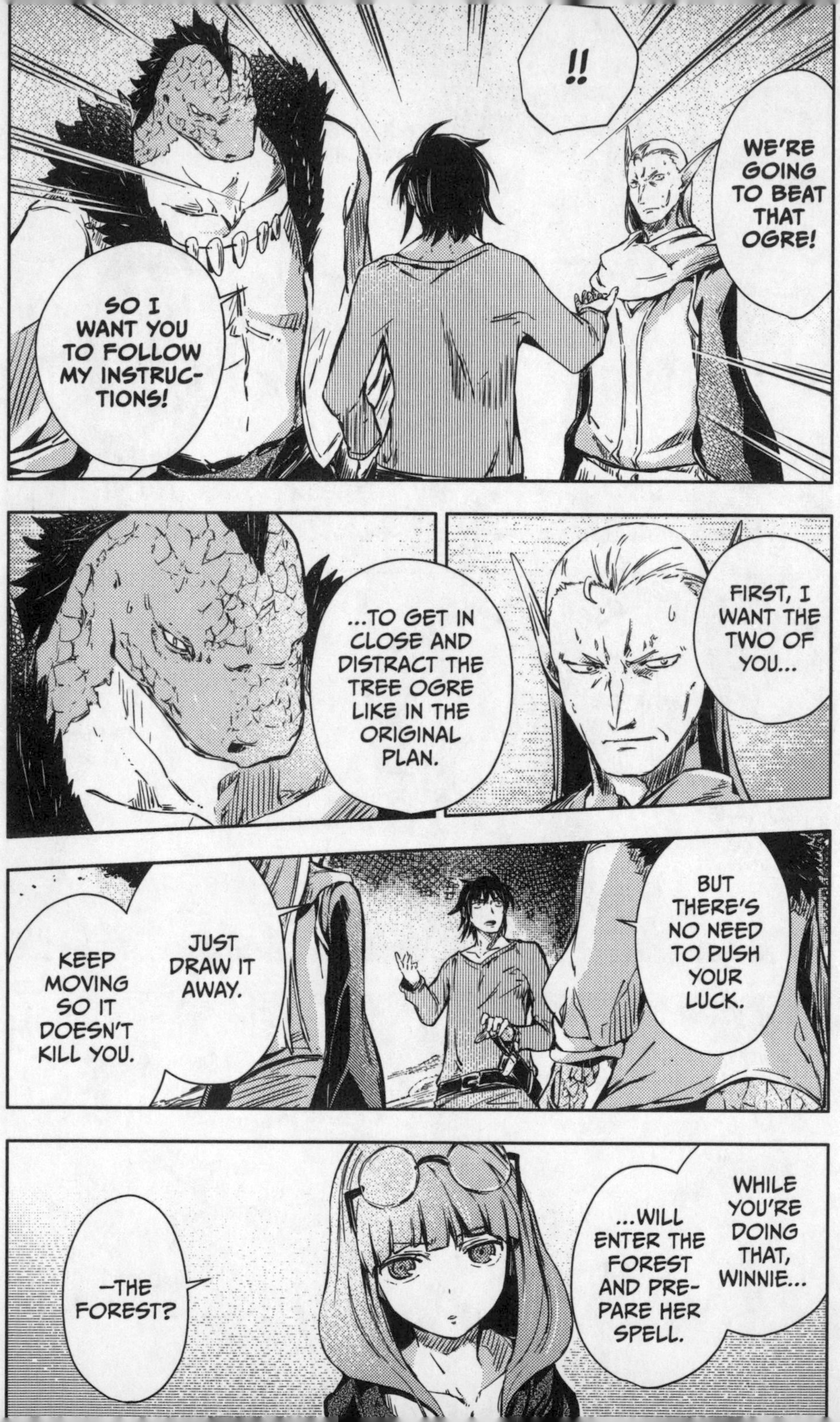
WE'RE GOING TO BEAT THAT OGRE!
!!
SO I WANT YOU TO FOLLOW MY INSTRUC-TIONS!
FIRST, I WANT THE TWO OF YOU...
...TO GET IN CLOSE AND DISTRACT THE TREE OGRE LIKE IN THE ORIGINAL PLAN.
BUT THERE'S NO NEED TO PUSH YOUR LUCK.
JUST DRAW IT AWAY.
KEEP MOVING SO IT DOESN'T KILL YOU.
WHILE YOU'RE DOING THAT, WINNIE...
...WILL ENTER THE FOREST AND PRE-PARE HER SPELL.
—THE FOREST?

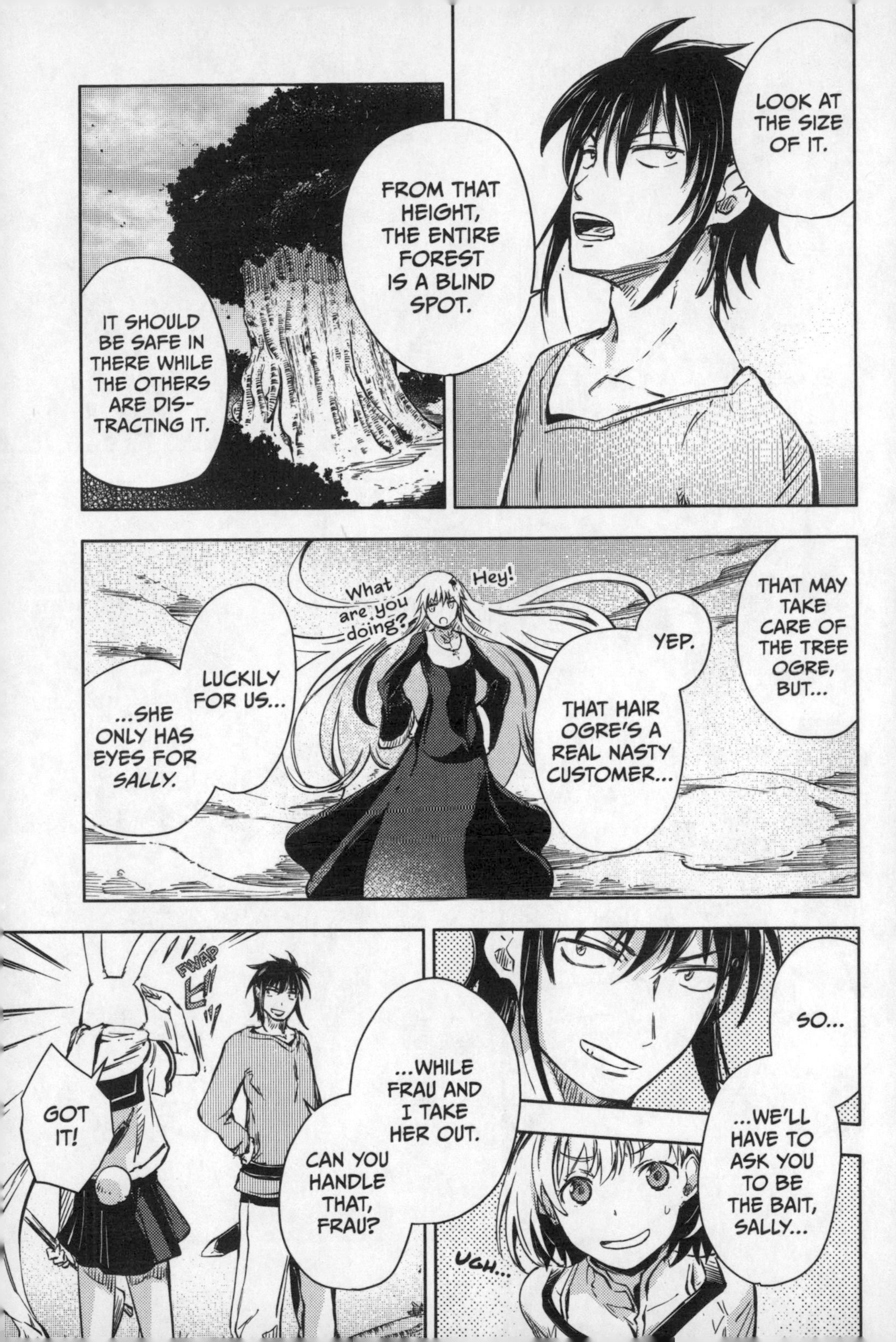
LOOK AT THE SIZE OF IT.
FROM THAT HEIGHT, THE ENTIRE FOREST IS A BLIND SPOT.
IT SHOULD BE SAFE IN THERE WHILE THE OTHERS ARE DIS-TRACTING IT.
THAT MAY TAKE CARE OF THE TREE OGRE, BUT...
YEP.
THAT HAIR OGRE'S A REAL NASTY CUSTOMER...
Hey!
What are you doing?
LUCKILY FOR US...
...SHE ONLY HAS EYES FOR SALLY.
SO...
...WE'LL HAVE TO ASK YOU TO BE THE BAIT, SALLY...
UGH...
...WHILE FRAU AND I TAKE HER OUT.
CAN YOU HANDLE THAT, FRAU?
FWAP
GOT IT!

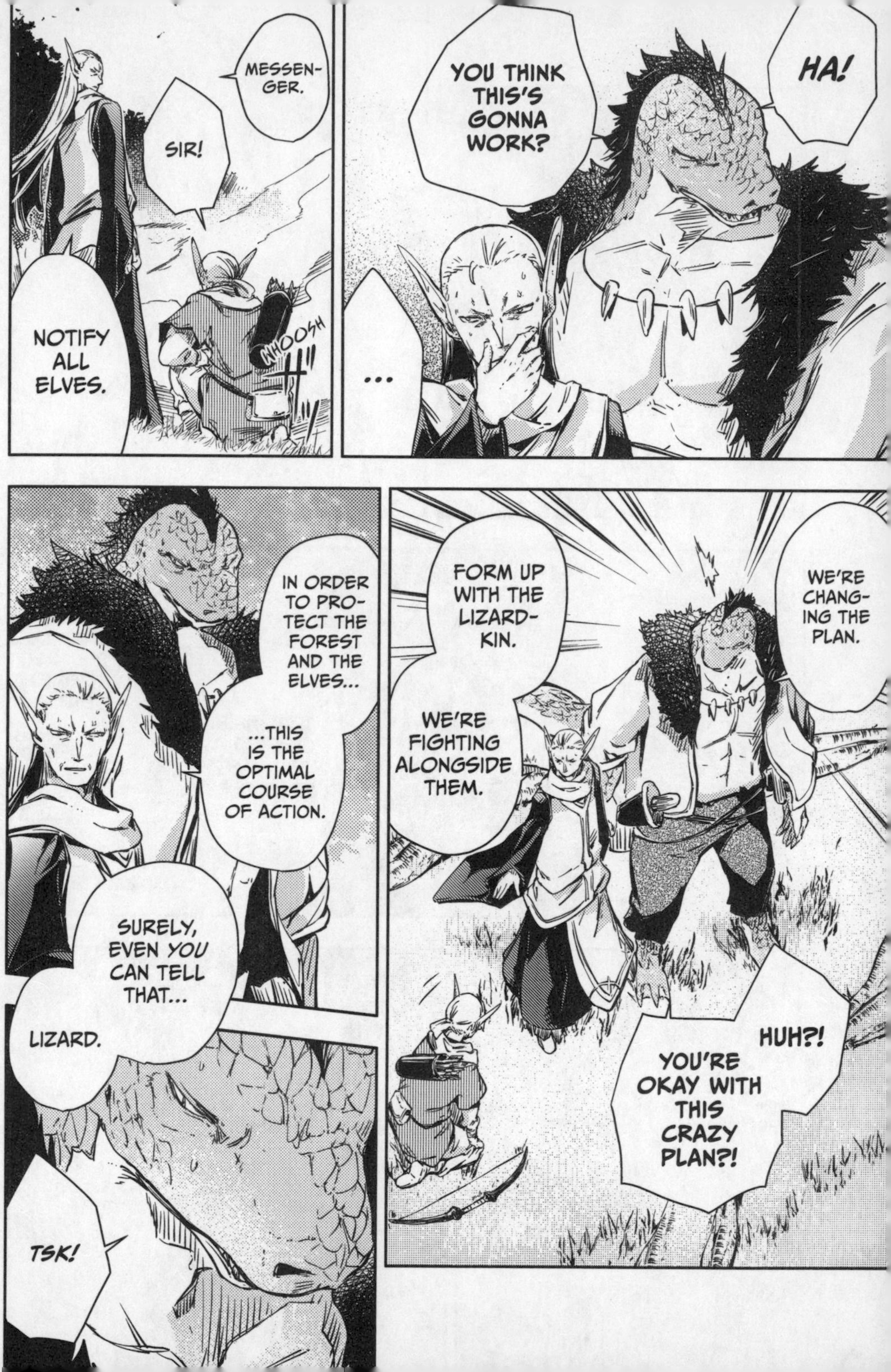
HA!
YOU THINK THIS'S GONNA WORK?
...
MESSENGER.
SIR!
NOTIFY ALL ELVES.
WHOOSH
WE'RE CHANGING THE PLAN.
FORM UP WITH THE LIZARDKIN.
WE'RE FIGHTING ALONGSIDE THEM.
HUH?! YOU'RE OKAY WITH THIS CRAZY PLAN?!
IN ORDER TO PROTECT THE FOREST AND THE ELVES...
...THIS IS THE OPTIMAL COURSE OF ACTION.
SURELY, EVEN *YOU* CAN TELL THAT...
LIZARD.
TSK!

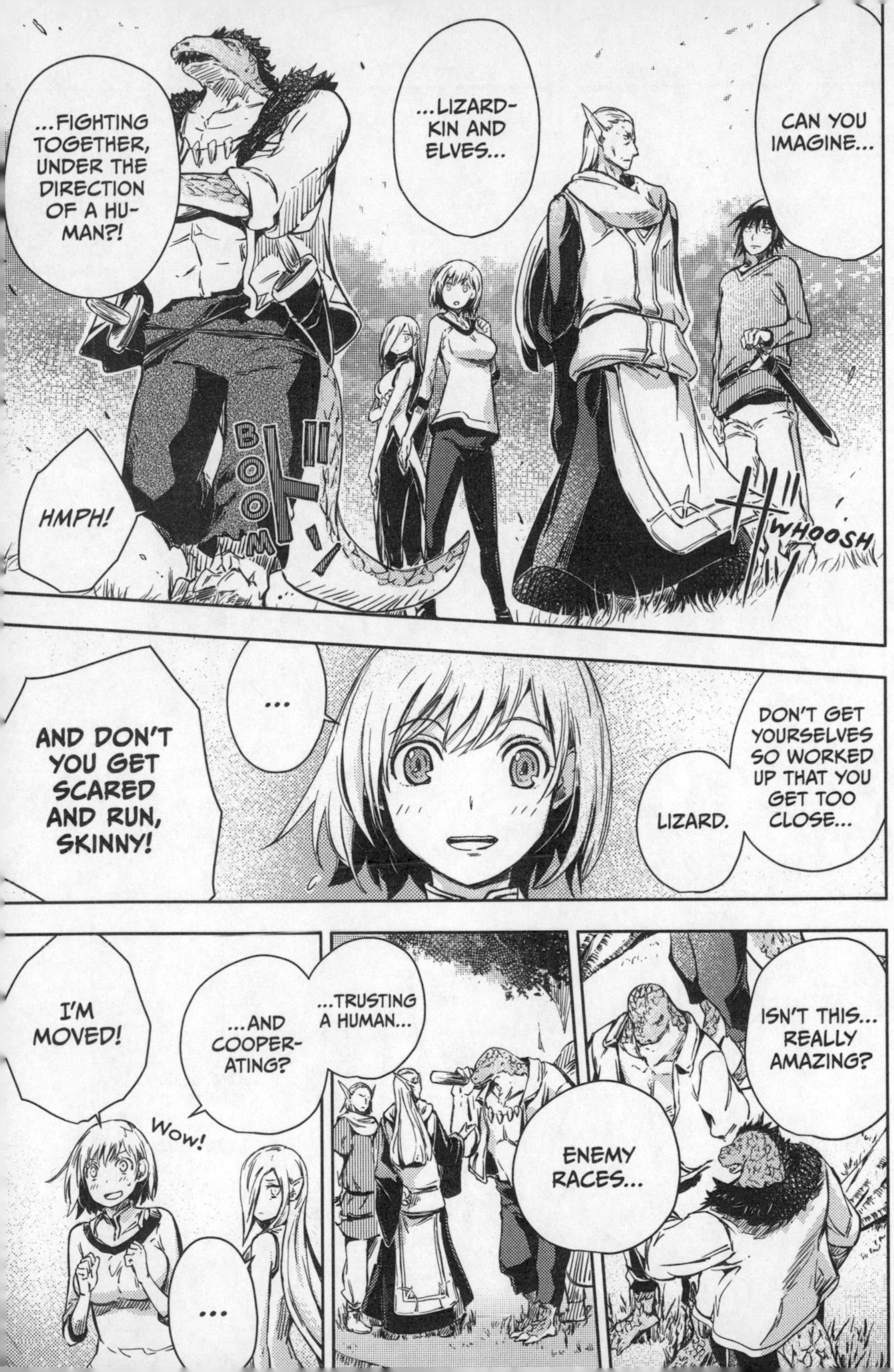
CAN YOU IMAGINE...
...LIZARD-KIN AND ELVES...
...FIGHTING TOGETHER, UNDER THE DIRECTION OF A HU-MAN?!
WHOOSH
BOOM
HMPH!
DON'T GET YOURSELVES SO WORKED UP THAT YOU GET TOO CLOSE...
LIZARD.
...
AND DON'T YOU GET SCARED AND RUN, SKINNY!
ISN'T THIS... REALLY AMAZING?
ENEMY RACES...
...TRUSTING A HUMAN...
...AND COOPER-ATING?
I'M MOVED!
Wow!
...

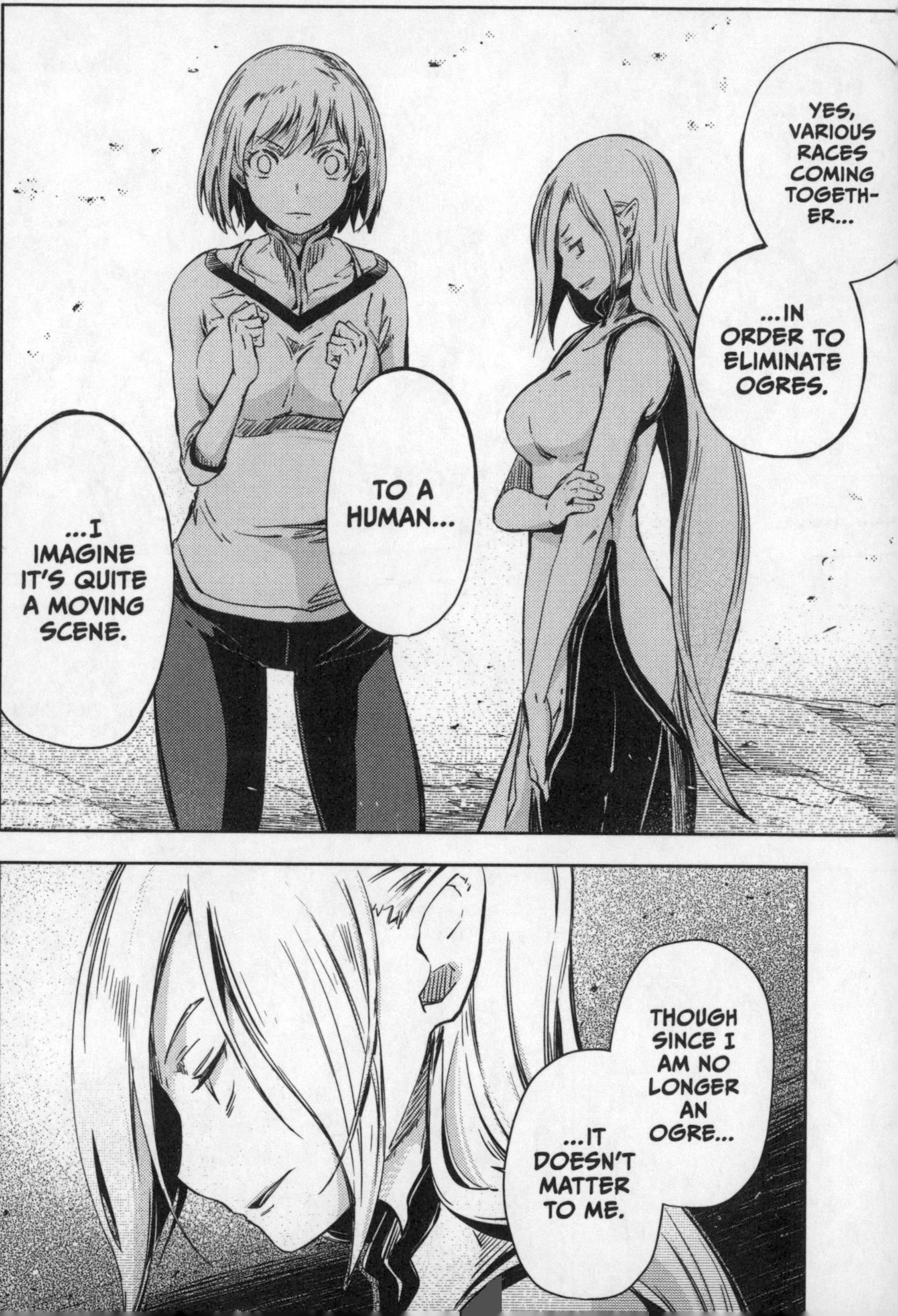
YES, VARIOUS RACES COMING TOGETH-ER...
...IN ORDER TO ELIMINATE OGRES.
TO A HUMAN...
...I IMAGINE IT'S QUITE A MOVING SCENE.
THOUGH SINCE I AM NO LONGER AN OGRE...
...IT DOESN'T MATTER TO ME.

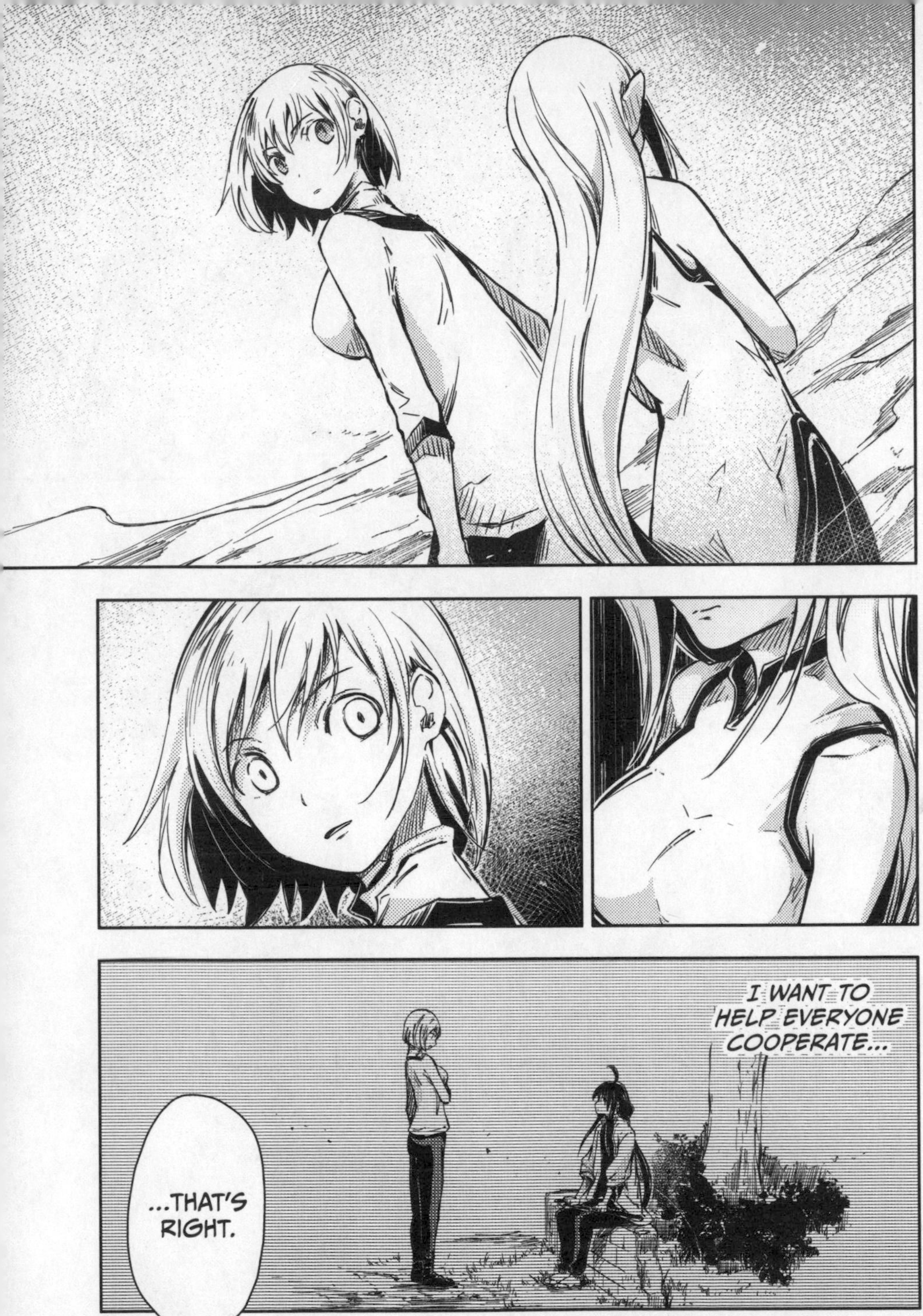
I WANT TO HELP EVERYONE COOPERATE...
...THAT'S RIGHT.

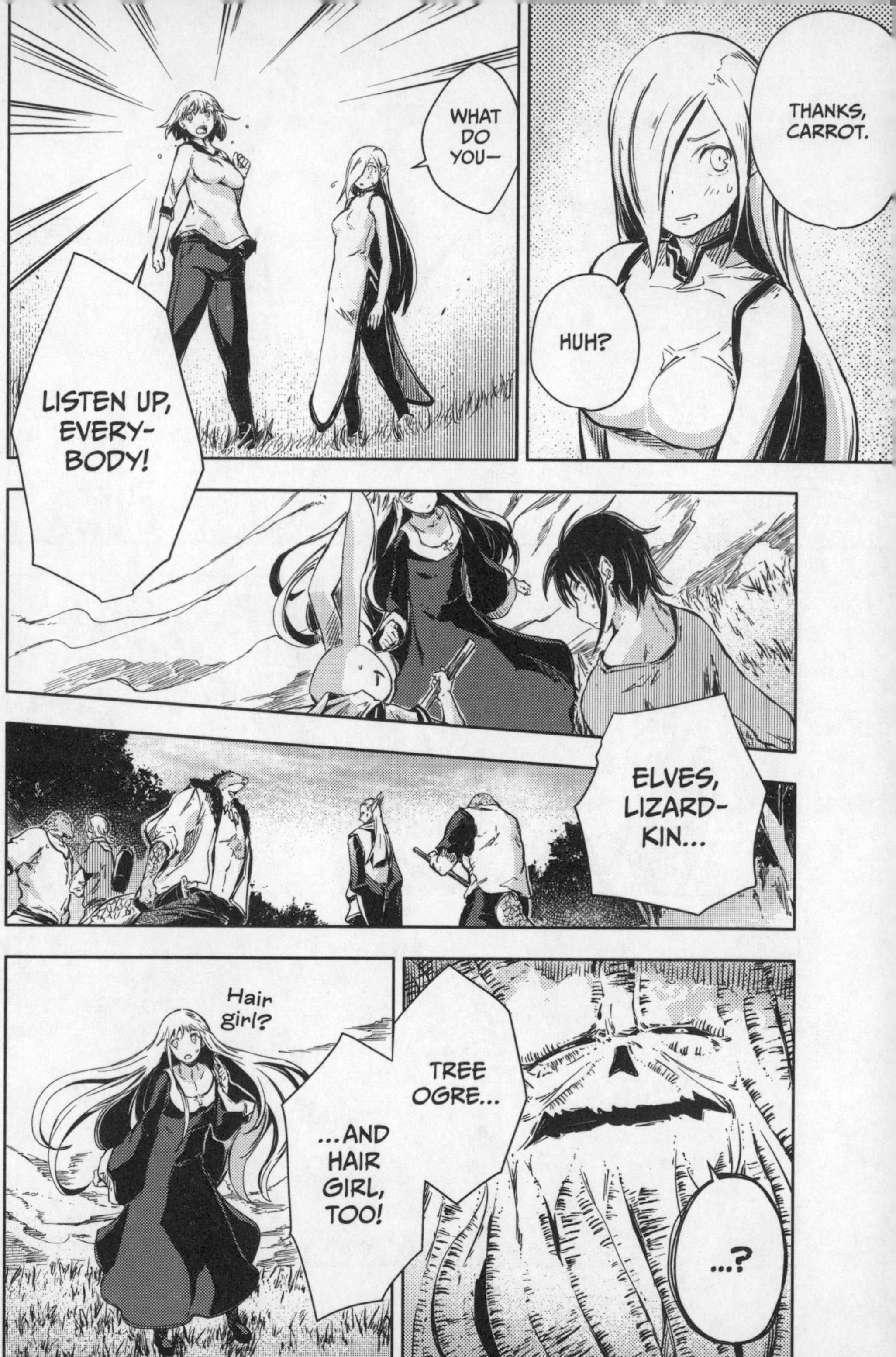
THANKS, CARROT.
HUH?
WHAT DO YOU—
LISTEN UP, EVERY-BODY!
ELVES, LIZARD-KIN...
TREE OGRE...
...AND HAIR GIRL, TOO!
...?
Hair girl?

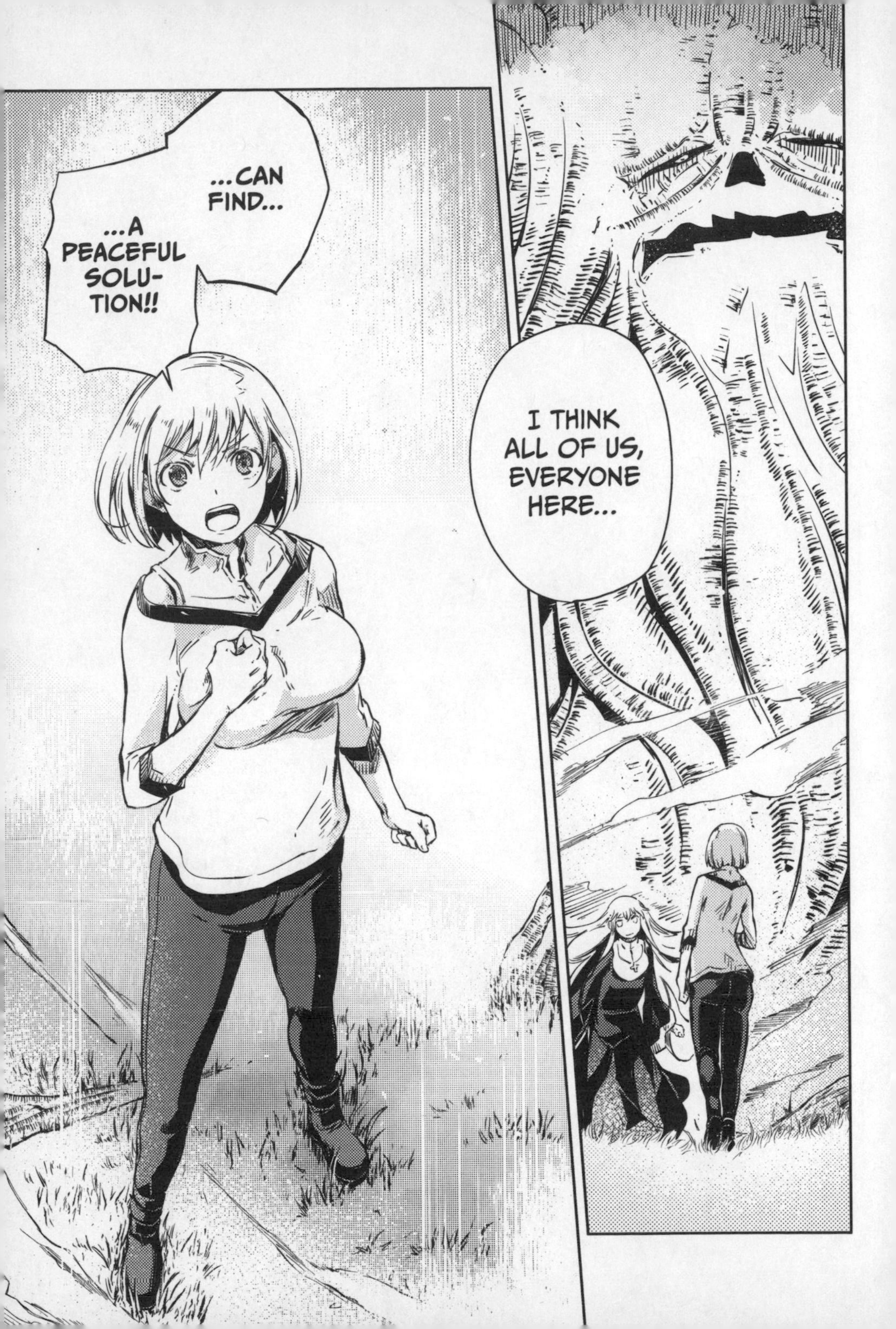
I THINK ALL OF US, EVERYONE HERE...
...CAN FIND...
...A PEACEFUL SOLU- TION!!

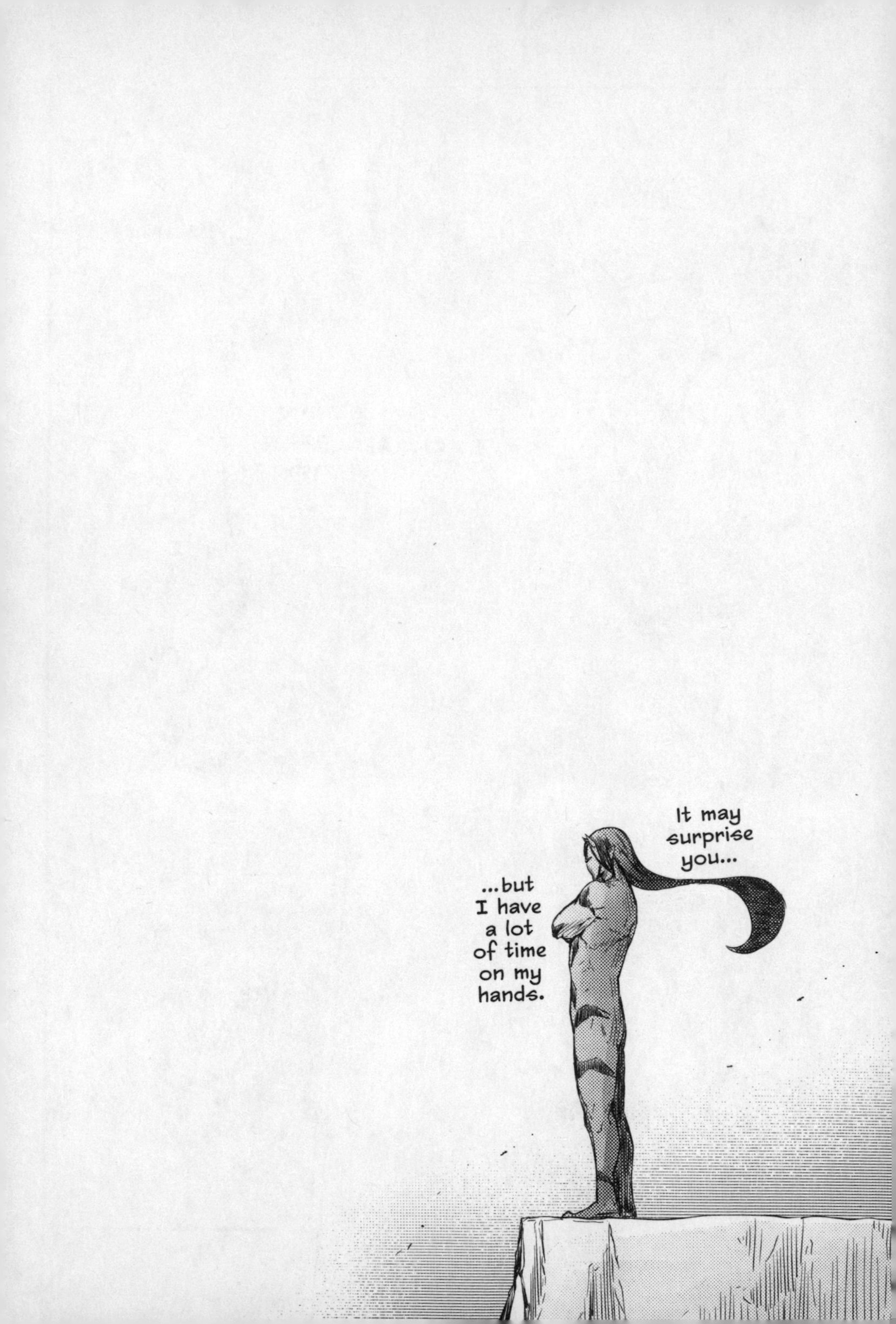
It may surprise you...
...but I have a lot of time on my hands.

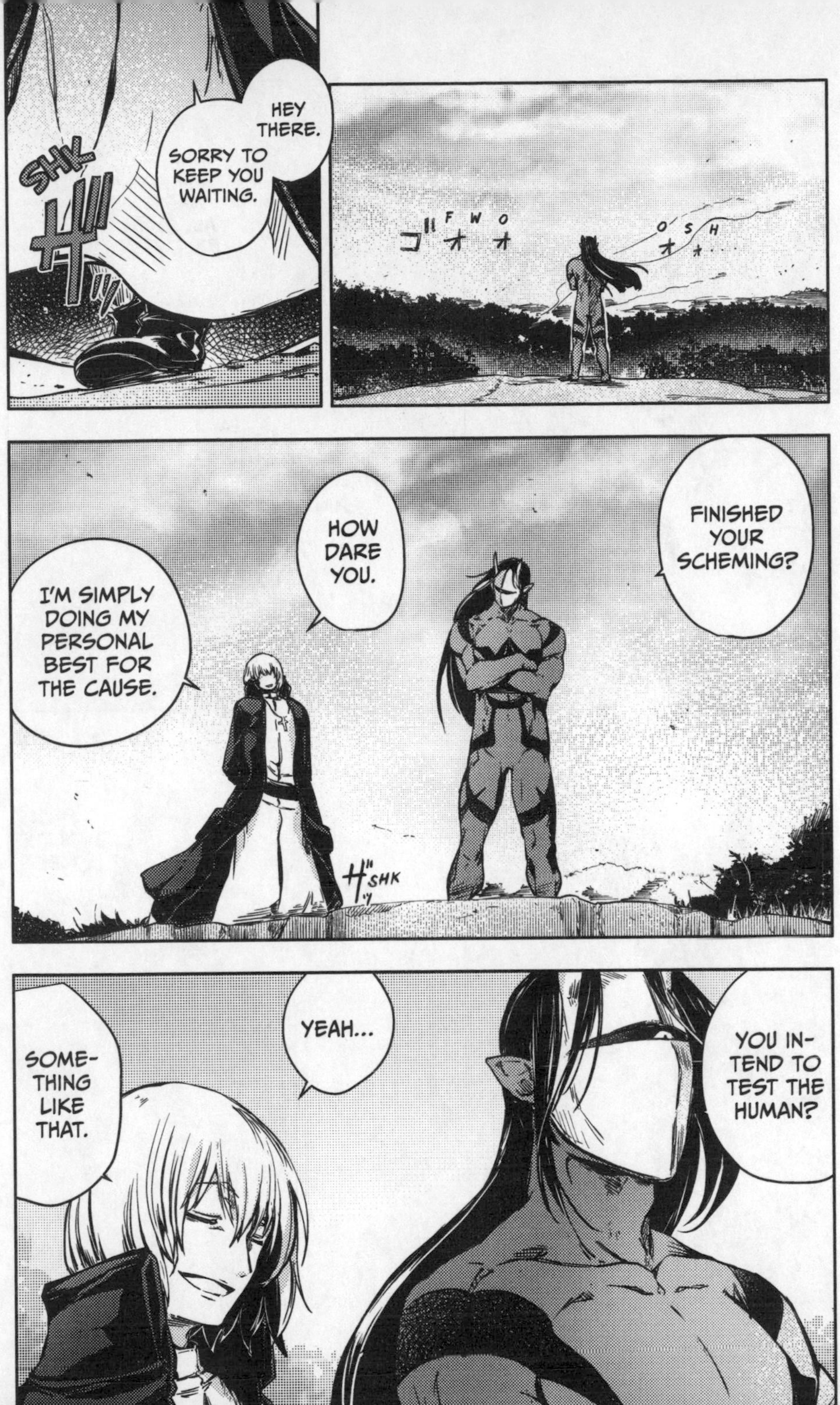
ゴオオ FWO
OSH
HEY THERE.
SORRY TO KEEP YOU WAITING.
SHK
FINISHED YOUR SCHEMING?
HOW DARE YOU.
I'M SIMPLY DOING MY PERSONAL BEST FOR THE CAUSE.
SHK
YOU IN-TEND TO TEST THE HUMAN?
YEAH...
SOME-THING LIKE THAT.

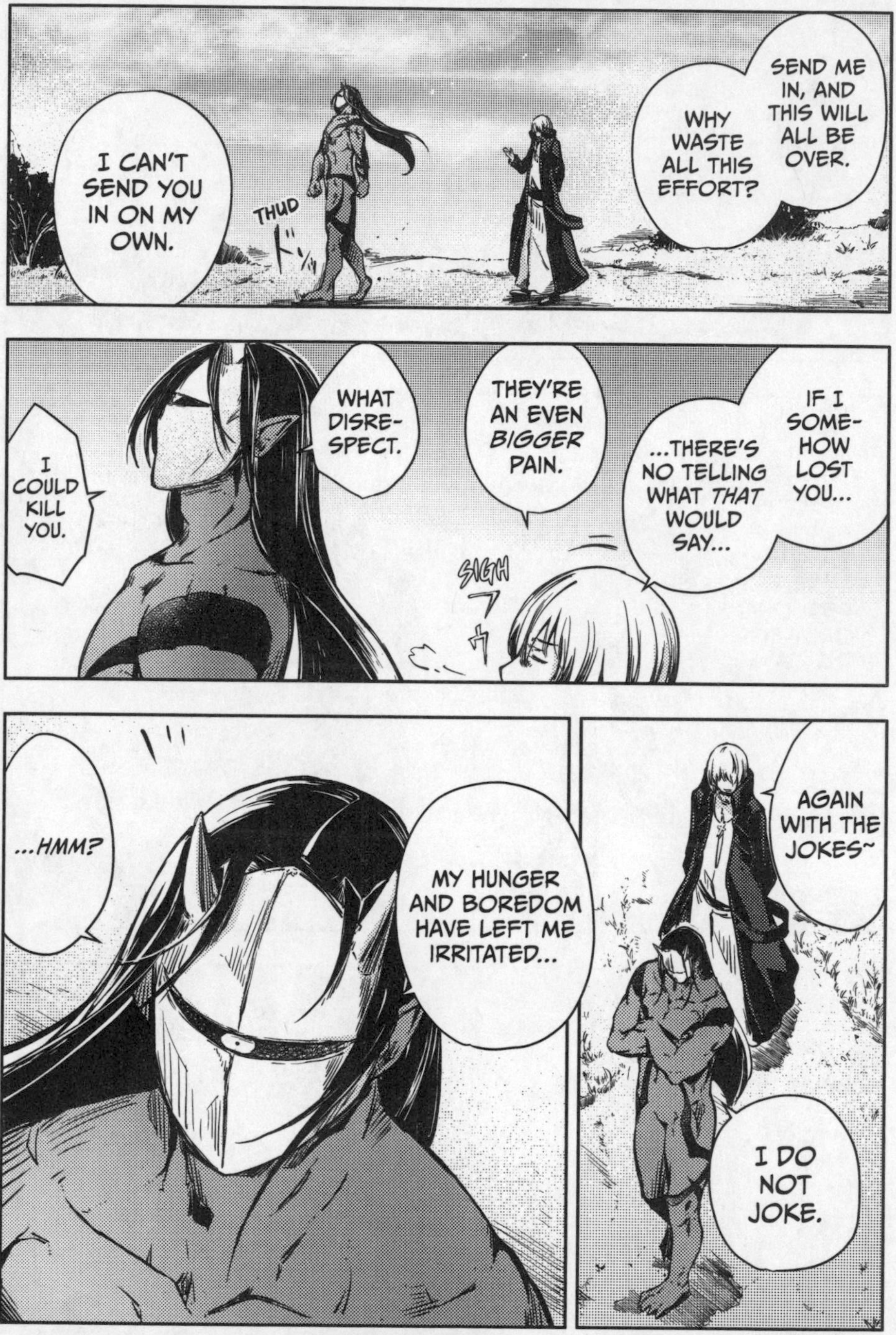
SEND ME IN, AND THIS WILL ALL BE OVER.
WHY WASTE ALL THIS EFFORT?
THUD
I CAN'T SEND YOU IN ON MY OWN.
IF I SOMEHOW LOST YOU...
...THERE'S NO TELLING WHAT *THAT* WOULD SAY...
THEY'RE AN EVEN *BIGGER* PAIN.
SIGH
WHAT DISRESPECT.
I COULD KILL YOU.
AGAIN WITH THE JOKES~
I DO NOT JOKE.
MY HUNGER AND BOREDOM HAVE LEFT ME IRRITATED...
...*HMM?*

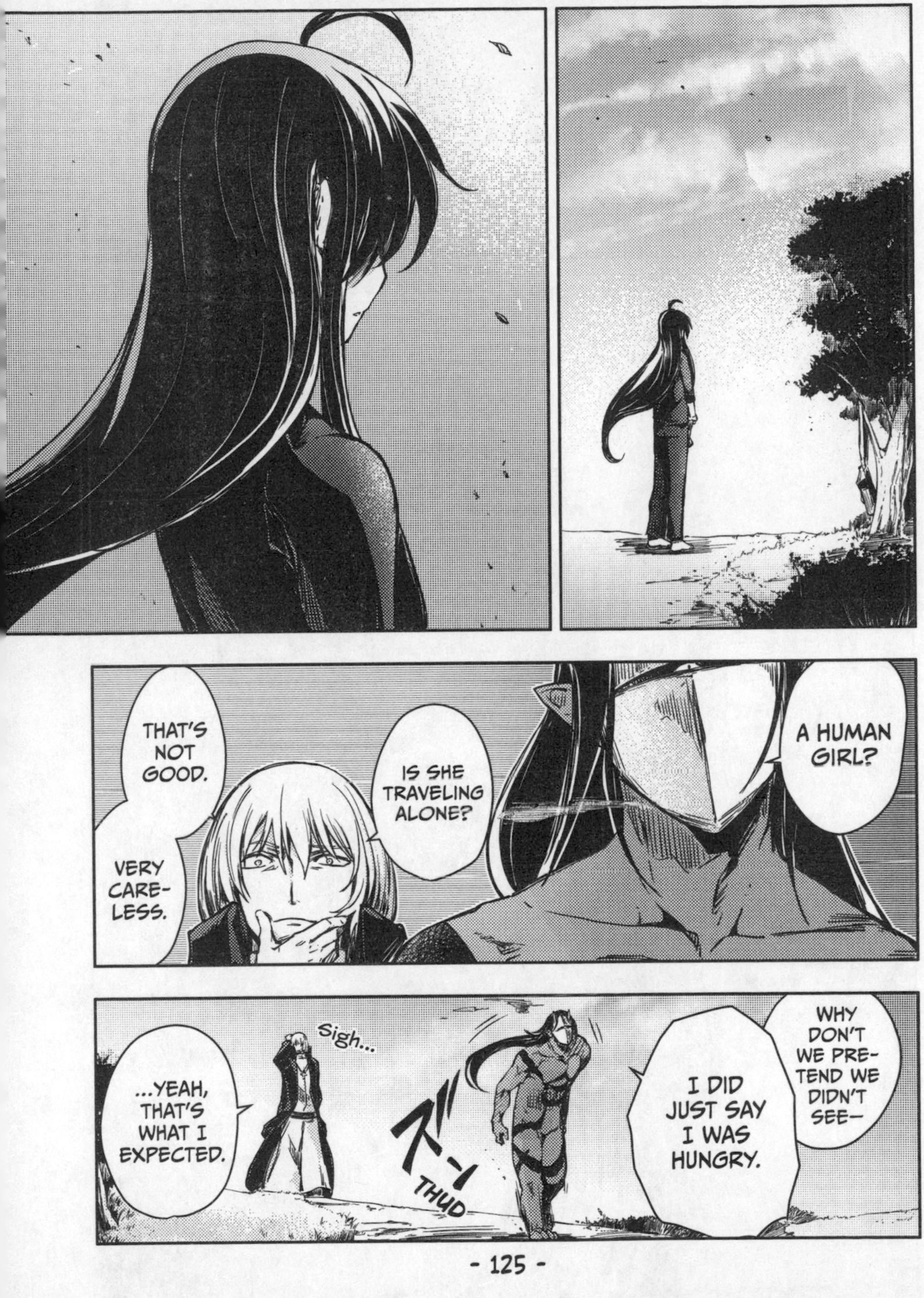
A HUMAN GIRL?
IS SHE TRAVELING ALONE?
THAT'S NOT GOOD.
VERY CARE-LESS.
WHY DON'T WE PRE-TEND WE DIDN'T SEE—
I DID JUST SAY I WAS HUNGRY.
THUD
Sigh...
...YEAH, THAT'S WHAT I EXPECTED.

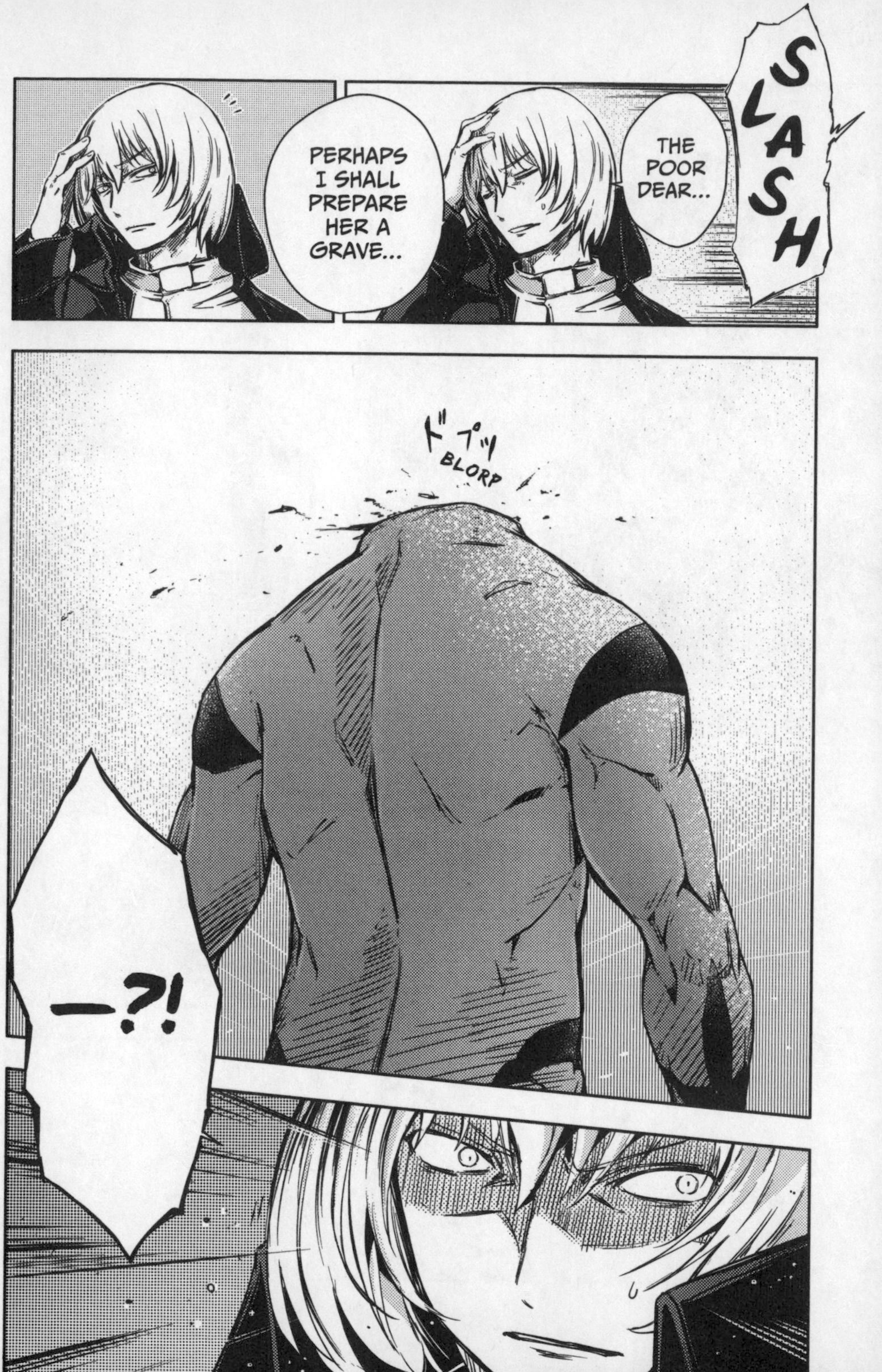
SLASH
THE POOR DEAR...
PERHAPS I SHALL PREPARE HER A GRAVE...
ドプッ
BLORP
—?!

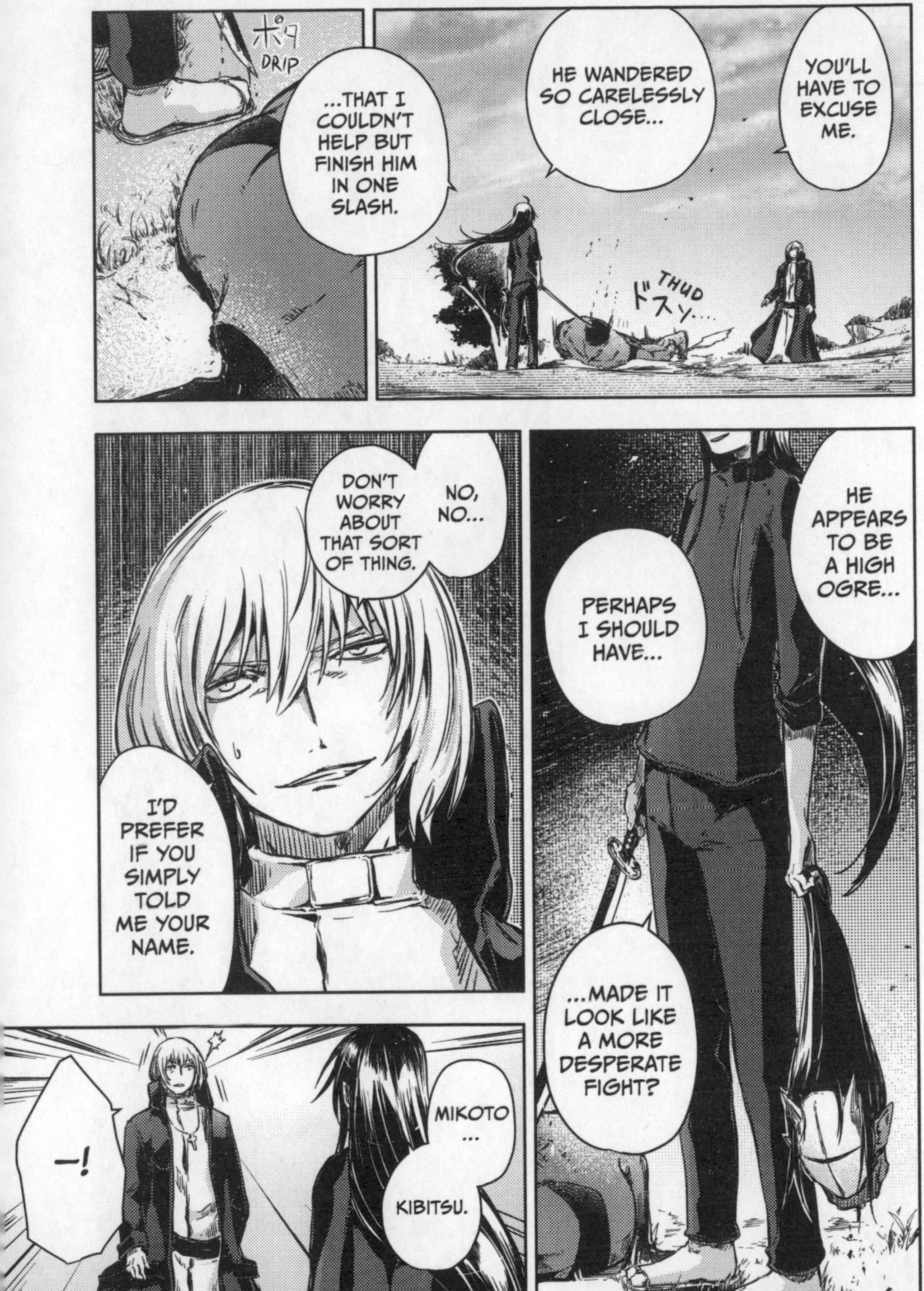
YOU'LL HAVE TO EXCUSE ME.
HE WANDERED SO CARELESSLY CLOSE...
ドスッ THUD
ポタ DRIP
...THAT I COULDN'T HELP BUT FINISH HIM IN ONE SLASH.
HE APPEARS TO BE A HIGH OGRE...
PERHAPS I SHOULD HAVE...
...MADE IT LOOK LIKE A MORE DESPERATE FIGHT?
NO, NO...
DON'T WORRY ABOUT THAT SORT OF THING.
I'D PREFER IF YOU SIMPLY TOLD ME YOUR NAME.
MIKOTO ...
KIBITSU.
—!

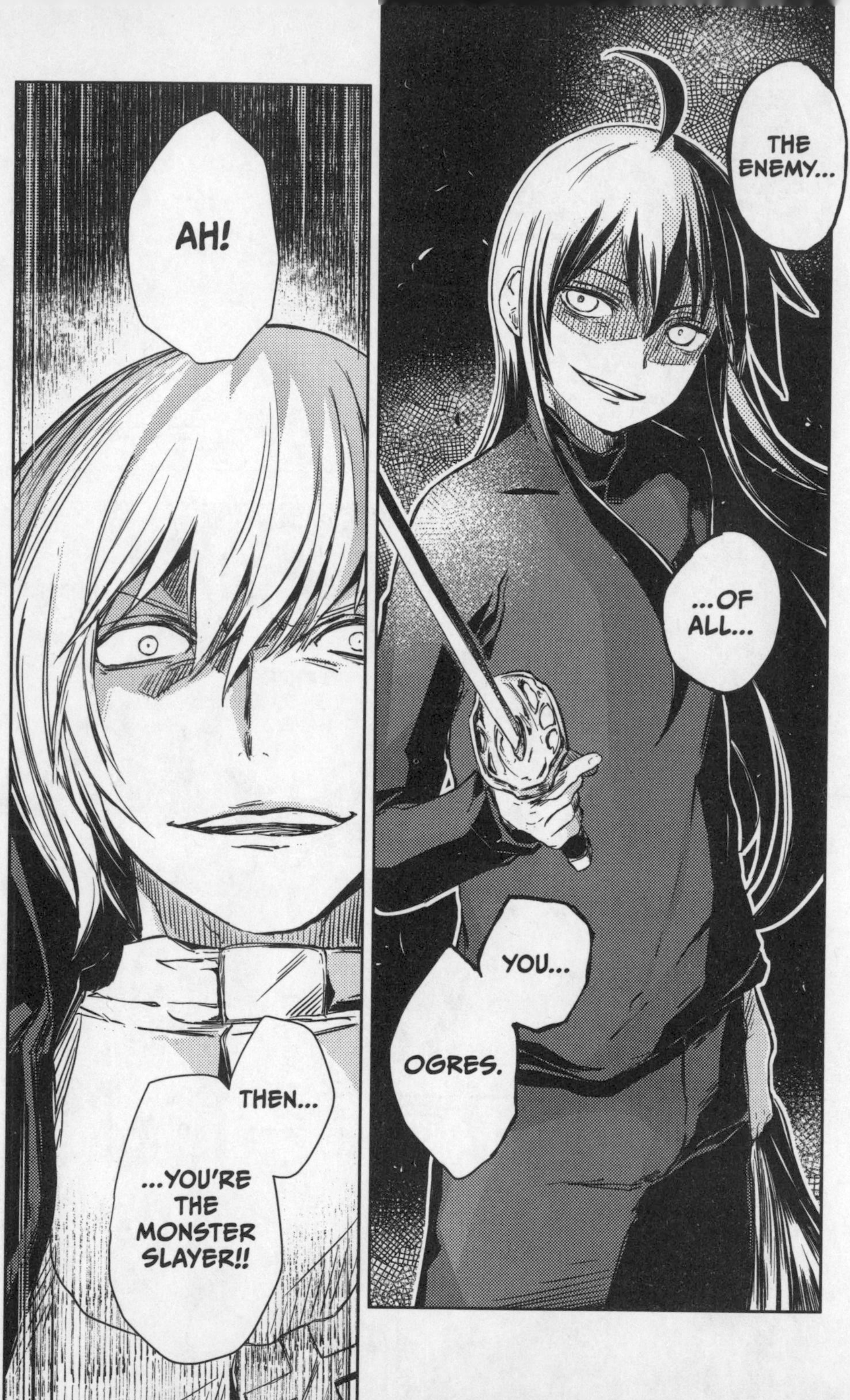
THE ENEMY...
...OF ALL...
YOU...
OGRES.
AH!
THEN...
...YOU'RE THE MONSTER SLAYER!!

# CHAPTER 11: SALLY AND OGRES

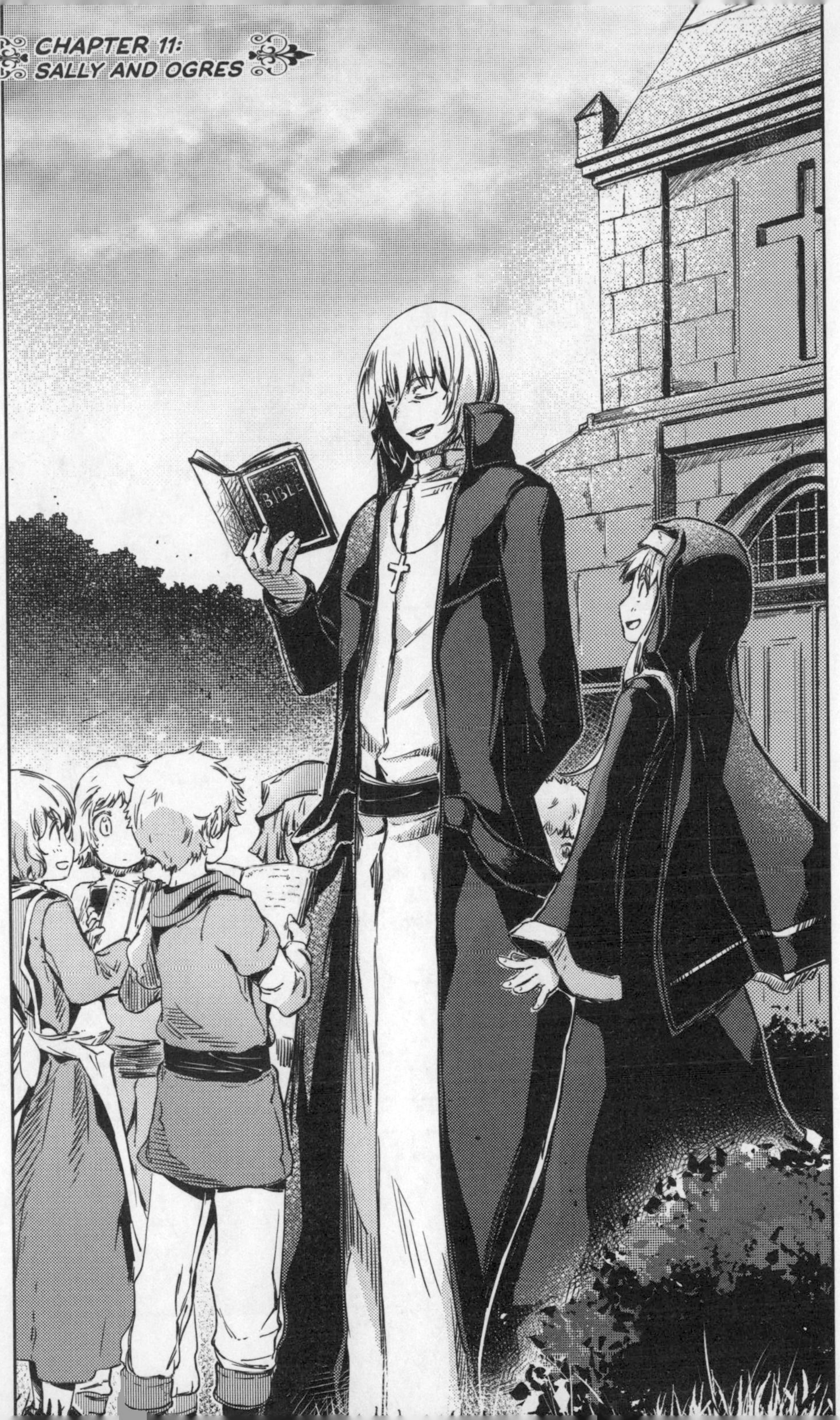
BIBLE

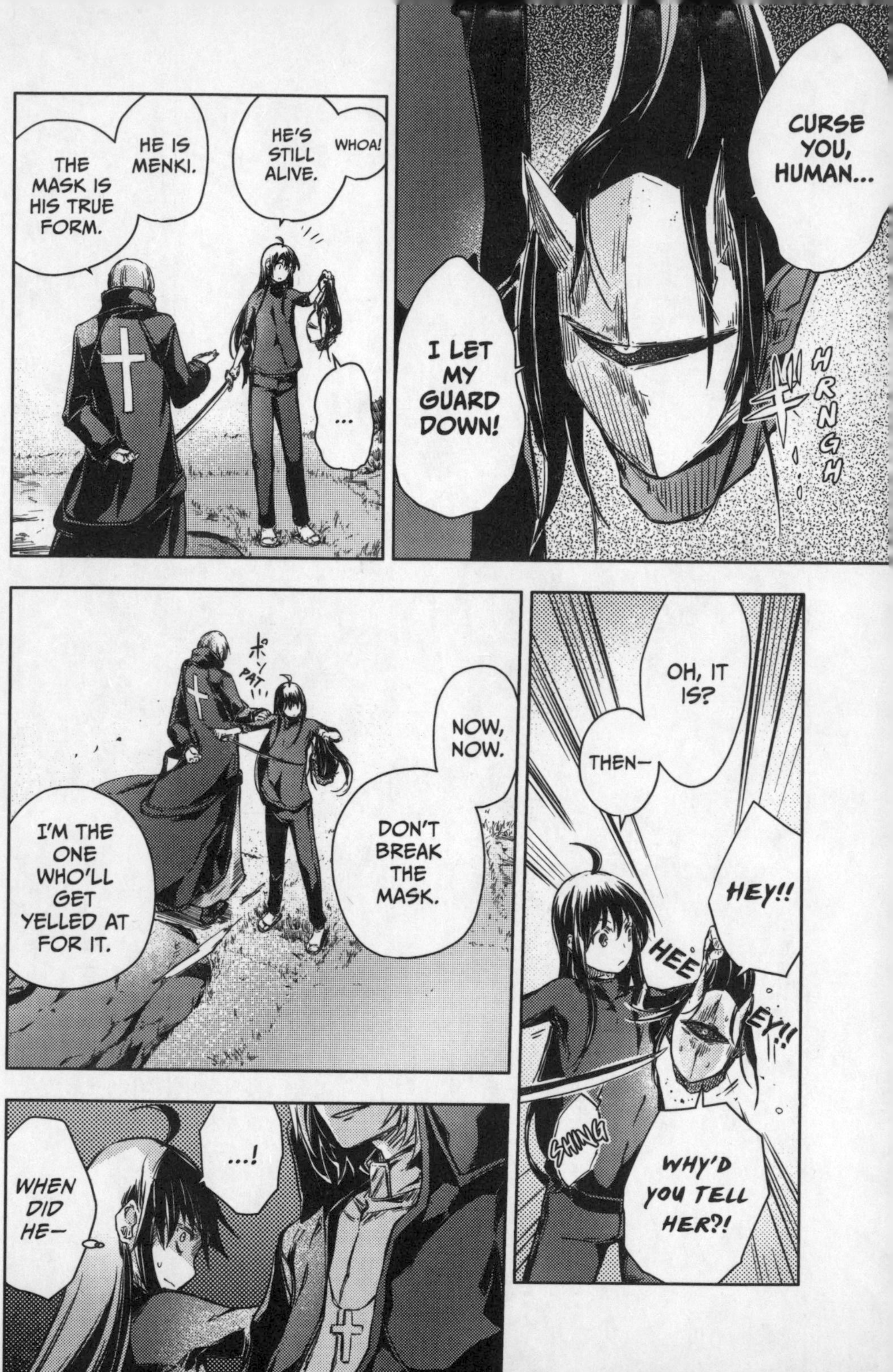
CURSE YOU, HUMAN...
I LET MY GUARD DOWN!
HRNGH
WHOA!
HE'S STILL ALIVE.
HE IS MENKI.
THE MASK IS HIS TRUE FORM.
...
OH, IT IS?
THEN—
HEY!!
HEE EY!!
SHING
WHY'D YOU TELL HER?!
PAT
NOW, NOW.
DON'T BREAK THE MASK.
I'M THE ONE WHO'LL GET YELLED AT FOR IT.
...!
WHEN DID HE—

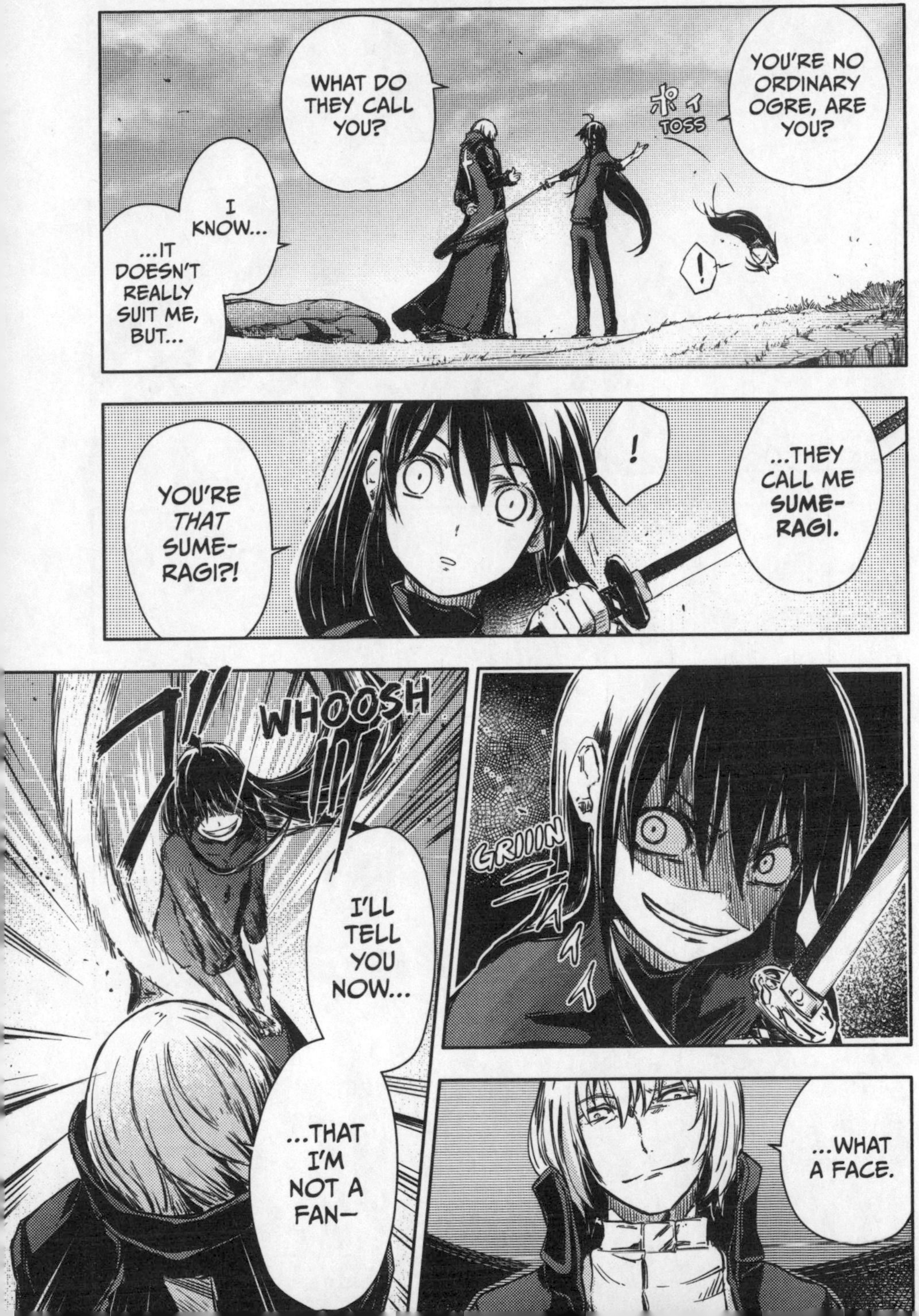
YOU'RE NO ORDINARY OGRE, ARE YOU?
ポイ TOSS
WHAT DO THEY CALL YOU?
!
I KNOW...
...IT DOESN'T REALLY SUIT ME, BUT...
...THEY CALL ME SUME-RAGI.
!
YOU'RE *THAT* SUME-RAGI?!
GRIIIN
...WHAT A FACE.
WHOOSH
I'LL TELL YOU NOW...
...THAT I'M NOT A FAN—

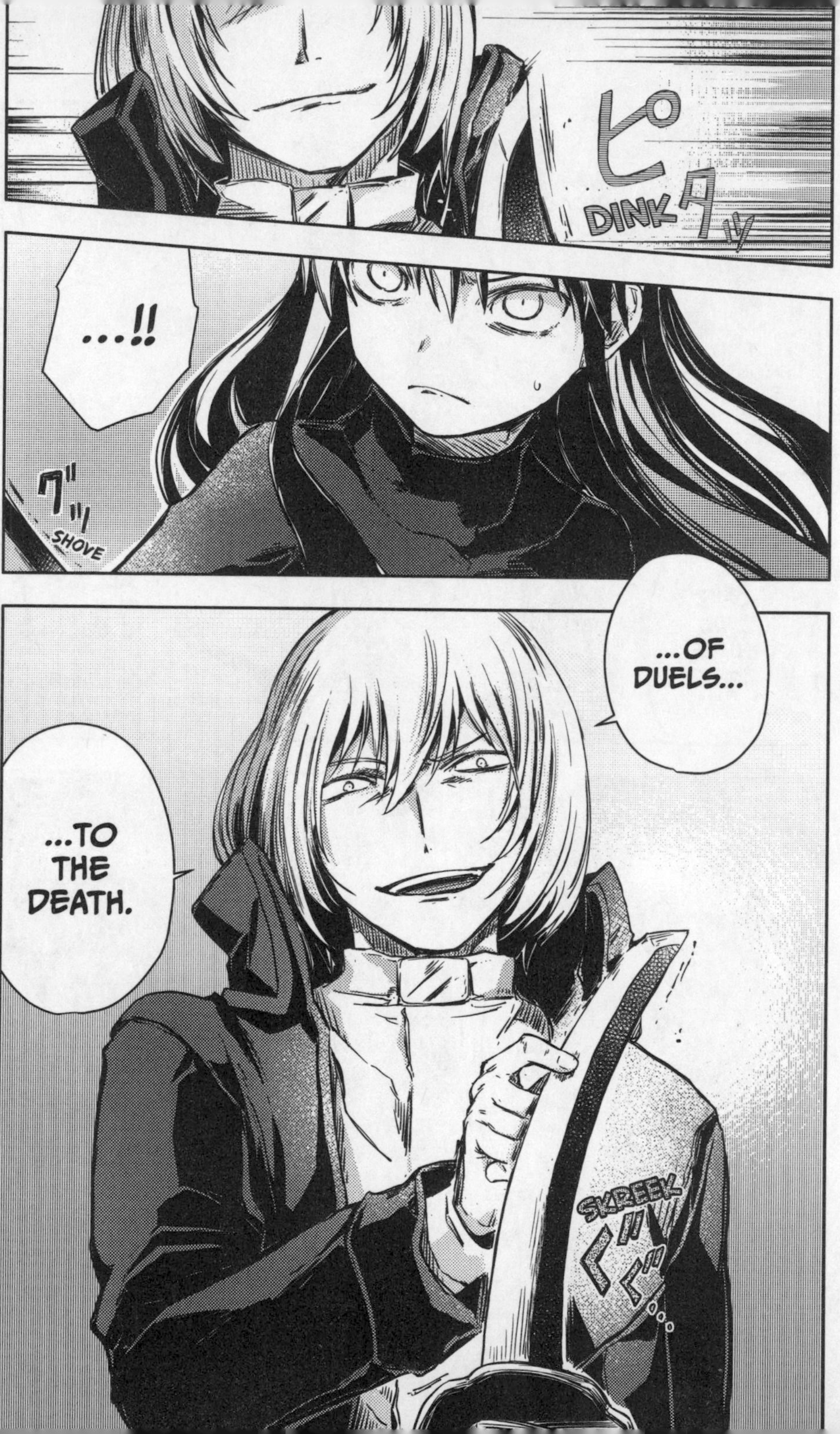
ピ
DINK タッ
...!!
グッ
SHOVE
...OF DUELS...
...TO THE DEATH.
SKREEK
ぐぐ

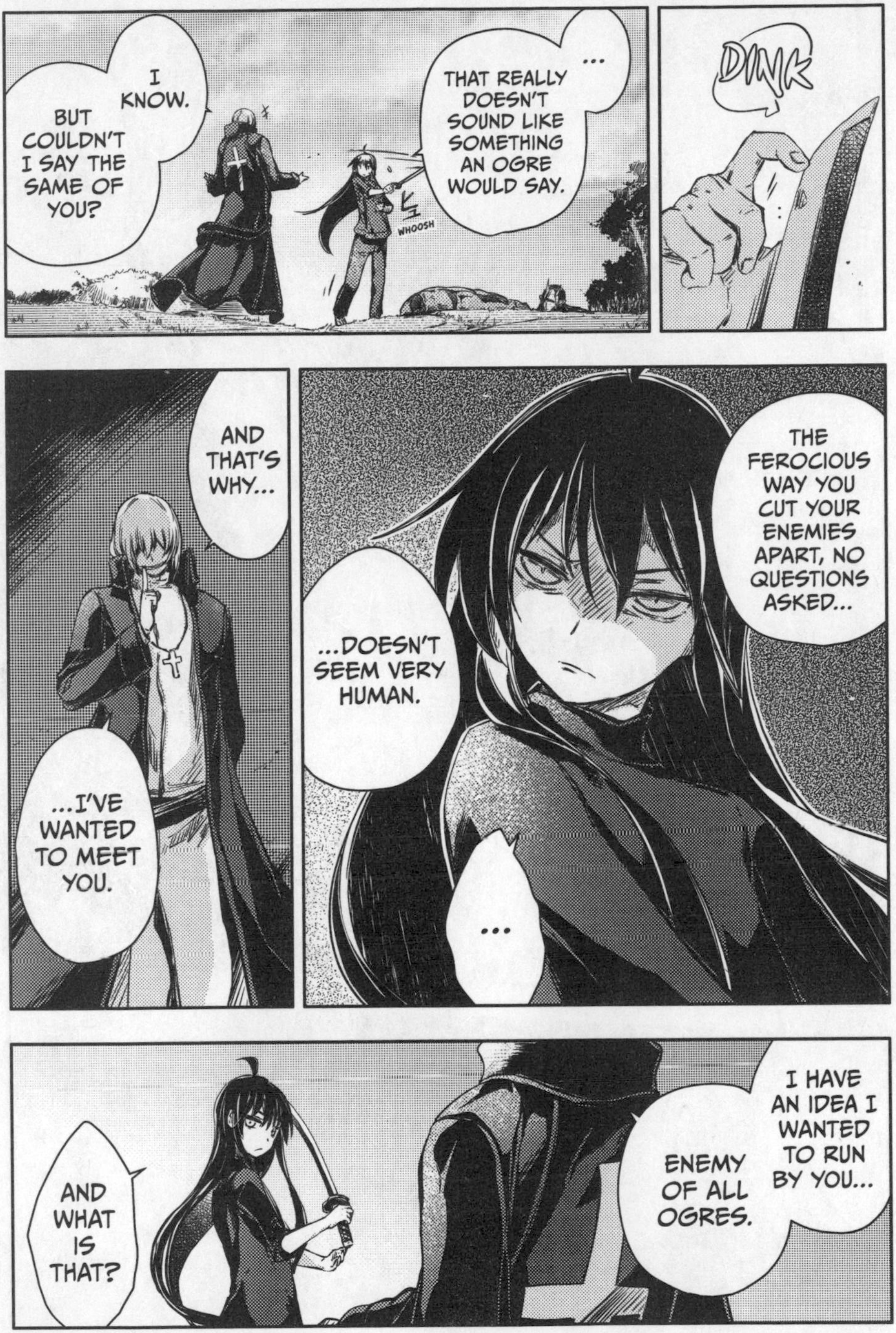
DINK
... THAT REALLY DOESN'T SOUND LIKE SOMETHING AN OGRE WOULD SAY.
WHOOSH
I KNOW. BUT COULDN'T I SAY THE SAME OF YOU?
THE FEROCIOUS WAY YOU CUT YOUR ENEMIES APART, NO QUESTIONS ASKED...
...DOESN'T SEEM VERY HUMAN.
...
AND THAT'S WHY...
...I'VE WANTED TO MEET YOU.
I HAVE AN IDEA I WANTED TO RUN BY YOU...
ENEMY OF ALL OGRES.
AND WHAT IS THAT?

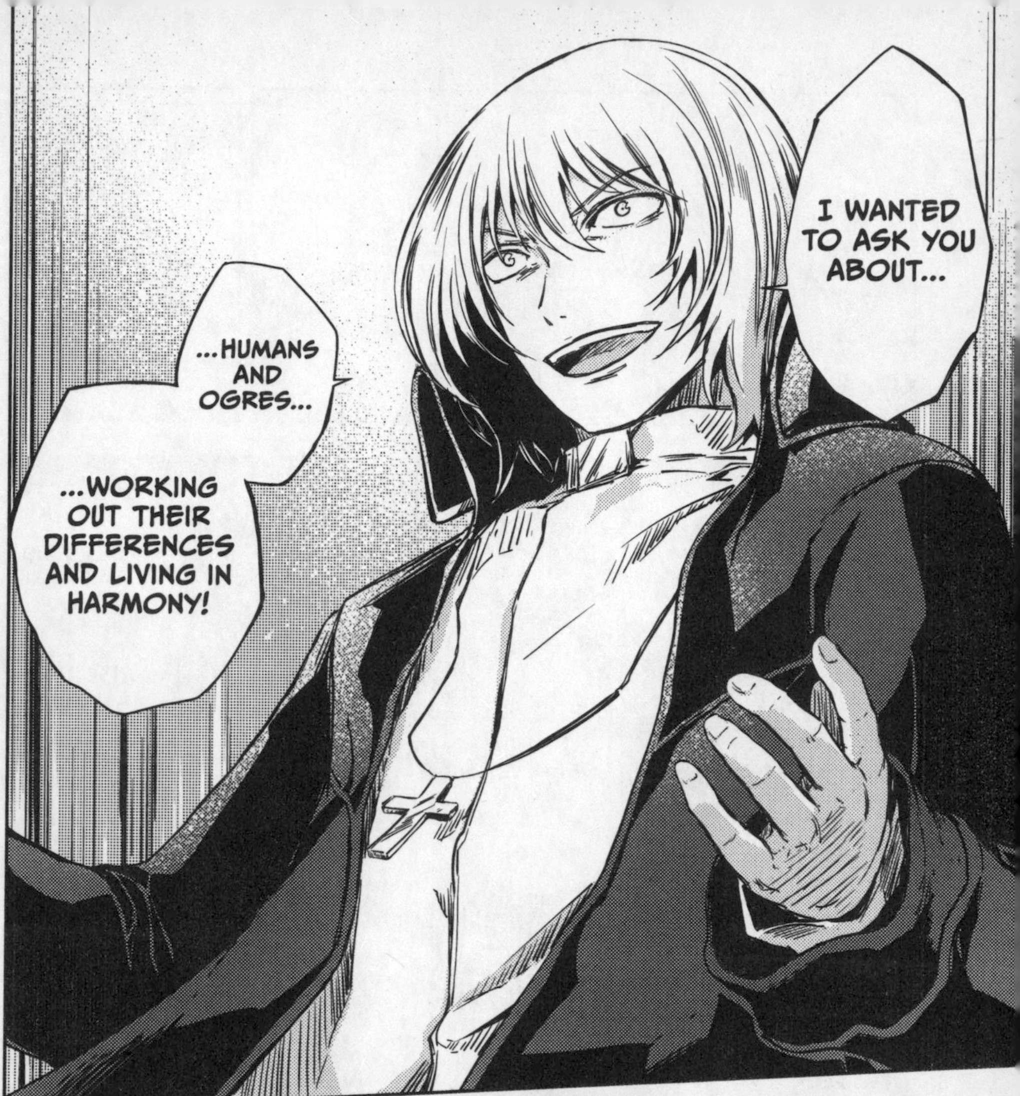
I WANTED TO ASK YOU ABOUT...
...HUMANS AND OGRES...
...WORKING OUT THEIR DIFFERENCES AND LIVING IN HARMONY!

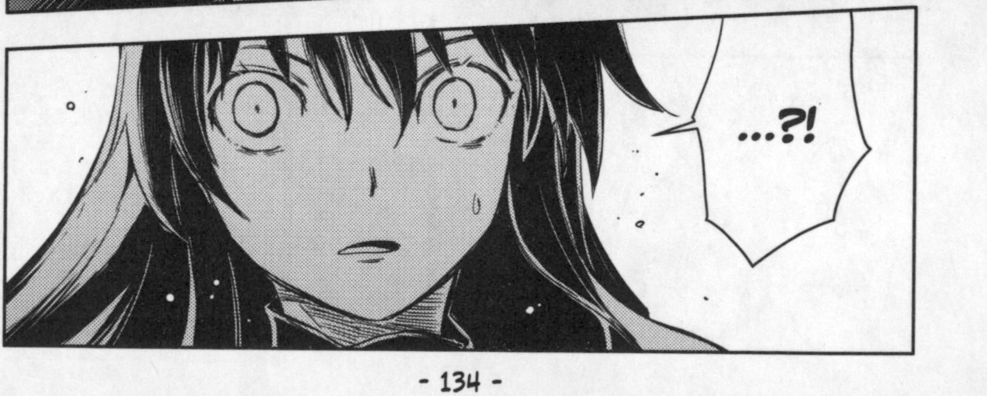
...?!

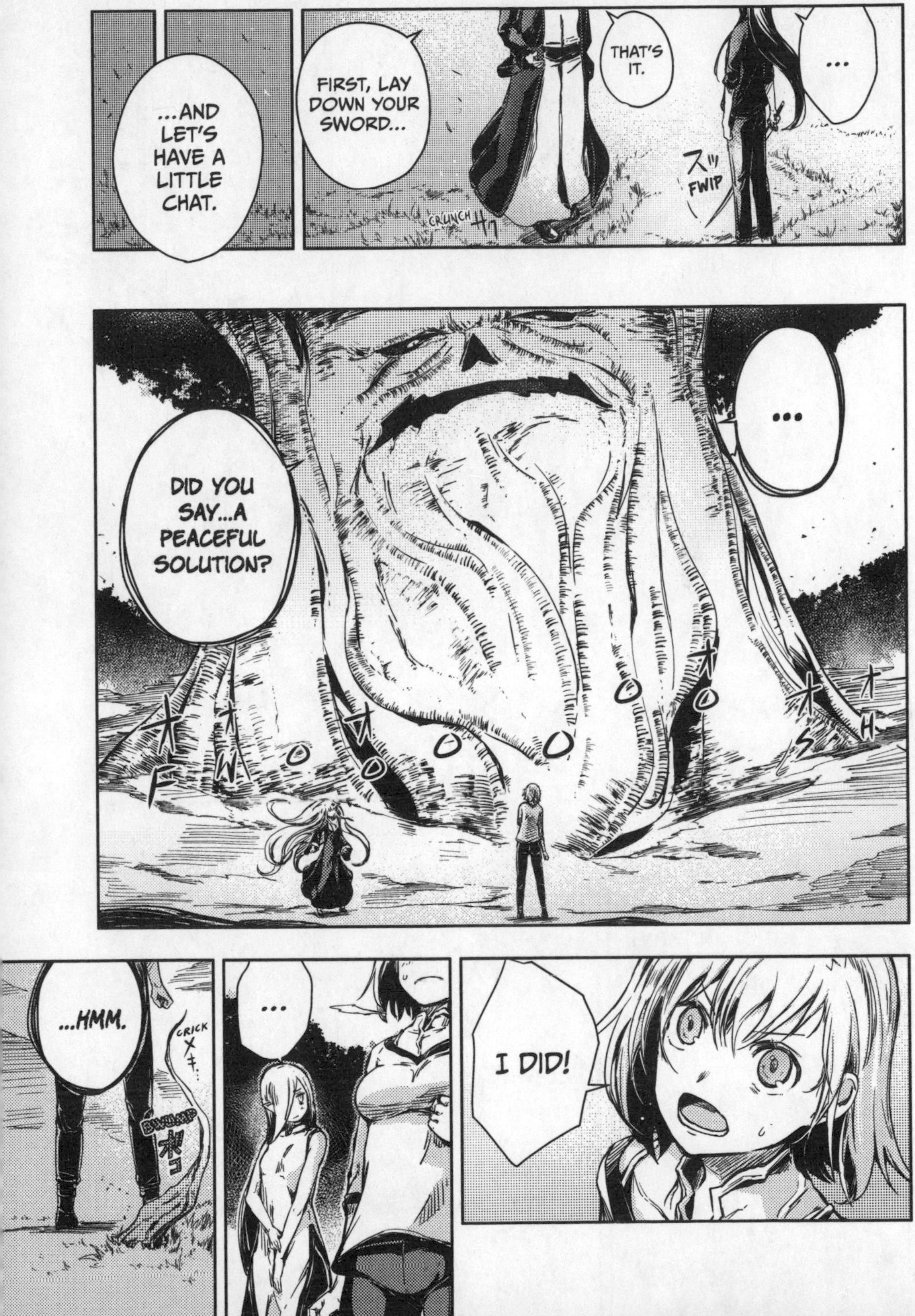
...
THAT'S IT.
FIRST, LAY DOWN YOUR SWORD...
FWIP
CRUNCH
...AND LET'S HAVE A LITTLE CHAT.
...
DID YOU SAY...A PEACEFUL SOLUTION?
FWOOOOOOSH
I DID!
...
...HMM.
CRICK

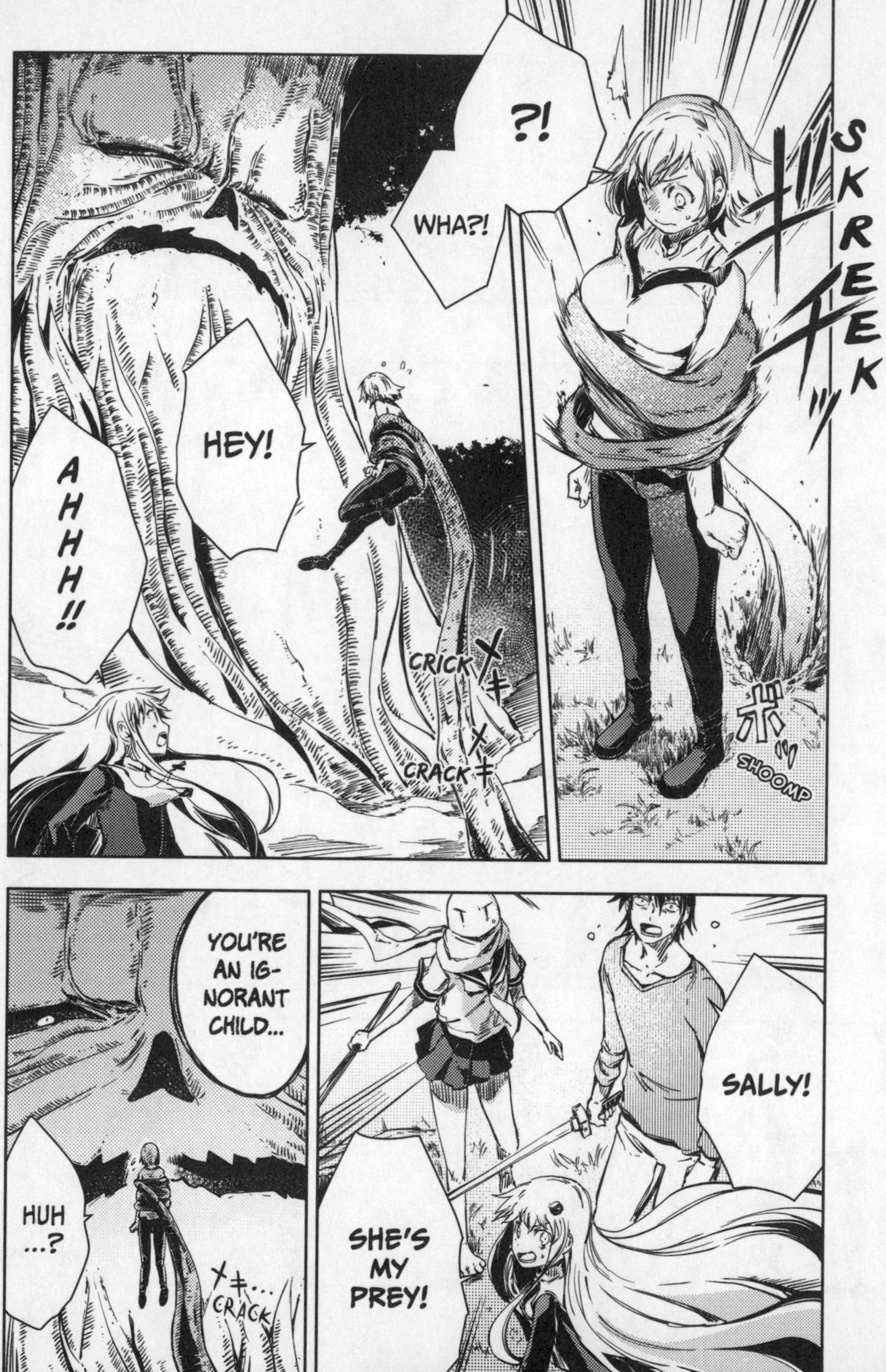
SKREEK
?!
WHA?!
SHOOMP
HEY!
AHHHH!!
CRICK
CRACK
SALLY!
SHE'S MY PREY!
YOU'RE AN IG-NORANT CHILD...
HUH ...?
CRACK

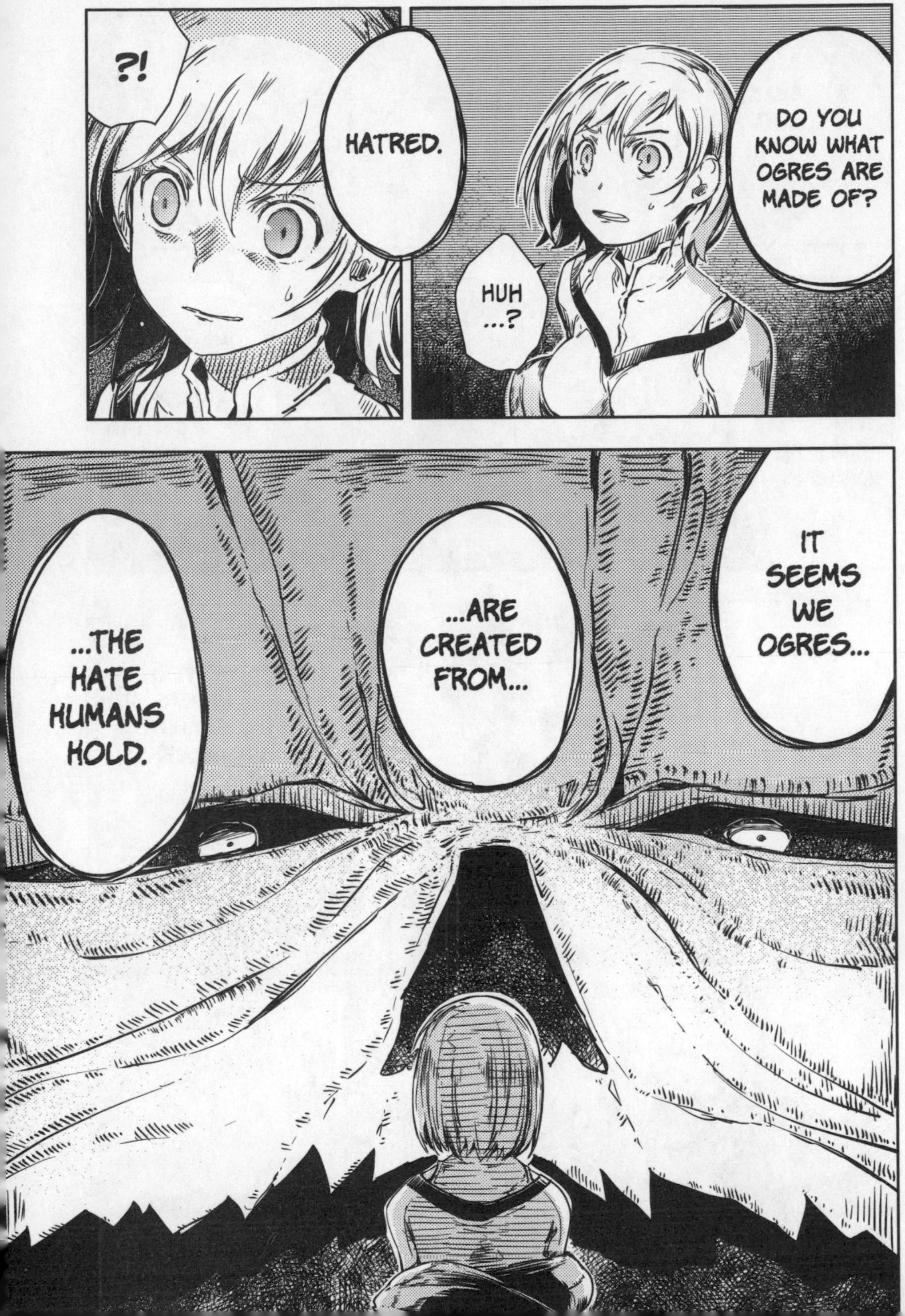
DO YOU KNOW WHAT OGRES ARE MADE OF?
HUH ...?
HATRED.
?!
IT SEEMS WE OGRES...
...ARE CREATED FROM...
...THE HATE HUMANS HOLD.

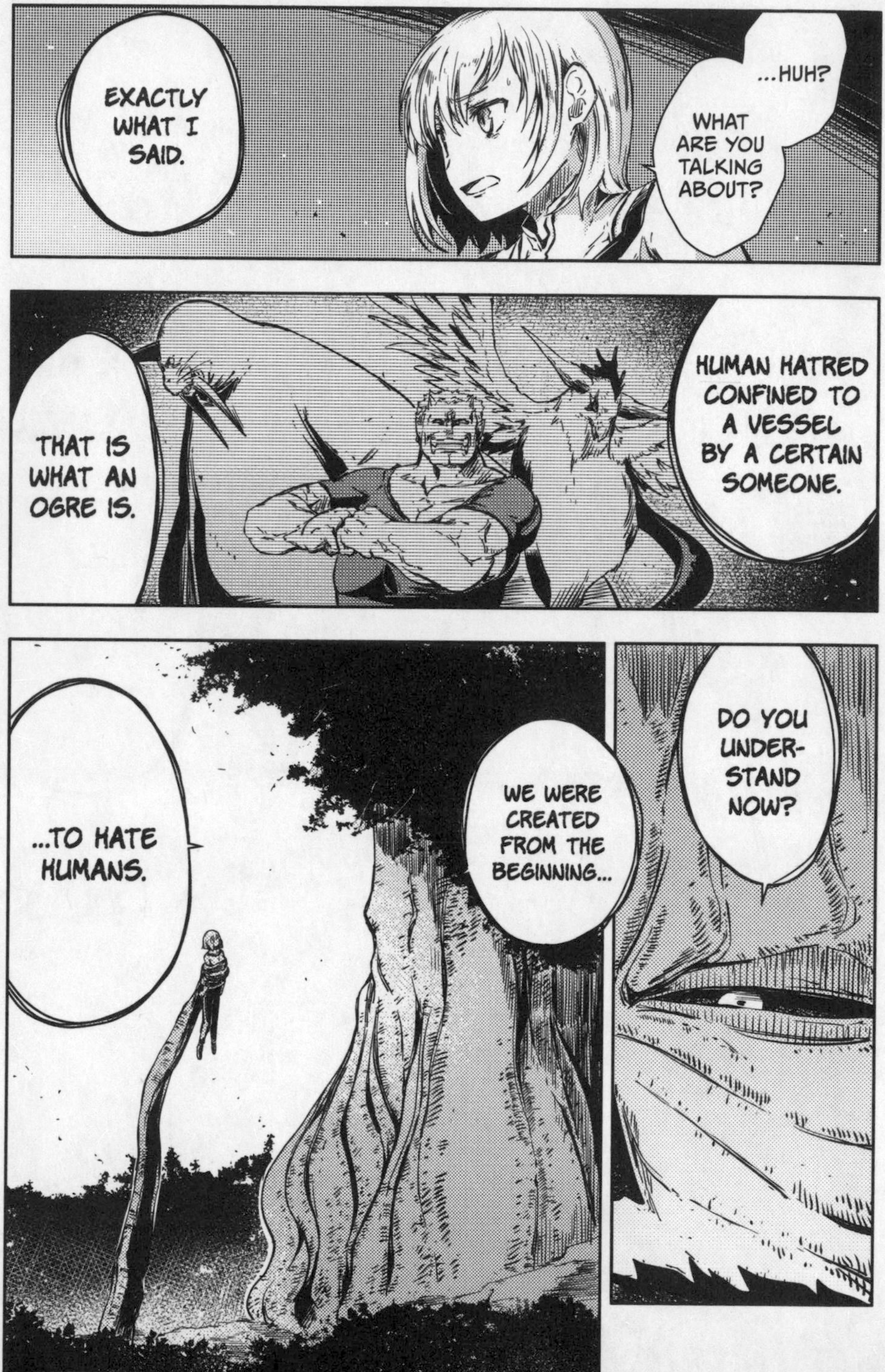
...HUH?
WHAT ARE YOU TALKING ABOUT?
EXACTLY WHAT I SAID.
HUMAN HATRED CONFINED TO A VESSEL BY A CERTAIN SOMEONE.
THAT IS WHAT AN OGRE IS.
DO YOU UNDER-STAND NOW?
WE WERE CREATED FROM THE BEGINNING...
...TO HATE HUMANS.

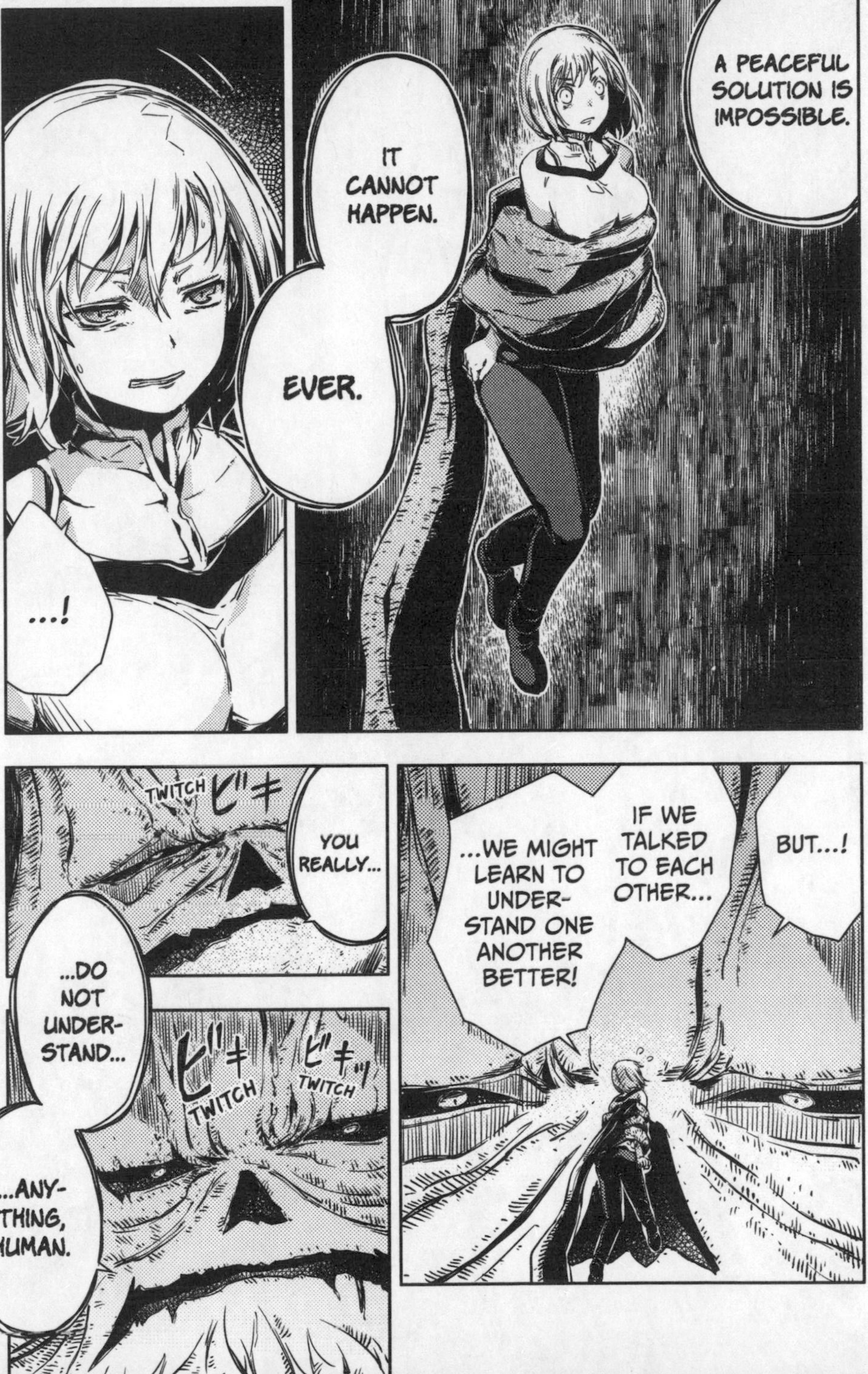
A PEACEFUL SOLUTION IS IMPOSSIBLE.
IT CANNOT HAPPEN.
EVER.
...!
BUT...!
IF WE TALKED TO EACH OTHER...
...WE MIGHT LEARN TO UNDERSTAND ONE ANOTHER BETTER!
TWITCH ビキ
YOU REALLY...
...DO NOT UNDERSTAND...
ビキッ TWITCH
ビキ TWITCH
...ANYTHING, HUMAN.

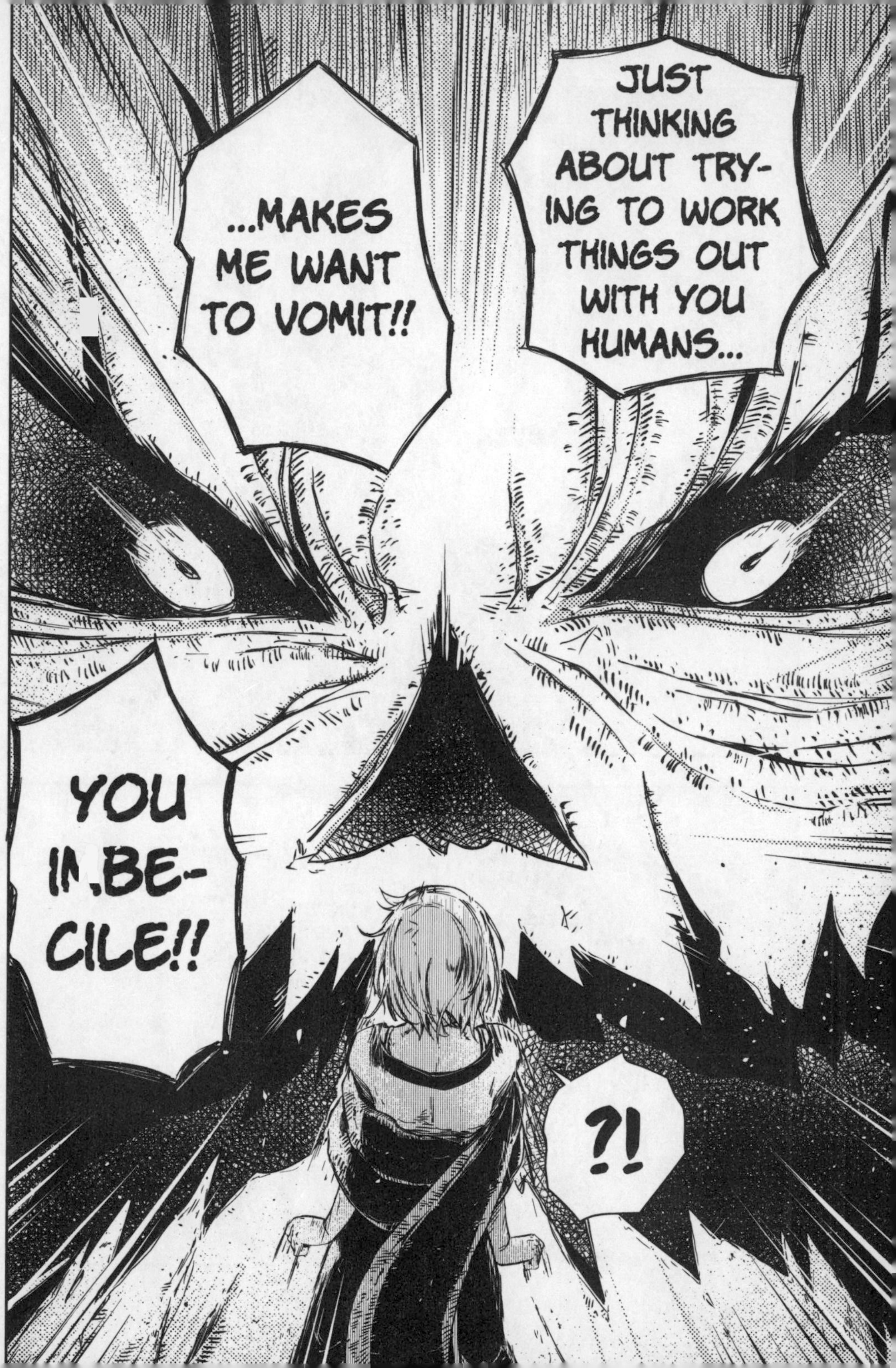
JUST THINKING ABOUT TRYING TO WORK THINGS OUT WITH YOU HUMANS...
...MAKES ME WANT TO VOMIT!!
YOU IMBECILE!!
?!

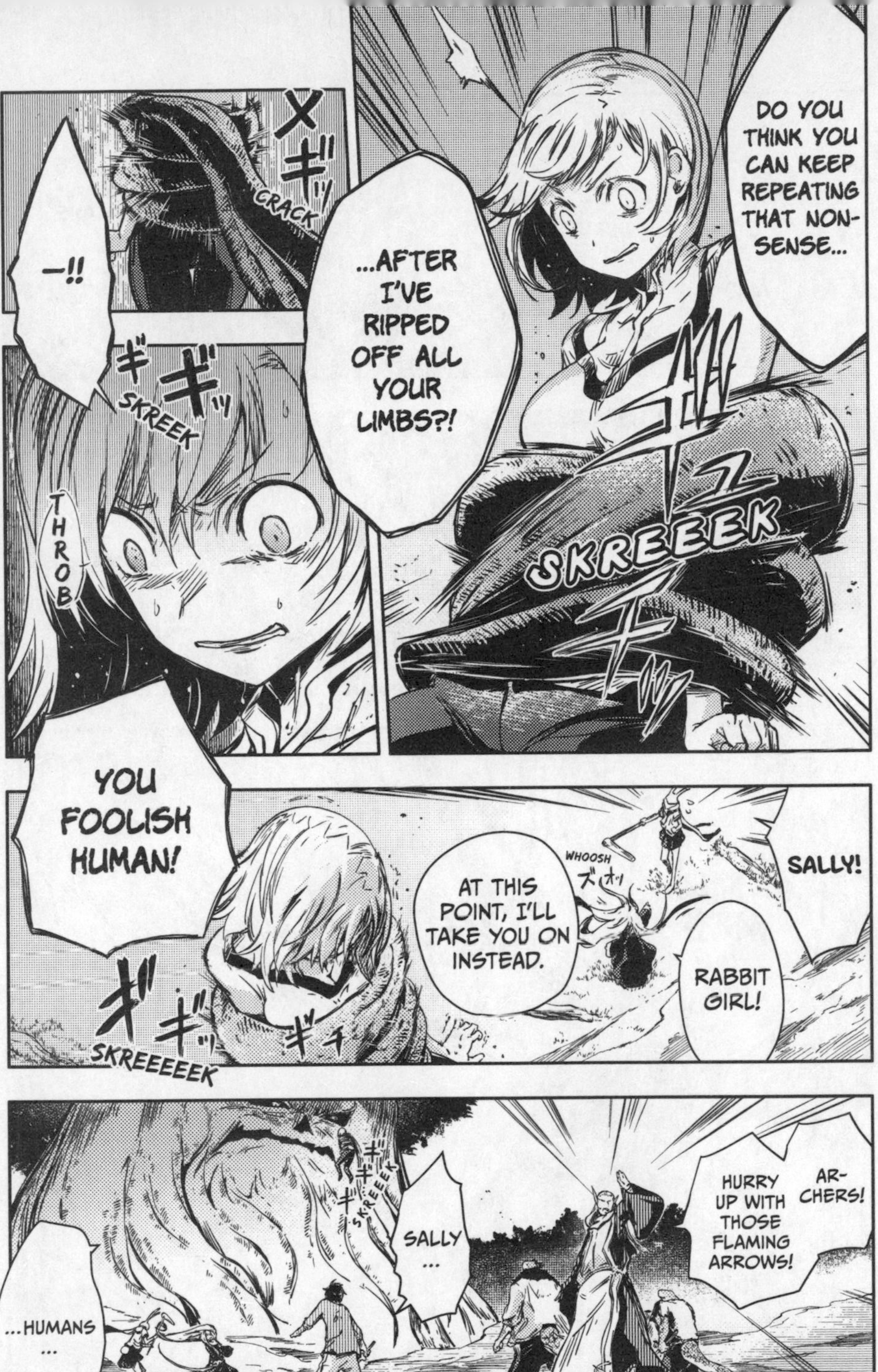
DO YOU THINK YOU CAN KEEP REPEATING THAT NON-SENSE...
...AFTER I'VE RIPPED OFF ALL YOUR LIMBS?!
SKREEEK
CRACK
—!!
SKREEK
THROB
SALLY!
RABBIT GIRL!
WHOOSH
AT THIS POINT, I'LL TAKE YOU ON INSTEAD.
YOU FOOLISH HUMAN!
SKREEEEEK
ARCHERS!
HURRY UP WITH THOSE FLAMING ARROWS!
SKREEEK
SALLY...
...HUMANS...

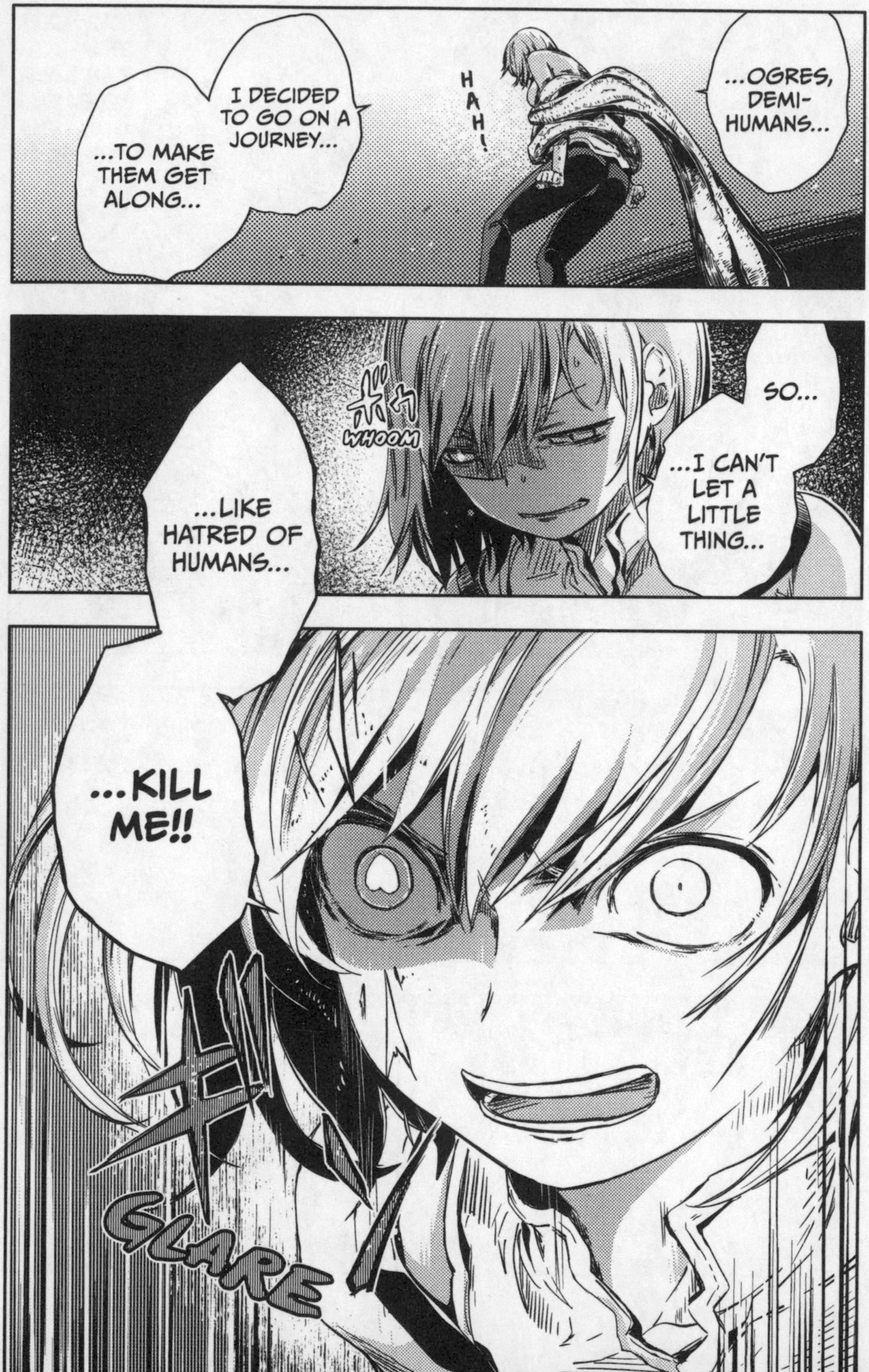
...OGRES, DEMI-HUMANS...
HAH!
I DECIDED TO GO ON A JOURNEY...
...TO MAKE THEM GET ALONG...
SO...
...I CAN'T LET A LITTLE THING...
WHOOM
...LIKE HATRED OF HUMANS...
...KILL ME!!
GLARE

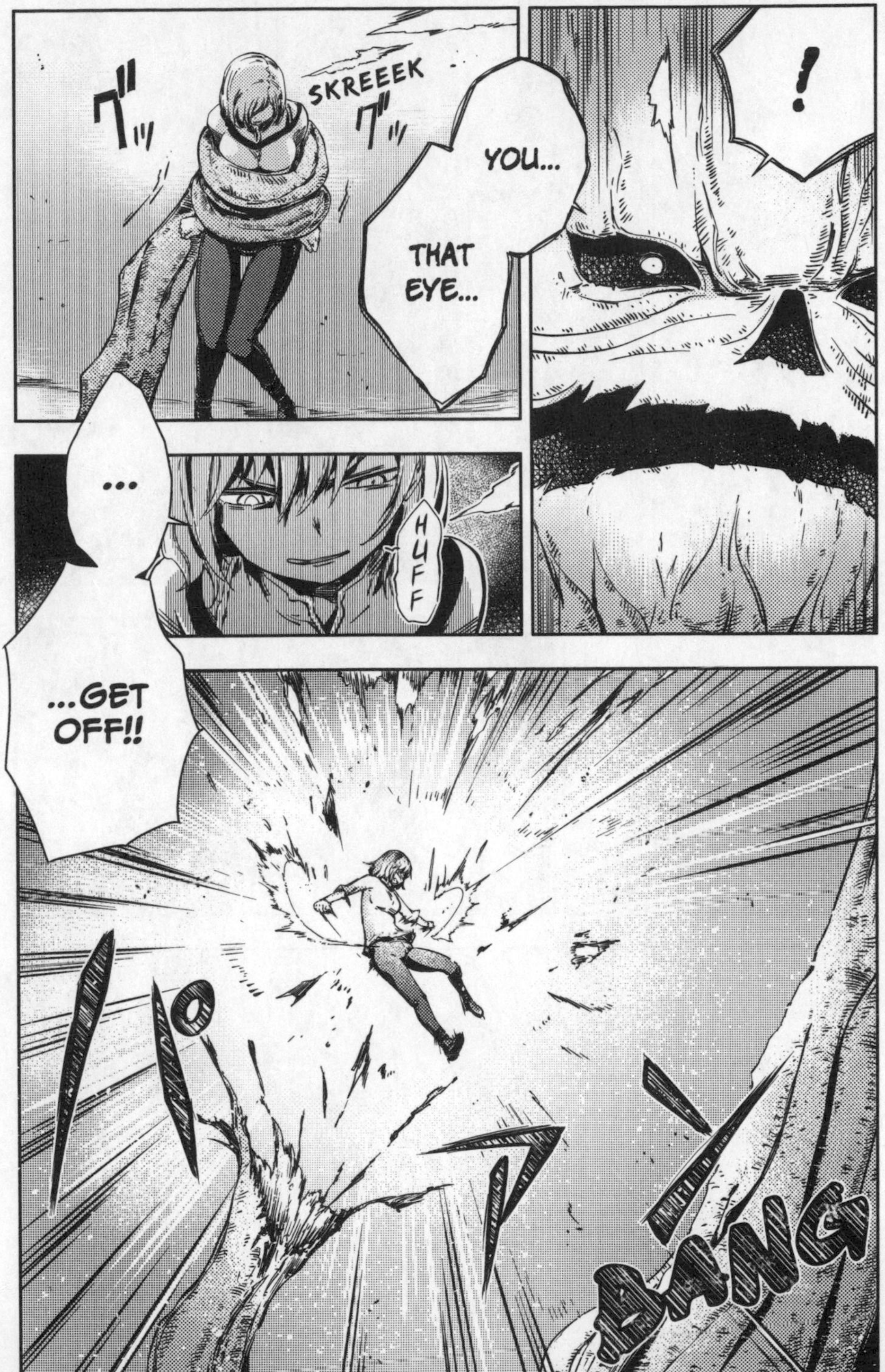
!
YOU...
THAT EYE...
SKREEEK
...
HUFF
...GET OFF!!
BANG

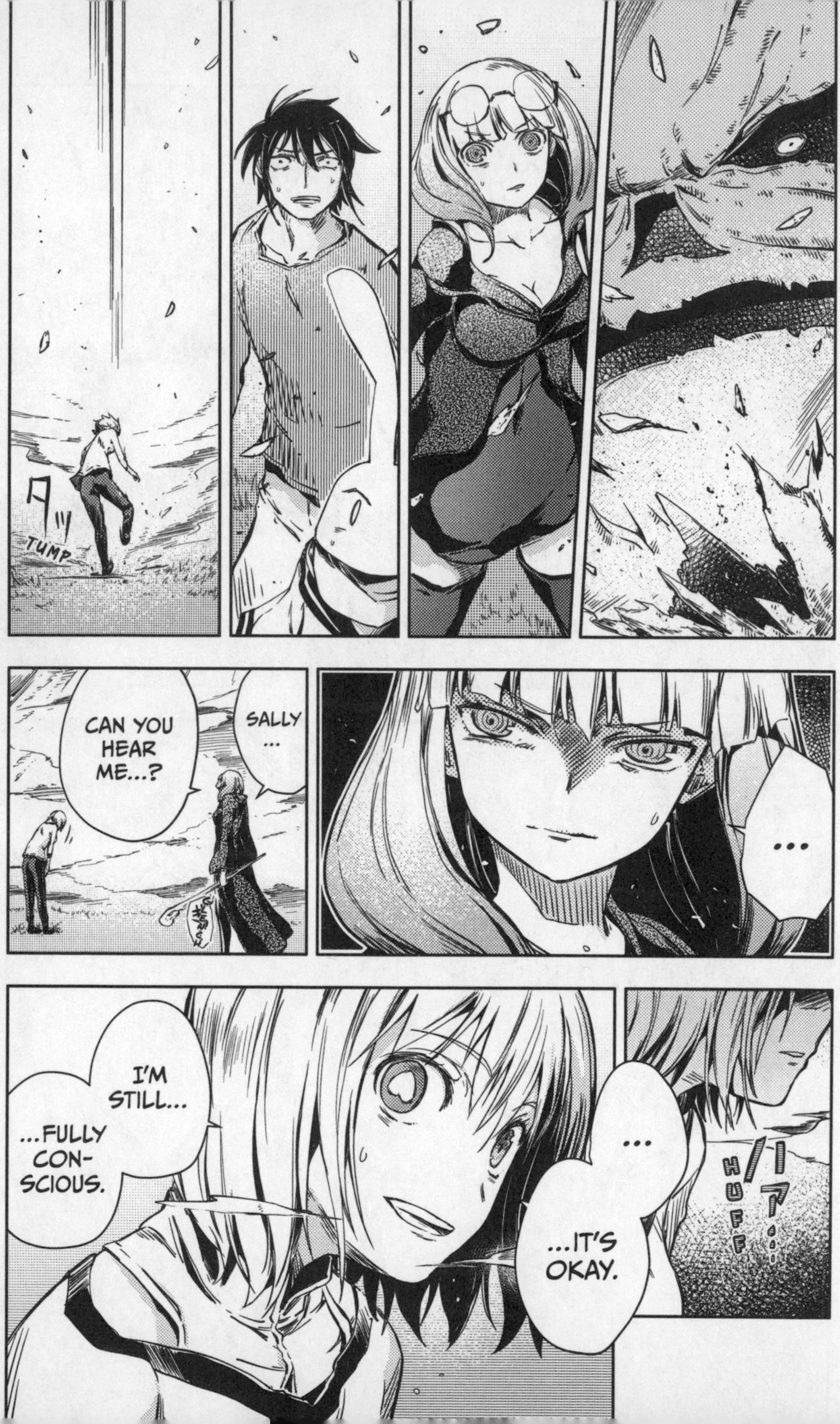
タッ
TUMP
...
SALLY ...
CAN YOU HEAR ME...?
ハァ…
HUFF
...
...IT'S OKAY.
I'M STILL...
...FULLY CON-SCIOUS.

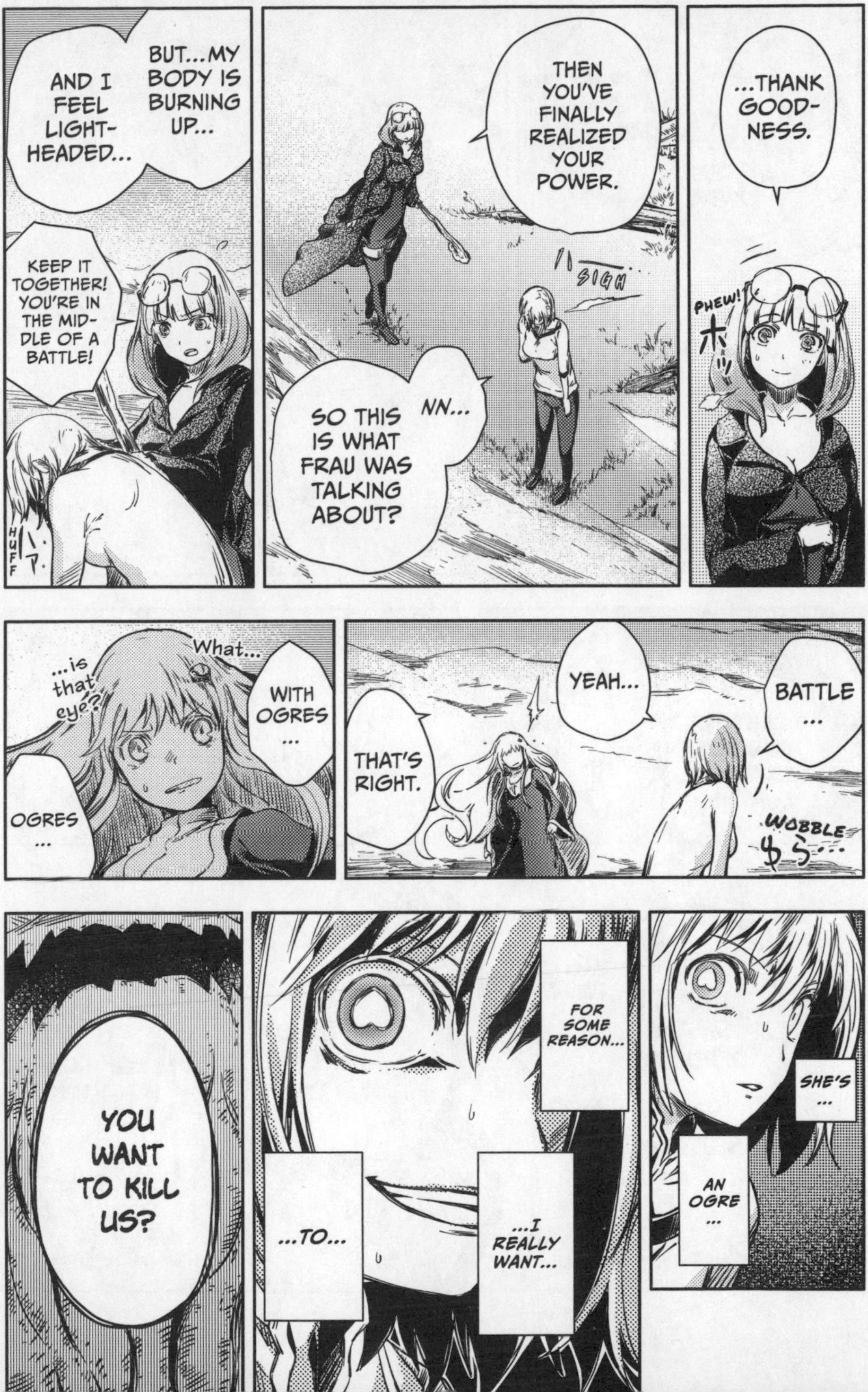
...THANK GOODNESS.
PHEW!
THEN YOU'VE FINALLY REALIZED YOUR POWER.
SIGH
NN...
SO THIS IS WHAT FRAU WAS TALKING ABOUT?
BUT...MY BODY IS BURNING UP...
AND I FEEL LIGHT-HEADED...
KEEP IT TOGETHER! YOU'RE IN THE MIDDLE OF A BATTLE!
HUFF
BATTLE ...
WOBBLE
YEAH...
THAT'S RIGHT.
What...
...is that eye?
WITH OGRES ...
OGRES ...
SHE'S ...
AN OGRE ...
FOR SOME REASON...
...I REALLY WANT...
...TO...
YOU WANT TO KILL US?

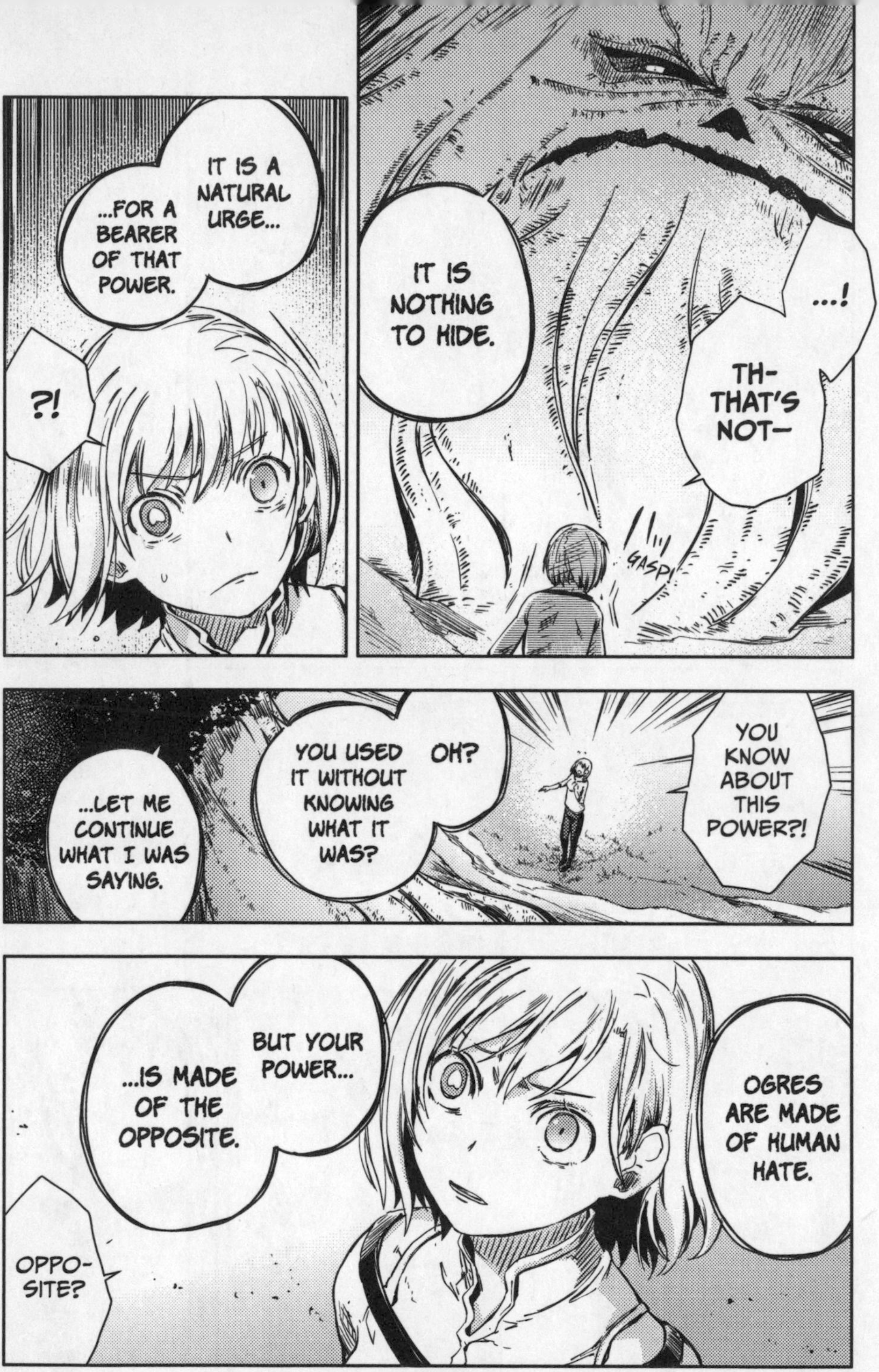
...!
TH- THAT'S NOT—
IT IS NOTHING TO HIDE.
GASP!
IT IS A NATURAL URGE...
...FOR A BEARER OF THAT POWER.
?!
YOU KNOW ABOUT THIS POWER?!
OH?
YOU USED IT WITHOUT KNOWING WHAT IT WAS?
...LET ME CONTINUE WHAT I WAS SAYING.
OGRES ARE MADE OF HUMAN HATE.
BUT YOUR POWER...
...IS MADE OF THE OPPOSITE.
OPPO- SITE?

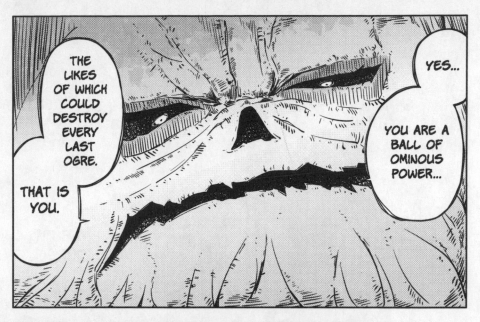

YES...

YOU ARE A BALL OF OMINOUS POWER...

THE LIKES OF WHICH COULD DESTROY EVERY LAST OGRE.

THAT IS YOU.

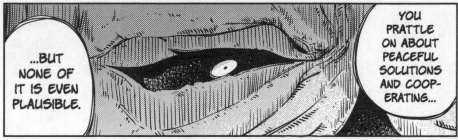

YOU PRATTLE ON ABOUT PEACEFUL SOLUTIONS AND COOP-ERATING...

...BUT NONE OF IT IS EVEN PLAUSIBLE.

LET IT BE KNOWN THAT...

...TO US OGRES...

...YOUR VERY EXISTENCE IS EVIL.

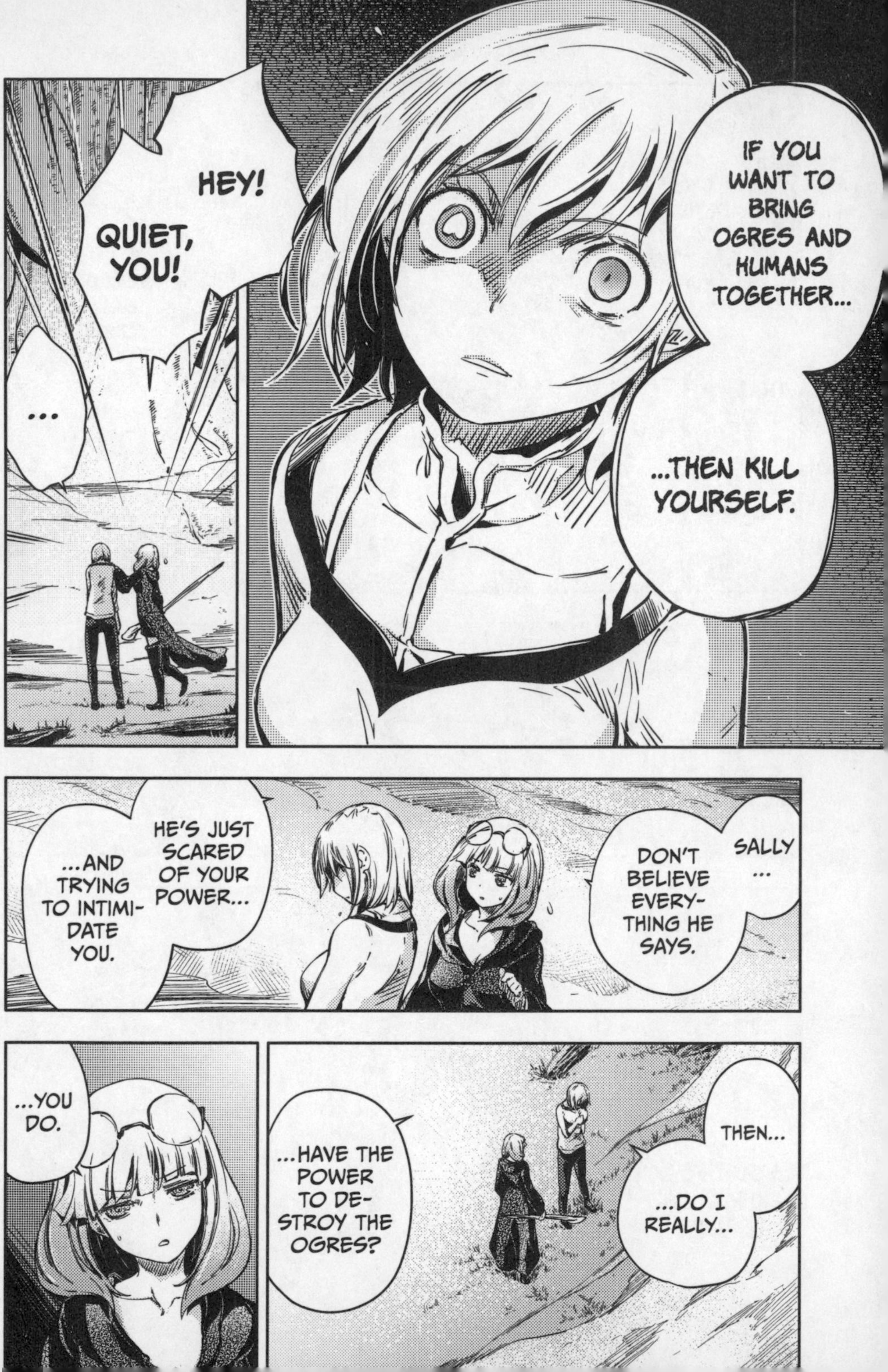
IF YOU WANT TO BRING OGRES AND HUMANS TOGETHER...
...THEN KILL YOURSELF.
HEY! QUIET, YOU!
...
SALLY...
DON'T BELIEVE EVERY-THING HE SAYS.
HE'S JUST SCARED OF YOUR POWER...
...AND TRYING TO INTIMI-DATE YOU.
THEN...
...DO I REALLY...
...HAVE THE POWER TO DE-STROY THE OGRES?
...YOU DO.

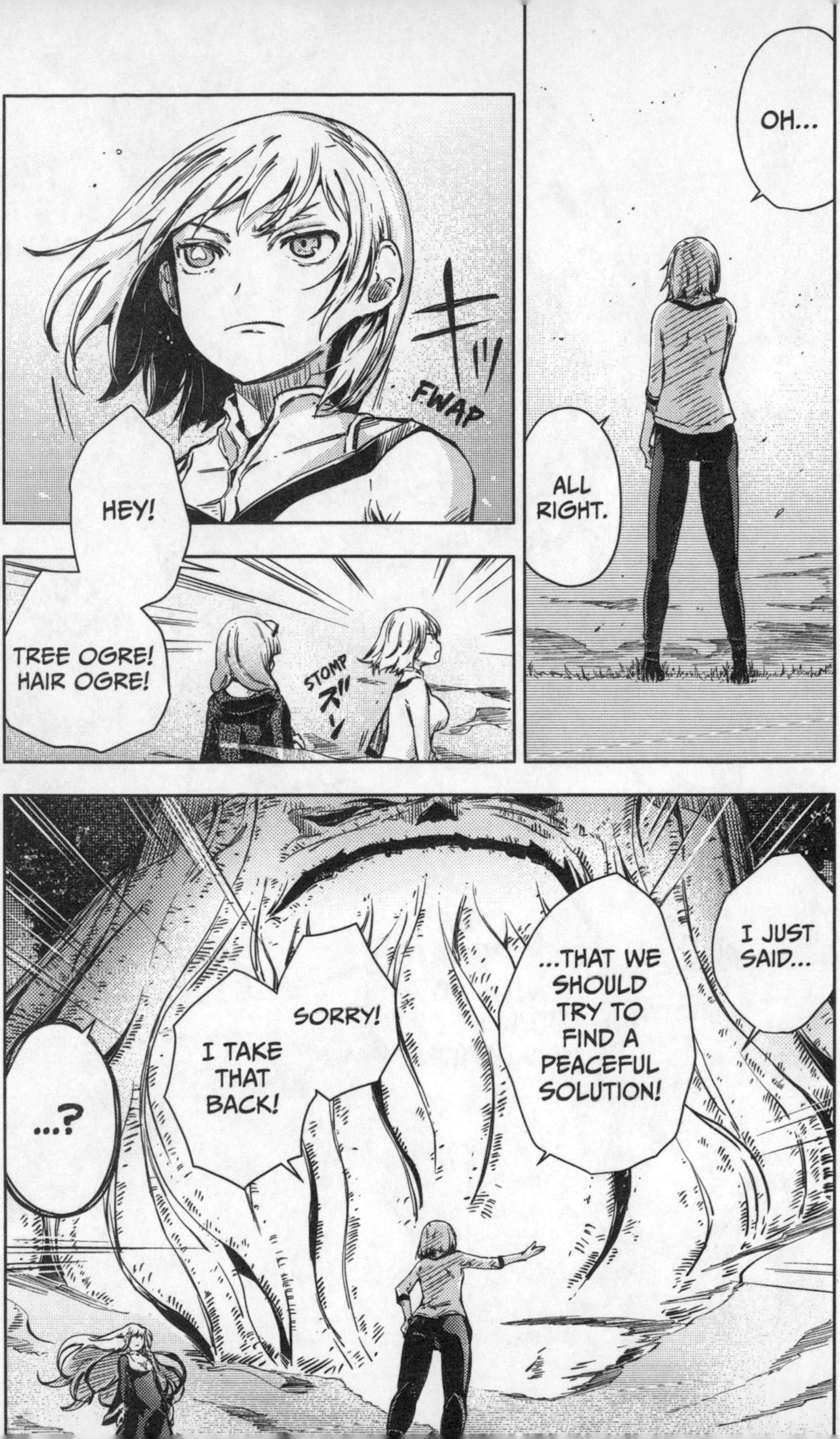
OH...
ALL RIGHT.
FWAP
HEY!
STOMP
TREE OGRE! HAIR OGRE!
I JUST SAID...
...THAT WE SHOULD TRY TO FIND A PEACEFUL SOLUTION!
SORRY! I TAKE THAT BACK!
...?

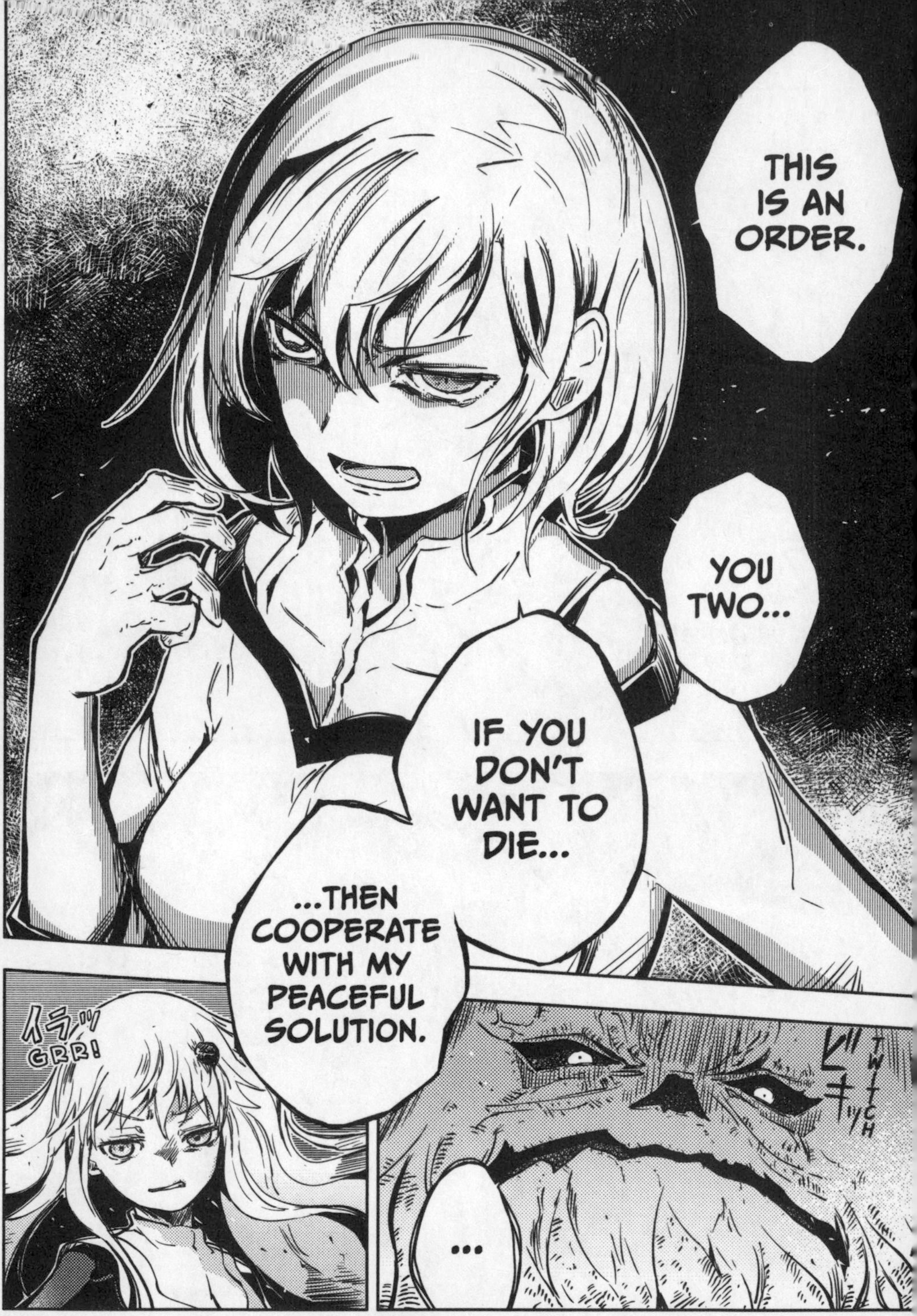
THIS IS AN ORDER.
YOU TWO...
IF YOU DON'T WANT TO DIE...
...THEN COOPERATE WITH MY PEACEFUL SOLUTION.
ビキッ TWITCH
...
イラッ GRR!

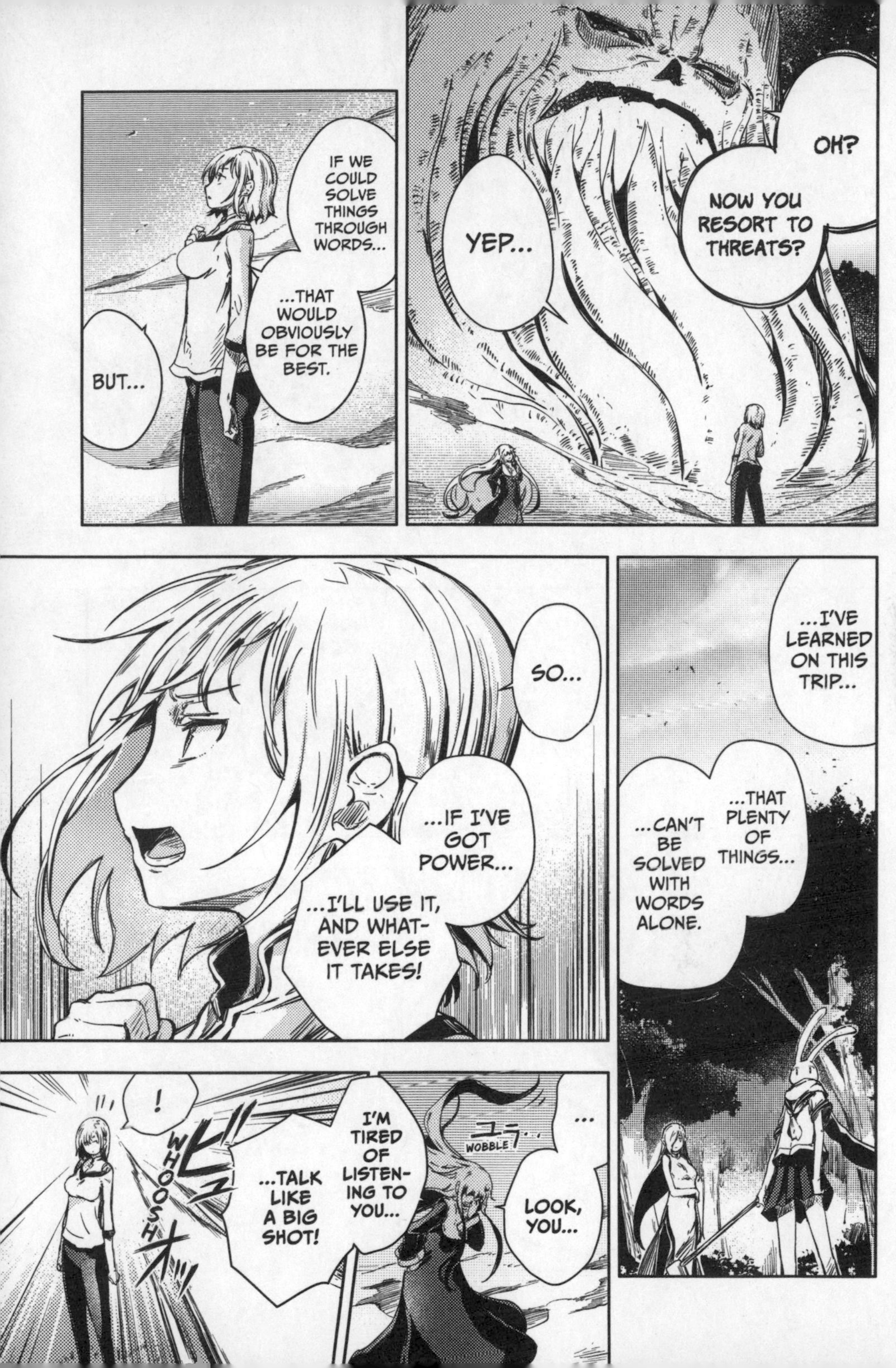
OH?
NOW YOU RESORT TO THREATS?
YEP...
IF WE COULD SOLVE THINGS THROUGH WORDS...
...THAT WOULD OBVIOUSLY BE FOR THE BEST.
BUT...
...I'VE LEARNED ON THIS TRIP...
...THAT PLENTY OF THINGS...
...CAN'T BE SOLVED WITH WORDS ALONE.
SO...
...IF I'VE GOT POWER...
...I'LL USE IT, AND WHATEVER ELSE IT TAKES!
...
LOOK, YOU...
WOBBLE
I'M TIRED OF LISTENING TO YOU...
...TALK LIKE A BIG SHOT!
!
WHOOSH

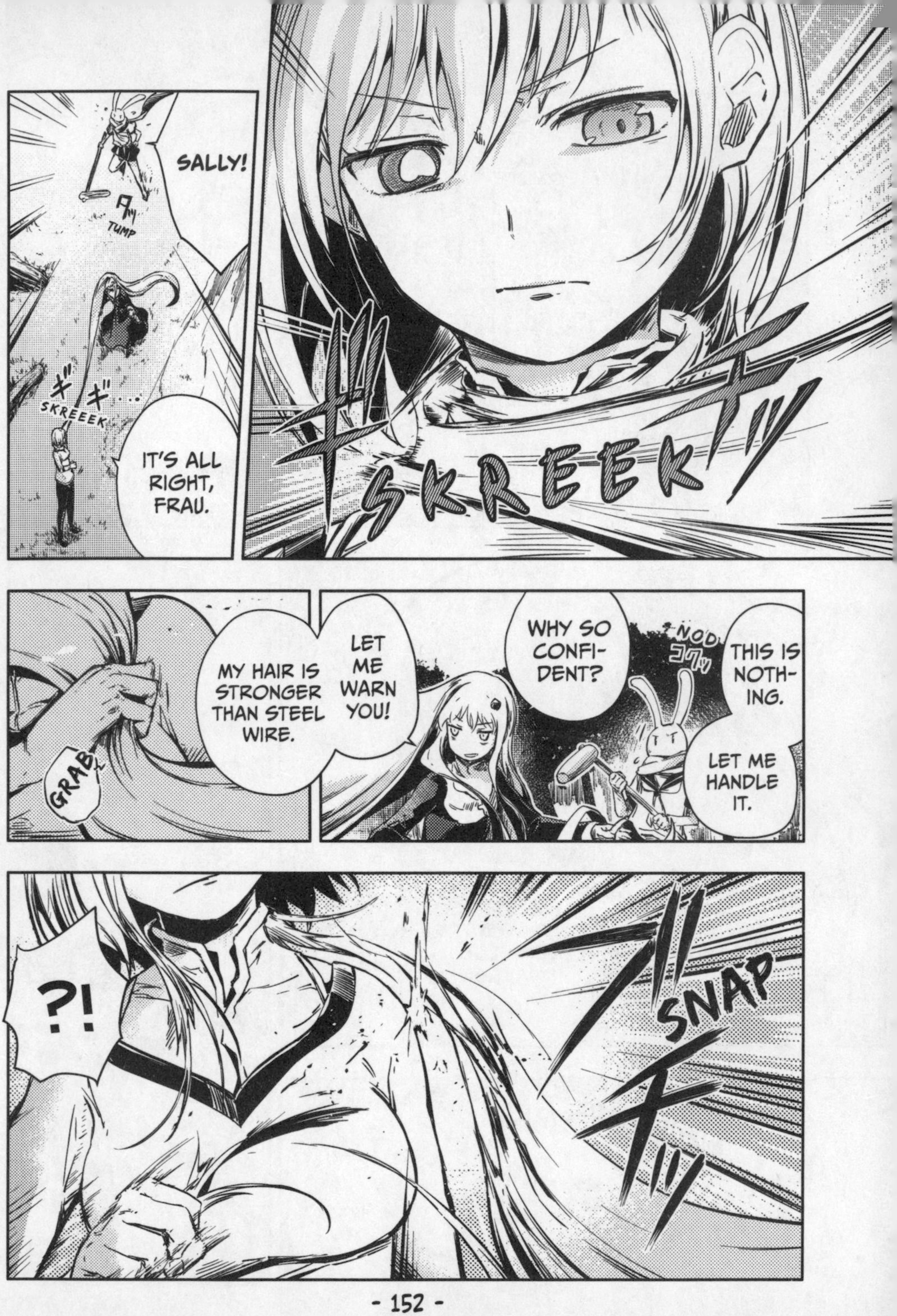
SKREEK
SALLY!
TUMP
SKREEEK
IT'S ALL RIGHT, FRAU.
THIS IS NOTHING.
LET ME HANDLE IT.
NOD
WHY SO CONFIDENT?
LET ME WARN YOU!
MY HAIR IS STRONGER THAN STEEL WIRE.
GRAB
SNAP
?!

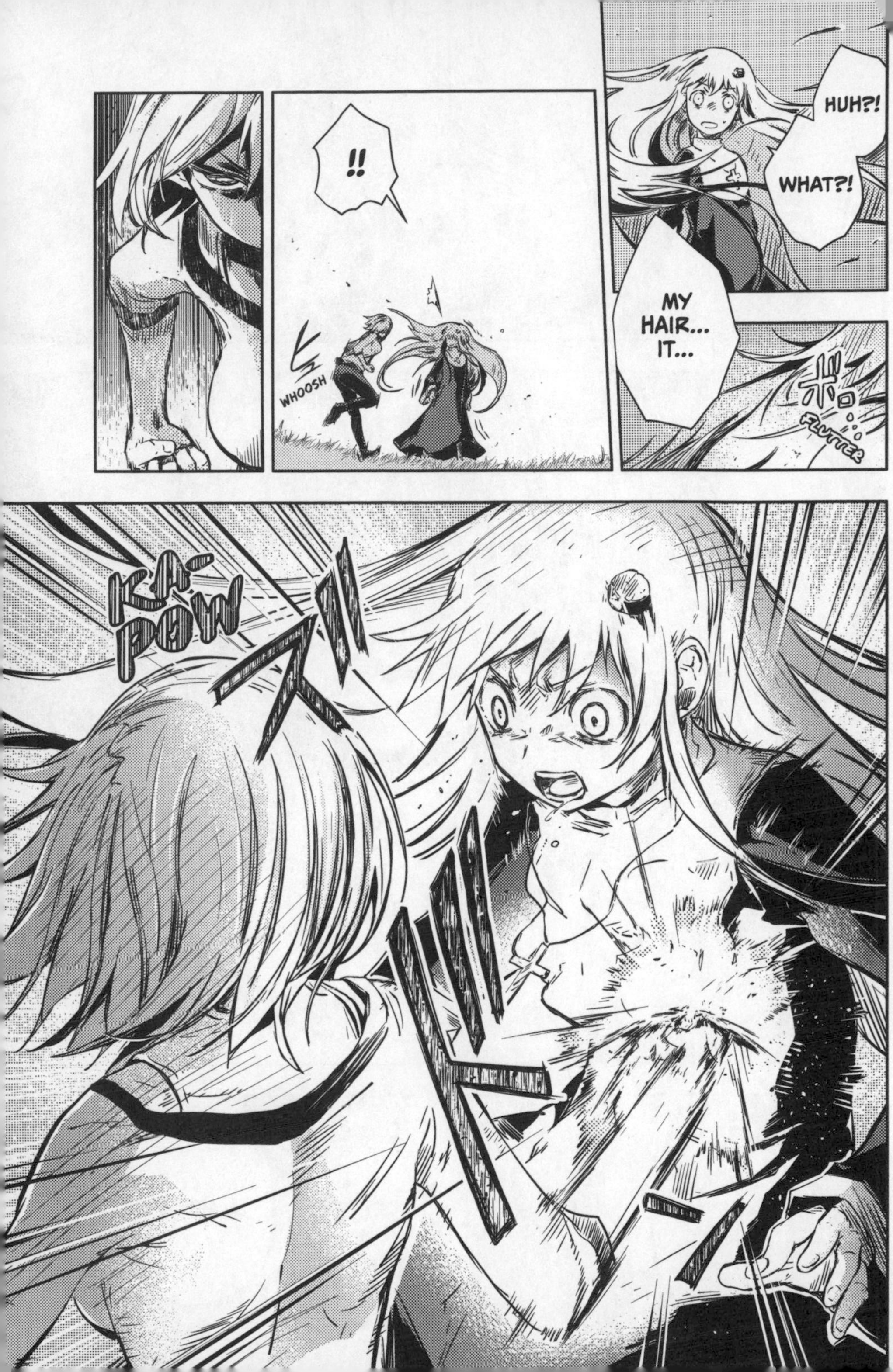
HUH?!
WHAT?!
MY HAIR... IT...
FLUTTER
!!
WHOOSH
KA-POW

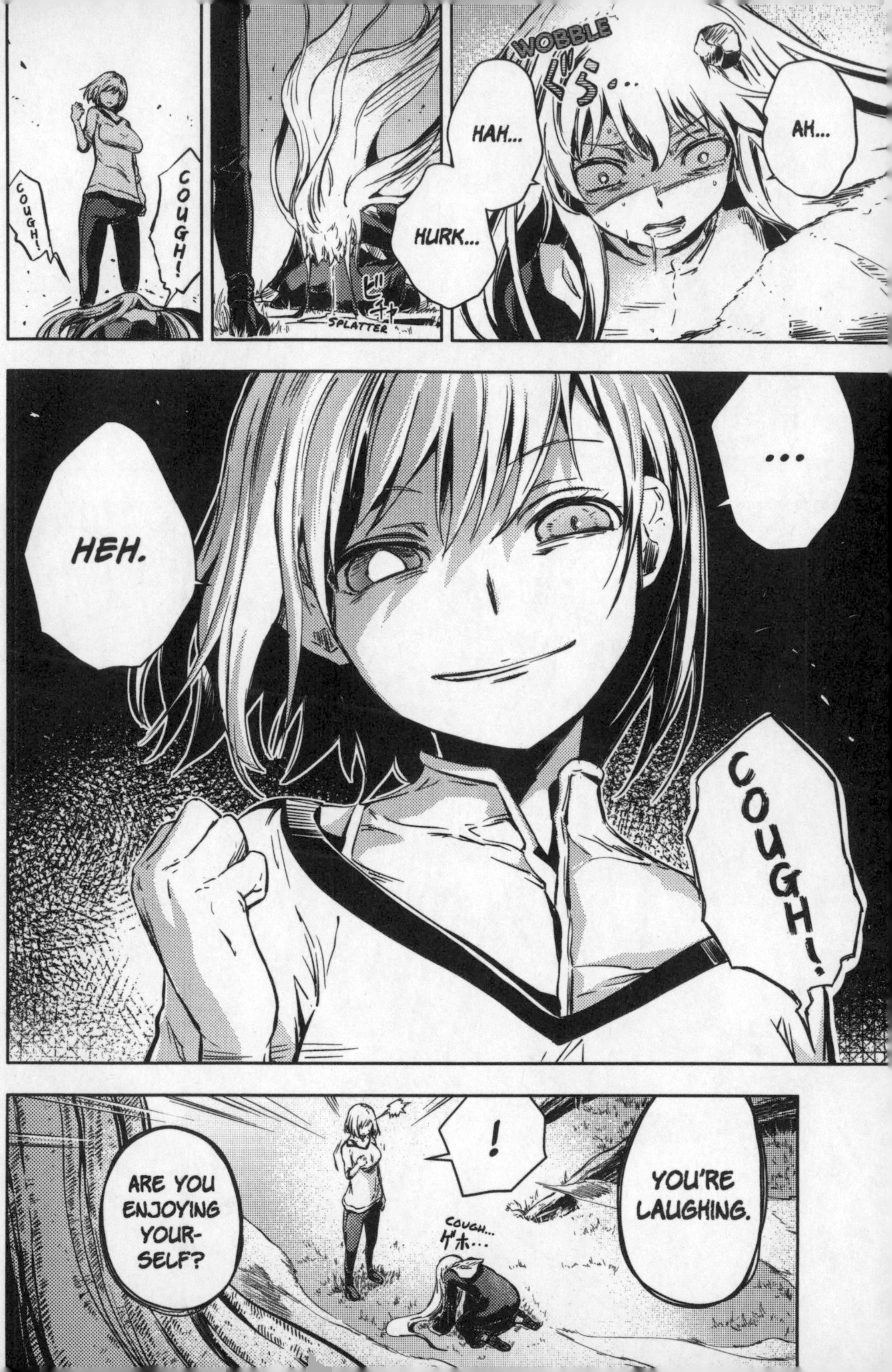
WOBBLE
ぐら...
AH...
HAH...
HURK...
ビチャ
SPLATTER
COUGH!
COUGH!
...
HEH.
COUGH!
YOU'RE LAUGHING.
!
COUGH...
ゲホ...
ARE YOU ENJOYING YOUR-SELF?

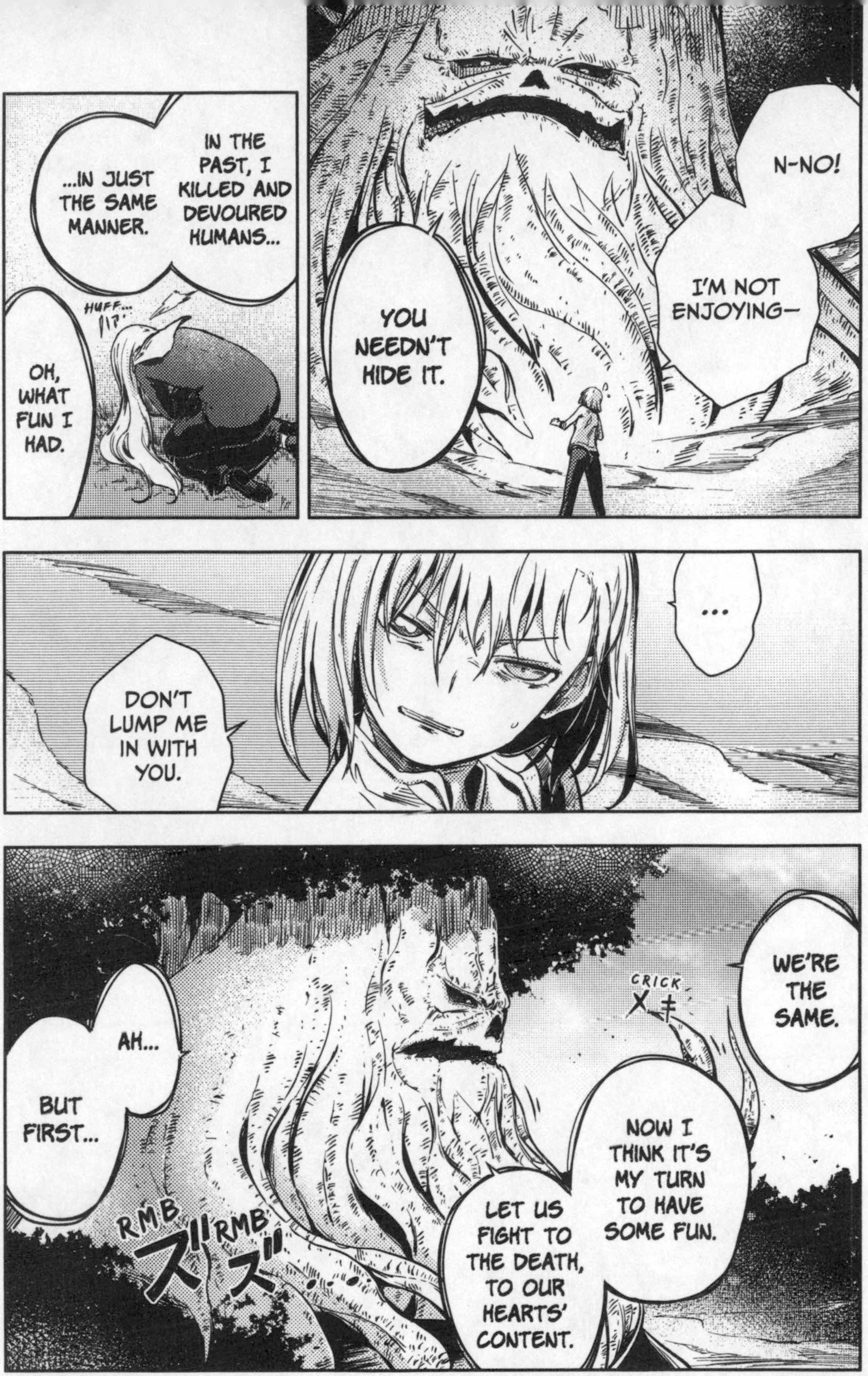
N-NO!
I'M NOT ENJOYING—
YOU NEEDN'T HIDE IT.
IN THE PAST, I KILLED AND DEVOURED HUMANS...
...IN JUST THE SAME MANNER.
HUFF...
!?
OH, WHAT FUN I HAD.
...
DON'T LUMP ME IN WITH YOU.
WE'RE THE SAME.
CRICK
NOW I THINK IT'S MY TURN TO HAVE SOME FUN.
LET US FIGHT TO THE DEATH, TO OUR HEARTS' CONTENT.
AH...
BUT FIRST...
RMB
RMB

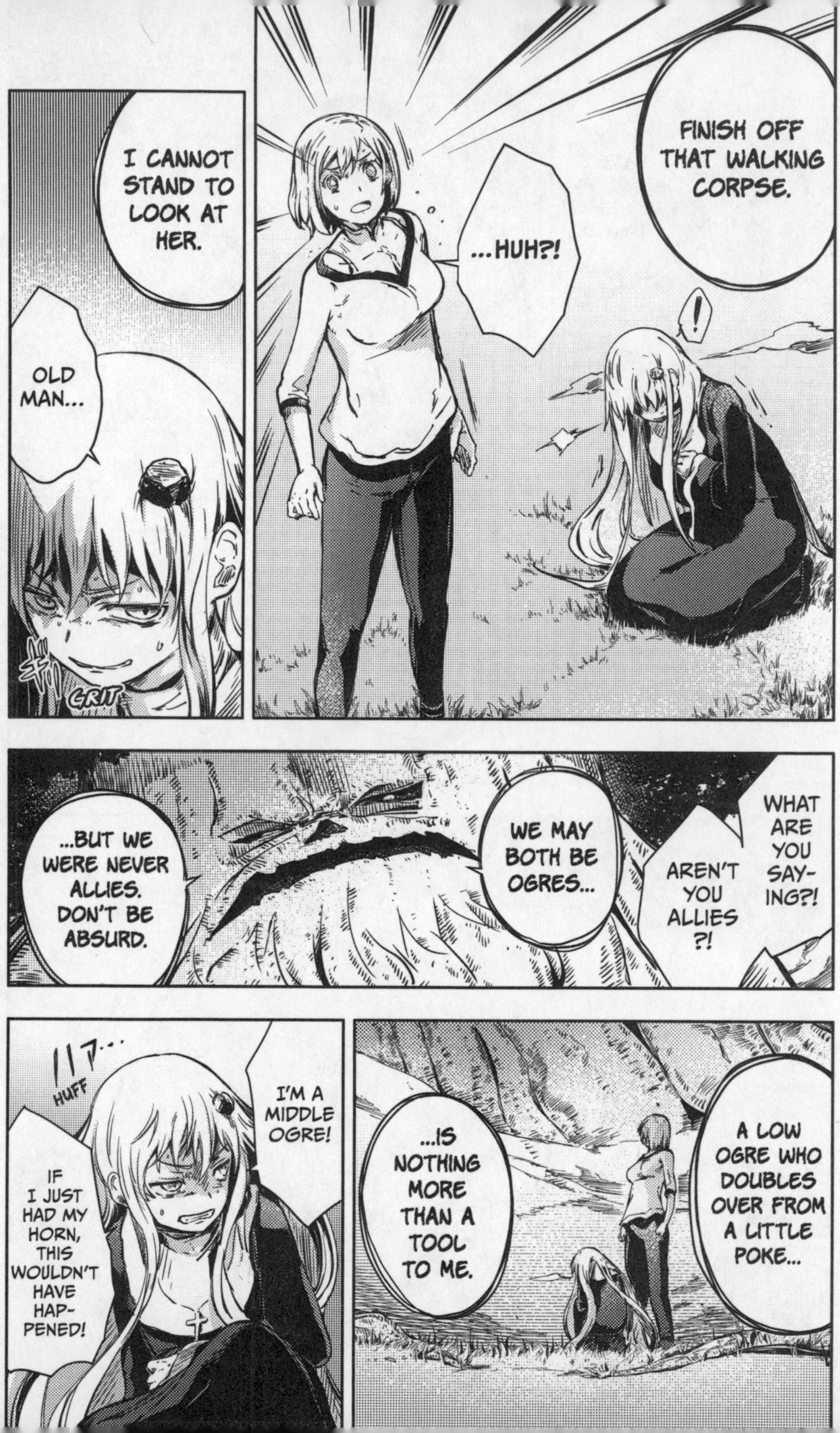
FINISH OFF THAT WALKING CORPSE.
...HUH?!
!
I CANNOT STAND TO LOOK AT HER.
OLD MAN...
GRIT
WHAT ARE YOU SAYING?!
AREN'T YOU ALLIES?!
WE MAY BOTH BE OGRES...
...BUT WE WERE NEVER ALLIES. DON'T BE ABSURD.
A LOW OGRE WHO DOUBLES OVER FROM A LITTLE POKE...
...IS NOTHING MORE THAN A TOOL TO ME.
I'M A MIDDLE OGRE!
HUFF
IF I JUST HAD MY HORN, THIS WOULDN'T HAVE HAPPENED!

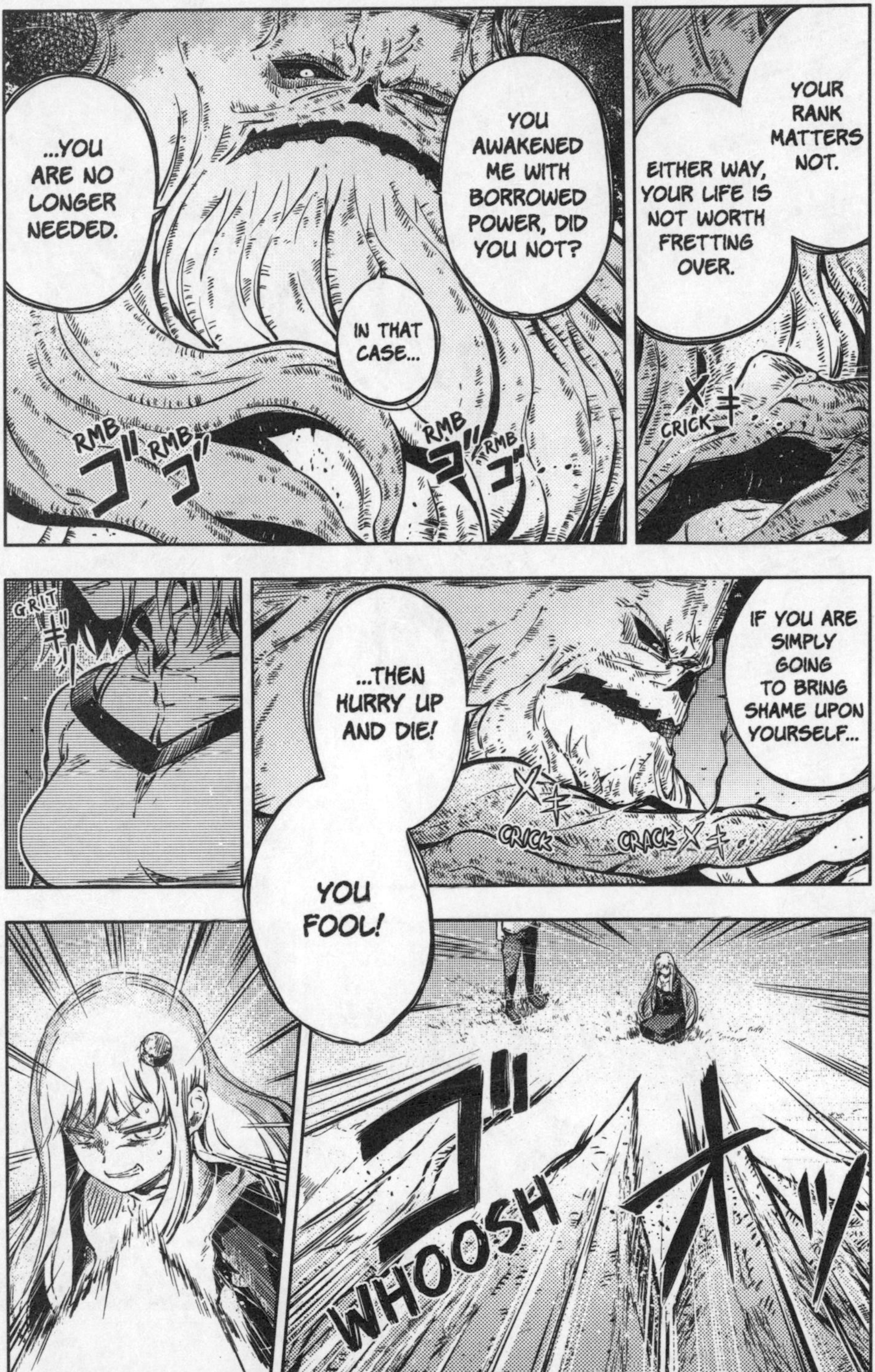
YOUR RANK MATTERS NOT.
EITHER WAY, YOUR LIFE IS NOT WORTH FRETTING OVER.
CRICK
YOU AWAKENED ME WITH BORROWED POWER, DID YOU NOT?
...YOU ARE NO LONGER NEEDED.
IN THAT CASE...
RMB
RMB
RMB
RMB
IF YOU ARE SIMPLY GOING TO BRING SHAME UPON YOURSELF...
...THEN HURRY UP AND DIE!
CRACK
CRICK
GRIT
YOU FOOL!
WHOOSH

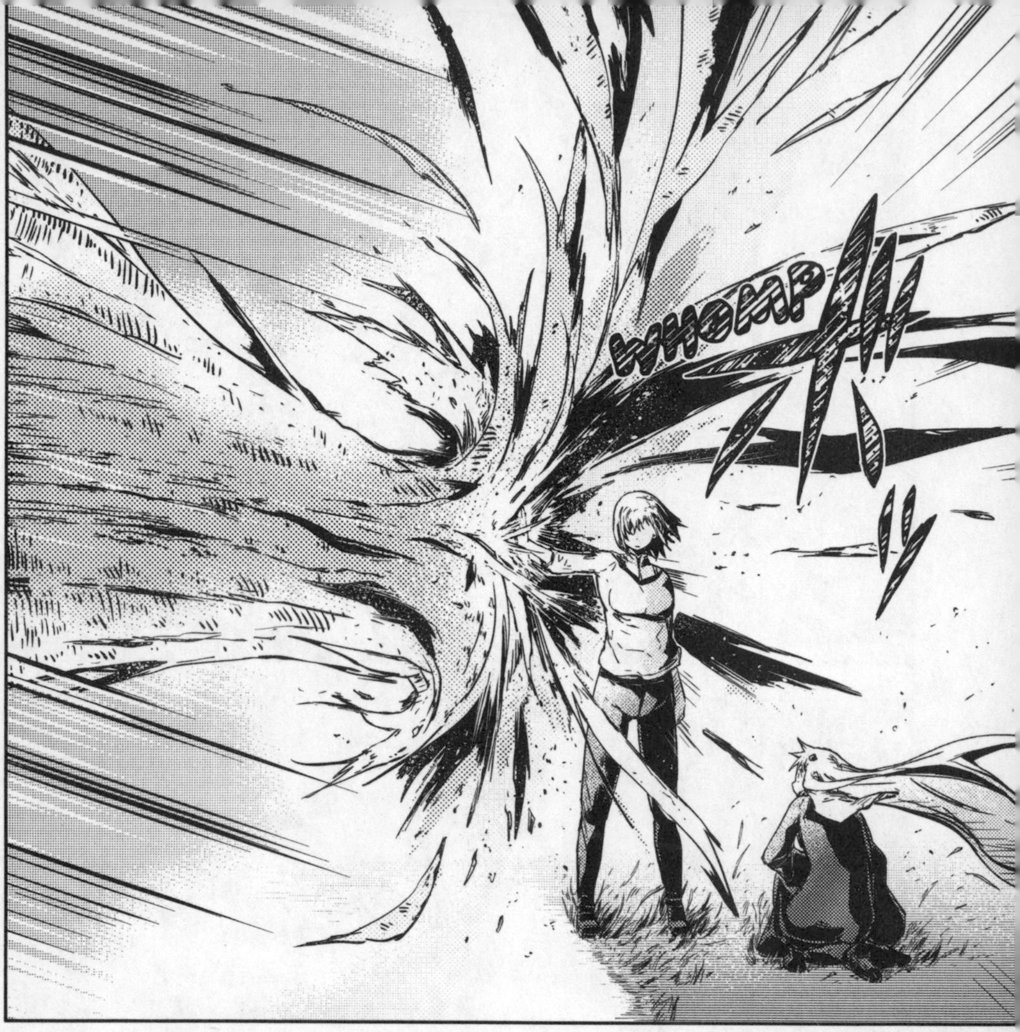
WHOMP
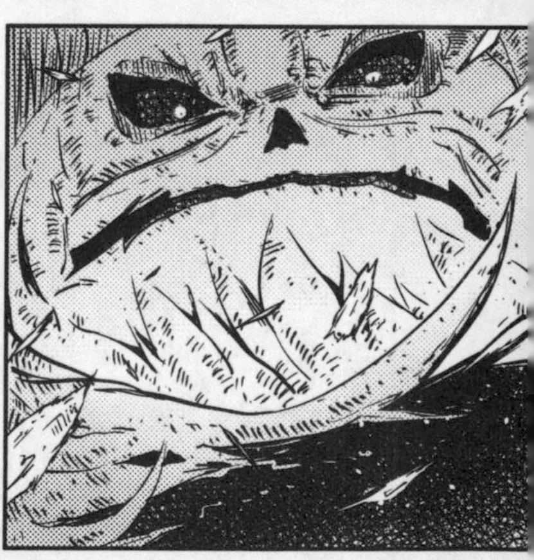
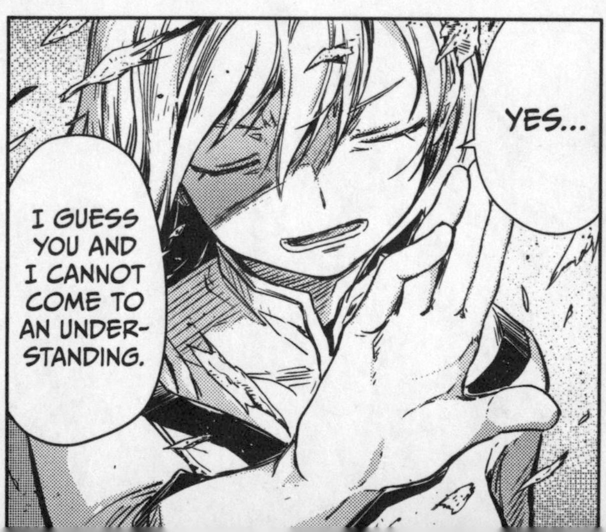
YES...
I GUESS YOU AND I CANNOT COME TO AN UNDER-STANDING.

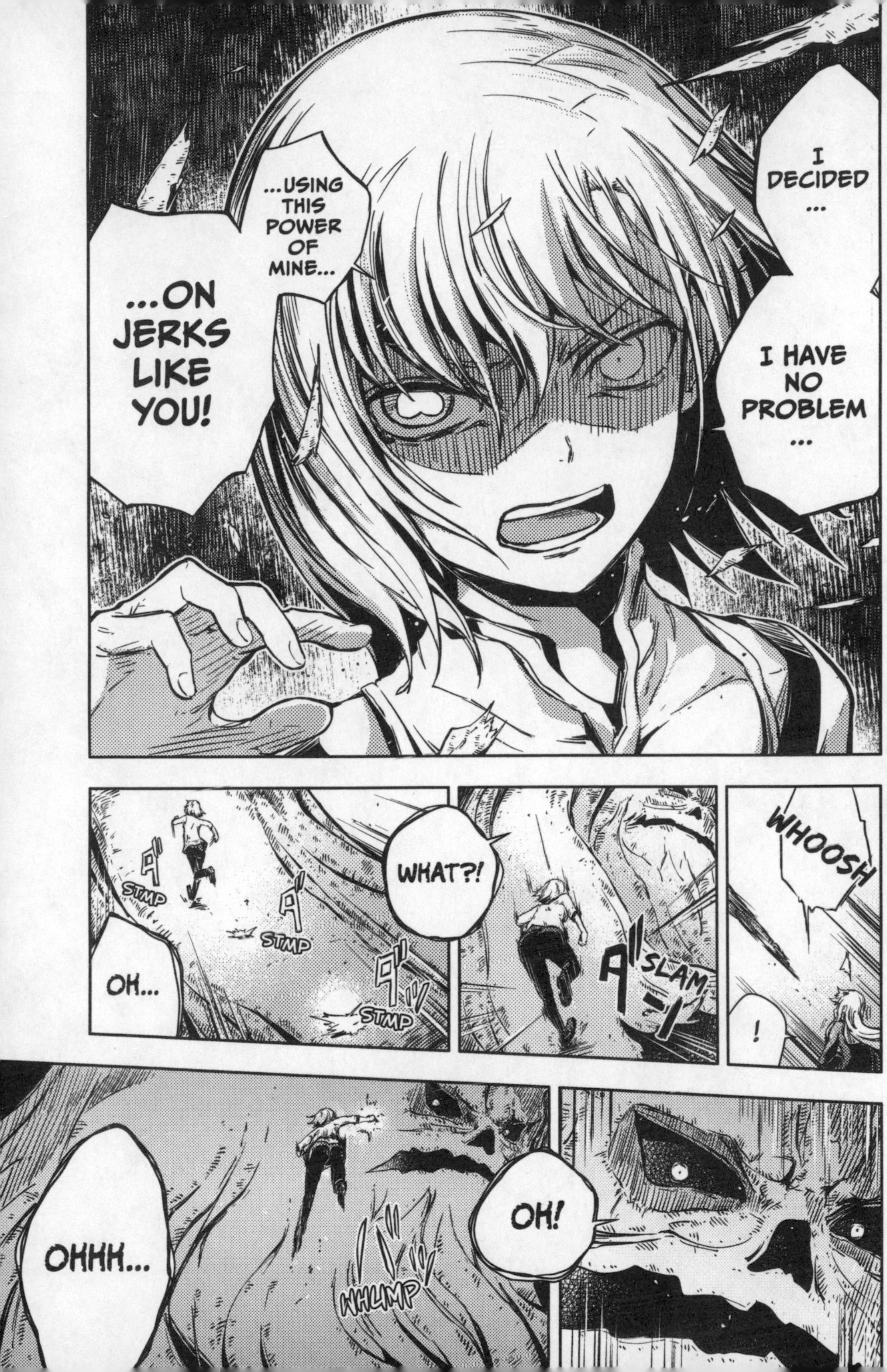
I DECIDED...
I HAVE NO PROBLEM...
...USING THIS POWER OF MINE...
...ON JERKS LIKE YOU!
WHOOSH
!
WHAT?!
SLAM
STMP
STMP
STMP
OH...
OH!
OHHH...
WHUMP

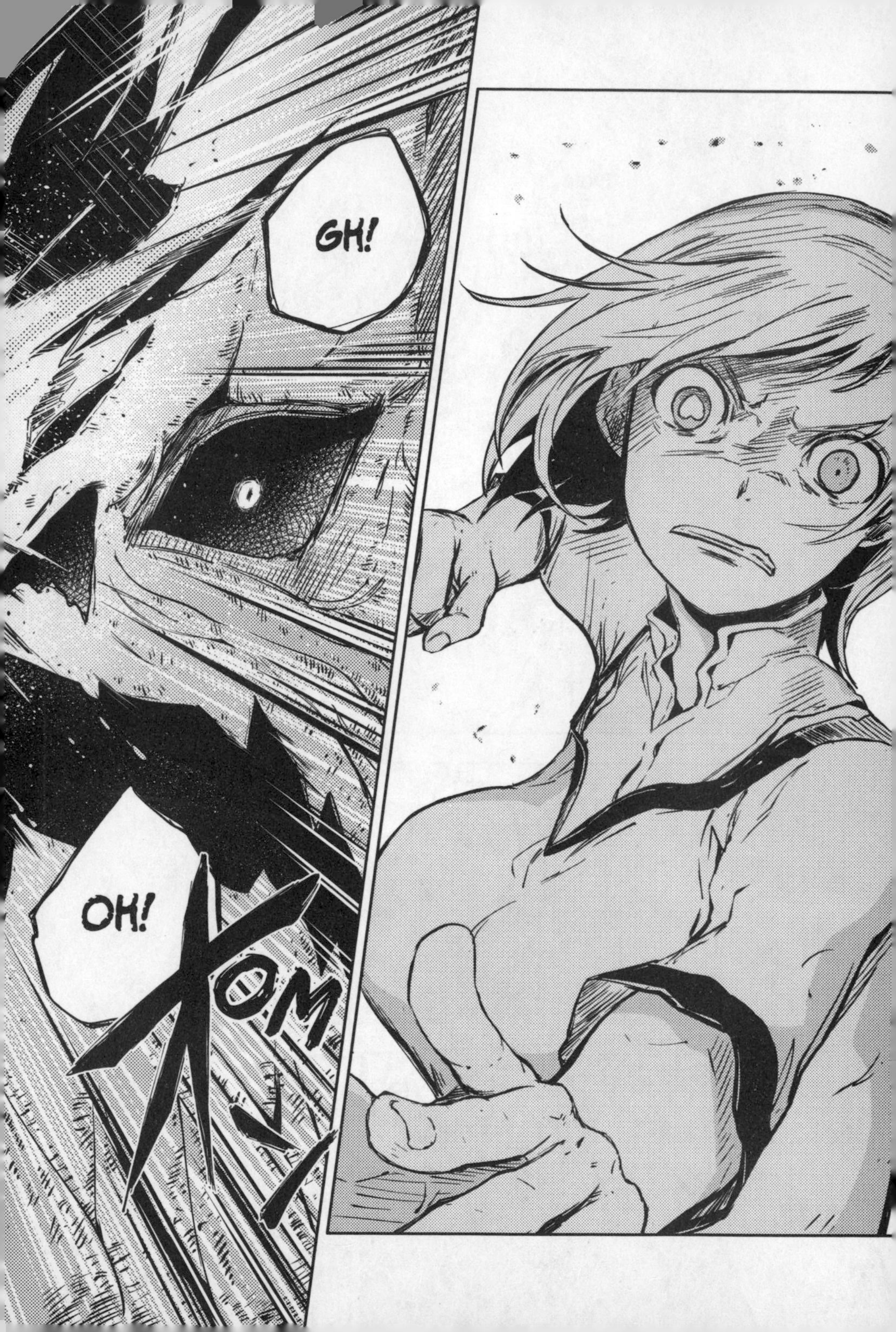
GH!
OH!
KOM

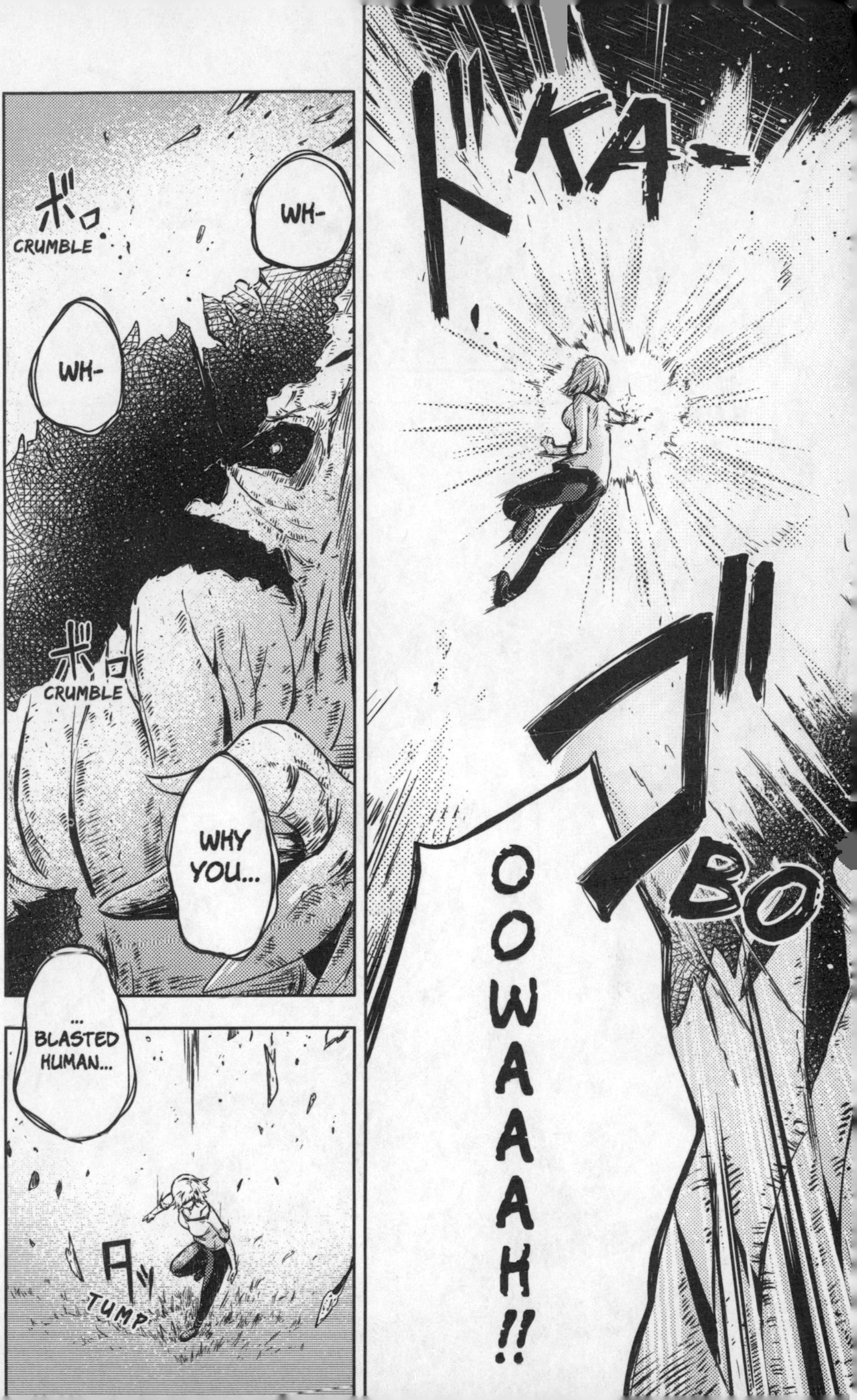

ドKA-
ゴ
BO
OOWAAAAH!!
WH-
ボロ
CRUMBLE
WH-
ボロ
CRUMBLE
WHY YOU...
...BLASTED HUMAN...
タッ
TUMP

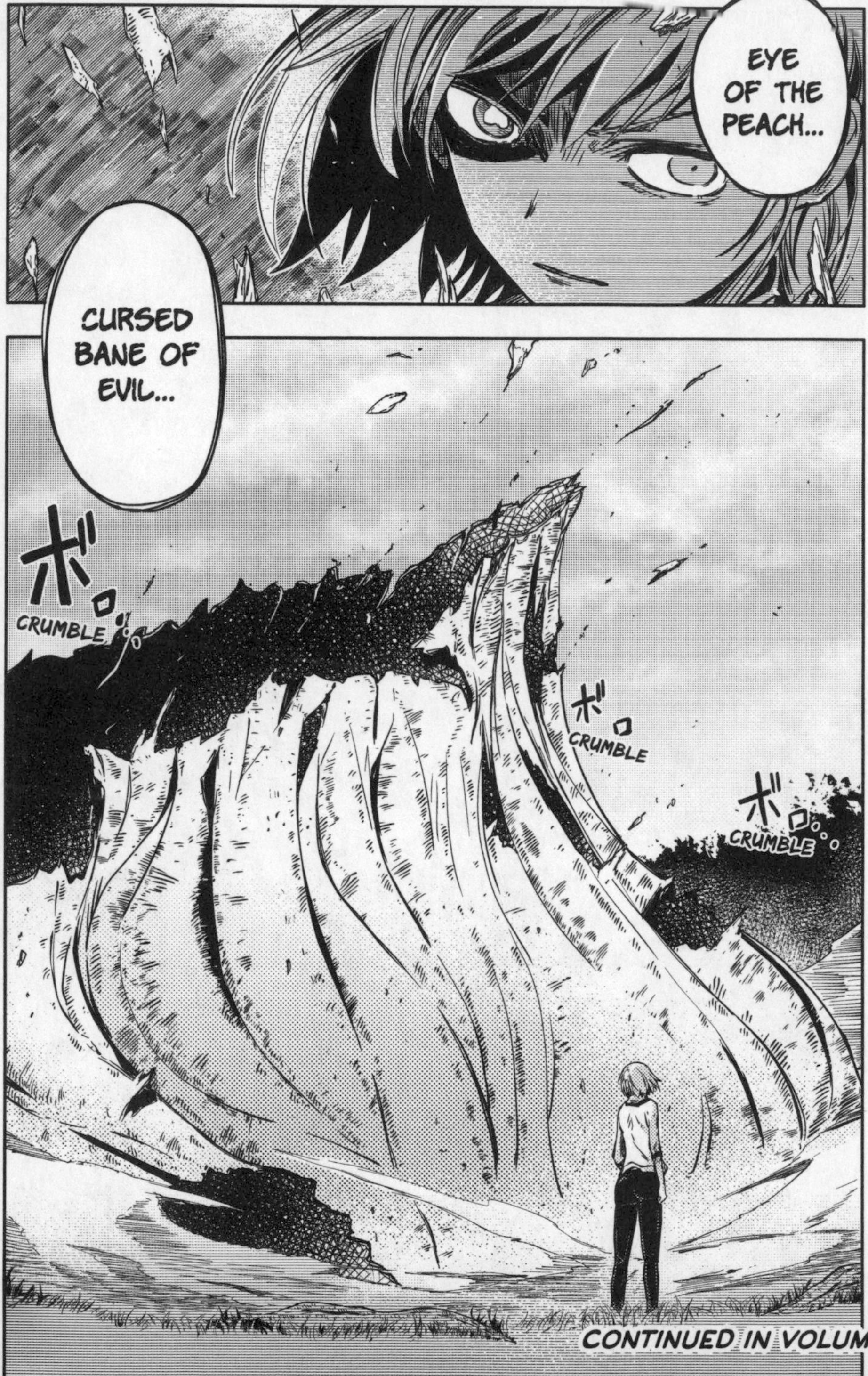
EYE OF THE PEACH...
CURSED BANE OF EVIL...
ボロ
CRUMBLE
ボロ
CRUMBLE
ボロ
CRUMBLE
CONTINUED IN VOLUME 4

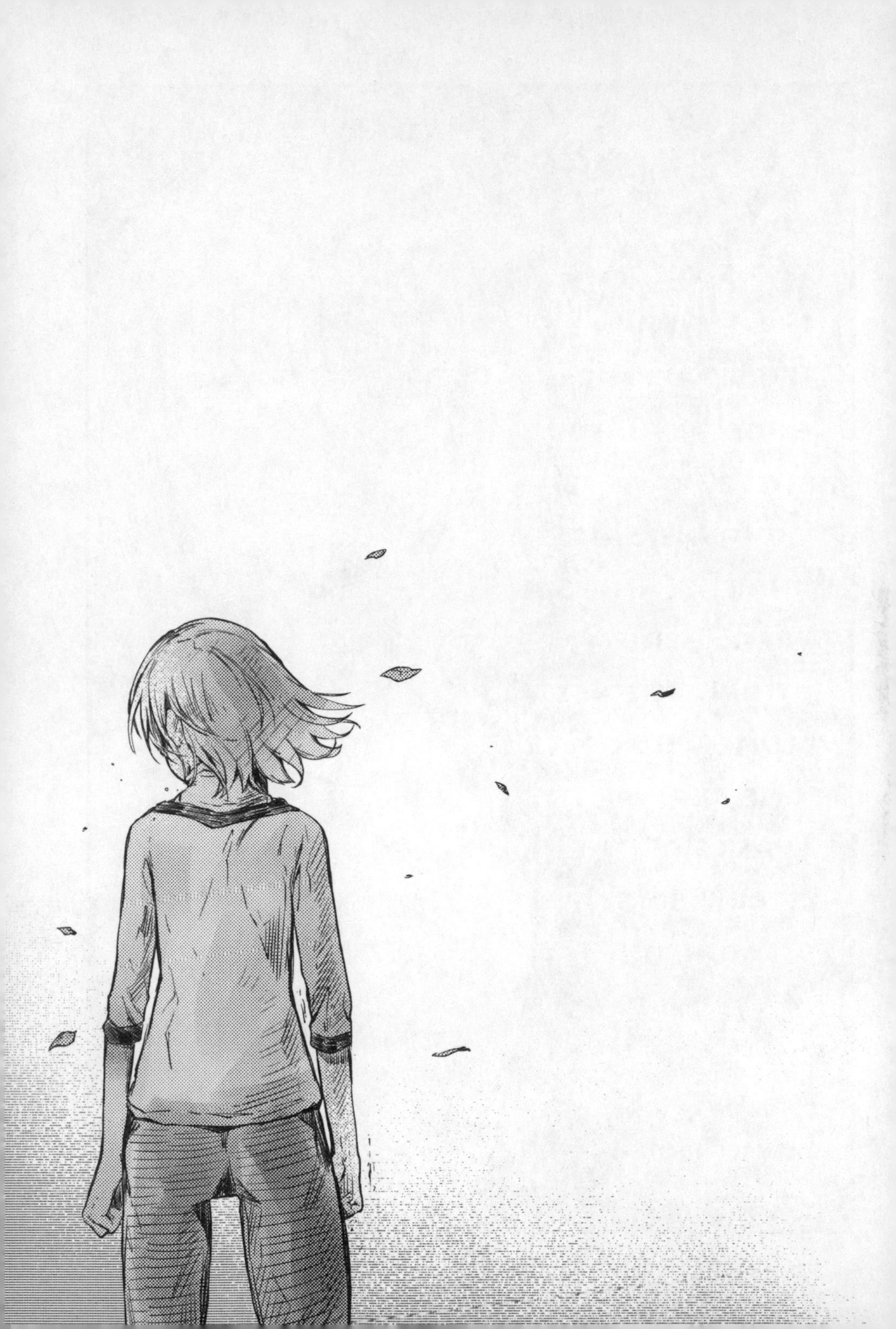

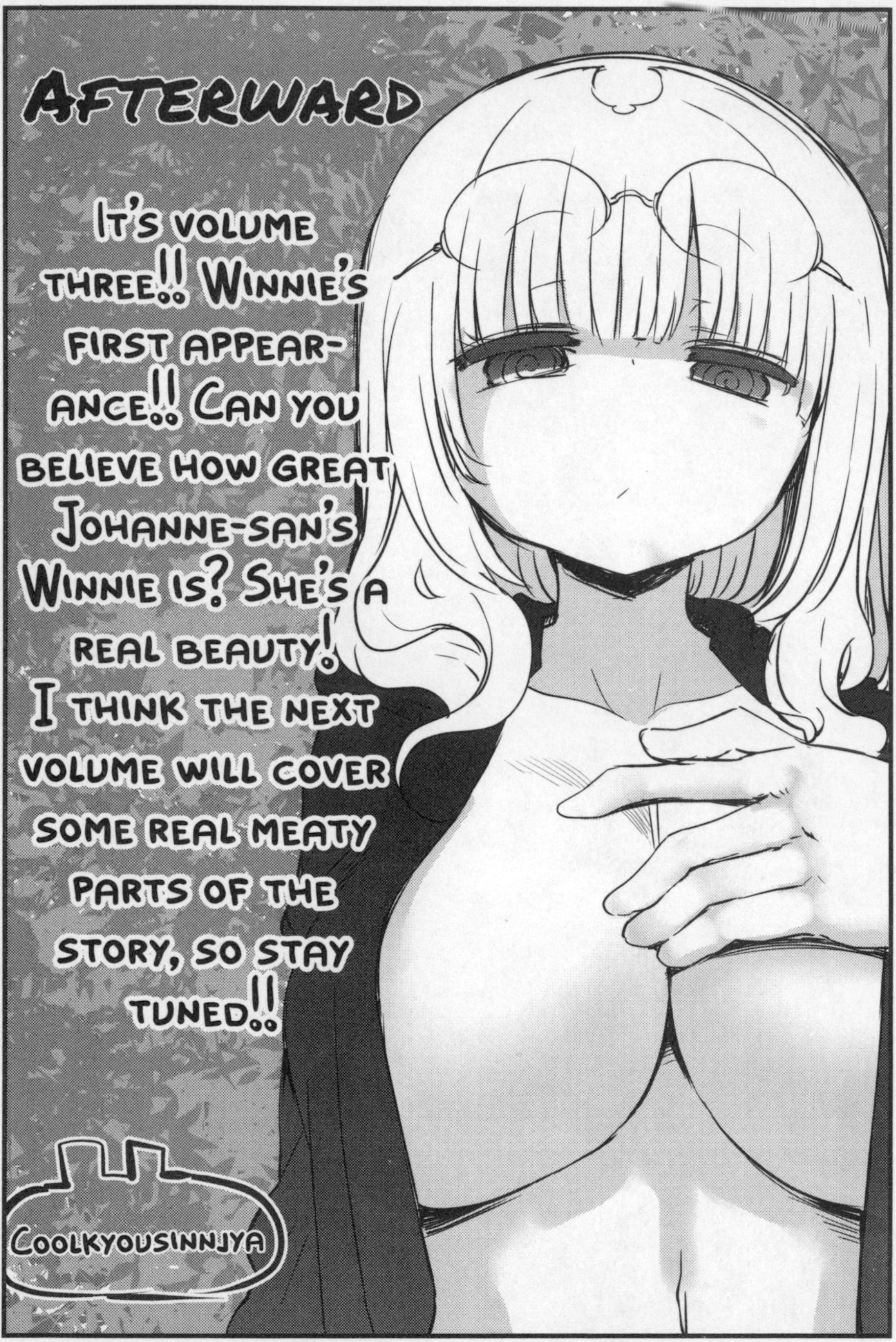
AFTERWARD
IT'S VOLUME THREE!! WINNIE'S FIRST APPEARANCE!! CAN YOU BELIEVE HOW GREAT JOHANNE-SAN'S WINNIE IS? SHE'S A REAL BEAUTY! I THINK THE NEXT VOLUME WILL COVER SOME REAL MEATY PARTS OF THE STORY, SO STAY TUNED!!
COOLKYOUSINNJYA

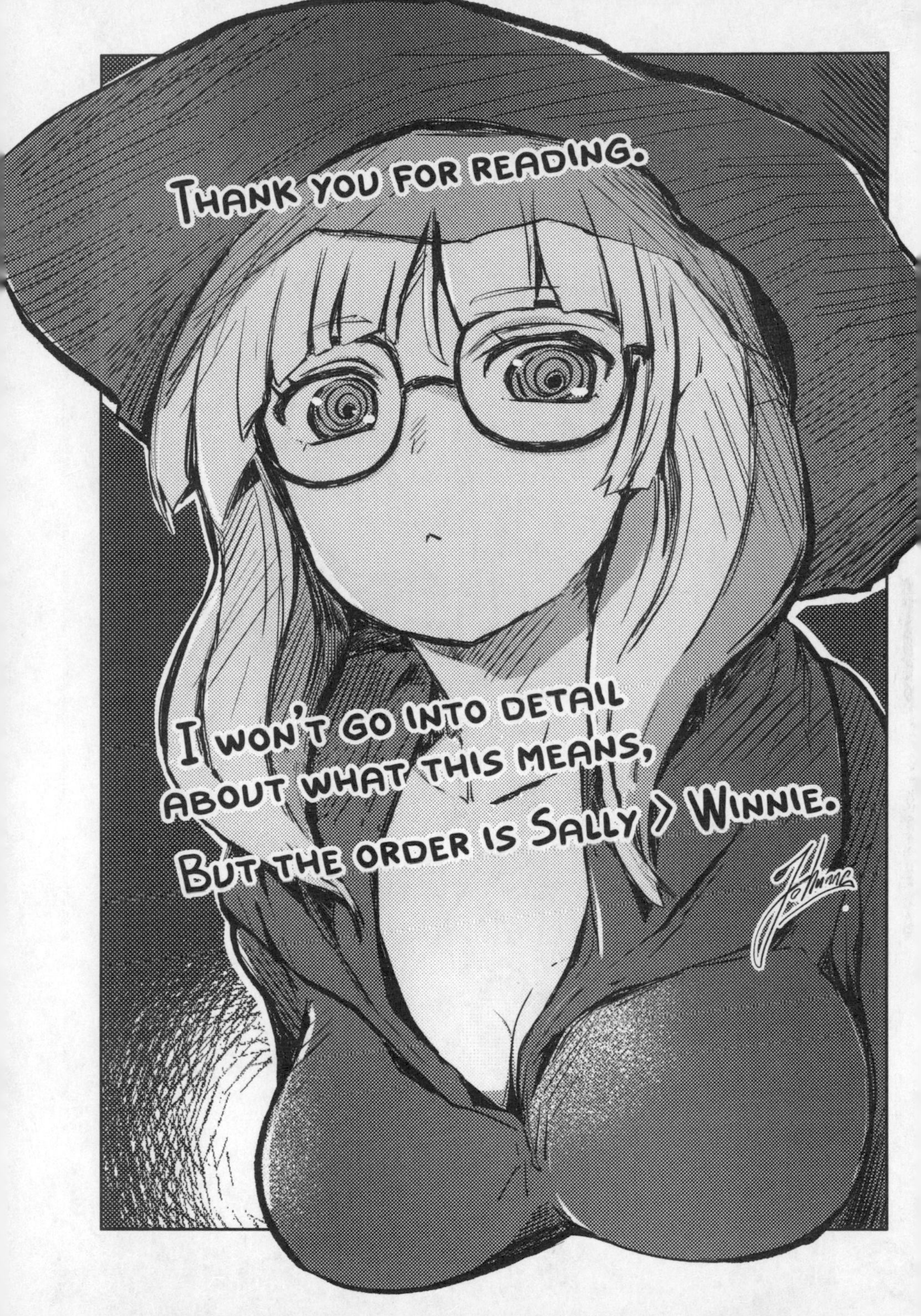
Thank you for reading.
I won't go into detail about what this means, but the order is Sally > Winnie.

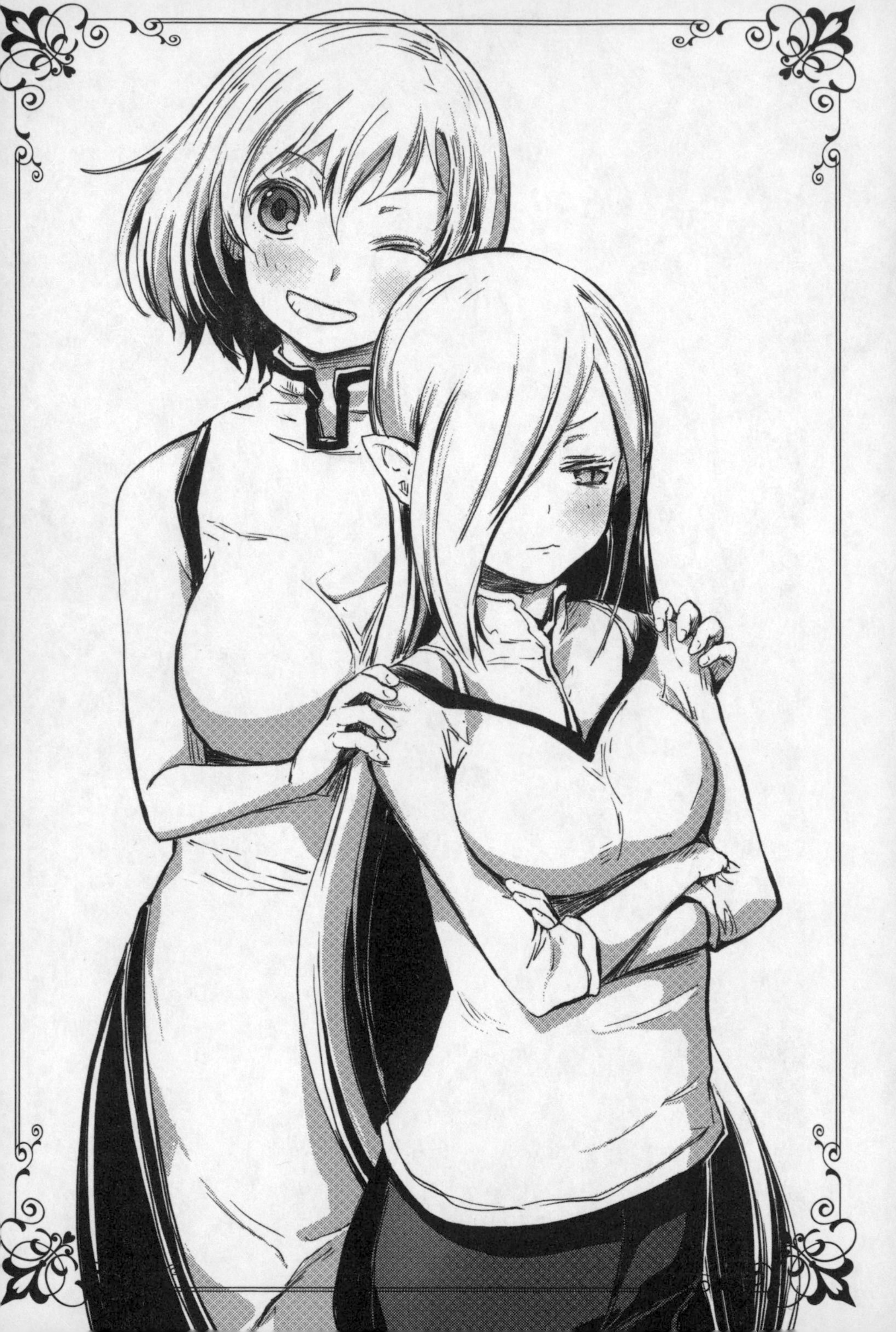

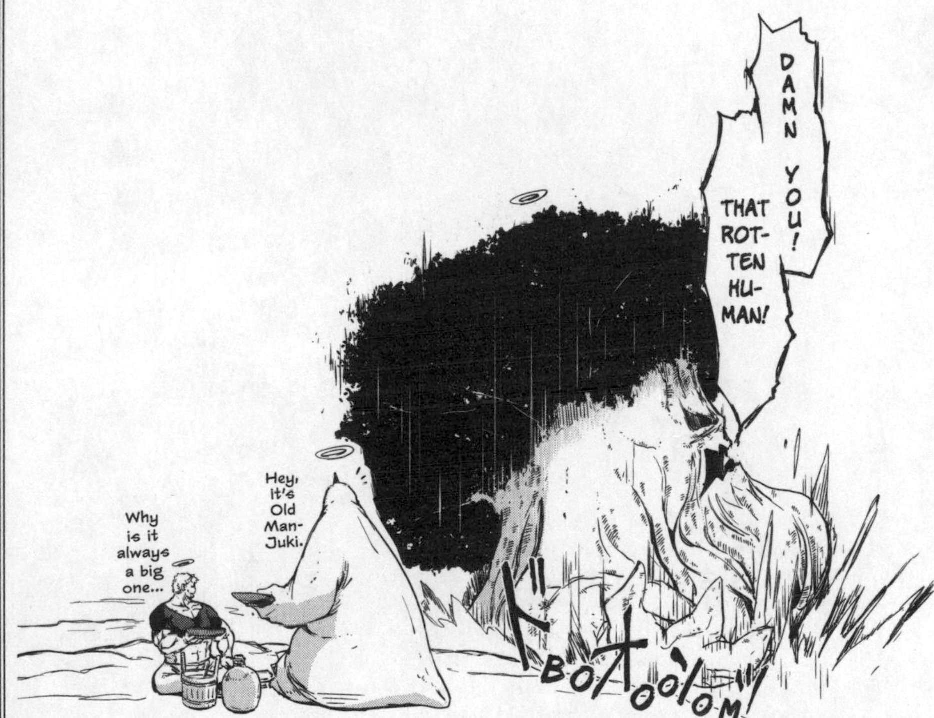
DAMN YOU!
THAT ROT-TEN HU-MAN!
BOOOOOM!
Hey, it's Old Man-Juki.
Why is it always a big one...

# CUTE ANIMALS AND LIFE LESSONS, PERFECT FOR ASPIRING PET VETS OF ALL AGES!

YUZU THE PET VET

1

BY MINGO ITO

In collaboration with NIPPON COLUMBIA CO., LTD.

Yuzu the Pet Vet © Mingo Ito / NIPPON COLUMBIA CO., LTD. / Kodansha Ltd.

For an 11-year-old, Yuzu has a lot on her plate. When her mom gets sick and has to be hospitalized, Yuzu goes to live with her uncle who runs the local veterinary clinic. Yuzu's always been scared of animals, but she tries to help out.  Through all the tough moments in her life, Yuzu realizes that she can help make things all right with a little help from her animal pals, peers, and kind grown-ups.

## Every new patient is a furry friend in the making!

**The adorable new odd-couple cat comedy manga from the creator of the beloved *Chi's Sweet Home*, in full color!**

# Sue & Tai-chan

### Konami Kanata

Sue is an aging housecat who's looking forward to living out her life in peace... but her plans change when the mischievous black tomcat Tai-chan enters the picture! Hey! Sue never signed up to be a catsitter! *Sue & Tai-chan* is the latest from the reigning meow-narch of cute kitty comics, Konami Kanata.

# PERFECT WORLD

### Rie Aruga

A TOUCHING NEW SERIES ABOUT LOVE AND COPING WITH DISABILITY

An office party reunites Tsugumi with her high school crush Itsuki. He's realized his dream of becoming an architect, but along the way, he experienced a spinal injury that put him in a wheelchair. Now Tsugumi's rekindled feelings will butt up against prejudices she never considered — and Itsuki will have to decide if he's ready to let someone into his heart...

"Depicts with great delicacy and courage the difficulties some with disabilities experience getting involved in romantic relationships... Rie Aruga refuses to romanticize, pushing her heroine to face the reality of disability. She invites her readers to the same tasks of empathy, knowledge and recognition."
—Slate.fr

"An important entry [in manga romance]... The emotional core of both plot and characters indicates thoughtfulness... [Aruga's] research is readily apparent in the text and artwork, making this feel like a real story."
—Anime News Network

KC
KODANSHA COMICS

# A SMART, NEW ROMANTIC COMEDY FOR FANS OF *SHORTCAKE CAKE* AND *TERRACE HOUSE!*

Living-Room Matsunaga-san © Keiko Iwashita / Kodansha Ltd.

A romance manga starring high school girl Meeko, who learns to live on her own in a boarding house whose living room is home to the odd (but handsome) Matsunaga-san. She begins to adjust to her new life away from her parents, but Meeko soon learns that no matter how far away from home she is, she's still a young girl at heart — especially when she finds herself falling for Matsunaga-san.

# Young characters and steampunk setting, like *Howl's Moving Castle* and *Battle Angel Alita*

Beyond the Clouds © 2018 Nicke / Ki-oon

A boy with a talent for machines and a mysterious girl whose wings he's fixed will take you beyond the clouds! In the tradition of the high-flying, resonant adventure stories of Studio Ghibli comes a gorgeous tale about the longing of young hearts for adventure and friendship!

**One of CLAMP's biggest hits returns in this definitive, premium, hardcover 20th anniversary collector's edition!**

CLAMP

1
Chobits
20TH ANNIVERSARY EDITION

"A wonderfully entertaining story that would be a great installment in anybody manga collection."
— Anime News Network

"CLAMP is an all-female manga-creating team whose feminine touch shows in this entertaining, sci-fi soa opera."
— Publishers Weekly

Poor college student Hideki is down on his luck. All he wants is a good job, a girlfriend, and his very own "persocom"—the latest and greatest in humanoid computer technology. Hideki's luck changes one night when he finds Chi—a persocom thrown out in a pile of trash. But Hideki soon discovers that there's much more to his cute new persocom than meets the eye.

KC
KODANSHA
COMICS

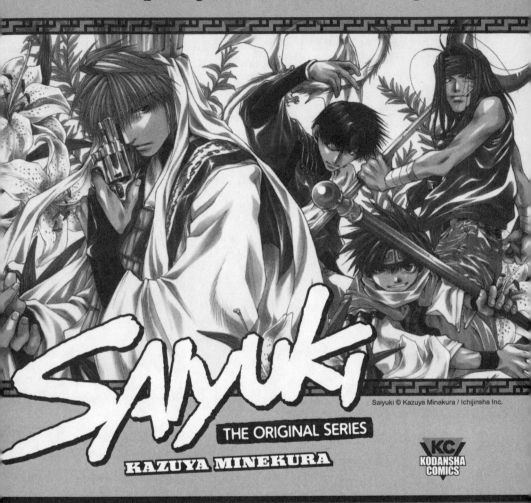

# THE SWEET SCENT OF LOVE IS IN THE AIR! FOR FANS OF OFFBEAT ROMANCES LIKE *WOTAKOI*

Sweat and Soap © Kintetsu Yamada / Kodansha Ltd.

In an office romance, there's a fine line between sexy and awkward... and that line is where Asako — a woman who sweats copiously — meets Koutarou — a perfume developer who can't get enough of Asako's, er, scent. Don't miss a romcom manga like no other!

A Kodansha Comics Trade Paperback Original
*Peach Boy Riverside 3* copyright © 2017 Coolkyousinnjya/Johanne
English translation copyright © 2021 Coolkyousinnjya/Johanne

Published in the United States by Kodansha Comics, an imprint of Kodansha USA Publishing, LLC, New York.

Publication rights for this English edition arranged through Kodansha Ltd., Tokyo.

First published in Japan in 2017 by Kodansha Ltd., Tokyo.

ISBN 978-1-64651-341-3

Original cover design by Tadashi Hisamochi (hive&co.,ltd.)

Printed in the United States of America.

www.kodansha.us

1st Printing
Translation: Steven LeCroy
Lettering: Andrew Copeland
Additional Lettering: Belynda Ungurath
Editing: Michal Zuckerman
YKS Services LLC/SKY Japan, Inc.
Kodansha Comics edition cover design by Adam Del Re

Publisher: Kiichiro Sugawara

Director of publishing services: Ben Applegate
Associate director of operations: Stephen Pakula
Publishing services managing editors: Madison Salters, Alanna Ruse
Production managers: Emi Lotto, Angela Zurlo
Logo and character art ©Kodansha USA Publishing, LLC